Group Politics

A New Emphasis

Group Politics
A New
Emphasis

Edward S. Malecki
*California State College,
Los Angeles*

H.R. Mahood
Memphis State University

Charles Scribner's Sons · *New York*

PREFACE

The primary aim of this volume of readings is to take into account critical developments in the area of group politics and to integrate selections reflecting these developments into a comparative framework. Through the comparative perspective the student can be sensitized to variations in group politics which are associated with variations in the social setting in which group politics take place.

In this volume the relationship between group politics and social setting is viewed in three basic ways: one, cross-sectional comparison *between* societies; two, cross-sectional comparison *within* societies; and three, longitudinal comparison within societies. The cross-sectional view between societies is aimed at sensitizing the student to the impact that different types of societies have on the scope and autonomy of group politics. The cross-sectional view within societies is aimed at increasing awareness of variations in the style and content of group politics taking place at different levels of the social structure within a society. The longitudinal view within societies is intended to direct the student's attention to the dynamic impact that changes over time in a society's social structure can have on the character of its group politics.

The three comparative viewpoints emphasized in this volume and the readings selected to reflect those perspectives respond to criticisms that the field of group politics has a one dimensional focus. The cross-sectional perspective between societies attempts to answer criticisms by students of comparative politics that the field of group politics is biased because it is almost solely based on studies of American group politics. The selections begin with readings which take a cross-sectional view of group politics in different types of societies. The perspective of cross-sectional comparison within societies responds to criticisms that the field of group politics focuses almost exclusively on the politics of the politically organized to the neglect of the study of the powerless and the unorganized located at the lower positions of the social structure. Within each of the four parts into which the entire set of readings is divided there are selections which deal with group politics among both the powerful and less powerful segments of society. The perspective of the longitudinal comparison of group politics attempts to answer criticisms that the field concentrates on the study of social and political statics at the expense of studying the dynamics of change. Selections in the beginning and final blocks of readings deal with comparisons of group politics at different points in time. Thus, the readings in this volume were selected to meet past criticisms of the field and to cover the three comparative perspectives.

The authors wish to acknowledge the various writers upon whose work they have drawn and the publishers who generously granted permission to reprint the articles used.

The authors share responsibility for the selection and editing of the articles. Edward Malecki assumed the major responsibility for the introductory comments and the outline.

CONTENTS

Part One

Social Structure and Group Politics

G ROUP politics involves the study of collective efforts to influence the authoritative allocation of values.[1] Typically this means collective efforts to enlist governmental authority on behalf of a collective goal or the extension of governmental legitimacy to collective activities. Traditionally group politics have been associated with the study of voluntary associations,[2] but increasingly attention has focused on the political role of corporate groups,[3] conflict groups,[4] and social movements.[5] Theoretically the most innovative development in the story of group politics is the recognition of the impact that differing societal settings have on the extent and nature of group politics.

Impact of Variations in Social Structures Between Societies

The most useful starting point for placing group politics into proper perspective is at the differentiation of societies in terms of their group setting. Societies differ in terms of the number and variety of groups found within

[1] For the general conception of politics as the authoritative allocation of values see David Easton. *The Political System* (New York: Alfred Knopf, 1953), Chapter 5. Contemporary thought views group politics as part of the total picture of politics, but for a statement equating group conflict with the authoritative allocation of values see Charles Hagan, "The Group in a Political Science," in *Approaches to the Study of Politics,* ed. Roland Young (Evanston, Ill.: Northwestern University Press, 1958), pp. 38-51.

[2] The best example is still David Truman, *The Governmental Process* (New York: Alfred Knopf, 1951).

[3] Andrew Hacker, "Power to Do What?" in *The Bias of Pluralism,* ed. William Connolly (New York: Atherton, 1969), pp 67-80; Morris Davis, "Some Neglected Aspects of British Pressure Groups," *Midwest Journal of Political Science,* VII (February 1963), 42-53.

[4] Ralf Dahrendorf, *Class and Class Conflict in Industrial Society* (Stanford, Calif.: Stanford University Press, 1959), Chapters 5 and 6. For an illustration of the behavior of conflict groups, see the Lipsky selection (pages 158–181).

[5] Murray Edelman, *The Symbolic Uses of Politics* (Urbana: University of Illinois Press, 1964), pp. 167-171; Seymour Martin Lipset, *Political Man* (Garden City, N. Y.: Doubleday, 1960); Joseph Gusfield, *Protest, Reform and Revolt: A Reader in Social Movements* (New York: John Wiley, 1970); for illustrations see the Kornhauser selection (pages 5-25), and the discussion of anomic interest group behavior in the LaPalombara selection (pages 253-267).

them. For example, all known societies have some form of a family group, but not all societies have formal voluntary associations. The elaborate division of labor found in industrialized societies tends to produce a greater variety and specificity of group politics than that found in agrarian societies.[6] There are a variety of political, economic, technological, and cultural conditions which shape the social structure of a society, but for most political analysis the social structure can be taken as a given aspect of the group setting which has an impact on the group politics of that society.

In the first selection William Kornhauser outlines the characteristics of four types of society in terms of a group typology. Strong autonomous groups render the elite accessible to the non-elite. Non-inclusive voluntary groups remove the availability of the non-elite to the elite by insulating them from elite penetration. Combining the criteria of accessibility of elites and availability of non-elite yields mass, pluralistic, traditional, and totalitarian societal types. In traditional and totalitarian societies the social structure limits the accessibility of the elites, reducing the scope of group demands on the input side of these political systems.[7] On the other hand in mass and pluralistic societies the social structure facilitates access to the elites, hence the scope of group politics is relatively broad in such systems.[8]

Most contemporary societies contain a mixture of traditional, transitional and modern cultural traits.[9] This cultural mixture is paralleled by a mixture of traditional, mass, and pluralistic or totalitarian social structures.[10] For example, while the "modern" nuclear family is distinguished from the extended family, the family of whatever type remains primarily an element of traditional social structure which is found in all types of society. Most societies also contain prisons and at least to that extent possess an element of totalitarian social structure. The key point to remember is that societies usually have mixed social structures and this mixture must be considered in the analysis of group politics.

The second selection, by Gabriel Almond and Sidney Verba, presents findings on the extent of membership in voluntary associations in five societies. Multiple memberships in autonomous voluntary associations are a critical feature of a pluralistic social structure. Their findings indicate that even in the United States, which is often cited as the model of pluralism, only one-third of the population maintains multiple group memberships. Additional findings also indicate that the political attitudes of individuals with group memberships differ from those of individuals without group memberships. These findings raise two questions. First, to what extent do differences in the extent of pluralism between societies affect the character of group politics. (This question also should be kept in mind when reading the materials in Part III on group impact on government.) Secondly, to what extent do the organized individuals in a society differ politically from the unorganized.

Impact of Variations of Social Structures Within Societies

The selections by Murray Edelman and William Gamson address the second question. Both agree that the organized are favored in the distribution of values in comparison to the unorganized. Edelman notes that the organized have a rational orientation to politics while the unorganized tend to have an emotional orientation. He also notes that the organized tend to obtain tangible benefits while the unorganized tend to receive symbolic values from the political process. Moreover, there is a tendency for the symbolic aspects of the distribution to keep the unorganized in a state of political quiescence.

The main thrust of the Gamson selection is the critical analysis of the structural features of the pluralistic segment of United States society which inhibit the solidarity and initial political organization among unrepresented groups. Gamson's analysis indicates that the existence of a substantial degree of pluralism in a society can be a major factor inhibiting the extension of representation to segments of society outside the pluralistic sector.

[6]Gabriel Almond and Bingham Powell, *Comparative Politics* (Boston: Little, Brown & Co., 1966), pp. 91-97.

[7]For an illustration in a totalitarian society see the Schwartz and Keech selection (pages 234-253), and for an illustration in a traditional setting, see the discussion of *parentela* in La-Palombara's selection (pages 253-267).

[8]For an illustration in a mass setting see the Lipsky selection (pages 158-181), and for illustrations in a pluralistic setting see the Beer and Froman selections (pages 221 and 203).

[9]Almond and Powell, pp. 63-64; and Gabriel Almond and James Coleman, eds., *The Politics of the Developing Areas* (Princeton: Princeton University Press, 1960), pp. 3-64.

[10]For example, C. Wright Mills, *The Power Elite* (New York: Oxford University Press, 1956), identified a mass setting at the bottom of United States society (Chapter 13), pluralistic at the middle (Chapter 11), and overall approaching a power elite or totalitarian condition (Chapter 12).

Conditions and Structure of Mass Society

William Kornhauser

Conditions of Mass Society

The aristocratic critique of mass society yields the idea of accessible elites, and the democratic critique yields the idea of available non-elites. We have shown that the consequences imputed to each are more likely to follow from a combination of both factors than from either one alone. This suggests a more general conception of mass society than that contained in the aristocratic or democratic version. *Mass society is a social system in which elites are readily accessible to influence by non-elites and non-elites are readily available for mobilization by elites.*

This conception of mass society may be better understood by comparing it with other types of societies. For this purpose, we shall consider communal society, pluralist society, and totalitarian society, insofar as they can be characterized by other combinations of the two variables of (a) accessibility of elites and (b) availability of non-elites. Access and availability vary in kind as well as in degree. For example, access to elites may be institutionalized or it may be direct; access can take the form of membership in elites or of selection of elites. These are some of the main *kinds* of access. There are important differences between social systems in respect to the kinds of access to elites (or the kinds of availability of non-elites) that predominate in each; this aspect of the problem will be explored subsequently. For the moment, we are concerned only with the *degree* of access and availability. As a rough indicator of the degree of access to elites we shall use the extent to which members of the society participate in the selection of elites, and as a comparable measure of the degree of availability of non-elites we may use the extent to which members of the society lack attachments to independent groups. Of each type of society we shall now ask only whether it involves high or low access to elites, high or low availability of non-elites.

Communal society requires inaccessible elites and unavailable non-elites if it is to sustain its traditional structure—as in certain medieval communities. Elites are inaccessible in that elite elements and standards are

SOURCE: From William Kornhauser, *The Politics of Mass Society* (Glencoe, Illinois: The Free Press, 1959), pp. 39-43, 74-101. © The Free Press, a corporation, 1959. Reprinted by permission of The Macmillan Company, and Routledge & Kegan Paul Ltd. (London).

selected and fixed by traditional ascription. Non-elites are unavailable in that people are firmly bound by kinship and community. Such a population is very difficult to mobilize unless powerful forces have eroded communal ties, as happened in the Late Middle Ages, when the incipient processes of urbanization and industrialization began their destruction of the medieval community, thereby unloosing portions of the population for participation in the various millennial movements that flourished during this period.

| | | AVAILABILITY OF NON-ELITES | |
		Low	High
ACCESSIBILITY OF ELITES	Low	communal society	totalitarian society
	High	pluralist society	mass society

Pluralist society requires accessible elites and unavailable non-elites if it is to sustain its freedom and diversity—as in certain liberal democracies. Elites are accessible in that competition among independent groups opens many channels of communication and power. The population is unavailable in that people possess multiple commitments to diverse and autonomous groups. The mobilization of a population bound by multiple commitments would require the breaking up of large numbers of independent organizations, as totalitarian movements have sought to do.

Mass society requires both accessible elites and available non-elites if it is to exhibit a high rate of mass behavior. Elites are accessible and non-elites are available in that there is a paucity of independent groups between the state and the family to protect either elites or non-elites from manipulation and mobilization by the other. In the absence of social autonomy at all levels of society, large numbers of people are pushed and pulled toward activist modes of intervention in vital centers of society; and mass-oriented leaders have the opportunity to mobilize this activism for the capture of power. As a result, freedom is precarious in mass society.

Totalitarian society requires an inaccessible elite and an available population if it is to sustain a system of total control from above—as in certain modern dictatorships. The elite is inaccessible in that elite elements are selected and fixed through co-optation, by virtue of a monopoly over the means of coercion and persuasion in the hands of those at the apex of the structure. The population is available in that its members lack all those independent social formations that could serve as a basis of resistance to the elite. Instead, the population is mobilized by the elite through multiple organizations taken over or created for that purpose.

These are abstract types of society; no large-scale society is purely communal, pluralist, mass, or totalitarian. However, any given society would appear to be like one type more than like other types. For example, large, complex societies always contain some pluralist elements, so that total control is impossible, even under totalitarian regimes. Yet some societies give much greater weight to pluralist elements than do others. They not only exhibit a much greater degree of institutional autonomy, but in addition, "it is acknowledged and guaranteed and finds support in the legal system, the ethos and the distribution of legitimate power" (Shils, 1956, p. 154).

A weakness of the two theories of mass society may be identified in light of the model of four types of society. Aristocratic critics fasten on popular access to elites as the distinguishing characteristic of mass society, and thereby confound pluralist society with mass society.[10] Democratic critics, on the other hand, fasten on the availability of atomized non-elites in their conception of mass society, and thereby confound totalitarian society with mass society.[11] By distinguishing mass society from totalitarian society, on the one side, and pluralist society, on the other, the model presented here would appear to be a more fruitful one for the examination of problems related to social structure and freedom.[12]

[10]Thus Lippmann (1956, p. 50) judges all democratic republics to be mass-dominated by virtue of their accessible elites: "It is significant, I think, certainly it is at least suggestive, that while nearly all the Western governments have been in deep trouble since the First World War, the constitutional monarchies of Scandinavia, the Low Countries, and the United Kingdom have shown greater capacity to endure, to preserve order with freedom, than the republics of France, Germany, Spain and Italy. . . . The evaporation of the imponderable powers, a total dependence upon the assemblies and the mass electorates, has upset the balance of powers between the two functions of the state. The executive has lost both its material and its ethereal powers. The assemblies and the mass electorates have acquired the monopoly of effective powers."

[11]Thus Mills states that all modern societies, including both democratic societies (especially the United States) and totalitarian societies (especially the Soviet Union), are "mass societies" in that they allegedly feature elite domination of atomized masses (1956, p. 310): "In all modern societies, the autonomous associations standing between the various classes and the state tend to lose their effectiveness as vehicles of reasoned opinion and instruments for the rational exertion of political will. Such associations can be deliberately broken up and thus turned into passive instruments of rule, or they can more slowly wither away from lack of use in the face of centralized means of power. But whether they are destroyed in a week, or wither in a generation, such associations are replaced in virtually every sphere of life by centralized organizations, and it is such organizations with all their new means of power that take charge of the terrorized or—as the case may be—merely intimidated, society of masses." (See also *ibid.*, p. 27.)

[12]DeGré also distinguishes between these three types of social systems. His distinction between totalitarian society and mass society closely parallels our own (1946, pp. 528-9): "Totalitarian society . . . has systematically destroyed all independent groups and autonomous opinion. It resembles the atomistic [i.e., mass] society in that the individual again operates without the backing of any group of his own. It differs from the atomistic [i.e., mass] society, however, in the fact that this time the atomized individual faces the full power of an omnipotent Leviathan state."

Our conception of mass society involves the following major proposition: *a high rate of mass behavior may be expected when both elites and non-elites lack social insulation; that is, when elites are accessible to direct intervention by non-elites, and when non-elites are available for direct mobilization by elites.*

•   •   •

Structure of Mass Society

We can conceive of all but the simplest societies as comprising three levels of social relations. The first level consists of highly personal or primary relations, notably the family. The third level contains relations inclusive of the whole population, notably the state. The second level comprises all intermediate relations, notably the local community, voluntary association, and occupational group. These intermediate relations function as links between the individual and his primary relations, on the one hand, and the state and other national relations, on the other hand. It must be emphasized that voluntary associations are not the only kind of intermediate relation; all organized relations that mediate between the family and the nation, such as local government and the local press, are classified as intermediate structures in the present study. Voluntary associations are used as the main empirical indicators of intermediate structures in this study because the best data are available for this kind of intermediate relation.

The logic of our model dictates that the structure of mass society must be of such a nature as to support a high rate of mass behavior by fulfilling the two requirements for mass behavior, namely, accessible elites and available non-elites. Such a structure may be shown to be one in which intermediate relations of community, occupation, and association are more or less inoperative, and therefore one in which the individual and primary group are directly related to the state and to nation-wide organizations. The members of mass society, then, are interconnected only by virtue of their common ties to national centers of communication and organization. It is in this sense that we speak of mass society as the *atomized* society.

Mass society lacks intermediate relations, but it is not to be conceived merely as the absence of social relations. The central feature of primary groups in mass society is not so much their internal weakness as it is their external *isolation* from the larger society. The isolation of primary groups means that by themselves they cannot provide the basis for participation in the larger society. Again, mass society is not to be thought of as lacking relations inclusive of the whole population. On the contrary, modern mass society possesses a highly *politicized* organization, as "everything that people know or feel Society will not undertake is simply heaped on to the . . . State" (Burckhardt, 1955, p. 203). This results in the centralization of the social structure, especially a centralized state. The centralization of communication and decision-making means that to the extent people do participate in the larger society, they must do so through the state, and other inclusive (nation-wide) structures.[24]

We shall elaborate this model of the structure of mass society by examining it on each of its three levels: (1) the weakness of intermediate relations, (2) the isolation of primary relations, and (3) the centralization of national relations.

WEAKNESS OF INTERMEDIATE RELATIONS

Weak intermediate relations leave elites and non-elites directly exposed to one another, and thereby invite widespread mass behavior; for in the absence of intermediate relations, participation in the larger society must be direct rather than filtered through intervening relationships.

The lack of strong independent groups undermines multiple proximate concerns, and thereby increases mass availability. Consider a man's relation to his work. While there often are important sources of intrinsic satisfaction derivable from the work itself, nevertheless the gratification derived from a sense of fellowship and control over the conditions of work are at least as important for firm occupational attachments. It is precisely these latter sources of interest and participation in work that require independent groups for their realization. Informal work groups supply some basis for fellowship and control at work, but with the growth in scale and complexity of the factory, office, and work institutions generally, they are insufficient. Therefore, all kinds of formal work associations, such as trade unions and professional associations, are needed.[25] To the extent that they fail to develop, or, at the other extreme, themselves grow so far out of the reach of their members as to no longer be capable of providing the individual with a sense of participation and control, people are less likely to find the whole sphere of work an interesting and rewarding experience. Consequently, people may cease to care about their work, though of course they continue to work, despite their alienation from their jobs.

Similar factors shape a man's relation to his community. Unless a variety of forms of associations are open to him, the individual is not likely to take an active interest in civic affairs—particularly in the metropolis, where the size of the population and the specialization of activities place a premium on

[24]Centralization, it must be emphasized, does not necessarily mean authoritarianism. Thus Lasswell and Kaplan (1950, pp. 224-5, 235) distinguish between "centralization" and "concentration" of power, and include the latter but exclude the former on a list of seven definitive characteristics of despotic as against democratic rule.

[25]Durkheim judged occupational groups to be the basic kind of intermediate organization in modern society (1958, pp. 1-41, 96-97).

voluntary associations as bases of political participation. Or, in the absence of associations such as the P.T.A. to provide channels of communication and influence between parents and school, the individual is less likely to develop or sustain interest and participation in the education of his children. Examples may be easily multiplied, but these are sufficient to suggest why independent groups are indispensable bases for the maintenance of meaningful proximate concerns.

The lack of a structure of independent groups also removes the basis for self-protection on the part of elites, because it permits direct modes of intervention to replace mediated participation in elites. In the first place, intermediate groups, even though they are independent of top elites, operate to protect these elites from arbitrary and excessive pressures by themselves being responsive to the needs and demands of people. They carry a large share of the burden of seeking to fulfill the interests of people who would otherwise have to rely exclusively on national agencies to minister to their needs. Secondly, the leaders of intermediate groups, irrespective of their particular aims (so long as these aims are not contrary to the integrity of the community), help to shore up the larger system of authority with which their own authority is inextricably bound. Third, intermediate groups help to protect elites by functioning as channels through which popular participation in the larger society (especially in the national elites) may be directed and restrained. In the absence of intermediate groups to act as representatives and guides for popular participation, people must act *directly* in the critical centers of society, and therefore in a manner unrestrained by the values and interest of a variety of social groups.

These reasons why the weakness of intermediate groups characterize mass society are at the same time reasons why the strength of such groups characterizes the pluralist society. A strong intermediate structure consists of stable and independent groups which represent diverse and frequently conflicting interests. The opposition among such groups restrains one another's power, thereby limiting the aggregate intervention in elites; that is, a system of social checks and balances among a plurality of diverse groups operates to protect elites as well as non-elites in ways we have indicated. Furthermore, the separation of the various spheres of society—for example, separation of religion and politics—means that access to elites in one sphere does not directly affect elites in other spheres. The various authorities are more or less autonomous in their own spheres, in that they are not directly determined in their membership or policy by authorities in other spheres. These same factors protect non-elites from elites, since independent groups guard their members from one another, and since overlapping memberships among groups, *each of which concerns only limited aspects of its members' lives,* restrains each group from seeking total domination over its membership.

The state in pluralist society also plays a vital role in support of individual freedom, for it is above all the state which has the capacity to safeguard the individual against domination by particular groups. Durkheim saw more profoundly than most that it is the *combination* of the state and what he called "secondary groups" that engenders individual liberty, rather than one or the other social structure alone. We shall quote him at length because he brings out with great clarity the special competence of each type of social structure for the advancement of individual freedom:

[The individual] must not be curbed and monopolised by the secondary groups, and these groups must not be able to get a mastery over their members and mould them at will. There must therefore exist above these local, domestic—in a word, secondary—authorities, some overall authority which makes the law for them all: it must remind each of them that it is but a part and not the whole and that it should not keep for itself what rightly belongs to the whole. The only means of averting this collective particularism and all it involves for the individual, is to have a special agency with the duty of representing the overall collectivity, its rights and its interests, vis-à-vis these individual collectivities. . . . It is solely because, in holding its constituent societies in check, it [the state] prevents them from exerting the repressive influences over the individual that they would otherwise exert. So there is nothing inherently tyrannical about State intervention in the different fields of collective life; on the contrary, it has the object and the effect of alleviating tyrannies that do exist. It will be argued, might not the State in turn become despotic? Undoubtedly, provided there was nothing to counter that trend. In that case, as the sole existing collective force, it produces the effects that any collective force not neutralized by any counter-force of the same kind would have on individuals. The State itself then becomes a leveller and repressive. And its repressiveness becomes even harder to endure than that of small groups, because it is more artificial. The State, in our large-scale societies, is so removed from individual interests that it cannot take into account the special or local and other conditions in which they exist. Therefore when it does attempt to regulate them, it succeeds only at the cost of doing violence to them and distorting them. It is, too, not sufficiently in touch with individuals in the mass to be able to mould them inwardly, so that they readily accept its pressure on them. The individual eludes the State to some extent—the State can only be effective in the context of a large-scale society—and individual diversity may not come to light. Hence, all kinds of resistance and distressing conflicts arise. The small groups do not have this drawback. They are close enough to the things that provide their *raison d'être* to be able to adapt their actions exactly and they surround the individuals closely enough to shape them in their own image. The inference to be drawn from this comment, however, is simply that *if that collective force, the State, is to be the liberator of the individual, it has itself need of some counterbalance; it must be restrained by other collective forces, that is, by . . . secondary groups . . . it is out of this conflict of social forces that individual liberties are born.* (Durkheim, 1958, pp. 62-3; italics added)

It has been said that medieval society was in fact essentially pluralist.[26] But of course medieval society did not permit democratic control. The con-

---

[26]See, for example, Kerr (1955, p. 4).

fusion here resides in the notion of pluralism: shall it be conceived as referring merely to a multiplicity of associations, or in addition, to a multiplicity of *affiliations?* Where individuals belong to several groups, no one group is *inclusive* of its members' lives. Associations have members with a variety of social characteristics (e.g., class and ethnic identities) and group memberships (e.g., trade unions may possess members who go to various churches, or even belong to church-affiliated trade union associations such as ACTU). Warner found that in Newburyport, Massachusetts, one-third of the 357 associations that were studied had members from three out of the six classes he identified, another third had members from four classes, and one-sixth from five or six classes. Almost two-thirds of the 12,876 members of associations belonged to associations in which four or more of the six classes were represented. Over three-fourths belonged to associations in which three or more of the ten ethnic groups were represented. Over one-half belonged to associations in which two or more of the four religious faiths were represented (Warner and Lunt, 1941, pp. 341, 346, 349). Such extensive *cross-cutting solidarities* favor a high level of freedom and consensus: these solidarities help prevent one line of social cleavage from becoming dominant, and they constrain associations to respect the various affiliations of their members lest they alienate them. Socially heterogeneous religious organizations are also important pluralistic agencies; they may be contrasted with situations in which religious and class lines tend to closely correspond, as in France where anti-clericalism is largely a working-class phenomenon. Political parties which draw their support from all major social segments constitute still another kind of cross-cutting solidarity. In this respect, the highly heterogeneous and decentralized American parties may be contrasted with the highly centralized, class-based Socialist parties and religious-based Catholic parties characteristic of European multiparty systems.

Our conception of pluralism includes that of multiple affiliations, which means that medieval society was not pluralist in our use of the term. So long as no association claims or receives hegemony over many aspects of its members' lives, its power over the individual will be limited. This is a vital point, because the authority of a private group can be as oppressive as that of the state.

A plurality of groups that are both independent and non-inclusive not only protects elites and non-elites from one another but does so in a manner that permits liberal democratic control. Liberal democratic control requires that people have *access* to elites, and that they exercise *restraint* in their participation. Independent groups help to maintain access to top-level decision-making by bringing organized pressure to bear on elites to remain responsive to outside influence. Each group has interests of its own in gaining access to elites, and has organized power not available to separate individuals for the implementation of these interests. These interests require not only that elites pay attention to the demands of the group, but also that other groups do not become so strong as to be able to shut off this group's access to the elite. Since independent groups seek to maintain their position by checking one another's power as well as the power of higher-level elites, the interaction of these groups helps to sustain access to decision-making processes in the larger society.

A plurality of independent groups also helps to regulate popular participation by integrating people into a wide range of proximate concerns. Where people possess multiple interests and commitments, attachments to remote objects, such as loyalty to the nation-state, are mediated by proximate relations.[27] Therefore, people in pluralist society engage in relatively little *direct* participation in national decisions, not because elites prevent them from doing so, but because they can influence decisions more effectively through their own groups. Furthermore, people tend to be *selective* in their participation, limiting their direct involvement in the larger society to matters that appear to them of particular concern in light of their values and interests. Since pluralist society engenders a variety of values and interests, self-selective involvement in national politics tends to limit the number of people who are vitally concerned with any given issue.

The intermediate structure of pluralist society helps to maintain access to elites by virtue of its *independence* from elites. The intermediate structure of totalitarian society, on the other hand, helps to prevent access to the elite by virtue of its *domination* by the elite. By means of intermediate groups instituted and controlled from above, the totalitarian regime is able to keep the population in a state of mobilization. Such organizations as Soviet trade unions have the primary function of activating and channelizing the energies of workers in directions determined by the regime. If there were no controlled intermediate organizations in all spheres of society, people would be free to regroup along lines independent of the regime. That is why it is of the utmost importance to totalitarian regimes to keep the population active in these controlled groups. Totalitarian regimes search out all independent forms of organizations in order to transform them or destroy them. In certain other societies, the natural decline of independent forms of association prepares the way for the rise of totalitarian movements.

The intermediate structure of communal society helps to maintain tra-

---

[27]See Grodzins (1956, pp. 29-30) for a discussion of the combination of direct and indirect ties to the nation-state in pluralist society: "National loyalty has a variety of roots. It springs from direct involvement in the nation's grandeur, from direct response to the symbols of the nation. It is an indirect product of satisfactory private life, loyalties to voluntary groups being transmitted to, and culminating in, national loyalty."

ditional authority and community in that its constituent groups are in-dependent of the highest elites, while at the same time exercising *inclusive* control over their members—who are not free to leave the group or to join another group.[28] This kind of intermediate structure is exemplified in the corporations of the Middle Ages.

> In the Middle Ages men thought and acted corporately. The status of every man was fixed by his place in some community—manor, borough, guild, learned University or convent. The villein and the monk scarcely existed in the eye of the law except through the lord of the manor and the Abbot of the monastery. . . . The unit of medieval society was neither the nation nor the individual but something between the two—the corporation. (Trevelyan, 1953, p. 239)

The corporation protected the individual from outside coercion—for example, from undue interference by the king; but at the same time, the individual had little control over his corporate group, for he had neither status nor rights apart from the group. "As a human being, or as an English subject, no man had 'rights' either to employment or to the vote, or indeed to anything very much beyond a little Christian charity"(Trevelyan, 1953, p. 239).

The intermediate structure corresponding to each of our four types of society has been analyzed along two dimensions: (a) the strength of inter-mediate social organizations, especially their capacity to operate as autonomous centers of power; and (b) the inclusiveness of intermediate organizations, that is, the extent to which they encompass all aspects of their members' lives. The results of our analysis may be summarized in the form of a diagram.

INTERMEDIATE GROUPS

		Strong	Weak
INTERMEDIATE GROUPS	Inclusive	communal society	totalitarian society
	Non-Inclusive	pluralist society	mass society

France provides a good illustration of a society in which intermediate relations are weak and non-inclusive. A closer look at this aspect of French life may help to clarify our conception of mass structure.

French society tends to be highly organized on the national level, in the form of a highly centralized state bureaucracy, and on the family level.

[28]Simmel has remarked that the "peculiar character of group formation in the Middle Ages" lies in the fact that "affiliation with a group absorbed the whole man" (1955, pp. 148-9).

There is a relative paucity of intermediate structures to link these two levels of life. Since voluntary associations are major forms of intermediation in the democratic society, the weakness of this social form in France, compared with England or the United States, is one important indication of the atomization of that society.

France has a long history of hostility toward voluntary associations:

> French tradition has not been favourable to the growth of associations. . . . It is only within the last thirty years that the bonds of a restraining vigilance have been finally relaxed. . . . It seems clear enough that what associations, whether religious or secular, were able to exist, were the offspring of a privilege tardily given and illiberally exercised. (Laski, 1919, p. 321)

Freedom of association was not granted full legal recognition until 1901; but even since that time, a marked retardation in voluntary organization has persisted in France. Arnold Rose reports, on the basis of interviews with a number of French leaders,

> the almost uniform impression that what social influence associations [those actively directed toward an outside purpose] there are in France are largely "paper" organizations and that even if they claim a large membership they do not involve the members' interests and emotions very deeply. . . . The general impression is that associations play but a small role, both in the functioning of the community or nation and in the lives of the average citizens. (1954, p. 77)

Another recent study of French society also observed "the relative scarcity of voluntary organizations in France as compared with the massive American proliferation of channels whereby individuals engage themselves in public enterprise."

> The absence of active civic participation is evident in all social classes in France. There are very few "clubs" of the sort developed by the upper social groups in Britain. Among the middle class there are few parallels of Rotary, Kiwanis, and Lions . . . [or of] the Parent-Teachers' Association, the League of Women Voters, and the Association of University Women. . . . Among the working class only the labour union has made any headway, but even it hardly touches the French worker in his daily life—offering him neither educational opportunities, recreational facilities, consumers' cooperatives, nor social diversions. (Lerner, 1957, p. 29)

Voluntary groups generally tend to be shut out from participation in the performance of vital social functions in France, with the consequence that they are incapable of helping to adapt people to changing social circumstances. This appears to be true for associations nominally oriented toward change as well as for associations with conservative ideologies; French trade unions and working-class parties, for example, frequently resist change just as strenuously as do agricultural organizations and business associations. A study of associations in two French communities arrives at the conclusion that French associations are less capable of mediating social change than are their American counterparts: "The association in the United States may be a mechanism for integrating or mediating change, but in the French community, associations appear to be oriented toward the prevention of change" (Gallagher, 1957, p. 159).

Harold Laski believed that the "division of French parties into a plethora of groups owes its origin less to any inherent naturalness or to a proved benefit in the performance of party-functions than to the possibility such division affords for the erection of a system of loyalties external to that of the state" (Laski, 1919, p. 322). Yet, even political parties do not absorb the attention of very many Frenchmen. When asked, "Do you think it would make much difference whether one party or another were in power?" thirty-nine per cent of a national sample answered negatively and an additional 12% had no opinion. In answer to the question, "Do questions concerning politics interest you?" only 10% indicated a great interest, 39% expressed little interest, and 51% said they had no interest at all (Rose, 1954, pp. 111-13). These data suggest that French political parties are not by themselves very effective links between a large portion of the population and the national society.

Local government in France also does not function as an independent intermediate structure, since it operates more as a part of the national bureaucracy than as an expression of the autonomy of the local community. The key agent of local government, the Prefect, is appointed by the Minister of the Interior and exercises the national government's powers in a local area (department). Since these powers are great, including as they do extensive executive and financial controls, local self-government is small. Local government is a mechanism of national authority, and not a basis for local participation and control. Therefore, it does not serve to involve the individual in the public realm, nor does it serve to protect the individual against control by the state.

> To an inconceivable degree Empire and Republic have completed the work of the monarchy and extinguished all trace of autonomy and independence in communes and departments. The first and most important answer to the question of who rules France must be that it is ruled by ninety agents [Prefects] of the Ministry of the Interior. (Luethy, 1957, p. 20)

The local community and parish in France may provide certain satisfactions for the individual. The cafe and public parks are bases of participation in the local community.[29] But institutions of this type, no matter

---

[29]See Rose (1954, pp. 105-6, 110, 112). Cf. Mannheim's statement: "France, too, has the smaller cities and the provinces as counter-forces to protect it against the mechanisms of mass society"

how much they may enrich communal life, are nevertheless not capable of linking either the individual or the community to the larger society. Furthermore, increasing geographic mobility is weakening these informal social relations. As for the parish, a recent inquiry notes that "the larger part of even rural France consists of 'parishes indifferent to Christian traditions' " and concludes that "the church does not have much hold over a majority of the French today" (Rose, 1954, pp. 106-7). The apparent ineffectiveness of local government, community, and parish as bases of participation in the larger society creates a social vacuum in French life. This may be a reason why a study of a French community, after reporting that associations are "generally not very important" and "cut into the lives of their members very little," nevertheless concludes that "without the associations, [people] would live in almost complete isolation."[30]

We may conclude from this brief analysis of French group life that independent social forms are more or less inoperative as sources of mediation between elites and non-elites. As a result, large numbers of people are available for mass appeals, as evidenced in the success of communism, Gaullism, and Poujadism in recent years. Since World War II no other Western democracy has witnessed such widespread mass attacks on the constitutional order. . . .

• • •

Germany appears to be similar to France and different from England and the United States in respect to the development of multiple independent groups that participate in the direction of public affairs. In a recent study of West German society, the author described the crucial differences between Germany, on the one side, and England and the United States, on the other, as follows:

> In Germany, there is a sharp break between the public and the private spheres. Political and social responsibility is an attribute of office, whether in the parliaments, the ministries, the churches, the trade-unions, or the interest-groups. What is more, within these various political structures a strong hierarchical spirit dominates, so that political responsibility and communication tend to be confined to the very heights of these institutions. In England and the United States, on the other hand, there is a gradation from public to private. Private association for public purposes is not confined to political parties and interest-groups, but includes a variety of general and special public-interest groups concerned with policy issues of all kinds at all levels of the governmental process. Power and communication are more or less decentralized within these organizations. . . .

(1940, p. 88); and Luethy's statement: "The empty and impoverished life of most French villages and provincial towns, whose monuments bear witness to a former vitality, is the result of [the centralization of French Society]" (1957, p. 20).

[30]Charles Bettleheim and S. Frère, *Une Ville Française Moyenne: Auxerre en 1950*, p. 282 (cited in Rose, 1954, p. 75).

The shortcomings of democratic society in Germany result from absence of such institutional pluralism. (Almond, 1957, pp. 238-9)

France and Germany suffer from the failure to have developed and sustained an intermediate structure of independent groups. The centralization of national organization is one major consequence. Conversely, whenever there is expropriation of major social functions by large organizations, smaller groups lose their reasons for existence (except perhaps as administrative agencies). This loss of function, in turn, undermines the meaning smaller groups possess for their participants. No group can lose its character-defining functions and remain a source of meaning and belonging. An organization whose performance falls far short of its avowed purposes loses meaning: the subjective response of the individual is tied to the objective role of the group. Thus, the role of local organization becomes attenuated as decision-making and communication shift toward a national center, with the consequence that rank and file members find little basis for participation in it. Similarly, the role of a job in the fashioning of a product becomes attenuated as that job becomes increasingly subdivided and removed from the worker's control, with the consequence that the individual finds little basis for a sense of workmanship and status in it.[31] In like manner, as the role of the local community in leisure activities progressively gives way to the national media of entertainment, the individual finds less to interest him in his community.[32] In sum, the attenuation of association, occupation, and community characterizes the intermediate structure of mass society.

ISOLATION OF PERSONAL RELATIONS

Personal as well as intermediate relations become increasingly peripheral to the central operations of the mass society. This is shown by the change in social position of the family from an extended kinship system to an *isolated* conjugal unit following upon the loss of many social functions. The family gives up its educational role to a public school system, its mutual aid role to a social security system, and so on. The loss of functions sharply limits the public meaning of the family, though not necessarily its private meaning, and diminishes its capacity for relating the individual to the larger society. Kinship units may be too narrow in scope and too far removed from the public realm to be able to provide an effective basis for developing interest and participation in it.

With this argument in mind, many students of mass society imply that

[31]Of the voluminous literature on the alienation of labor, the writings of Karl Marx are especially noteworthy (n. d., pp. 395-400, 708-9). See also Fromm (1953, pp. 125-31, 177-84) and Arendt (1958, pp. 248-57).

[32]On the alienation of leisure, see Fromm (1953, pp. 131-7) and Riesman (1953, pp. 315-45).

mass society lacks family ties as well as intermediate social relations. This view is open to serious question. In the first place, since the family by itself is inherently incapable of linking the individual to large-scale society, it is theoretically unnecessary to assume that such relations are absent in order to have a mass society. In other words, it is entirely possible to have a society in which there are family ties but which is still a mass society due to the lack of intermediate relations. Furthermore, since the individual who is *totally* isolated (that is, without even family ties) for long periods is not likely to possess that minimum of personal organization required by collective activity, the loss of all family life leads to personal deviance—in the extreme case, mental disorders and suicides—rather than to mass behavior. But it is mass behavior which marks the mass society.

• • •

Thus, there are good theoretical and empirical reasons (although the data are far from conclusive) for not assuming that the loss of family life is a necessary condition underlying mass tendencies. Rather, we contend that it is the *isolation* of the family and other primary groups which marks the mass society.

Since social isolation, as the term will be used herein, refers to the lack of social relations to the larger society, individuals may be isolated even though they possess family ties—so long as the family groups in turn are not linked to the larger society in any firm way. For isolated families (or other kinds of primary associations, such as friendship groups) cannot by themselves provide the basis for understanding or managing the impersonal environment with which the individual also must grapple. Therefore, whereas the isolation of a small group does not entail the isolation of its members from one another, the individual member of such a group may nevertheless be isolated from the common life of the "great society." A central proposition of this study states that meaningful and effective participation in the larger society requires a structure of groups intermediate between the family and the nation; and the weakness of such a structure creates a vulnerability to mass movements. Participation in small but isolated groups such as the family is no substitute for participation in intermediate groups and may even be favorable to participation in mass movements, since the individual is more likely to engage in new ventures when he receives support from his close associates, and because the member of even a small group is a more accessible target for mass agitation than is a completely unattached person. In other words, the totally isolated individual (that is, the person without *any* social ties) will be unable to maintain his personal organization sufficiently to engage in cooperative ventures of any kind, whereas the individual who has personal ties but no broader ties in the society is more likely to be available for mass movements.[35]

[35]For further discussion of this point, see Part III, pp. 217-18.

CENTRALIZATION OF NATIONAL RELATIONS

The organizing principle of large-scale mass society centers on the national level. This is indicated by the proliferation of governmental functions in previously autonomous spheres of activity, by the growth of national organizations, and by the concomitant shift in power from local to national centers. Structures on the national level develop in response to the size and complexity of society; they expropriate functions formerly reserved to intermediate groups and the family. Modern mass society is characterized by the great degree to which this transference has taken place, so that the state and national organization assume the central role in the direction of all kinds of collective activity. Mass society finds a major basis of integration in large-scale organization. Therefore, we would be misconstruing mass society if we were to describe it as a state of social disorganization.

National organization that is centralized at the expense of smaller forms of association helps to create amorphous masses. People are more easily manipulated and mobilized when they become directly and exclusively dependent on the national organization for the satisfaction of interests otherwise also met in proximate relations. When the national organization is atomized, its members find it increasingly difficult to orient themselves to the larger society. They cannot understand the workings of the overall system, in part because "there are far fewer positions from which the major structural connections between different activities can be perceived, and fewer men can reach these vantage points" (Mannheim, 1940, p. 59). Furthermore, increasing distance between centers of decision and daily life make it more difficult for people to grasp the meaning of issues at stake. Faced with the impersonality and incomprehensibility of national relations, and at the same time lacking an independent group life, the individual may withdraw from participation in the larger society. Or he may act in spite of the lack of group relations. Certain spheres of mass society are based on such unmediated participation of large numbers of individuals.

Large-scale communication is based on mass participation when it is divorced from intermediate relations, and prevails over other modes that are anchored in such relations. Agencies of large-scale communication are not necessarily mass media, however. They become so when they lose their ties to local and personal forms of communication. Mere growth in size of these agencies makes mass relations more probable (but certainly not inevitable), as it encourages national centralization and discourages local relations of those who manage the media.[36] Thus, the genuine community

[36]The change in the *Manchester Guardian*, a leading English newspaper, has been considered in this light (Taylor, 1957, p. 12). *"The Manchester Guardian* . . . has ceased to represent Manchester except in name . . . it is now a national paper pure and simple. . . . The London office provides most of the paper. . . . Now the editor plays little part in local politics."

newspaper forms a link in the local chain of gossip and discussion, as its staff members participate in face-to-face relations with their readers. By contrast, the mass media lack such intermediate associations; as a result, instead of sharing a community of value and interest with their audience, they substitute organizational and market relations on a national level.

In general, formal organizations are to be identified as mass organizations, not by their size, but when they lack intermediate units which have some autonomy from the central leadership. In the absence of a structure of smaller groups, formal organizations themselves become remote from their members. That is, they get beyond the reach of their members, and as a result cannot deeply influence them nor command their allegiance in the face of competition for member loyalties. Consequently, members of excessively bureaucratized organizations may become mobilized by totalitarian elites. This is illustrated by the Nazi success in capturing many youth groups in Germany during the 1920's.

Prior to World War I, Germany witnessed a great upsurge of youth movements, filled with young men and women who were alienated from existing religion, politics, business, education, art, literature, and family life. The youth movement themselves were "at bottom random, 'goalless,' but persistent attempts to replace the crumbled value system . . . with another which would in some way focus the longing for a sacred experience" (Becker, 1946, p. 51). But the pre-war youth movement sank into routine in the early 1920's. Esoteric and intimate aspects of the movement became commonplace. The initially spontaneous charismatic leadership grew matter-of-fact and even traditional. The tendency toward tutelage by adults created centralized and routinized office staffs for many youth organizations. The whole movement became bureaucratized. Hitler, Goebbels, and Rosenberg seized the opportunity to exploit the widespread yearning for action on the part of both leaders and members of the youth movements. By 1923, the Nazis proclaimed the establishment of the Greater German Youth Movement to capture these restive youths. Funds were appropriated for an intensive propaganda campaign. By the end of 1924, Nazi youth groups were shooting up throughout Upper Saxony. After Hitler announced the creation of the Hitler Youth as a party auxiliary at the 1926 party convention, the organization spread rapidly (Becker, 1946, pp. 145-6).

Members or clients of an organization who are alienated from the leadership are favorite targets for mass movements. Communist successes among unemployed trade unionists in England during the depression have been related to the lack of close ties between the central Trade Union Congress and the local Trades Councils. In the absence of effective communication and organic bonds, the national leadership was insufficiently responsive to the distress of its members, with the result that the local organizations "were left without either lead or help from the centre and were thus easily led to back the Communists" (Cole, 1948, p. 148). Communist (and Nazi) penetration of the unemployed ranks in Germany likewise was facilitated by poor relations between trade union leadership and the ranks, in this instance in part because union functions were being absorbed by the state. German trade union connections with the workers were "unquestionably weakened by the increased activity of the state in the regulation of wages and conditions of unemployment." The vast array of economic functions administered by the state induced workers to believe they no longer needed unions (F. Newmann, 1936, pp. 31-2). At the same time rank and file members were becoming less and less committed to their unions, the leadership of both the trade unions and the Social Democratic party was becoming more and more entrenched and entwined in the government apparatus (Schorske, 1955, pp. 127-8). As a result, there developed "an increasing gap between what the average worker hoped and expected, and what was being said and done by the reformist, government-affiliated bureaucracy of the SPD and the unions" (Kirchheimer, 1957, p. 138). Membership in the socialist unions declined, and, especially as unemployment rose, both the Communists and the Nazis won increasing working-class support.

When, on the other hand, unions have developed strong locals, clubs, and the like, which perform important economic and social functions for their members, these members possess multiple relations to the organization, and to the larger social order—commitments they are not likely to endanger by supporting extremist movements. A study of the International Typographical Union shows how independent subgroup formation not only ties printers to the union, but also how it facilitates democratic processes within it (Lipset *et al.*, 1956). The I.T.U. is perhaps the most democratic union in America. Its distinguishing feature is a permanent two-party system, which guarantees an ever-present source of criticism of and alternative leadership to the incumbent administration. The two parties are not the only independent groups within the union to relate the rank and file leadership, however. In addition, and supportive of the party-system as well as the union, there are strong and relatively autonomous locals, large enough to protect their members from undue outside coercion, and small enough to provide an interpersonal basis for participation in the union's affairs. Furthermore, the printers possess a flourishing "occupational community," organized around a plurality of independent benevolent organizations, newspapers, athletic teams, lodges, social clubs, and informal relations. Although these subgroups are not part of the union, nor explicitly political in any way, they serve to increase political participation in the union (for example, by increasing contact of non-political printers with those who already are active in union politics), to train new union leaders (especially as a result of filling their own leadership needs for club officials), and to give their members a greater stake in maintaining the social order of the occupation, including the union and its party system. In short, through parties, locals, clubs, and friendships, as well as a result of other factors (such as the insulation of the printing occupation from other manual trades), printers develop multiple ties to their work, their union, and the larger social order of which they are a part.

Nisbet argues that unless all kinds of large-scale organizations are rooted in partially autonomous subgroups, they intensify rather than counteract the process of atomization:

> The labor union, the legal or medical association, or the church will become as centralized and as remote as the national State itself unless these great organizations are rooted in the smaller relationships which give meaning to the ends of the large associations. . . . Only thus will the large formal associations remain important agencies of order and freedom in democracy. (Nisbet, 1953, p. 277)

Large-scale organizations that fail to develop or sustain independent subgroups tend to be characterized by low levels of membership participation. Because they are not close enough to their members to allow for effective participation, mass organizations engender widespread apathy. Furthermore, the lack of a pluralist structure within organizations, like its absence in the larger society, not only discourages membership participation. It also discourages the formation of an informed membership, the development of new leadership, and the spread of responsibility and authority, so that the wide gap between the top and the bottom of mass organizations tends to be bridged by manipulation.[37]

At the same time that mass relations permit extensive manipulation of people by elites, they also encourage manipulation of elites by non-elites. Elites are more directly influenced by non-elites in the absence of intermediate groups because they are less insulated. Elites lose their insulation since demands and impulses of large numbers of people that formerly were sublimated and fulfilled by intermediate groups now are focused directly on the national level. Higher elites absorb functions formerly reserved to intermediate elites and therefore no longer can depend on these groups to siphon off popular pressures and to regulate participation. Furthermore, popular participation in the higher elites is all the stronger and less restrained for being in part a substitute for diversified participation in intermediate groups—especially in times of crisis.

In conclusion, the growth of centralized organizations at the expense of intermediate groups constrains both elites and non-elites to engage in efforts to directly manipulate the other. Media of communication that command the attention of millions of people simultaneously are major

---

[37]Cf. Selznick (1952, p. 290).

instruments of this manipulation by those who command them, but also by the audience upon which their success or failure directly is dependent. Centralized decision-making also may cut two ways: if the populace can make its voice felt more easily when it can influence directly one master decision, rather than having to influence many smaller decisions to achieve the same result, then by the same token elites also may grasp one major lever of power more readily than many smaller ones. Centralization of decision-making functions does not preclude direct intervention either by the mass or the elite, although it certainly does prevent people from expressing and implementing *individual* views on public matters. When centralized national relations are combined with weak intermediate relations and isolated family relations, elites are unprotected from mass pressures and masses are unprotected from elite pressures. The structure of mass society thus provides extensive opportunity for mass movements. The character of that structure may now be summarized.

Social groups larger than the family and smaller than the state operate to link elites and non-elites, so that the nature of these groups shapes the political relation. Where intermediate groups do not exist or do not perform important social functions, elites and non-elites are directly dependent on one another: there is non-mediated access to elites and direct manipulation of non-elites. This kind of social arrangement leaves society vulnerable to anti-democratic movements based on mass support. Centralized national groups do not mitigate mass availability; neither do isolated primary groups. For the one relationship is too remote and the other is too weak to provide the individual with firm bases of attachment to society. This is the situation of mass society.

Where many social groups are operative, the question is whether they are autonomous, that is, free from domination by other groups, and of limited scope, that is, influential with respect to only limited aspects of their members' lives. Where groups are influential with respect to the whole of their members' lives (for example, where "the status of every man was fixed by his place in some community—manor, borough, guild, learned University or convent" [Trevelyan, 1953, p. 239]), the political structure tends to be authoritarian but not totalitarian, since each community is to some degree independent and therefore capable of limiting the power of a central elite. This is the situation of more complex communal societies, such as medieval society with its corporations that protected the individual from undue external interference, for example, by the monarchy, but that did not give him much leeway with respect to the corporate authority itself.

Where, on the other hand, social groups are not only inclusive of their members' lives but also are themselves controlled by a central elite, then the political structure tends to be totalitarian. For in this case the individual is available to the central elite through his intermediate affiliations, which are instituted by the elite precisely for this purpose. Thus, whereas the medieval guild could help prevent the state from easy manipulation of its members by virtue of the guild's independence of the king, the state-dominated trade union is an instrument of the political elite for the mobilization of workers (as in the Soviet Union today). Where the trade union is not only independent of the state, but in addition the worker is not under the domination of his union except with reference to limited areas of life, then it supports a liberal democratic rule. The trade union must fulfill important social functions, however, for otherwise it becomes merely another organization without the ability to define and protect its members' position in the larger society. Intermediate groups whose functions have been absorbed by national structures mark the mass society. A wide variety of independent, limited-function organizations permits democratic control but also insulates both elite and non-elite from undue interference in the life of the other. This is the situation of pluralist society.

Social arrangements may encourage tendencies that transform the political system. This is especially true of the mechanisms of mass society, for they permit an abundance of mass movements. A major objective of this study is to identify the social origins and social bases of mass movements. On the basis of our model of mass society, we expect to find that mass movements are facilitated by the atomization of social relations, since unattached people are disposed to engage in mass action. . . .

Organizational Membership and Civic Competence

Gabriel Almond / Sidney Verba

A civic culture, we have argued, rests upon a set of nonpolitical attitudes and nonpolitical affiliations. Many of these attitudes that we have discussed—general attitudes toward other people, sense of social trust—have

SOURCE: From Gabriel Almond and Sidney Verba, "Organizational Membership and Civic Competence" in *The Civic Culture: Political Attitudes and Democracy in Five Nations* (Princeton: Princeton University Press, 1963), Chapter 11, pp. 300-322 (omission of Table 6, p. 308; 10 lines, p. 316; Table 10 plus 6 lines, p. 315). Copyright © 1963 by Princeton University Press. Reprinted by permission of Princeton University Press.

little explicit political content, and many of the affiliations we have dealt with—primary group affiliations in particular—are quite distant from the political system. Our concentration on this level of social structure has not meant to imply that larger, secondary, nonpolitical groups—voluntary associations are the main example—play an insignificant role in the democratic polity. Quite the contrary: though primary associations play an important role in the development of a citizen's sense of political competence and reflect an incipient capability to aggregate one's demands with others, they would, by themselves, represent a weak link between the individual and the polity. As Kornhauser has pointed out, primary groups are still small and powerless compared with the mass institutions of politics. Larger institutions, close enough to the individual to allow him some participation and yet close enough to the state to provide access to power, are also a necessary part of the democratic infrastructure.[1]

Voluntary associations are the prime means by which the function of mediating between the individual and the state is performed. Through them the individual is able to relate himself effectively and meaningfully to the political system. These associations help him avoid the dilemma of being either a parochial, cut off from political influence, or an isolated and powerless individual, manipulated and mobilized by the mass institutions of politics and government. The availability of his primary groups as a political resource in times of threat gives him an intermittent political resource. Membership in voluntary associations gives him a more structured set of political resources, growing out of his varied interests.

If the citizen is a member of some voluntary organization, he is involved in the broader social world but is less dependent upon and less controlled by his political system. This is so for several reasons. The association of which he is a member can represent his needs and demands before the government. It can make the government more chary of engaging in activities that would harm the individual. Furthermore, communications from central governmental authorities are mediated by the associational memberships of the individual. This is because individuals tend to interpret communications in terms of their memberships in social groupings— i.e., they are likely to reject communications that are unfavorable to the association to which they belong—and also because they may also receive communications from their associations and are thereby provided with alternate channels of political communication. Above all, from the point of view of the individual member, affiliation with some voluntary organization appears to have significant effects on his political attitudes. We shall try to specify these effects in this chapter.

In dealing with the data on associational membership, we must consider one further point. Associational membership may involve a low level of

[1]William Kornhauser, *The Politics of Mass Society*, Glencoe, Ill., 1959.

individual participation and competence: associations may be quite large; opportunities for participation limited. Thus the existence of a high frequency of membership may tell us more about the political institutions of a society than it does about the state of citizenship in that society. For the latter we shall have to know somewhat more about the nature of the membership—how active individuals are in their organizations and what effects their memberships have upon them.

The Distribution of Voluntary Association Membership

Voluntary association membership is more widespread in some countries than in others. This is apparent from Table 1. In the United States over half the respondents are members of some such organization.[2] In Britain and Germany somewhat less than half the respondents are members of some organization, while in Italy and Mexico the proportions are 29 per cent and 25 per cent, respectively.

TABLE 1   Membership in Voluntary Associations, by Nation

Nation	(%)	(No.)*
United States	57	(970)
Great Britain	47	(963)
Germany	44	(955)
Italy	29	(995)
Mexico	25	(1,007)

*Numbers in parentheses refer to the bases upon which percentages are calculated.

To what sorts of organizations do individuals in the five countries belong? The range of specific organizations is wide. But Table 2 suggests some of the main types. In all countries organizations representing economic interests—unions, business organizations, farm organizations, and, perhaps, professional organizations—are frequently reported. Social organizations are mentioned by 10 per cent or more of our sample in the United States, Britain, and Germany; and in the United States religious, civic-political, and fraternal organizations are also mentioned by 10 per

[2] These data are based on responses to this question: "Are you a member of any organizations now—trade or labor unions, business organizations, social groups, professional or farm organizations, cooperatives, fraternal or veterans' groups, athletic clubs, political, charitable, civic or religious organizations, or any other organized group? Which ones?" The amount of voluntary association membership depends heavily upon the wording of the question and on the definition given the respondent of a voluntary association. The inclusion of trade unions, for instance, results in a somewhat higher figure than has been found in other studies. However, what is relevant here is not the absolute level of membership in any one nation, but the relative position of each of the five nations. What is significant, then, is that the same question was asked in all five nations.

cent or more of the respondents. One point to note is that the extent of "politicization" of these organizations, that is, the extent to which they are overtly engaged in politics, probably varies greatly. Some of the economic organizations are obviously deeply politicized; some of the social ones may be completely nonpolitical. We shall return below to the implications of this for political attitudes.

TABLE 2 Membership in Various Types of Organizations, by Nation (in per cent)

Organizations	U.S.	U.K.	Germany	Italy	Mexico
Trade unions	14	22	15	6	11
Business	4	4	2	5	2
Professional	4	3	6	3	5
Farm	3	0	4	2	0
Social	13	14	10	3	4
Charitable	3	3	2	9	6
Religious*	19	4	3	6	5
Civic-political	11	3	3	8	3
Cooperative	6	3	2	2	0
Veterans	6	5	1	4	0
Fraternal**	13				
Other	6	3	9	6	0
Total per cent members	57	47	44	30	24
Total number of respondents	970	963	955	995	1,007

*This refers to church-related organizations, not to church affiliation itself.
**U.S. only.

TABLE 3 Percentage of Respondents Who Belong to Some Organization, by Nation and Sex

Nation	Total		Male		Female	
	(%)	(No.)*	(%)	(No.)	(%)	(No.)
United States	57	(970)	68	(455)	47	(515)
Great Britain	47	(963)	66	(460)	30	(503)
Germany	44	(955)	66	(449)	24	(506)
Italy	30	(995)	41	(471)	19	(524)
Mexico	24	(1,007)	43	(355)	15	(652)

*Numbers in parentheses refer to the bases upon which percentages are calculated.

The distribution of organizational membership is also interesting. If we look at the proportion of men and women who are members of some organizations, we see some striking results (see Table 3). The national differences in the number of individuals participating in associations can be largely explained by differences in the proportion of women who report such membership. Thus the high level of associational membership in the

United States depends to a large extent on the high level of female participation. If only males are considered, associational participation in the United States is no more frequent than it is in Britain or Germany. It is, in fact, striking how similar the frequency of membership is among the three nations: about two-thirds of male respondents in each of the three nations report such membership. Among females, on the other hand, participation in the United States is substantially more frequent than in Britain and about twice as frequent as in Germany. In Mexico and Italy the level of participation by both males and females is lower than in the other three countries. However, a similar relationship between frequency of male participation and frequency of female participation is found in all nations except the United States; that is, men participate in voluntary organizations about two to three times as frequently as do women. In terms of the participatory role of women, then, the United States differs substantially from the other four countries, for American women, though they participate less frequently than American men in voluntary associations, do not differ from men in this respect as much as do women in other countries.

Just as men participate more frequently in voluntary associations, so do individuals with higher education. This is seen in Table 4. In all countries there is a sharp increase in organizational membership as one moves up the educational ladder. Among those with primary school education, memberships are much less frequent than among those with higher education. This suggests one of the reasons for the close relationship be-

TABLE 4 Percentage of Respondents Who Belong to Some Organization, by Nation and Education

Nation	Total (%)	(No.)*	Prim. or Less (%)	(No.)	Some Sec. (%)	(No.)	Some Univ. (%)	(No.)
United States	57	(970)	46	(339)	55	(443)	80	(188)
Great Britain	47	(963)	41	(593)	55	(322)	92	(24)
Germany	44	(955)	41	(792)	63	(124)	62	(26)
Italy	30	(995)	25	(692)	37	(245)	46	(54)
Mexico	24	(1,007)	21	(877)	39	(103)	68	(24)

*Numbers in parentheses refer to the bases upon which percentages are calculated.

tween education and political competence. Education has compound effects upon political competence. Not only does the more highly educated individual learn politically relevant skills within the school, but he also is more likely to enter into other nonpolitical relationships that have the effect of further heightening his political competence. Associational membership is one form of such nonpolitical participation. The individual with less education, and therefore less political competence, is also less likely to enter into the sorts of relationships that would tend to develop political competence in later years. The data, then, do suggest that the various functions performed by voluntary associations are performed more frequently for those with higher education.[3]

We are interested in the way in which voluntary association membership affects political attitudes. But the types of associations we are dealing with are many and varied, and one would expect different effects from membership in different types of organization. One way in which the organizations vary is in the extent to which they are concerned with public affairs. Some of the associations are purely social, others are directly and overtly politically oriented. One can argue—and, indeed, this is one of the major hypotheses about voluntary association membership—that membership in even a nonpolitical organization will affect political attitudes. The experience with social interaction within the organization; the opportunity to participate in the decisions of the organization (if there is such participation); and the general broadening of perspectives that occurs in any sort of social activity—all would be expected to increase an individual's potential for political involvement and activity. Nevertheless, one would also expect to find that those organizations more directly involved in politics would have greater effects on the political perspectives of their members.[4]

Unfortunately, our data do not allow us objectively to divide the voluntary organizations into different types, based on the degree to which they take an active political role. We do, however, know whether or not the individual member perceives of his organization as taking some part in politics. Respondents were asked if any organization they belonged to was "in any way concerned with governmental, political, or public affairs; for instance, do they take stands on or discuss public issues or try to influence governmental decisions?" It must be remembered that this question probes the perceptions of the respondents: it asks for their own definition of political affairs. Furthermore, many members may not be aware of the activities of their organizations. A member of a veterans' group that is actively lobbying for veterans' benefits or for certain foreign policies may perceive his group in essentially social terms. Thus these data do not neces-

[3]Similar data could be presented for the distribution of organizational membership among the occupational strata. Higher occupational status generally involves more frequent voluntary association membership, though the relationship is not as close as that between education and affiliation.

[4]Similarly, such organizations would probably also have greater effects of the operation of the political system. Even those that take no active role in politics—do not press for legislation, are politically unconcerned—may have a significant role in political decisions. Their very existence as *potential* political organizations may affect the decisions of government officials in ways that would not happen if these particular groups were not organized. Yet all else being equal, one would expect an overtly political group to have more of an impact on political decisions.

sarily reflect the actual state of political activity by voluntary associations. But we are interested in the impact of membership in political and non-political organizations on political attitudes, and so these data on the individual's perception of the political role of his organization may be sufficient.

Table 5 reports the frequency with which respondents in our five countries perceive that their organizations take some part in politics. In the United States about one in four respondents belongs to an organization that he perceives to be involved in politics.[5] This proportion falls off to six per cent in Italy. Though the nations differ in the percentage of the *total population* who perceive that an organization of theirs is involved in political affairs (column 1), the proportion of *organizational members* who hold this perception is strikingly uniform among the nations (column 2). With the exception of Italy, approximately the same proportion of organizational members in each country — 40 to 45 per cent — perceives itself to be part of a politically active organization. For about one-fifth of the Italian members and about two-fifths of the members in each of the other nations, being part of an organization does involve (in terms of the individual's awareness) recruitment into the political system.

TABLE 5   Respondents Who Believe an Organization of Theirs Is Involved in Political Affairs, by Nation

Nation	% of Total Population		% of Organizational Members	
	(%)	(No.)*	(%)	(No.)
United States	24	(970)	41	(551)
Great Britain	19	(963)	40	(453)
Germany	18	(955)	40	(419)
Italy	6	(995)	20	(291)
Mexico	11	(1,007)	46	(242)

*Numbers in parentheses refer to the base upon which percentages are calculated.

Organizational Membership and Political Competence

Political and Nonpolitical Organizations. What effect, if any, does organizational membership have on political attitudes? Do those individuals

[5]That the frequency with which an individual reports affiliation with a political organization varies with his definition of politics is suggested by a finding made by Woodward and Roper: 31 per cent of their sample responded positively to the question, "Do you happen to belong to any organizations that sometimes take a stand on housing, better government, school problems, or other public issues?" In contrast, 24 per cent in our sample answered our question positively. The difference may be due to the fact that many of our respondents would not consider "school problems" a political question. See Julian L. Woodward and Elmo Roper, "Political Activity of American Citizens," *American Political Science Review,* XLIV (1950), pp. 872-85.

who are members of some organization differ in their political perspectives from those who are not members? And does membership in any sort of organization, political as well as nonpolitical, affect one's political views? Or is it only membership in a politically relevant organization that influences one's perspectives on politics? The political attitudes we are interested in are those associated with democratic citizenship, as we have defined it. If organizational membership fosters the development of a democratic citizenry, one would expect the members, in comparison with those who are not members, to feel more confident of their ability to influence the government, to be more active in politics, more "open" in their political opinions, and, in general, more committed to democratic values.

Let us look first at the relationship between organizational membership and the individual's sense of ability to influence the government. This sense of competence, we have suggested earlier, is a major attitudinal variable in understanding the political perspectives of the individual, and it has significant implications for a wide range of other important political attitudes. The proportion of respondents receiving high scores on the subjective competence scale among (1) those respondents who are members of organizations they consider to be involved in politics, (2) those who are members of nonpolitical organizations, and (3) those who are members of no organization. The results are striking, and quite uniform from nation to nation. In all nations those respondents who are members of no organization are generally lower in the scale than are organizational members. And among organizational members, those respondents who consider their organization to be involved in politics are most likely to receive high scores on the scale. In Great Britain, for instance, 80 per cent of the members of a politically oriented organization are to be found in the highest three scores of the subjective competence scale; 69 per cent of the members of a nonpolitical organization are in these top three categories; while only 56 per cent of those who belong to no organization can be found in the highest categories of the scale. In Italy 77 per cent of the members of politically oriented organizations score high on the scale, in contrast with 49 per cent of those who belong to nonpolitical organizations, and 34 per cent of those who belong to no organization.

Both subjective competence and the frequency of organizational membership are related to educational attainment, thus it is important to note that this relationship between membership and sense of ability to influence the government persists when educational level is held constant. Only among British respondents with higher education is there a reversal of the trend: those respondents who are members of a nonpolitical organization score slightly better on the subjective competence scale than do the respondents who are members of a political organization. But the expected pattern is quite strong among British respondents in the lower educational group, and on both educational levels elsewhere.

. . . Such membership is indeed related to a citizen's self-confidence. The individual who belongs to an organization, compared with one who does not, is more likely to feel competent to influence the government. . . . The kind of organization one belongs to also makes a difference. Those who are members of a politically related organization are more likely to feel competent in their relations with the government than are those who belong to a nonpolitical organization. But the most striking finding is the contrast between those who are members of organizations that they do not perceive as being political and those who are members of no organization. In all nations, on both levels of education, those who are members of a non-political organization are more likely to feel subjectively competent than are those who belong to no organization. This, then, appears to confirm the fact that latent political functions are performed by voluntary associations, whether these organizations are explicitly political or not. Those who are members of some organization, even if they report that it has no political role, have more political competence than those who have no such membership.

A similar pattern is reported in Table 7. Members of politically oriented organizations report more often than the other respondents that they discuss politics. This is to be expected, and it appears in all five nations and on both levels of education (with the exception of the Mexican respondents with higher education, where there is a slight reversal). And, as with the data on subjective competence, the individual who is a member of a non-political organization is more likely to report he discusses politics than is the individual who belongs to no organization. Thus in Germany; 88 per cent of those who belong to a political organization discuss politics, in contrast with 70 per cent of the members of a nonpolitical organization. And both these percentages contrast with the figure that represents the frequency of such discussions among nonmembers: 47 per cent. Organizational membership, apparently, even if explicitly nonpolitical, makes it more likely that an individual will have a sense of ability to participate in politics and that he will actually participate in political discussion.

Organizational membership also seems to expand an individual's range of political opinion. In Table 8 we compare members of politically oriented organizations, members of nonpolitical organizations, and nonmembers, according to their willingness to express opinions on a variety of political questions. Members of political organizations were most likely to respond to all six questions; members of nonpolitical organizations and nonmembers followed in order. In Italy, for example, 68 per cent of the members of some politically oriented organization answered all six questions in this series, in contrast with 36 per cent of those who were members of a non-

TABLE 7   Percentage of Respondents Who Discuss Politics among Members of Political and Nonpolitical Organizations, by Nation and Education

Nation	Total			Primary or Less			Secondary or More		
	Member Political Organiz. % No.*	Member Nonpolitical Organiz. % No.	Non-member % No.	Member Political Organiz. % No.	Member Nonpolitical Organiz. % No.	Non-member % No.	Member Political Organiz. % No.	Member Nonpolitical Organiz. % No.	Non-member % No.
United States	89 (228)	79 (322)	66 (418)	86 (91)	66 (163)	56 (263)	92 (137)	92 (160)	82 (156)
Great Britain	81 (193)	76 (257)	62 (510)	77 (97)	69 (144)	59 (352)	86 (86)	84 (112)	71 (148)
Germany	88 (172)	70 (246)	47 (534)	86 (137)	66 (184)	44 (471)	94 (32)	83 (63)	76 (55)
Italy	79 (56)	39 (254)	25 (701)	64 (25)	30 (148)	18 (519)	90 (31)	54 (85)	45 (183)
Mexico	64 (103)	61 (139)	31 (765)	61 (79)	54 (101)	27 (697)	74 (24)	79 (36)	59 (67)

*Numbers in parentheses refer to the bases upon which percentages are calculated.

TABLE 8 Percentage of Respondents Willing to Express Opinions on All Six Political Attitude Questions* among Members of Political and Nonpolitical Organizations, by Nation and Education

	Total			Primary or Less			Secondary or More		
Nation	Member Political Organiz. No.**	Member Nonpolitical Organiz. % No.	Non-member % No.	Member Political Organiz. % No.	Member Nonpolitical Organiz. % No.	Non-member % No.	Member Political Organiz. % No.	Member Nonpolitical Organiz. % No.	Non-member % No.
United States	78 (228)	66 (322)	53 (418)	62 (91)	54 (163)	44 (263)	89 (137)	79 (160)	69 (156)
Great Britain	70 (193)	61 (257)	46 (510)	68 (97)	58 (144)	45 (352)	73 (86)	65 (112)	51 (148)
Germany	68 (172)	52 (246)	38 (534)	65 (137)	48 (184)	35 (471)	81 (32)	64 (63)	63 (55)
Italy	68 (56)	36 (234)	20 (701)	56 (25)	26 (148)	13 (519)	77 (31)	52 (85)	39 (183)
Mexico	75 (103)	60 (139)	40 (765)	71 (79)	60 (101)	37 (697)	87 (24)	62 (36)	63 (67)

*The six questions used to compute the "range of opinion" index were as follows: 1. One sometimes hears that some people or groups have so much influence on the way the government is run that the interests of the majority are ignored. Do you agree or disagree that there are such groups? 2. We know that the ordinary person has many problems that take his time. In view of this, what part do you think the ordinary person ought to play in the community affairs of his town or district? 3. People speak of the obligations that they owe to their country. In your opinion, what are the obligations that every man owes his country? 4. Some people say that campaigning is needed so the public can judge candidates and issues. Others say that it causes so much bitterness and is so unreliable that we'd be better off without it. What do you think—is it needed or would we be better off without it? 5. The ——— party now controls the government. Do you think that its policies and activities would ever seriously endanger the country's welfare? Do you think that this probably would happen, that it might happen, or that it probably wouldn't happen? 6. Same as question 5, but with reference to chief opposition party.

**Numbers in parentheses refer to the bases upon which percentages are calculated.

political organization, and 20 per cent of those who belonged to no organization at all.

Membership in an organization, political or not, appears therefore to be related to an increase in the political competence and activity of the individual.[7] The member, in contrast with the nonmember, appears to approximate more closely what we have called the democratic citizen. He is competent, active, and open with his opinions.

Active and Passive Membership. One reason why organizational membership might be expected to effect political competence and activity is that the members of such organizations receive training for participation within the organization, and this training is then transferable to the political sphere. According to this argument, a member of an organization will have greater opportunity to participate actively within the organization than he would have within the larger political system. Organizations are, in a sense, small political systems, and both the skill in participation and the expectation that one can participate increase the individual's competence vis-á-vis the political system. Furthermore—and this is one of the most important effects imputed to organizational membership—training within these organizations means that there are alternate channels of recruitment into politics. If opportunities to participate in organizations did not exist, all such training for participation would have to take place within the political system itself, and would be dominated by the more general norms of that system. The existence of alternate channels means that the recruitment into political activity will not be as closely controlled by incumbent elites. In this way organizational participation leads to greater pluralism.

But we cannot assume that membership in a voluntary association necessarily involves active participation by the member. Many of these organizations are large and complex; to the individual member, perhaps they are as large and complex, with as distant centers of power, as his nation. Many of these organizations are centrally controlled, and allow little room for individual participation. Membership, then, offers very little training for political participation. A member of a large, centrally organized trade union, for example, may feel as passive a participant in his organization as does a subject in a large, authoritarian nation; and he may in fact have as little voice.

To trace the impact of organizational membership on political attitudes, therefore, it is important to consider the extent to which individuals take active roles in their organizations. The gross membership figures tell us nothing about this participation. In order to have some estimate of the

[7]This relationship between group membership and political efficacy and activity is reported in some of the studies carried on by the Survey Research Center, and in other community studies. See Robert E. Lane, *Political Life,* p. 188.

extent to which membership involves active participation, those respondents who reported membership were asked if they took any active role within their organization: in particular, whether they had ever held any form of official position, high or low, in a local branch or in some central office.

The data bring out more striking differences among countries than did the figures on gross membership (see Table 9). In the United States 26 per cent of the respondents report that they have held some such position in an organization. In Britain the proportion, though lower (13 per cent), is substantially above that in the other countries (7 to 8 per cent). This suggests that the effect of voluntary associations upon the nature of citizenship may differ significantly from one country to another. In some countries there is a relatively large stratum of individuals who more or less actively participate in the decision making of voluntary associations; elsewhere,

TABLE 9   Respondents Who Report They Have Ever Been an Officer in One of their Organizations, by Nation

Nation	% of Total Population		% of Organizational Members	
	(%)	(No.)*	(%)	(No.)
United States	26	(970)	46	(551)
Great Britain	13	(963)	29	(453)
Germany	7	(955)	16	(419)
Italy	7	(995)	23	(291)
Mexico	8	(1,007)	34	(242)

*Numbers in parentheses refer to the bases upon which percentages are calculated.

organizational membership may be relatively formal and lacking in participatory opportunities. Organizations in which there is some opportunity for the individual to take an active part may be as significant for the development of democratic citizenship as are voluntary organizations in general.

These considerations add another link to our discussion of the nature of participation in the five countries. In particular, they point to a sharp distinction between the nature of participation in Germany, on the one hand, and Great Britain and the United States, on the other. All three countries are relatively high on organizational membership, especially among males. Yet the differences in the proportions of members who are active participating members (as measured by whether or not they have ever held an official position) are sharp. If we look at the second column of Table 9 (the proportion of members who have held some official position), we see that 46 per cent of American members and 29 per cent of British members have held some official position in one of the organizations to which they belong, while only 16 per cent of the German members have had experience in active participation. (In fact, the percentage of active group members is lower in Germany than in Mexico or Italy—although in the latter two countries we are dealing with a much smaller population of group members.) Here again is a reflection of the tendency for participation in Germany to be widespread but not intense. It tends to be formal in nature and involves little direct individual commitment and activity. Formal organizations in Germany, like those in Britain and the United States, are widespread and important in policy determination. But they differ in the degree to which they afford opportunities for their members to participate in decisions. Once again we find that in Germany the structures of a democratic system are well developed, but they do not yet play significant roles in the perspectives and behavior of citizens. They are elements of a democratic political structure; they are not yet assimilated into a democratic political culture.

●   ●   ●

It is of particular interest that the German pattern of frequent organizational membership, coupled with infrequent participation within the organization, is relatively uniform among all the German subgroups. While German males are members of organizations as frequently as are British or American males, and while Germans in particular educational groups are members as frequently as are their British or American counterparts, in no subgroup on Table 11 do we find German respondents as frequently active within their organization as are American and British respondents. . . .

TABLE 11   Organizational Members Who Were Ever Officers, by Nation and Education

Nation	Total (%)	(No.)*	Prim. or Less (%)	(No.)	Some Sec. (%)	(No.)	Some Univ. (%)	(No.)
United States	46	(551)	31	(156)	44	(245)	64	(150)
Great Britain	29	(453)	23	(241)	31	(176)	64	(22)
Germany	16	(419)	12	(321)	24	(79)	38	(16)
Italy	23	(291)	13	(173)	36	(91)	38	(26)
Mexico	33	(242)	30	(181)	39	(44)	52	(17)

*Numbers in parentheses refer to the bases upon which percentages are calculated.

The extent to which organizational membership involves some sort of active participation within that organization appears to vary significantly from nation to nation, and within nations among sex and educational groupings as well. Not all members take an active role in their organization. Furthermore, the extent to which an individual is active in the organization seems to be related to his political perspectives. This is suggested clearly in Table 12. Again we use the subjective competence score to measure this relationship (though measures of political activity would give similar results). Those organizational members who have held active posi-

TABLE 12   Percentage of Respondents Who Scored Highest in Subjective Competence* by the Extent of their Activity in Organizations, by Nation and Education

Nation	Total			Primary or Less			Secondary or More		
	Active Member % No.**	Passive Member % No.	Non-member % No.	Active Member % No.	Passive Member % No.	Non-member % No.	Active Member % No.	Passive Member % No.	Non-member % No.
United States	82 (253)	66 (298)	54 (418)	68 (98)	55 (166)	46 (263)	85 (165)	80 (132)	69 (156)
Great Britain	84 (130)	69 (320)	55 (510)	86 (56)	66 (184)	52 (352)	84 (69)	73 (127)	62 (148)
Germany	72 (65)	55 (353)	37 (534)	69 (39)	50 (282)	35 (471)	80 (25)	74 (69)	55 (55)
Italy	76 (66)	48 (224)	34 (701)	53 (32)	44 (150)	29 (519)	74 (43)	56 (73)	49 (183)
Mexico	68 (83)	42 (159)	33 (765)	63 (56)	39 (124)	32 (697)	76 (27)	49 (33)	46 (67)

*I.e., those who received three highest scores on the subjective competence scale.

**Numbers in parentheses refer to the bases upon which percentages are calculated.

tions in their organizations are more likely than rank-and-file members to receive high scores on this scale. In Italy, for instance, 76 per cent of these respondents who report some active participation within their organization score in the top three categories of our scale of subjective competence, in contrast with 48 per cent of the more passive organizational members. However, even passive membership, when compared with nonmembership, appears to be associated with an increased sense of political competence. Whereas 48 per cent of the passive members score in the top three categories of the subjective competence scale, only 34 per cent of the nonmembers are in the higher levels. And the pattern for Italy is apparent in all nations, for individuals on both educational levels and for men and women. Apparently both the type of organization one belongs to and the intensity of one's activity within it are related to one's political attitudes. Yet organizational membership per se appears to have a residual effect on political competence and activity. The passive member as well as the member of a nonpolitical organization still differ from the individual who reports no such membership.[9]

These findings strongly support the proposition associated with the theory of mass society, that the existence of voluntary associations increases the democratic potential of a society. Democracy depends upon citizen participation, and it is clear that organizational membership is directly related to such participation. The organizational member is likely to be a self-confident citizen as well as an active one. We can also specify somewhat more precisely the inpact on political competence of various types of organizational membership. Membership in a *politically oriented* organization appears to lead to greater political competence than does membership in a nonpolitical organization, and *active* membership in an organization has a greater impact on political competence than does passive membership. This fact is important because it helps explain the differential effect of organizational membership among the nations. Lipset, using data from a variety of surveys, points out that the frequency of voluntary association membership is about as great in such stable democracies as the

[9]In 1948 the American military government in Germany conducted a survey among German youth to evaluate how effective the newly formed youth organizations were in the inculcation of democratic attitudes. They found that there was relatively little difference between youth club members and nonmembers in their adherence to democratic attitudes. For instance, 58 per cent of the youth club members and 55 per cent of the nonmembers believed it was better for a club to have a leader elected by majority rule rather than appointed. In contrast, 72 per cent of the club members whose own club leaders were elected favored election of leaders, in comparison with 48 per cent of the club members whose own leaders were appointed. Apparently the nature of the authority structure in the youth club had a greater effect on youth attitudes than did the fact of membership per se. See Office of Military Government for Germany (US), Opinion Survey Report No. 99, March 5, 1948, "A Report on German Youth." The survey of youth is based on 2,337 interviews with respondents between the ages of 10 and 25 years.

United States, Britain, and Sweden as it is in the relatively less stable democracies of Germany and France—a finding that seems to challenge the idea of a connection between stable democracy and organizational membership.[10] Our data for the United States, Britain, and Germany confirm that the rates of membership are similar for the three nations. In Britain and the United States organizational membership much more frequently involves active participation within the organization than it does in Germany, where relatively few members appear to take an active part. And, as our data further show, the degree of activity within an organization has an effect upon political attitudes. The active member is more likely to be the competent democratic citizen.[11]

Multiple Membership. One other aspect of organizational participation must be considered to round out our picture of the differing patterns of participation and the impact of that participation on political attitudes among the nations. This is the number of organizations to which individuals belong. If one considers merely the frequency of membership and nonmembership among the nations, one finds some striking differences, yet this does not indicate the full extent of the differences in the amount of organizational participation. Nations differ, not only in the frequency with which respondents report membership, but also—and perhaps even more strikingly—in the frequency with which individuals report membership in more than one organization. This fact is illustrated in Table 13. In the United States about one-third of our total sample are members of more than one organization and, indeed, 9 per cent of the sample are members of four or more organizations. In Britain 16 per cent of the total sample are members of more than one organization. The figure falls off to 12 per cent of the total in Germany, 6 per cent in Italy, and 2 per cent in Mexico. Though on many measures of participation Great Britain and the United States were quite similar, on the question of organizational membership the impressions of many observers prove correct. Organizational participation in the United States, both in the total number who are members and the number who are members of several organizations, is much higher than that of any other country. This is reflected in the proportion of the total sample who are multiple members, as well as in the proportion of organization members who are members of more than one organization. In the United States 55 per cent of organizational members belong to more

[10]See Lipset, *Political Man,* p. 67.

[11]We have no data that are comparable for Sweden or France, the other two nations cited by Lipset; but descriptions of French voluntary associations strongly suggest that, like the German and unlike the American and British, they tend to be highly centralized and to allow little opportunity for active participation. See in particular Arnold Rose, *Theory and Method in the Social Sciences,* Minneapolis, 1954, p. 74, and M. Crozier, "La France, Terre du Commandement," *Esprit,* xxv (1957), 779-98.

than one organization. The other figures are: Britain, 34 per cent; Germany, 27 per cent; Italy, 20 per cent, and Mexico, 8 per cent.

TABLE 13   Respondents Who Belong to One or More Organizations, by Nation (in per cent)

Per Cent who	U.S.	U.K.	Germany	Italy	Mexico
Belong to one organization	25	31	32	24	23
Belong to two organizations	14	10	9	5	2
Belong to three organizations	9	4	2	1	0
Belong to four or more organizations	9	2	1	*	*
Total per cent multiple members	32	16	12	6	2
Total per cent members	57 (970)*	47 (963)	44 (955)	30 (995)	25 (1007)

*Numbers in parentheses refer to the bases upon which percentages are calculated.

The number of organizations to which an individual belongs also affects his political competence. Organizational membership appears to have a cumulative effect: that is, membership in one organization increases an individual's sense of political competence, and membership in more than one organization leads to even greater competence. This relationship is apparent in Table 14. Those who belong to an organization show higher political competence than those who are members of no organization, but the members of more than one organization show even higher competence than those whose affiliation is limited to one. And in their political competence multiple members differ from members of a single organization about as much as, if not more than, single members differ from nonmembers.

What we have shown so far is that voluntary associations do play a major role in a democratic political culture. The organizational member, compared with the nonmember, is likely to consider himself more competent as a citizen, to be a more active participant in politics, and to know and care more about politics. He is, therefore, more likely to be close to the model of the democratic citizen. We have also shown that it makes a difference which type of organization an individual belongs to; political organizations yield a larger political "dividend" than do nonpolitical organizations. And it makes a difference how active an individual is within his own organization: the active member displays a greater sense of political competence than does the passive member. But perhaps the most striking finding is that any membership—passive membership or membership in a nonpolitical organization—has an impact on political competence. Membership in some association, even if the individual does not consider the membership politically relevant and even if it does not involve his

TABLE 14 Percentage of Respondents Who Scored Highest in Subjective Competence* among Members of One or More Organizations, by Nation and Education

Nation	Total			Primary or Less			Secondary or More		
	Multiple Member % No.**	Single Member % No.	Non-member % No.	Multiple Member % No.	Single Member % No.	Non-member % No.	Multiple Member % No.	Single Member % No.	Non-member % No.
United States	81 (314)	64 (242)	55 (418)	72 (106)	55 (150)	46 (263)	85 (208)	78 (92)	68 (156)
Great Britain	80 (160)	70 (294)	56 (510)	82 (77)	65 (165)	52 (352)	80 (79)	74 (119)	62 (148)
Germany	71 (111)	52 (308)	37 (534)	66 (82)	48 (239)	35 (471)	90 (27)	69 (68)	73 (55)
Italy	74 (55)	49 (240)	34 (701)	58 (26)	46 (150)	29 (519)	89 (28)	54 (90)	49 (183)
Mexico	61 (22)	50 (220)	34 (765)	[82 (11)]	45 (169)	32 (697)	[42 (10)]	64 (50)	48 (67)

*I.e., those who received three highest scores on the subjective competence scale.
**Numbers in parentheses refer to the bases upon which percentages are calculated.

active participation, does lead to a more competent citizenry. Pluralism, even if not explicitly political pluralism, may indeed be one of the most important foundations of political democracy.

Symbols and Political Quiescence

Murray Edelman

Few forms of explanation of political phenomena are more common than the assertion that the success of some group was facilitated by the "apathy" of other groups with opposing interests. If apathy is not an observable phenomenon in a political context because it connotes an individual's mental state, quiescence is observable. It is the purpose of this paper to specify some conditions associated with political quiescence in the formation of business regulation policies. Although the same general conditions are apparently applicable to the formation of public policies in any area, the argument and the examples used here focus upon the field of government regulation of business in order to make the paper manageable and to permit more intensive treatment.

Political quiescence toward a policy area can be assumed to be a function either of lack of interest—whether it is simple indifference or stems rather from a sense of futility about the practical prospects of securing obviously desirable changes—or of the satisfaction of whatever interest the quiescent group may have in the policy in question. Our concern here is with the forms of satisfaction. In analyzing the various means by which it can come to pass, the following discussion distinguishes between interests in resources (whether goods or freedoms to act) and interests in symbols connoting the suppression of threats to the group in question. Few political scientists would doubt, on the basis of common sense evidence, that public policies have value to interested groups both as symbols and as instruments for the allocation of more tangible values. The political process has been much less thoroughly studied as a purveyor of symbols, however; and there is a good deal of evidence, to be presented below, that symbols are a more central

SOURCE: Murray Edelman, "Symbols and Political Quiescence," *American Political Science Review*, LIV (September 1960), 695-704. Reprinted by permission.

component of the process than is commonly recognized in political scientists' explicit or implicit models.[1]

Three related hypotheses will be considered:

1. The interests of organized groups in tangible resources or in substantive power are less easily satiable than are interests in symbolic reassurance.
2. Necessary conditions associated with the occurrence of the later type of interest are:
   (a) the existence of economic conditions in some measure threatening the security of a large group;
   (b) the absence of organization for the purpose of furthering the common interest of that group;
   (c) widespread political responses suggesting the prevalence of inaccurate, oversimplified, and distorted perceptions of the issue.
3. The pattern of political activity represented by lack of organization, distorted perception, interests in symbolic reassurance, and quiescence is a key element in the ability of organized groups to use political agencies in order to make good their claims on tangible resources and power, thus continuing the threat to the unorganized.

Available evidence bearing on these hypotheses will be marshalled as follows. First, some widely accepted propositions regarding group claims, quiescence, and techniques for satisfying group interests in governmental regulation of business will be summarized. Next, some pertinent experimental and empirical findings of other disciplines will be considered. Finally the paper will explore the possibility of integrating the various findings and applying them to the propositions listed above.

I

If the regulatory process is examined in terms of a divergence between political and legal promises on the one hand and resource allocations and group reactions on the other hand, the largely symbolic character of the entire process becomes apparent. What do the studies of government regulation of business tell us of the role and functions of that amorphous group who have an interest in these policies in the sense that they are affected by them, but who are not rationally organized to pursue their interest? The following generalizations would probably be accepted by most students, perhaps with occasional changes of emphasis:

1. Tangible resources and benefits are frequently not distributed to unorganized political group interests as promised in regulatory statutes and the propaganda attending their enactment.

---

[1]Harold Lasswell is a major exception, and some of his contributions will be noted.

This is not true of legal fictions, but rather of the values held out to (or demanded by) groups which regard themselves as disadvantaged and which presumably anticipate benefits from a regulatory policy. There is virtually unanimous agreement among students of the anti-trust laws, the Clayton and Federal Trade Commission acts, the Interstate Commerce acts, the public utility statutes and the right-to-work laws, for example, that through much of the history of their administration these statutes have been ineffective in the sense that many of the values they promised have not in fact been realized. The story has not been uniform, of course; but the general point hardly needs detailed documentation at this late date. Herring,[2] Leiserson,[3] Truman,[4] and Bernstein[5] all conclude that few regulatory policies have been pursued unless they proved acceptable to the regulated groups or served the interests of these groups. Within the past decade Redford,[6] Bernstein,[7] and others have offered a "life cycle" theory of regulatory history, showing a more or less regular pattern of loss of vigor by regulatory agencies. For purposes of the present argument it need not be assumed that this always happens but only that it frequently happens in important cases.[8]

2. When it does happen, the deprived groups often display little tendency to protest or to assert their awareness of the deprivation.

The fervent display of public wrath, or enthusiasm, in the course of the initial legislative attack on forces seen as threatening "the little man" is a common American spectacle. It is about as predictable as the subsequent lapse of the same fervor. Again, it does not always occur, but it happens often enough to call for thorough explanation. The leading students of regulatory processes have all remarked upon it; but most of these scholars, who ordinarily display a close regard for rigor and full exploration, dismiss this highly significant political behavior rather casually. Thus, Redford declares that, "In the course of time the administrator finds that the initial

[2]E. Pendleton Herring, *Public Administration and the Public Interest* (New York, 1936), p. 213.

[3]Avery Leiserson, *Administrative Regulation: A Study in Representation of Interests* (Chicago: The University of Chicago Press, 1942), p. 14.

[4]David Truman, *The Governmental Process* (New York, 1951), ch. 5.

[5]Marver Bernstein, *Regulating Business by Independent Commissions* (New York: Princeton University Press, 1955), ch. 3.

[6]Emmette S. Redford, *Administration of National Economic Control* (New York, 1952), pp. 385-386.

[7]*Op. cit.*, note 5 above.

[8]In addition to the statements in these analytical treatments of the administrative process, evidence for the proposition that regulatory statutes often fail to have their promised consequences in terms of resource allocation is found in general studies of government regulation of business and in empirical research on particular statutes. As an example of the former see Clair Wilcox, *Public Policies Toward Business* (Chicago, 1955). As examples of the latter see Frederic Meyers, *'Right to Work' in Practice* (New York: Fund for the Republic, 1959); Walton Hamilton and Irene Till, *Antitrust in Action*, TNEC Monograph 16 (Washington: GPO, 1940).

public drive and congressional sentiment behind his directive has wilted and that political support for change from the existing pattern is lacking."[9]

Although the presumed beneficiaries of regulatory legislation often show little or no concern with its failure to protect them, they are nevertheless assumed to constitute a potential base of political support for the retention of these statutes in the law books. The professional politician is probably quite correct when he acts on the assumption that his advocacy of this regulatory legislation, in principle, is a widely popular move, even though actual resource allocations inconsistent with the promise of the statutes are met with quiescence. These responses (support of the statute; apathy toward failure to allocate resources as the statute promises) define the meanings of the law so far as the presumed beneficiaries are concerned.[10] It is the frequent inconsistency between the two types of response that is puzzling.

3. The most intensive dissemination of symbols commonly attends the enactment of legislation which is most meaningless in its effects upon resource allocation. In the legislative history of particular regulatory statutes the provisions least significant for resource allocation are most widely publicized and the most significant provisions are least widely publicized.

The statutes listed under Proposition 1 as having promised something substantially different from what was delivered are also the ones which have been most intensively publicized as symbolizing protection of widely shared interests. Trust-busting, "Labor's Magna Carta" (the Clayton Act), protection against price discrimination and deceptive trade practices, protection against excessive public utility charges, tight control of union bureaucracies (or, by other groups, the "slave labor law"), federal income taxation according to "ability to pay," are the terms and symbols widely disseminated to the public as descriptive of much of the leading federal and state regulation of the last seven decades; and they are precisely the descriptions shown by careful students to be most misleading. Nor is it any less misleading if one quotes the exact language of the most widely publicized specific provisions of these laws: Section 1 of the Sherman Act, Sections 6 and 20 of the Clayton Act, or the closed shop, secondary boycott, or emergency strike provisions

[9]Redford, *op. cit.*, p. 383. Similar explanations appear in Herring, *op. cit.*, p. 227, and Bernstein, *op. cit.*, pp. 82-83. Some writers have briefly suggested more rigorous explanations, consistent with the hypotheses discussed in this paper, though they do not consider the possible role of interests in symbolic reassurance. Thus Truman calls attention to organizational factors, emphasizing the ineffectiveness of interest groups "whose interactions on the basis of the interest are not sufficiently frequent or stabilized to produce an intervening organization and whose multiple memberships, on the same account, are a constant threat to the strength of the claim." Truman, *op. cit.*, p. 441. Multiple group memberships are, of course, characteristic of individuals in all organizations, stable and unstable; and "infrequent interactions" is a phenomenon that itself calls for explanation if a common interest is recognized. Bernstein, *loc. cit.*, refers to the "undramatic nature" of administration and to the assumption that the administrative agency will protect the public.

[10]*Cf.* the discussion of meaning in George Herbert Mead, *Mind, Self and Society* (Chicago: University of Chicago Press, 1934), pp. 78-79.

of Taft-Hartley, for example. In none of these instances would a reading of either the text of the statutory provision or the attendant claims and publicity enable an observer to predict even the direction of future regulatory policy, let alone its precise objectives.

Other features of these statutes also stand as the symbols of threats stalemated, if not checkmated, by the forces of right and justice. Typically, a preamble (which does not pretend to be more than symbolic, even in legal theory) includes strong assurances that the public or the public interest will be protected. And the most widely publicized regulatory provisions always include other nonoperational standards connoting fairness, balance, or equity.

If one asks, on the other hand, for examples of changes in resource allocations that have been influenced substantially and directly by public policy, it quickly appears that the outstanding examples have been publicized relatively little. One thinks of such legislation as the silver purchase provisions; the court definitions of the word "lawful" in the Clayton Act's labor sections; the procedural provisions of Taft-Hartley and the Railway Labor Act; the severe postwar cuts in Grazing Service appropriations; and changes in the parity formula requiring that such items as interest, taxes, freight rates and wages be included as components of the index of prices paid by farmers.

Illuminating descriptions of the operational meaning of statutory mandates are found in Truman's study and in Earl Latham's *The Group Basis of Politics*.[11] Both emphasize the importance of contending groups and organizations in day-to-day decision-making as the dynamic element in policy formation; and both distinguish this element from statutory language as such.[12]

We are only beginning to get some serious studies of the familiarity of voters with current public issues and of the intensity of their feelings about issues; but successful political professionals have evidently long acted on the assumption that there is in fact relatively little familiarity, that expressions of deep concern are rare, that quiescence is common, and that, in general, the congressman can count upon stereotyped reactions rather than persistent, organized pursuit of material interests on the part of most constituents.[13]

4. Policies severely denying resources to large numbers of people can be pursued indefinitely without serious controversy.

[11]Truman, *op. cit.*, pp. 439-446; Earl Latham, *The Group Basis of Politics* (Ithaca: Cornell University Press, 1952), ch. 1.

[12]The writer has explored this effect in labor legislation in "Interest Representation and Labor Law Administration," *Labor Law Journal*, Vol. 9 (1958), pp. 218-226.

[13]Evidence for these propositions is contained in the writer's study of congressional representation, still not completed or published. See also Lewis A. Dexter, "Candidates Must Make the Issues and Give Them Meaning," *Public Opinion Quarterly*, Vol. 10 (1955-56), pp. 408-414.

The silver purchase policy, the farm policy, and a great many other subsidies are obvious examples. The anti-trust laws, utility regulations, and other statutes ostensibly intended to protect the small operator or the consumer are less obvious examples; though there is ample evidence, some of it cited below, that these usually support the proposition as well.

The federal income tax law offers a rather neat example of the divergence between a widely publicized symbol and actual resource allocation patterns. The historic constitutional struggle leading up to the Sixteenth Amendment, the warm defenses of the principle of ability to pay, and the frequent attacks upon the principle through such widely discussed proposals as that for a 25 per cent limit on rates have made the federal tax law a major symbol of justice. While the fervent rhetoric from both sides turns upon the symbol of a progressive tax and bolsters the assumption that the system is highly progressive, the bite of the law into people's resources depends upon quite other provisions and activities that are little publicized and that often seriously qualify its progressive character. Special tax treatments arise from such devices as family partnerships, gifts *inter vivos*, income-splitting, multiple trusts, percentage depletion, and deferred compensation.

Tax evasion alone goes far toward making the symbol of "ability to pay" hollow semantically though potent symbolically. While 95 per cent of income from wages and salaries is taxed as provided by law, taxes are actually collected on only 67 per cent of taxable income from interest, dividends, and fiduciary investments and on only about 36 per cent of taxable farm income.[14] By and large, the recipients of larger incomes can most easily benefit from exemptions, avoidances and evasions. This may be desirable public policy, but it certainly marks a disparity between symbol and effect upon resources.

II

These phenomena are significant for the study of the political process for two reasons. First, there is a substantial degree of consistency in the group interest patterns associated with policies on highly diverse subject matters. Second, they suggest that nonrational reaction to symbols among people sharing a common governmental interest is a key element in the process. The disciplines of sociology, social psychology, and semantics have produced some pertinent data on the second point; and to some of this material we turn next.

Harold Lasswell wrote three decades ago that "[P]olitics is the process by which the irrational bases of society are brought out into the open." He

[14]Randolph E. Paul, "Erosion of the Tax Base and Rate Structure," in Joint Committee on the Economic Report, *Federal Tax Policy for Economic Growth and Stability*, 84th Cong., 1st sess., 1955, pp. 123-138.

marshalled some support in case studies for several propositions that have since been confirmed with richer and more direct experimental evidence. "The rational and dialectical phases of politics," he said, "are subsidiary to the process of redefining an emotional consensus." He argued that "widespread and disturbing changes in the life-situation of many members of society" produces adjustment problems which are resolved largely through symbolization; and he suggested that "[P]olitical demands probably bear but a limited relevance to social needs."[15]

The frame of reference suggested by these statements is sometimes accepted by political scientists today when they study voting behavior and when they analyze the legislative process. Its bearing on policy formation in the administrative process is not so widely recognized. It is true that cognition and rationality are central to administrative procedures to a degree not true of legislation or voting. But this is not at all the same thing as saying that administrative policies or administrative politics are necessarily insulated from the "process of redefining an emotional consensus."

Let us consider now some experimental findings and conclusions specifying conditions under which groups or personality types are prone to respond strongly to symbolic appeals and to distort or ignore reality in a fashion that can be politically significant.

1. People read their own meanings into situations that are unclear or provocative of emotion. As phrased by Fensterheim, "The less well defined the stimulus situation, or the more emotionally laden, the greater will be the contribution of the perceiver."[16] This proposition is no longer doubted by psychologists. It is the justification for so-called projective techniques and is supported by a great deal of experimental evidence.

Now it is precisely in emotionally laden and poorly defined situations that the most widely and loudly publicized public regulatory policies are launched and administered. If, as we have every reason to suppose, there is little cognitive familiarity with issues, the "interest" of most of the public is likely to be a function of other socio-psychological factors. What these other factors are is suggested by certain additional findings.

2. It is characteristic of large numbers of people in our society that they see and think in terms of stereotypes, personalization, and oversimplifications; that they cannot recognize or tolerate ambiguous and complex

---

[15]*Psychopathology and Politics* (Chicago: University of Chicago Press, 1930), pp. 184, 185.

[16]Herbert Fensterheim, "The Influence of Value Systems on the Perception of People," *Journal of Abnormal and Social Psychology*, Vol. 48 (1953), p. 93. Fensterheim cites the following studies in support of the proposition: D. Krech and R. S. Crutchfield, *Theory and Problems of Social Psychology* (New York, 1948); A. S. Luchins, "An Evaluation of Some Current Criticisms of Gestalt Psychological Work on Perception," *Psychological Review*, Vol. 58 (1951), pp. 69-95; J. S. Bruner, "One Kind of Perception: A Reply to Professor Luchins," *Psychological Review*, Vol. 58 (1951), pp. 306-312; and the chapters by Bruner, Frenkel-Brunswik, and Klein in R. R. Blake and G. V. Ramsey, *Perception: An Approach to Personality* (New York, 1951).

situations; and that they accordingly respond chiefly to symbols that over-simplify and distort. This form of behavior (together with other character-istics less relevant to the political process) is especially likely to occur where there is insecurity occasioned by failure to adjust to real or perceived prob-lems.[17] Frenkel-Brunswik has noted that "such objective factors as economic conditions" may contribute to the appearance of the syndrome, and hence to its importance as a widespread group phenomenon attending the formula-tion of public policy.[18] Such behavior is sufficiently persistent and wide-spread to be politically significant only when there is social reinforcement of faith in the symbol. When insecurity is individual, without communica-tion and reinforcement from others, there is little correlation with ethno-centricity or its characteristics.[19]

A different kind of study suggests the extent to which reality can become irrelevant for persons very strongly committed to an emotion-satisfying symbol. Festinger and his associates, as participant-observers, studied a group of fifteen persons who were persuaded that the world would come to an end on a particular day in 1956 and that they as believers would be carried away in a flying saucer. With few exceptions the participants refused to give up their belief even after the appointed day had passed. The Fes-tinger study concludes that commitment to a belief is likely to be strength-ened and reaffirmed in the face of clear disproof of its validity where there is a strong prior commitment (many of the individuals involved had actu-ally given away their worldly goods) and where there is continuing social support of the commitment by others (two members who lost faith lived in environments in which they had no further contact with fellow-members of the group; those who retained their faith had continued to see each other). What we know of previous messianic movements of this sort supports this hypothesis.[20]

3. Emotional commitment to a symbol is associated with contentment and quiescence regarding problems that would otherwise arouse concern.

It is a striking fact that this effect has been noticed and stressed by care-ful observers in a number of disparate fields, using quite different data and

[17]Among the leading general and experimental studies dealing with the phenomenon are: M. Rokeach, "Generalized Mental Rigidity as a Factor in Ethnocentrism," *Journal of Abnormal and Social Psychology,* Vol. 43 (1948), pp. 259-277; R. R. Canning and J. M. Baker, "Effect of the Group on Authoritarian and Non-authoritarian Persons," *American Journal of Sociology,* Vol. 64 (1959), pp. 579-581; A. H. Maslow, "The Authoritarian Character Structure," *Journal of Social Psychology,* Vol. 18 (1943), p. 403; T. W. Adorno and others, *The Authoritarian Per-sonality* (New York, 1950); Gerhart Saenger, *The Psychology of Prejudice* (New York, 1953), pp. 123-138; Erich Fromm, *Escape from Freedom* (New York, 1941); R. K. Merton, *Mass Per-suasion* (New York, 1950).

[18]Else Frenkel-Brunswik, "Interaction of Psychological and Sociological Factors in Political Behavior," [*American Political Science*] *Review,* Vol. 46 (1952), pp. 44-65.

[19]Adorno, *op. cit.*

[20]Leon Festinger, Henry Riecken, and Stanley Shachter, *When Prophecy Fails* (Minneapolis: University of Minnesota Press, 1956).

methods. Adorno reports it as an important finding of the *Authoritarian Personality* study:

> Since political and economic events make themselves felt apparently down to the most private and intimate realms of the individual, there is reliance upon stereotype and similar avoidances of reality to alleviate psychologically the feeling of anxiety and uncertainty and provide the individual with the illusion of some kind of intellectual security.[21]

In addition to the support it gets from psychological experiment, the phenomenon has been remarked by scholars in the fields of semantics, organizational theory, and political science. Albert Salomon points out that "Manipulation of social images makes it possible for members of society to believe that they live not in a jungle, but in a well organized and good society."[22] Harold Lasswell put it as follows:

> It should not be hastily assumed that because a particular set of controversies passes out of the public mind that the implied problems were solved in any fundamental sense. Quite often a solution is a magical solution which changes nothing in the conditions affecting the tension level of the community, and which merely permits the community to distract its attention to another set of equally irrelevant symbols. The number of statutes which pass the legislature or the number of decrees which are handed down by the executive, but which change nothing in the permanent practices of society, is a rough index of the role of magic in politics. . . . Political symbolization has its catharsis function. . . .[23]

Chester Barnard, an uncommonly astute analyst of his own long experience as an executive, concluded that:

> Neither authority nor cooperative disposition . . . will stand much overt division on formal issues in the present stage of human development. Most laws, executive orders, decisions, etc., are in effect formal notice that all is well—there is agreement, authority is not questioned.[24]

Charles Morris, a leading logician and student of semantics, has analyzed the role of language in shaping social behavior and inculating satisfaction with existing power relationships. He points to the possibility that exploited groups will "actively resist changes in the very sign structure by which they are exploited." Defining such behavior as "socially pathic," he makes the following comment:

[21]Adorno, *op. cit.,* p. 665.

[22]Albert Salomon, "Symbols and Images in the Constitution of Society," in L. Bryson, L. Finkelstein, H. Hoagland and R. M. MacIver (eds.), *Symbols and Society* (New York, 1955), p. 110.

[23]Lasswell, *op. cit.,* p. 195.

[24]Chester I. Barnard, *The Functions of the Executive* (Cambridge: Harvard University Press, 1938), p. 226.

The signs in question may relieve certain anxieties in the members of society with respect to the social behavior in which they are engaged, and so be cherished for this satisfaction even though the signs hinder or even make impossible the actual realization of the goals of such social behavior itself.[25]

Kenneth Burke makes much the same point. Designating political rhetoric as "secular prayer," he declares that its function is "to sharpen up the pointless and blunt the too sharply pointed."[26] Elsewhere, he points out that laws themselves serve this function, alleging that positive law is *itself* "the test of a judgment's judiciousness."[27]

4. An active demand for increased economic resources or fewer political restrictions on action is not always operative. It is, rather, a function of comparison and contrast with reference groups, usually those not far removed in socio-economic status.

This is, of course, one of the most firmly established propositions about social dynamics; one that has been supported by macro-sociological analysis,[28] by psychological experiment,[29] and by observation of the political process, particularly through contrast between politically quiescent and protest or revolutionary activity.[30]

The proposition helps explain failure to demand additional resources where such behavior is socially sanctioned and supported. It also helps explain the insatiability of the demand by some organized groups for additional resources (*i.e.*, the absence of quiescence) where there is competition for such resources among rival organizations and where it is acquisitiveness that is socially supported.

5. The phenomena discussed above (the supplying of meaning in vague situations, stereotypes, oversimplification, political quiescence) are in large measure associated with social, economic, or cultural factors affecting large segments of the population. They acquire political meaning as group phenomena.

Even among the psychologists, some of whom have at times been notably insensitive to socialization and environment as explanations and phases of the individual "traits" they claim to "identify" or "isolate," there are impressive experimental findings to support the proposition. In analyzing the interview material of his *Authoritarian Personality* study, Adorno concluded that "our general cultural climate" is basic in political ideology and in

[25]Charles Morris, *Signs, Language and Behavior* (New York, 1946), pp. 210-211.

[26]Kenneth Burke, *A Grammar of Motives* (New York, 1945), p. 393.

[27]*Ibid.*, p. 362.

[28]Mead, *op. cit.;* Ernst Cassirer. *An Essay on Man* (New Haven: Yale University Press, 1944).

[29]See James G. March and Herbert A. Simon, *Organizations* (New York, 1958), pp. 65-81, and studies cited there.

[30]See, *e.g.*, Murray Edelman, "Causes of Fluctuations in Popular Support for the Italian Communist Party since 1946," *Journal of Politics*, Vol. 20 (1958), pp. 547-550; Arthur M. Ross, *Trade Union Wage Policy* (Berkeley and Los Angeles: University of California Press, 1948).

stereotyped political thinking; and he catalogued some standardizing aspects of that climate.[31] His finding, quoted above, regarding the relation of symbols to quiescence is also phrased to emphasize its social character. Lindesmith and Strauss make a similar point, emphasizing the association between symbols and the reference groups to which people adhere.[32]

Another type of research has demonstrated that because interests are typically bound up with people's social situation, attitudes are not typically changed by *ex parte* appeals. The function of propaganda is rather to activate socially rooted interests. One empirical study which arrives at this conclusion sums up the thesis as follows:

> Political writers have the task of providing "rational" men with good and acceptable reasons to dress up the choice which is more effectively determined by underlying social affiliations.[33]

George Herbert Mead makes the fundamental point that symbolization itself has no meaning apart from social activity: "Symbolization constitutes objects . . . which would not exist except for the context of social relationships wherein symbolization occurs."[34]

III

These studies offer a basis for understanding more clearly what it is that different types of groups expect from government and under what circumstances they are likely to be satisfied or restive about what is forthcoming. Two broad patterns of group interest activity *vis-à-vis* public regulatory policy are evidently identifiable on the basis of these various modes of observing the social scene. The two patterns may be summarized in the following shorthand fashion:

1. Pattern A: a relatively high degree of organization—rational, cognitive procedures—precise information—an effective interest in specifically identified, tangible resources—a favorably perceived strategic position with respect to reference groups—relatively small numbers.

2. Pattern B: shared interest in improvement of status through protest

---

[31]Adorno, *op. cit.*, p. 655.

[32]Alfred R. Lindesmith and Anselm L. Strauss, *Social Psychology* (New York, 1956), pp. 253-255. For a report of another psychological experiment demonstrating that attitudes are a function of group norms, see I. Sarnoff, D. Katz, and C. McClintock, "Attitude-Change Procedures and Motivating Patterns," in Daniel Katz and others (eds.), *Public Opinion and Propaganda* (New York, 1954), pp. 308-9; also Festinger *et al.*, *op. cit.*

[33]Paul F. Lazarsfeld, Bernard Berelson and Ilazel Gaudet, *The People's Choice* (New York, 1944), p. 83. For an account of an experiment reaching the same conclusion see S. M. Lipset, "Opinion Formation in a Crisis Situation," *Public Opinion Quarterly*, Vol. 17 (1953), pp. 20-46.

[34]Mead, *op. cit.*, p. 78.

activity—an unfavorably perceived strategic position with respect to reference groups—distorted, stereotyped, inexact information and perception—response to symbols connoting suppression of threats—relative ineffectiveness in securing tangible resources through political activity—little
organization for purposeful action—quiescence—relatively large numbers.

It is very likely misleading to assume that some of these observations can
be regarded as causes or consequences of others. That they often occur together is both a more accurate observation and more significant. It is also
evident that each of the patterns is realized in different degrees at different
times.

While political scientists and students of organizational theory have gone
far toward a sophisticated description and analysis of Pattern A, there is
far less agreement and precision in describing and analyzing Pattern B and
in explaining how it intermeshes with Pattern A.

The most common explanation of the relative inability of large numbers
of people to realize their economic aspirations in public policy is in terms
of invisibility. The explanation is usually implicit rather than explicit, but
it evidently assumes that public regulatory policy facilitating the exploitation of resources by knowledgeable organized groups (usually the "regulated") at the expense of taxpayers, consumers, or other unorganized groups
is possible only because the latter do not know it is happening. What is
invisible to them does not arouse interest or political sanctions.

On a superficial level of explanation this assumption is no doubt valid.
But it is an example of the danger to the social scientist of failure to inquire
transactionally: of assuming, in this instance, (1) that an answer to a questioner, or a questionnaire, about what an individual "knows" of a regulatory
policy at any point in time is in any sense equivalent to specification of a
group political interest; and (2) that the sum of many individual knowings
(or not-knowings) as reported to a questioner is a *cause* of effective (or ineffective) organization, rather than a consequence of it, or simply a concomitant phase of the same environment. If one is interested in policy formation, what count are the assumptions of legislators and administrators
about the determinants of future political disaffection and political sanctions. Observable political behavior, as well as psychological findings,
reveals something of these assumptions.

There is, in fact, persuasive evidence of the reality of a political interest,
defined in this way, in continuing assurances of protection against economic
forces understood as powerful and threatening. The most relevant evidence
lies in the continuing utility of old political issues in campaigns. Monopoly
and economic concentration, anti-trust policy, public utility regulation,
banking controls, and curbs on management and labor are themes that party
professionals regard as good for votes in one campaign after another, and
doubtless with good reason. They know that these are areas in which con-

cern is easily stirred. In evaluating allegations that the public has lost "interest" in these policies the politician has only to ask himself how much apathy would remain if an effort were made formally to repeal the antitrust, public utility, banking, or labor laws. The answers and the point become clear at once.

The laws may be repealed in effect by administrative policy, budgetary starvation, or other little publicized means; but the laws as symbols must stand because they satisfy interests that are very strong indeed: interests that politicians fear will be expressed actively if a large number of voters are led to believe that their shield against a threat has been removed.

More than that, it is only as symbols of this sort that these statutes have utility to most of the voters. If they function as reassurances that threats in the economic environment are under control, their indirect effect is to permit greater exploitation of tangible resources by the organized groups concerned than would be possible if the legal symbols were absent. Those who are deprived become defenders of the very system of law which permits the exploiters of resources to act effectively.

To say this is not to assume that everyone objectively affected by a policy is simply quiescent rather than apathetic or even completely unaware of the issue. It is to say that those who are potentially able and willing to apply political sanctions constitute the politically significant group. It is to suggest as well that incumbent or aspiring congressmen are less concerned with individual constituents' familiarity or unfamiliarity with an issue as of any given moment than with the possibility that the interest of a substantial number of them *could* be aroused and organized if he should cast a potentially unpopular vote on a bill or if a change in their economic situations should occur. The shrewder and more effective politicians probably appreciate intuitively the validity of the psychological finding noted earlier: that where public understanding is vague and information rare, interests in reassurance will be all the more potent and all the more susceptible to manipulation by political symbols.

The groups that succeed in using official agencies as instrumentalities to gain the resources they want are invariably organized so as to procure and analyze pertinent information and then act rationally. Most voters affected by the regulatory policy are certain on the other hand to secure distorted information, inadequate for intelligent planning of tactics or strategy.

We have already noted that it is one of the demonstrable functions of symbolization that it induces a feeling of well-being: the resolution of tension. Not only is this a major function of widely publicized regulatory statutes, but it is also a major function of their administration. Some of the most widely publicized administrative activities can most confidently be expected to convey a misleading sense of well-being to the onlooker because they suggest vigorous activity while in fact signifying inactivity or protection of the "regulated."

One form this phenomenon takes is noisy attacks on trivia. The Federal Trade Commission, for example, has long been noted for its hit-and-miss attacks on many relatively small firms involved in deceptive advertising or unfair trade practices while it continues to overlook much of the really significant activity it is ostensibly established to regulate: monopoly, interlocking directorates, and so on.[35]

Another form it takes is prolonged, repeated, well-publicized attention to a significant problem which is never solved. An excellent example is the approach of the FCC to surveillance of program content in general and to discussions of public issues on the air in particular. In the postwar period we have had the Blue Book, the Mayflower Policy, the abolition of the Mayflower Policy, and the announcement of a substitute policy; but the radio or television licensee is in practice perfectly free, as he has been all along, to editorialize, with or without opportunity for opposing views to be heard, or to eschew serious discussion of public affairs entirely.

The most obvious kinds of dissemination of symbolic satisfactions are to be found in administrative dicta accompanying decisions and orders, in press releases, and in annual reports. It is as common here as in labor arbitration to "give the rhetoric to one side and the decision to the other." Nowhere does the FCC wax so emphatic in emphasizing public service responsibility, for example, as in decisions permitting greater concentration of control in an area, condoning license transfers at inflated prices, refusing to impose sanctions for flagrantly sacrificing program quality to profits, and so on.[36]

The integral connection is apparent between symbolic satisfaction of the disorganized, on the one hand, and the success of the organized, on the other, in using governmental instrumentalities as aids in securing the tangible resources they claim.

Public policy may usefully be understood as the resultant of the interplay among groups.[37] But the political and socio-psychological processes discussed here mean that groups which would otherwise present claims upon resources may be rendered quiescent instead by their success in securing nontangible values. Far from representing an obstacle to organized producers and sellers, they become defenders of the very system of law which

[35]*Cf.* Wilcox, *op. cit.*, pp. 281, 252-255.

[36]Many examples may be found in the writer's study entitled *The Licensing of Radio Services in the United States, 1927 to 1947* (Urbana: University of Illinois Press, 1950).

[37]For discussions of the utility of this view to social scientists, see Arthur F. Bentley, *The Process of Government* (1908; New York: The Principia Press, reprint 1949); Truman, *op. cit.* But *cf.* Stanley Rothman, "Systematic Political Theory," [*American Political Science*] *Review*, Vol. 54, pp. 15-33 (March, 1960).

permits the organized to pursue their interests effectively, at the expense of the disorganized or unorganized.

Thurman Arnold has pointed out how the anti-trust laws perform precisely this function:

> The actual result of the antitrust laws was to promote the growth of great industrial organizations by deflecting the attack on them into purely moral and ceremonial channels . . . every scheme for direct control broke to pieces on the great protective rock of the antitrust laws . . . .
>
> The antitrust laws remained as a most important symbol. Whenever anyone demanded practical regulation, they formed an effective moral obstacle, since all the liberals would answer with a demand that the antitrust laws be enforced. Men like Senator Borah founded political careers on the continuance of such crusades, which were entirely futile but enormously picturesque, and which paid big dividends in terms of personal prestige.[38]

Arnold's subsequent career as Chief of the Anti-trust Division of the Department of Justice did as much to prove his point as his writings. For a five-year period he instilled unprecedented vigor into the Division, and his efforts were widely publicized. He thereby unquestionably made the laws a more important symbol of the protection of the public; but despite his impressive intentions and talents, monopoly, concentration of capital, and restraint of trade were not seriously threatened or affected.

This is not to suggest that signs or symbols in themselves have any magical force as narcotics. They are, rather, the only means by which groups not in a position to analyze a complex situation rationally may adjust themselves to it, through stereotypization, oversimplification, and reassurance.

There have, of course, been many instances of effective administration and enforcement of regulatory statutes. In each instance it will be found that organized groups have had an informed interest in effective administration. Sometimes the existence of these groups is explicable as a holdover from the campaign for legislative enactment of the basic statute; and often the initial administrative appointees are informed, dedicated adherents of these interests. They are thus in a position to secure pertinent data and to act strategically, helping furnish "organization" to the groups they represent. Sometimes the resources involved are such that there is organization on both sides; or the more effective organization may be on the "reform" side. The securities exchange legislation is an illuminating example, for after Richard Whitney's conviction for embezzlement key officials of the New York Stock Exchange recognized their own interest in supporting controls over less scrupulous elements. This interest configuration doubt-

---

[38]*The Folklore of Capitalism* (New Haven: Yale University Press, 1937), pp. 212, 215, 216.

less explains the relative popularity of the SEC both with regulated groups and with organized liberal groups.

IV

The evidence considered here suggests that we can make an encouraging start toward defining the conditions in which myth and symbolic reassurance become key elements in the governmental process. The conditions[39] are present in substantial degree in many policy areas other than business regulation. They may well be maximal in the foreign policy area, and a similar approach to the study of foreign policy formation would doubtless be revealing.

Because the requisite conditions are always present in some degree, every instance of policy formulation involves a "mix" of symbolic effect and rational reflection of interests in resources, though one or the other phenomenon may be dominant in any particular case. One type of mix is exemplified by such governmental programs outside the business regulation field as public education and social security. There can be no doubt that these programs do confer important tangible benefits upon a very wide public, very much as they promise to do. They do so for the reasons suggested earlier. Business organizations, labor organizations, teachers' organizations, and other organized groups benefit from these programs and have historically served to focus public attention upon the resources to be gained or lost. Their task has been all the easier because the techniques for achieving the benefits are fairly readily recognizable.

But the financing of these same programs involves public policies of a different order. Here the symbol of "free" education and other benefits, the complexity of the revenue and administrative structure, and the absence of organization have facilitated the emergence of highly regressive payroll, property, and head taxes as the major sources of revenue. Thus, business organizations, which by and large support the public schools that provide their trained personnel and the social security programs that minimize the costs of industrial pensions, pay relatively little for these services; while the direct beneficiaries of the "free" programs pay a relatively high proportion of the costs. Careful analysis of the "mix" in particular programs should prove illuminating.

If the conditions facilitating symbolic reassurance are correctly specified, there is reason to question some common assumptions about strategic variables in policy formulation and reason also to devise some more imaginative models in designing research in this area. The theory discussed here suggests, for example, a tie between the emergence of conditions promoting

[39]They are listed above under "Pattern B."

interests in symbolic reassurance and widened freedom of policy maneuver
for those attempting to assert leadership over the affected group. It implies
that the number of adherents of a political interest may have more to do
with whether the political benefit offered is tangible or symbolic than with
the quantity or quality of tangible resources allocated. It suggests that the
factors that explain voting behavior can be quite different from the factors
that explain resource allocations through government. The fact that large
numbers of people are objectively affected by a governmental program
may actually serve in some contexts to weaken their capacity to exert a
political claim upon tangible values.

A number of recent writers, to take another example, have suggested
that it is the "Independence" of the independent regulatory commissions
which chiefly accounts for their tendency to become tools of the groups they
regulate. The hypotheses suggested here apply to regulatory programs
administered in cabinet departments as well; and their operation is discernible in some of these programs when the specified conditions are present. The Grazing Service and the Anti-trust Division are examples.

In terms of research design, the implications of the analysis probably lie
chiefly in the direction of emphasizing an integral tie of political behavior
to underlying and extensive social interaction. Analysts of political dynamics must have a theory of relevance; but the directly relevant may run
farther afield than has sometimes been assumed. Political activities of all
kinds require the most exhaustive scrutiny to ascertain whether their
chief function is symbolic or substantive. The "what" of Lasswell's famous
definition of politics is a complex universe in itself.

Stable
Unrepresentation
in American
Society

William A. Gamson

A democratic political system must be able to handle two great problems if
it is to be maintained successfully: the danger of tyranny or domination by
a minority, and the problem of responsiveness to unmet or changing needs

SOURCE: William A. Gamson, "Stable Unrepresentation in American Society," *The American
Behavioral Scientist*, XII (November-December 1968), 15-21. Reprinted by permission of the
publisher, Sage Publications, Inc.

among its citizens. The theory of pluralist democracy has the virtue of explaining how a political system can handle both of these problems simultaneously. It is an elegant model of a political system, and it has provided, for a number of years, an influential and even dominant interpretation of American politics.

To the extent that the American political system approximates the pluralist model, it is argued, it will produce regular and orderly change with the consent of the governed. Those who argue for this interpretation are not unaware of urban riots and the considerable history of violent conflict in this country. However, they tend to view such events as abnormalities or pathologies arising from the gap between an always imperfect reality and an ideal abstract model. In other words, the occasional, admitted failures of American democracy to produce orderly change are caused by departures from the ideal conditions of pluralism. Furthermore, even a well-functioning thermostat sometimes produces temperatures which are momentarily too hot or too cold as it goes about giving us the proper temperature.

The pluralist interpretation of the American political system seems to make sense of a great body of historical and contemporary experience. Yet there is reason to doubt that it captures the full truth; rather, it is a partial truth that misses or blurs certain problems and paints an overly sanguine picture of the operation of power in American society. These limitations have given rise to a growing body of criticism of the pluralist interpretation and some attempts at alternative formulations. This paper represents such an effort with the provisional attempt at an alternative model which I have labeled "stable unrepresentation."

The Pluralist Model

There is a vast literature on pluralism and the American political system, and this brief discussion will not attempt to do it justice. A particularly coherent and convincing statement of the case is made in Dahl's *Pluralist Democracy in the United States* (1967). Now Dahl is no mindless celebrator of the genius of American politics; he paints his subject with all her warts and blemishes. But the important point is that this darker side of American politics is, with a major exception discussed below, viewed as blemish and not as the essence of his subject.

Dahl suggests (1967: 24) that the "fundamental axiom in the theory and practice of American pluralism is . . . this: Instead of a single center of sovereign power there must be multiple centers of power, none of which is or can be wholly sovereign." Why is this so important? Because the "existence of multiple centers of power . . . will help to tame power, to secure the consent of all, and to settle conflicts peacefully."

The brilliance of pluralist thinking is illustrated by its ability to handle multiple problems simultaneously—the prevention of dominance by a single group or individual, responsiveness to the needs of its citizens, and the prevention of extreme or violent conflict. It deals with two very different threats to the political system. The first threat is that the delicate balance of competition will be destroyed by a temporarily ascendant group that will use its ascendancy to crush its competitors. The second threat is that in the stalemate of veto groups and countervailing power, there will be ineffective government leading to an accumulation of discontent that will destroy the legitimacy and threaten the stability of the existing system.

We can examine the pluralist answer by addressing the question of how an ideal pluralist system functions. To operate properly, pluralist political institutions require an underlying pluralist social structure and values as well. More specifically, the following conditions should prevail:

1. *Procedural consensus.* There is acceptance of the "culture" of constitutional democracy. One operates within the rules, the rules are considered generally fair, and defeats are accepted because of the strong legitimacy attached to the manner of resolving conflicts. Dahl goes even further than procedural consensus and argues for a good deal of substantive consensus as well. "In the United States, there is a massive convergence of attitudes on a number of key issues that divide citizens in other countries. As one result, ways of life are not seriously threatened by the policies of opponents" (1967: 326).

2. *Cross-cutting solidarities.* Individuals have strong identifications and affiliations with solidarity groups at different levels below the total society—primary groups, community, clan, complex organization, religious group, ethnic group, social class, and so forth. Furthermore, these solidarities overlap and cut across each other in a complex web which creates multiple memberships linking individuals with different sets of others.

3. *Open access to the political arena.* There are no barriers to a group getting a hearing. Dissatisfied groups are encouraged to translate their dissatisfaction into political demands, find coalition partners among other powerful groups, and create political reforms which remedy the unsatisfactory conditions. As Dahl argues (1967: 24): "Because even minorities are provided with opportunities to veto solutions they strongly object to, the consent of all will be won in the long run." The political institutions offer multiple points at which to pursue one's demands. "The institutions . . . offer organized minorities innumerable sites in which to fight, perhaps to defeat, at any rate to damage an opposing coalition" (Dahl, 1967: 329).

4. *Balance of power or countervailing power operates.* There is a sufficiently large number of groups that no one group can dominate. Coalitions are fluid and impermanent, being formed more or less *de novo* for each issue or, at least, for each class of issues. Furthermore, issues partition groups in different ways, so that many groups not in a present coalition are potential coalition partners on subsequent issues. "Because one center of power is set against another," Dahl writes (1967: 24), "power itself will be tamed, civilized, controlled, and limited to decent human purposes, while coercion, the most evil form of power, will be reduced to a minimum."

When these assumptions are met, it is argued, neither tyranny nor rigidity will result. No group will become dominant, for several reasons. First, it will exercise self-restraint in exploiting any temporary ascendancy for normative reasons. The institutions "generate politicians who learn how to deal gently with opponents, who struggle endlessly in building and holding coalitions together, who doubt the possibilities of great change, who seek compromises" (Dahl, 1967: 329). Thus the political process encourages a normative commitment to a set of rules which would be violated by dealing too ruthlessly with an opponent.

Second, self-restraint is encouraged by long-run self-interest. In a world of constantly shifting coalitions, it is feckless to antagonize groups which may be tomorrow's allies on some other set of issues. Third, self-restraint is encouraged by short-run self-interest. Because of the nature of cross-cutting solidarities, any temporarily ascendant group is likely to include many members who belong as well to those groups who might be the victims of the abuse of power. In such a situation, any efforts to use power to injure or destroy the power of opponents are automatically threats to the *internal stability* of the groups that would attempt such action.

Finally, if self-restraint is not sufficient, efforts to achieve domination will encourage neutral and uninvolved groups to join an opposing coalition which controls greater resources than the temporarily ascendant group or coalition. Power which threatens to get out of hand stimulates countervailing power.

Many of the same pluralist conditions help to produce responsiveness as well. The critical element in this argument is that in the normal operation of the political system, dissatisfied groups are encouraged to organize and translate their dissatisfaction into concrete political demands. Several elements in the political system lead to such encouragement. First, competitive elections assure that political parties will woo dissatisfied groups that have achieved some degree of organization, either to broaden their base of support or to prevent the allegiance of such groups to their competitor. Second, existing interest groups with similar or overlapping interests will facilitate organization of such dissatisfied groups, seeing in them new allies. Third, multiple points of access to the political system will encourage participation by making available many sites for possible influence. Fourth, such organization and participation will be encouraged by the normative commitment of existing competitors to open access.

Thus, no group will long remain unrepresented, and it will find its entry into the political arena smoothed and facilitated by powerful allies who find it useful to do so for their own purposes. There will be no need for such groups to violate the existing rules of democratic politics to bring about the remedy of legitimate grievances.

This, then, is the case for pluralism. It is a subtle and persuasive argu-

ment with roots going back to James Madison and extending through an
array of subsequent political theorists. In criticizing it and in attempting
to formulate an alternative, I intend no denial of the great intellectual
insights into the workings of political systems in general, and of American
politics in particular, which we owe to this body of thought.

Flaws in the Pluralist Heaven

"The flaw in the pluralist heaven," writes Schattschneider (1960: 35),
"is that the heavenly chorus sings with a strong upper-class accent. Probably about 90% of the people cannot get into the pressure system." In one
form or another, this theme is present in most writing which is critical of
pluralist theory.

No pluralist, of course, asserts that influence is dispersed over the whole
political community. Dahl acknowledges, for example, that "there exists a
threshold beyond which low standing is a severe handicap in gaining influence over key governmental decisions; this threshold occurs approximately at the line dividing white-collar from blue-collar occupations"
(Dahl, 1961). Nevertheless, contrasting evaluations may be made of this
fact of differential participation in political life.

Many pluralist critics see it as a serious problem for the long-run success
of a democratic political system. But Walker (1966: 291) suggests that most
defenders of pluralist theory tend to view "widespread apathy [as] merely a
fact of political life, something to be anticipated. . . ." Furthermore, apathy
may be viewed as having important positive functions for a democratic
political system, making possible easier shifts in political power and removing from participation elements of the political community with the
weakest normative commitment to democratic politics. Walker contrasts
this view with that of the "classical democrats" for whom "political apathy
is an object of intense concern because the overriding moral purpose of
the classical theory is to expand the boundaries of the political community
and build the foundations for human understanding through participation
by the citizens in the affairs of their government" (1966: 291).

One line of criticism of pluralist theory has centered on the ability of
pluralist politics to handle the problem of dominance. This theme is given
classical expression in Mills' *The Power Elite* (1956). Mills argues for the
existence of a level of power operation not touched by pluralist assumptions. The pluralist model, Mills grants, is applicable to a middle level of
power, but a series of really major decisions are dominated by a small
group which is not subject to the constraints operating at the middle level.

Mills' argument is vulnerable at a number of points, in large part because of his emphasis on the issue of dominance. As Pilisuk and Hayden
argue (1965: 78): "Where Mills' theory is most awkward is in his asser-

tions that the elite can, and does, make its decisions against the will of others and regardless of external conditions. . . . What is attributed to the elite is a rather fantastic quality: literal omnipotence." Pilisuk and Hayden attempt to remedy this weakness in Mills while preserving his major insights by making the argument (1965: 92) in more sophisticated, institutional terms rather than in terms of a "ruling group."

> In the United States there is no ruling group . . . Nor is there any easily discernible ruling institutional order, so meshed have the separate sources of elite power become. But there is a social structure which is organized to create and protect power centers with only partial accountability. . . . We are describing the current system as one of overall "minimal accountability" and "minimal consent." We mean that the role of democratic review, based on popular consent, is made marginal and reactive. Elite groups are minimally accountable to publics and have a substantial, though by no means maximum, freedom to shape popular attitudes.

Having argued for the imbeddedness of a military-industrial complex in mainstream American institutions and mores, they conclude that "Our concept is not that American society contains a ruling military-industrial complex. Our concept is more nearly that American society *is* a military-industrial complex" (1965: 98).

Some of this criticism may be accepted by pluralists in a form that gives it a more appealing face. Concentration of power is necessary, it can be argued, to enjoy the fruits of leadership. Where substantial consensus exists on goals, many issues reflect technical problems. Agger, Goldrich, and Swanson write (1964: 76):

> Pluralists take the position, specifically or implicitly, that . . . major decisional options are not shaped by an influential ruling elite so much as they are by "technical" factors which, assuming there is a desire for "functional rationality," would lead rational men to similar choice situations or decisional outcomes, regardless of socio-economic class or official position.

If the collective interest is to be served, then the social system needs specialists in goal attainment to exercise disproportionate influence on its behalf (cf. Parsons, 1960). In this view, to see such essential leadership functions as "undemocratic," in some way, is to impose an ideology on an essential fact of social life: concentration of power is necessary for efficient goal attainment. Many social scientists sympathetic to the pluralist argument probably share the view which Dahl (1961: 321) attributes to members of the political stratum. "Public involvement may seem undesirable . . . for alterations in the prevailing norms are often subtle matters, better obtained by negotiation than by the crudities and over-simplifications of public debate."

This defense of pluralism is, I believe, an important one, but it deals with only one part of the attack. The fortress remains impregnable on the issue of *dominance,* but it is considerably more vulnerable on the issue of *responsiveness.*

There are two separate lines of attack on the responsiveness of a pluralist political system. One emphasizes the incremental nature of the changes which are fostered by pluralism, but questions the ability of the system to make major or radical shifts on the occasions when these may be necessary. The second line of criticism raises doubts about the completeness of even incremental responses to many portions of the population. We may consider each of these arguments in turn.

Pluralism, Dahl points out (1967: 190, 329) makes for a politics

> that brings about reform [more] through mutual adjustment and a gradual accumulation of incremental changes than through sweeping programs of comprehensive and coordinated reconstruction. . . . [The] institutions place a high premium on strategies of compromise and conciliation, on a search for consensus. They inhibit and delay change until there is wide support; they render comprehensive change unlikely.

The other side of this coin is that the institutions

> also foster delay in coming to grips with questions that threaten severe conflict. It is true that delay may provide precious time during which a seemingly severe problem may change its shape, become more manageable, even disappear. But postponement may also inhibit leaders from facing a problem squarely and searching for decisive solutions—solutions that may be forced upon them many years later when they can no longer delay [Dahl, 1967: 295].

At this point, Dahl joins the critics of pluralism, not simply because he suggests its imperfections but because he views these imperfections as a possible part of the *normal* operation of pluralist institutions rather than as an aberration. By preventing early and drastic changes in policy, pluralist institutions may "prolong and exacerbate severe conflict" instead of preventing it. Thus, the recurrent violence in American political life is less a product of departures from the ideal pluralist model and more an outgrowth of the regular and orderly operation of pluralist institutions.

Tilly (1968) arrives at an argument with similar implications via a quite different route. He is concerned with the conditions for collective violence and is at least as much focused on the European experience as the American. Consequently, he makes his argument not simply in terms of pluralist institutions but for political systems more generally. "Membership in the polity gives important advantages to a group," Tilly argues; "exclusion is costly." Consequently, the "entry of a new group into the polity tends to produce collective violence" because:

(a) The existing members resist with the coercive means under their control
(b) The aspiring members make or reinforce their claims to membership by the use of violence
(c) Each one defines the action of the other as illegitimate and as thus requiring and justifying extraordinary means of coercion.

Tilly doesn't suggest any special vulnerability of pluralist political institutions to such outcomes, but neither does he assume any special ability to respond to and accommodate excluded groups. Pluralist political systems, like other polities, can be expected to produce collective violence as part of their normal operations "where new groups are acquiring membership in the political community, or old groups are losing it."

These arguments do not preclude a good deal of short-run responsiveness to the needs of the citizenry in a pluralist society. However, important questions have been raised about such incremental responsiveness as well. Etzioni (1968) makes a useful distinction between flexibility and responsiveness. "Political and societal flexibility," he writes (1968: 506), "are not co-extensive with responsiveness, as they indicate a capacity only to adapt to changing power relations and not necessarily to members' needs." High political flexibility in a society means a "close 'fit' between the distributions of political and societal power" (1968: 513). It is quite possible, Etzioni argues, for a society to achieve a consensus—even with broad participation in its formation—without any "assurance that the resulting policy, action, or societal structure will not be alienating." This can happen because "differences in power lead to inauthentic consensus in support of patterns which are not responsive . . . to the needs of the weak. Substantial equality is a prerequisite for the relative neutralization of power and for the building of authentic, non-coerced consensus and, hence, for responsiveness" (1968: 517).

While flexibility without responsiveness is bad, political rigidity is even worse. "An important expression of political rigidity," Etzioni points out (1968: 513), "is the political overrepresentation of societally powerful collectivities and the underrepresentation of weaker collectivities; that is, the political conversion process further magnifies differences in societal power, adding some of the autonomous power of the state to already powerful collectivities."

In these terms, pluralist political institutions are subject to important rigidities at worst and to flexibility without responsiveness at best. "All interests are not equally represented in the bargaining arena," Presthus argues (1964: 31). "Real competition on any specific issues is limited to relatively few powerful groups. . . . These structural facets of contemporary pluralism mean that bargaining often proceeds among a presidium of elites, which disadvantages unorganized segments of society." Furthermore, Schattschneider argues (1960: 34) that this condition is an integral part of

the pressure system, not a remedial imperfection. "To suppose that everyone participates in pressure-group activity and that all interests get themselves organized in the pressure system is to destroy the meaning of this
form of politics. The pressure system makes sense only as the political
instrument of a segment of the community . . . ; if everybody got into the
act, the unique advantages of this form of organization would be destroyed,
for it is possible that if all interests could be mobilized the result would be
a stalemate."

Lowi's critique of "interest group liberalism" (1967) can also be seen as
an argument for the limited responsiveness of pluralist politics. Lowi concludes that the "rules-of-the-game heavily weight access and power in favor
of the established interests, just as American parliamentary rules-of-the-
game have always tended to make Congress a haven for classes in retreat"
(1967: 21). Rather than containing built-in features that keep the system
responsive and self-corrective, a reliance on bargaining among organized
interests encourages: "(1) The atrophy of institutions of popular control;
(2) the maintenance of old and creation of new structures of privilege; and
(3) conservatism, in several senses of the word," (Lowi, 1967: 18). Given
the existence of a "strong tendency, supported by a great deal of conscious
effort, to keep confrontation to a minimum . . . ," Lowi concludes (1967: 22)
that "it cannot be assumed that the conditions necessary for the self-cor-
rection system necessarily exist."

Perhaps the most subtle and fundamental argument of all against the
alleged responsiveness and corrective features contained in a pluralist
political system is made by Olson (1965) in *The Logic of Collective Action*. Olson argues that it is not rational for an individual to band together
with others of similar interest to pursue their collective interest. "Class-
oriented action will not occur if the individuals that make up a class act
rationally. If a person is in the bourgeois class, he may well want a government that represents his class. But it does not follow that it will be in his
interest to work to see that such a government comes to power. If there is
such a government he will benefit from its policies, whether or not he has
supported it, for by Marx's own hypothesis it will work for his class interests. Moreover, in any event one individual bourgeois presumably will
not be able to exercise a decisive influence on the choice of a government.
So the *rational* thing for a member of the bourgeoisie to do is to ignore his
class interests and to spend his energies on his *personal* interests" (Olson,
1965: 105).

Suffering and discontent will not inevitably lead to organized political
pressure. "The unorganized groups, the groups that have no lobbies and
exert no pressure, are among the largest groups in the nation, and they
have some of the most vital common interests. Migrant farm laborers are a
significant group with urgent common interests, and they have no lobby

to voice their needs. . . ." Neither logic nor empirical observation suggests that we can safely assume that groups with unmet needs will organize politically. "The rational individual in the economic system does not curtail his spending to prevent inflation . . . because he knows, first, that his own effort would not have a noticeable effect, and second, that he would get the benefits of any price stability that others achieved in any case. For the same two reasons, the rational individual in the large group in a sociopolitical context will not be willing to make any sacrifices to achieve the objectives he shares with others. There is accordingly no presumption that large groups will organize to act in their common interest. Only when groups are small, or when they are fortunate enough to have an independent source of selective incentives, will they organize to achieve their objectives" (Olson, 1965: 165-166).

The writers quoted above point to some important limits of pluralism. But we must go beyond poking holes in pluralism to the construction of an alternative model of the operation of the American political system. Some of the works discussed above have attempted to do this, and the model presented here is particularly indebted to Pilisuk and Hayden (1965).

Stable Unrepresentation

The alternative proposed here begins by accepting the existence of a high degree of competition in American politics on many and important issues. Furthermore, it does not seriously challenge the pluralist interpretation on the prevention of tyranny, but challenges it on the issue of responsiveness. My central argument is that the American political system normally operates to prevent incipient competitors from achieving full entry into the political arena. Far from there being built-in mechanisms which keep the system responsive, such groups win entry only through the breakdown of the normal operation of the system or through demonstration on the part of challenging groups of a willingness to violate the "rules-of-the-game" by resorting to illegitimate means for carrying on political conflict.

Any political system must handle discontented groups in some fashion. Such discontent can be handled either by some modification of the content of policies or by some effort to control the discontented group. One response attempts to remove pressure from dissidents by yielding ground (i.e., outcome modification), the other by directing counter-influence, or social control.

Social control will generally be preferred to outcome modification since, if it is successful, it will maximize the maneuverability of the recipient of pressure. Such maneuverability has three attractions (Gamson, 1968: 115):

1. It allows the incumbent authority to exercise his own personal preference. He is free to act as he pleases and to do what he thinks best, within the limits of his role but without the additional limits imposed by influence.
2. If he has no particular preferences, the freedom from influence on a given issue enables him to use his authority as a resource to influence other decisions on which he has a partisan interest. In other words, successful social control increases the resources of authorities by allowing them discretion in the areas in which they exercise authority; such freedom allows them to use their authority as an inducement or constraint on other authorities whom they would influence. . . .
3. Effective social control increases slack resources. This means that influence is cheaper. . . . [One] can influence at bargain rates when the competition has been removed by effective social control.

Thus, the normal response of the political system in this model is some form of social control rather than the encouragement of political organization and political influence by discontented groups, leading to an eventual response to their political demands. The social control techniques available to authorities are varied and effective. Thus, it is possible for stability to be achieved for considerable periods of time during which substantial unmet needs are present among many members of the society. This results in a situation in which large numbers of citizens are outside of the political arena in which competition and influence occur; they are doing little about it; and they are essentially invisible to those who actively participate in the political system. This situation can be described as one of stable unrepresentation; it breaks down under certain conditions, and genuine responses and changes occur, but the normal operation of the political system serves to amplify the power of those groups which already possess it.

A brief vocabulary will be useful in developing this model of stable unrepresentation. *Solidary groups* are "collections of individuals who think in terms of the effect of political decisions on the aggregate and feel that they are in some way personally affected by what happens to the aggregate" (Gamson, 1968: 35). Examples include ethnic groups, religious groups, some occupational groups, and so forth. Such solidary groups differ in their degree of cohesiveness or solidarity. Solidarity is promoted by symbolic expressions of the group as a collectivity, treatment as a group by others, a common style of life, norms, and values, and a high rate of interaction among members. *Interest groups* "are the formally organized manifestations of solidary groups. They may serve as the vehicle for the exercise of influence by such groups and, in addition, they perform important functions in building and maintaining the solidarity of their constituency and in creating potential influence in such a constituency" (Gamson, 1968: 36). The *authorities* are "those who, for any given social system, make binding decisions in that system. . . . A decision is binding if either it is accepted as binding (for whatever reason) *or,* if it is not accepted, legitimate force can be used to implement the decision" (Gamson, 1968: 21-22). The particular authorities we are concerned with here are those at the national level.

Feeling that they are affected in the same way by the political system, solidary groups are likely to develop similar attitudes of trust toward different political objects. It is possible, therefore, to characterize a solidary group as possessing particular attitudes of trust in spite of some degree of variance among individual members. The political trust of a solidary group is its perception of the efficiency of the political system in achieving collective goals and its bias in handling conflicts of interest. It is difficult to disentangle a group's perceptions of fairness from its perceptions of efficiency and, therefore, it is desirable to define trust in a way that combines the two dimensions. "This can be done by defining a 'preferred' outcome for a solidary group as the one it regards as most favorable to its interests when they conflict with other groups *or* as the most efficient for the system as a whole. Its political trust can be defined as the probability, P_b that the political system . . . will produce preferred outcomes even if left untended. In other words, it is the probability of getting preferred outcomes without the group doing anything to bring them about" (Gamson, 1968: 54).

Any solidary group may be characterized by a particular value (or range of values) of P_b. These values are continuous, of course, but it is useful to describe three pure points of *confidence, neutrality,* and *alienation.* "*Confidence* is the belief that for any given decision, $P_b = 1.0$. Confidence in authorities means that they are perceived as the group's agents, that the group members identify with them. . . . *Neutrality* is the belief that for any given decision, $P_b = 0.5$. There are different processes by which one can arrive at this state of neutrality. It may involve a view of the political system as composed of highly variable and erratic objects, potent but unpredictable in producing preferred outcomes. . . . Alternatively, there may be little salience to political objects. . . . *Alienation* is the belief that for any given decision, $P_b = 0$. Alienation from authorities means that they are regarded as incompetent and stupid in achieving collective goals and biased against the group in handling conflicts of interests. They are anti-agents of the group, the agents of groups with conflicting goals" (Gamson, 1968: 54-56).

Using these terms, we can define a represented and an unrepresented group. A *represented group* is any solidary group meeting either of the following conditions:

1. There exists some significant set of authorities in whom the group has political confidence, *or*
2. There exists some interest group in which the solidary group has confidence, *and* there exists some significant set of authorities in which this interest group has confidence.

An *unrepresented group* is any group meeting neither of the above conditions. It is worth noting that the unit here is not really the individual *qua* individual. As Tilly (1968) puts it: "The 'members' of the polity . . . do not include all identifiable groups within the society and need not include all persons within the society. For example, a Muslim longshoreman may belong to a political bloc in Pakistan by virtue of being a Muslim, but not by virtue of being a longshoreman. Later, longshoreman may acquire membership in the polity—'political identify'—*qua* longshoreman, thus giving Muslim longshoremen two modes of participation in Pakistani politics." Similarly, a Negro automobile worker might be a member of one represented group as unionized worker and a member of an unrepresented group as urban ghetto dweller. The collection of represented groups and authorities will be called the *competitive establishment.*

To restate the stable unrepresentation model in these terms, it argues that the American political system normally functions to (1) keep unrepresented groups from developing solidarity and politically organizing, and (2) discourage their effective entry into the competitive establishment if and as they become organized. The competitive establishment is boundary-maintaining, and the boundary-maintaining process involves various kinds of social control.

Examples of forces which discourage solidarity and initial political organization include: (1) lack of access to information about the effects of political decisions; (2) lack of politically experienced and skilled leadership; (3) the "culture of subordination" (Paige, 1968), including self-blame ideologies which locate sources of dissatisfaction in the individual's shortcomings or in irremediable states of nature and society rather than in politically remediable features of the social system; (4) low rates of interaction and organizational participation which might encourage the development of solidarity; (5) lack of financial resources; (6) pursuit of personal rather than group interest (see Olson, 1965); (7) lack of personal trust toward each other among members of the solidary group; and (8) "opiates" which divert energies from political paths.

If these handicaps aren't sufficient, there is further discouragement from members of the competitive establishment. Unrepresented groups tend to be poor in resources and rich in demands, making them poor coalition partners. They will expect to share in the rewards of a coalition disproportionately to the resources they contribute to it. Specific actions which serve to discourage the inclusion of unrepresented groups include: (1) attempts to undermine the legitimacy of their interest groups by discrediting them; (2) harassment of leaders; (3) drawing-off of interest group leaders into established organizations, thus removing the dependency of such leaders on the unrepresented solidary group (cooptation); (4) appeals to the constituency of unrepresented groups "over the head" of its leaders, urging members and potential members of interest groups to reject these groups as their representatives; and (5) incrementalism in the resolution of major policy issues.

Incrementalism helps to avoid competition by allowing major allocations to be determined by a large number of small, compartmentalized decisions. The smallness of each individual decision encourages a "live and let live" posture among potential competitors (tariff decisions or defense procurement decisions are examples of this). By removing these areas from extensive competition, interest groups which are affected by the overall result of multiple decisions find no obvious point at which they may assert some interest. "Above everything," Schattschneider writes (1960: 140), "the people are powerless if the political enterprise is not competitive. It is the competition of political organizations that provides the people with the opportunity to make a choice."

No implication is intended in the above discussion that there is any conscious, deliberate effort on the part of represented groups to keep newcomers out. Incrementalism, for example, may be nothing more than the unanticipated consequence of increasing differentiation of function and decision-making. To argue that it has the effect of decreasing competition and, thus, of helping to maintain stable unrepresentation, is not to argue that it *arose* for this reason or was designed by any individual or group as an instrument for that purpose. In short, the argument that an action or an institution serves to maintain stable unrepresentation does not depend on the *motivation* of the participants but on the *consequence* of discouraging the translation of grievances into political demands which can be effectively pursued through political action.

Conclusion

If pluralism is not the whole truth of American politics, neither is stable unrepresentation. It is not offered here as a complete model of the operation of the American political system, but as an heuristic device with two purposes. First, it attempts to construct an alternative which captures a significant part of the operation of American politics which is missed by the pluralist model. Second, it is designed to move us beyond the question of which description is more accurate or valid to the more interesting and answerable question of the *conditions* under which a political system tends to follow one or the other model.

I am not prepared at this point to answer this question, but it is the subject of research in which I am currently engaged (see Gamson, study in progress). I hope, however, to illustrate some possible answers by suggesting four hypotheses about the conditions under which stable unrepresentation breaks down. Each hypothesis has already been mentioned or implied in the earlier discussion, but they are restated here in the context of this new question. Conditions under which stable unrepresentation breaks down may also be viewed as conditions which encourage responsiveness by the political system.

1. *Crises in the achievement of collective goals.* A breakdown in the ability of a political system to achieve collective goals may lead to a breakdown in the effectiveness of social control. This may encourage groups that would not normally have done so to press demands (Cf. Parsons, 1964). Such crises might come from external sources (for example, foreign threats), from ill-conceived foreign adventures, or from a cumulative inadequacy of responses to internal needs. This hypothesis suggests that crises provide an occasion for the mobilization of power by relatively weak groups and, subsequently, for greater responsiveness to their demands.

2. *Resort to Violence.* Any group of even moderate size has an important constraint resource—the ability to make trouble. They may be deterred from using this resource by the probability of counter measures, but when desperation is present or controls break down, this may change. This hypothesis suggests that the willingness of unrepresented solidary group members to utilize their capacity to make trouble for others will increase the responsiveness of the political system.

3. *Planning and coordination attempts by authorities.* Efforts toward broader planning, toward cost-effectiveness studies of total operations and the establishment of priorities, may have the incidental and unintended consequence of increasing the degree of competition. Although there is no intention to do so, they create boundary-maintaining problems for represented groups by making the effects of previous incremental decisions more salient to those affected by them. This hypothesis suggests that coordination efforts open the arena to new competitors and thus lead to greater responsiveness to groups which were formerly excluded.

4. *Prior non-political organization.* Olson (1965: 132-133) suggests that: "The common characteristic which distinguishes all of the large economic groups with significant lobbying organizations is that these groups are also organized for some *other* purpose. The large and powerful economic lobbies are in fact the by-products of organizations that obtain their strength and support because they perform some function in addition to lobbying for collective goods. . . : The lobbies of the large economic groups are the by-products of organizations that have the capacity to 'mobilize' a latent group with 'selective incentives.' " This hypothesis suggests that groups which organize and secure a constituency around some nonpolitical service, and then apply their resources to the political arena, will find the system more responsive than those who attempt to organize around political demands.

Hopefully, by exploring such hypotheses with data on contemporary and historical groups, we may be able to understand the limits of pluralism. And in moving beyond the pluralist framework, we may eventually be able to reach a more complete understanding of the operation of power in American society.

References

Agger, R. et al. (1964) *The Rulers and the Ruled.* New York: Wiley.

Dahl, R. (1961) *Who Governs?* New Haven: Yale Univ. Press.

———— (1967) *Pluralist Democracy in the United States: Conflict and Consent.* Chicago: Rand-McNally.

Etzioni, A. (1968) *The Active Society.* New York: Free Press.

Gamson, W. (1968) *Power and Discontent.* Homewood, Ill.: Dorsey Press.

———— (study in progress) "Political processes and social change in the United States" (National Science Foundation, GS-1991). Ann Arbor: Univ. of Michigan, Center for Research on Conflict Resolution.

Lowi, T. (1967) "The public philosophy: interest-group liberalism." *Am. Pol. Sci. Rev.* 61 (March): 5-24.

Mills, C. W. (1956) *The Power Elite.* New York: Oxford Univ. Press.

Olson, M., Jr. (1965) *The Logic of Collective Action.* Cambridge, Mass.: Harvard Univ. Press.

Paige, J. (1968) "Collective violence and the culture of subordination." Unpub. Ph.D. dissertation, Univ. of Michigan.

Parsons, T. (1960) "The distribution of power in American society." Pp. 199-225 in T. Parsons (ed.) *Structure and Process in Modern Societies.* New York: Free Press.

———— (1964) "Some reflections on the place of force in social process." Pp. 33-70 in H. Eckstein (ed.) *Internal War.* New York: Free Press.

Pilisuk, M. and T. Hayden (1965) "Is there a military industrial complex which prevents peace?" *J. Social Issues* 21 (July): 67-117.

Presthus, R. (1964) *Men at the Top.* New York: Oxford Univ. Press.

Schattschneider, E. (1960) *The Semi-Sovereign People.* New York: Holt, Rinehart and Winston.

Tilly, C. (1968) "The changing place of collective violence" in M. Richter (ed.) *Social Theory and Social History.* Cambridge, Mass.: Harvard Univ. Press.

Walker, J. (1966) "A critique of the elitist theory of democracy." *Am. Pol. Sci. Rev.* 60 (June): 285-295.

Part Two
Politics
Within
Groups

To the extent that groups participate in the authoritative allocation of values in a society, an understanding of their internal politics is a necessary prerequisite to an understanding of the distributive system of the society. When groups make demands or render support to the political system, or when groups receive benefits or incur deprivations from the system, they function as political subsystems which mediate between the larger system and the individual. The study of the internal politics of groups can indicate who is likely to be benefitted or pay the costs which accrue to the group as a whole. The study of internal politics can also point out whose preferences are likely to be articulated as group policy and how stable such policies are likely to be for the group.

A useful way of interpreting the evidence on internal politics is to view groups as private governments.[1] In the first selection Grant McConnell analyzes a variety of studies on politics within groups from the perspective of private governments. McConnell raises two basic issues. First, he discusses the theoretical question of whether or not the type of governments at the private level must be compatible with the type of government at the public level.[2] Specifically, does democracy in public government require democracy in private governments? Secondly, he raises the empirical question of the extent of democratic government among private associations. Many groups such as corporations, churches, and lobbyist front groups with subscriber-type memberships do not base their claims of authority on the democratic ethos and have an oligarchical distribution of power.[3] In addition, many groups such as unions, trade associations, farm

[1]For summaries of research on internal politics of groups in addition to the selections in this part, see David Truman, *The Governmental Process* (New York: Alfred Knopf, 1951), Chapters 5 and 6; Abraham Holtzman, *Interest Groups and Lobbying* (New York: Macmillan, 1966), Chapter 2; Harmon Zeigler, *Interest Groups in American Society* (Englewood Cliffs, N. J.: Prentice-Hall, 1964), pp. 93-232; and Seymour Martin Lipset, *Political Man* (Garden City, N. Y.: Doubleday, 1960), Chapter 12. In addition, studies of foreign countries frequently summarize the evidence for those countries; see, for example, Joseph LaPalombara, *Interest Groups in Italian Politics* (Princeton: Princeton University Press, 1964), Chapter 5.

[2]The terms public government and private government are being used here as identifying labels. A number of writers including McConnell are extremely critical of the orthodox interpretation that the public-private distinction is theoretically meaningful. In addition to McConnell's *Private Power and American Democracy*, see Theodore Lowi, "The Public Philosophy: Interest Group Liberalism," *American Political Science Review*, LXI (March 1967), 5-24; Michael Brenner, "Functional Representation and Interest Group Theory," *Comparative Politics*, II (October 1969), 11-134; and Edward Malecki, "The Role of Executive Based Issue Organizations in Policy Making," *Public Administration*, XXIX (December 1970), 356-367.

[3]For a critical view of internal corporate power structures see Robert Presthus, *The Organ-*

organizations, professional associations, and various civic and recreational groups purport to be dedicated to the ideal of democratic organization, but with rare exceptions also exhibit oligarchical power structures. The evidence clearly indicates that private government is almost always oligarchical in character.

The consequences flowing from the existence of an oligarchical power structure are not necessarily unidirectional. One direction in which such a power structure can be used by the leadership is that of manipulating the group's membership into a monolithic unity conforming to the leaders' interests. On the other hand, the power structure can segregate the rank-and-file from the leadership, resulting in systematic differences in attitudes and values between the leadership and the rank-and-file. Each of these outcomes corresponds to a type of government. The monolithic group is similar to the manipulated consensus associated with totalitarian governments.[4] In this type of group the rank-and-file are highly active and have virtually parallel interests with the leadership. The group with segregated value sets is similar to a society with an authoritarian regime.[5] In this type of group the leadership is much more active than the rank-and-file and systematically differs from the rank-and-file in attitudes and values.

The Luttbeg and Zeigler selection presents findings on the degree of unity between leaders and rank-and-file in the Oregon Education Association. They found that the leaders are more active, more liberal, and more willing to expand the activities of the group than the rank-and-file.[6] The differences in organizational position of leaders and rank-and-file also is related to misperception of rank-and-file attitudes by the leadership. The leaders consistently see the bulk of the rank-and-file as more conservative and restrained than they actually are.[7] The segregated activity patterns

izational Society (New York: Random House, 1962), and for a favorable view see Edwin Epstein, *The Corporation in American Politics* (Englewood Cliffs, N. J.: Prentice-Hall, 1969), Chapter 9.

[4]See the Kornhauser selection (pages 5-25) for a review description of totalitarian societies. Keep in mind the distinction between groups in totalitarian societies and totalitarian-type groups.

[5]For a description of this type of society see Juan Linz, "An Authoritarian Regime: Spain," in *Reader in Political Sociology*, ed. by Frank Lindenfeld (New York: Funk & Wagnalls, 1968), pp. 129-148. Since authoritarian regimes are most frequently found in traditional societies the leader-follower relations are quite similar to those of traditional societies outlined in the Kornhauser selection.

[6]Studies of various unions have also found the leadership more active and politically oriented than the bread-and-butter oriented rank-and-file. See Arnold Rose, *Union Solidarity* (Minneapolis: University of Minnesota Press, 1952); H. Rosen and R. A. Rosen, *The Union Member Speaks* (Englewood Cliffs, N. J.; Prentice-Hall, 1955); A. Tannenbaum and R. Kahn, *Participation in Union Locals* (Evanston, Ill.: Row & Peterson, 1958); A. Kornhauser, H. Sheppard, and A. Mayer, *When Labor Votes* (New York: University Books, 1956); and Jack Seidman, *et al.*, *The Worker Views His Union* (Chicago: University of Chicago Press, 1958).

[7]For similar research on legislators' perception of their constituents' attitudes see Warren

and attitude sets clearly fit the authoritarian type of oligarchy. Studies of other organizations suggest that this is the dominant organizational mode.[8]

The leadership of organizations with authoritarian power structures control resources which usually give them the capacity to prevent internal changes initiated by the rank-and-file.[9] In the typical case of group political activities, the authoritarian power structure is sufficient for the maintenance of the leadership's viewpoints. Few political activities taken in the name of specific groups require mass mobilization of the membership. The popularity of grass roots lobbying among established associations has declined sharply in frequency and importance in recent decades.[10] Demonstrations and rallies, while frequently dramatic in temporary impact, are, nevertheless, infrequent political strategies of established groups and short-lived strategies for politically weak groups.[11] Mass mobilization of membership in election campaigns is generally attempted only by a few mass membership groups such as the AFL-CIO and even these activities occur only once a year or less. Thus, typical political strategies of groups do not require frequent attempts of manipulating the rank-and-file into a cohesive unity by the leadership.[12]

For those political strategies which require some degree of cohesiveness among group members, a variety of constraints limit the degree to which the leadership can persuade the rank-and-file to adopt their viewpoint. Campbell, Converse, Miller, and Stokes have carefully analyzed the conditions under which relatively formalized groups influence the electoral

Miller and Donald Stokes, "Constituency Influence in Congress," *American Political Science Review,* LVII (March 1963), 45-56; and for perceptions of legislative leaders, see Harlan Hahn, "Leadership Perceptions and Voting Behavior in a One-Party Legislative Body," *Journal of Politics,* XXXII (February 1970), 140-155.

[8]See the studies cited in footnotes 1 and 6.

[9]There are times when conflict among the leadership enables the rank-and-file to play an effective role in group policy making. The Abel-McDonald fight in the Steelworkers Union represents one of these relatively rare occurrences. See George McManus, *The Inside Story of Steel Wages and Prices, 1959-1967* (Philadelphia: Chilton Book Co., 1967), pp. 117-162.

[10]Charles Clapp, *The Congressman* (Garden City, N. Y.: Doubleday Anchor Books, 1963), pp. 194-196; see the selection by Milbrath (pages 182-195) on the relative importance of various lobbying techniques.

[11]See the selection by Lipsky (pages 158-181) on the importance of protest demonstrations as a political resource of groups.

[12]There has been a strong tendency among group theorists to stress the importance of group cohesion as a major condition of political effectiveness. See, for example, Truman, Chapters 5 and 6. It is, however, cohesion among the leadership, not cohesion of the group as a whole, which is usually important for political effectiveness since rank-and-file disagreement with leadership policy is rarely manifested. This analysis is supported by the recognition that effective political action is frequently associated with small groups simply because cohesion is more difficult to achieve in large groups. See Phillip Monypenny, "Political Science and the Study of Groups: Notes to Guide a Research Project," *Western Political Quarterly,* VII (June 1954), 183-201; and for a recent formulation on how calculations of individual rationality inhibit cohesiveness of large groups, see Mancur Olson, *The Logic of Collective Action* (New York: Schocken, 1965).

decisions of their members.[13] Among the factors isolated by their analysis are the distinctiveness of the group values, the degree of identification to the group by the member, and the proximity of the group to politics which is related to the transmission of group standards to members and the saliency of political events to those standards. Since participation, agreement with group standards, and strong identification are all correlated, the leadership's influence is usually restricted to mobilizing like-minded rank-and-file rather than converting group dissidents to the leaders' viewpoints. For example, union leadership usually finds it easier to obtain rank-and-file support for strikes than for political activities.[14] This differential support directly reflects the rank-and-file's concern for bread-and-butter issues and low concern for obtaining political objectives through the union. Thus, the rank-and-file's low capacity for influencing the leadership is paralleled by the leadership's low capacity for changing the rank-and-file. These combined incapacities typically yield status quo oriented internal group politics.

Politics within formally organized groups constitutes only part of the total picture of politics within groups. In the next selection Campbell, Converse, Miller, and Stokes extend their analysis to a study of social class in American electoral politics. The same general factors are at work on the leaders' ability to influence other class members as are present in more formalized groups. In the case of social class, the ambiguity of class standards, the frequently low political salience of economic events, the weak group identification of class members, and the lack of a clearly designated class leadership combine to reduce the influence of the implicit "natural" leadership of the business community over the middle class and the labor unions over the working class. In both instances their class leadership is weak and primarily restricted to activating class voting behavior among businessmen and unions rather than respectively among the middle class and working class as a whole. As a general rule one can expect that in the absence of a formalized class grouping with explicit leadership (e.g., mass based socialist or labor parties), politics within social class groupings will remain narrow in scope and weak in influence.[15]

[13]Angus Campbell, Philip Converse, Warren Miller, and Donald Stokes, *The American Voter*, abridged ed. (New York: Wiley, 1964), Chapter 11.

[14]See the studies cited in footnote 6. In addition, see Harry Scoble, "Organized Labor in Electoral Politics: Some Questions for the Discipline," *Western Political Quarterly*, XVI (September 1963), 666-685; and Nicholas Masters, "The Organized Labor Bureaucracy as a Base of Support for the Democratic Party," *Law and Contemporary Problems*, XXVII (Spring 1962), 252-265; and Schley Lyons, "Labor in City Politics: The Case of the Toledo United Auto Workers," *Social Science Quarterly*, XLIX (March 1969), 816-828.

[15]See for example Gerald Lenski, *Power and Privilege* (New York: McGraw-Hill, 1966), Chapter 10.

Private
Government

Grant McConnell

I

Massive endorsement of the private association as an essential of democracy is one of the most striking features of American political thought. Freedom of association has virtually become a fundamental guarantee of the Constitution. The ideas of self-government and self-regulation have entered deeply into the doctrines of the political order, and they have been institutionalized to an unheralded degree. The private association, moreover, has been linked with the values of decentralization and federalism. It has also been pictured as the source of stability in politics and held up as the medium of the public interest. Most frequently, however, it has been seen as the guarantor of liberty. This is the most essential part of the general argument, and any examination of the doctrine must deal with this claim.

There is no doubt that pluralism belongs in the liberal tradition. The pluralist attack upon the state's assertion of unlimited power was one of the most incisive ever made. The defense of the private association against attempts to suppress it or to subordinate it to the state has almost always been a defense of liberty itself; the elaboration of this defense by pluralist writers has provided some of the noblest statements on constitutionalism and the limits of state action. Pluralist discussions of law carried important insights on the roots of law in sources other than compulsion. Moreover, the pluralists for the most part spoke out of a genuine dedication to individual liberty. Perhaps the most important aspect of pluralist doctrine in the present context is its adherence to the distinction between the state and society, a distinction closely related to that between the public and the private spheres of life.

There can be equally little doubt that the preference of those American writers who are sometimes classed as pluralists is for liberty. More conspicuously, however, the private associations of the United States have fought with great vigor to protect themselves from government encroachments. The organizations of business and labor have been the most vociferous in this regard, but perhaps the churches have made greater contributions;

SOURCE: From Grant McConnell, *Private Power and American Democracy* (New York: Alfred A. Knopf, 1966), pp. 119-154. Copyright © 1966 by Alfred A. Knopf, Inc. Reprinted by permission of the publisher. Footnotes have been deleted.

certainly separation of church and state is a more firmly established principle in America than in most countries.

When all this has been recognized, however, some very important questions remain. Since the private association has made its claim against the state in the name of liberty, how has the liberty of the individual fared vis-à-vis the private association? If the private association is to maintain the right of self-government and self-regulation, how is it governed itself? What is its conception of government within its own boundaries? These questions were not asked by the pluralists, and only comparatively recently have they been asked by more than a few others. Nevertheless, they are not easily avoidable today.

Since early in the present century enthusiasts for the private association have been confronted with Robert Michels' very troubling analysis of the sociology of membership organizations. Ostensibly, his work dealt with political parties, and his concrete information related almost wholly to the social democratic parties of central Europe. The sweep of his work, however, was much broader, extending by implication to all organizations in which membership could be said to exist. Michels' thesis was one of the boldest and most provocative in all of social science: the "iron law of oligarchy"—who says organization says oligarchy. Nevertheless, for long periods of time, it has been ignored. Not that Michels was an obscure figure, nor that his argument, despite its somewhat disorderly presentation, was easily disposed of. From time to time Michels' work has been rediscovered and the controversy begun anew. Refutations have been offered, but the need for further refutation seems consistently to remain.

Michels' argument was phrased in perhaps too sensational terms. A generalization framed as an "iron law" invites the discovery of exceptions, particularly when it runs contrary to popular and cherished beliefs. Nevertheless, this "law" was supported with the citation of many factors of which increasing numbers of people have had personal experience. The argument rested, first, upon the characteristics of organization, and organization in the twentieth century was increasingly becoming the setting for the myriad activities in which Americans engaged. The situation was not new. Indeed, Alexis de Tocqueville, with his extraordinary prescience, had remarked during the previous century on the American propensity for forming associations. Where in Europe some large undertaking appeared, a prominent nobleman stood at its head; in America a similar undertaking would have an association of equals established for its furtherance. This trait was incalculably more intensified in the twentieth century, when national associations were formed for everything from abrasives and absorbent paper to Zionism and zirconium; a thousand-page volume could do little more than list them and the addresses of their headquarters, and it took no account of the multitude of local groups organized for seemingly every purpose the human mind could conceive. Thus many people had direct experience of the behavior of organizations, although few were willing to question the official doctrine about it. But such of those few who encountered Michels' argument found disturbing corroboration from their personal experience with many modern American associations.

Michels deliberately limited the scope of his work on private associations to the social democratic parties—those presumed to be most wholeheartedly devoted to a democratic ideal. If democracy existed in organizations, where more logical to look for it than among these parties? Or if it were not to be found there, what hope was there of finding it elsewhere?

Michels' entire work rested on a distinction between leaders and led that to a certain extent recalled the Marxist distinction between classes and was akin to ideas about the elite. The particular dimension he traced was formal organization. Organization requires leadership, since as a matter of technical necessity direct government by the membership is "mechanically" impossible. Moreover, because of their sheer incompetence without leaders, the masses or membership need, approve, and even crave leadership. The leaders control not merely by virture of their superior abilities and the submissive tendencies of the masses, but also by an array of simple but crucial devices. The list of members, the files, the organization press—the apparatus of organization—all are in the leaders' hands.

To the extent that the "iron law of oligarchy" means that leadership is inevitable in organization it is a truism; but there is a much more disturbing implication in the argument. Leaders develop within a different milieu from members. They engage in different activities and come to enjoy a different status. Most important, they acquire different interests. Organization becomes conservative; leaders tend to identify their own interests with those of the organization and seek to preserve the foundations of their own position, thus laying the foundation for conflict of interests between leaders and led. The identity that is commonly assumed to exist among the interests of all within the organization is therefore false. And in contests between leaders and led, the former have virtually all the advantages.

Plainly, this argument is very sweeping. It is also very disturbing, particularly for those drawn to the pluralist belief that the freedom and self-determination of private associations are close to the essence of democracy. If private associations themselves should be undemocratic, as the Michelian thesis would seem to assert, how can they be essential to democracy?

Perhaps the simplest answer offered to this question is that the internal arrangements of the private associations are irrelevant to the question. In the first place, so the argument goes, the private associations as centers of power stand in opposition to the assumption of total power by any all-encompassing tyranny. With such associations in vigorous and separate existence, a sudden *Putsch* or mob action is insufficient to assume complete domination over the nation. Totalitarianism is defeated unless it can either absorb or destroy the private associations; hence, it is argued, private associations preserve democracy against the totalitarian threat.

The contention has much merit if the threat of totalitarianism is considered imminent. Certainly, twentieth-century experience indicates that totalitarianism is an evil greater than almost any other. By comparison with what went on in Hitler's Germany and Stalin's Russia occasional breaches of the democratic ideal inside private associations in America are insignificant. The force of this argument diminishes, however, if the threats of totalitarianism in America appear remote. On a lesser score, this ground for indifference to the internal arrangements of the private associations stands against the pluralist argument that the private associations are schools in democracy for the larger community. If such they are to be, they can hardly be other than models for behavior in the larger arena of national politics.

Another reason sometimes offered for dismissing Michels' charge is that the private associations are mutually countervailing—a modern gloss on the argument of Madison and his colleagues in the Federalist Papers. It tends to merge with the preceding contention that private associations are barriers to totalitarianism, but it goes somewhat further: by opposing each other, private associations supposedly check any overly greedy attempts by particular associations to extend their power. One association protects against another to the extent that in the large community democracy is insured.

This argument is relevant to the fear that one or more associations may exploit the general public. Except under special and unusual circumstances, however, it does not bear on the problem Michels posed. A trade union and a corporation may check each other in the making of decisions affecting the scale of wages and production costs; a high-tariff interest group may find itself confronted by a low-tariff interest group. Yet although each of these contests and the many others commonplace in modern political life may protect the economy and the polity from the extremist policies that might be followed if opposing or countervailing private groups were not active, they do not protect the members of any of these groups when they are threatened by their own organizations. To provide such protection, countervailing organizations would have to exist *inside* the associations, or, alternatively, there would have to be very nearly parallel or rival associations between which members might move without being deprived of the benefits that go with association membership.

In practice, however, private associations tend to be jealous of rivals. They seek to prevent the rise of competitors in the fields they have marked as their own. Often, when such rivals do exist, there is bitter conflict between them, conflict that has as its object the destruction of one or the other. Sometimes, when the conflict cannot be brought to this point, an accommodation takes place and jurisdictional boundries are agreed upon, so that as a result the condition of monopoly is restored. An entire ethos within the American labor movement holds "dual unionism" to be the worst of sins, but this ethos is not unique to labor; it is found to some degree among farm organizations, veterans' organizations, and others. The appeal made to support this ethos is for unity. The fear is that with two or more organizations in a particular field, competition among them may lead one to appeal to a common foe, with consequent losses to the interests the organizations and their members share. In one degree or another many, if not most, private associations see themselves arrayed against some external enemy and are warring organizations.

If it is unrealistic to look for an escape from the problem through paralless or rival associations, there remains the first alternative: to look inside the associations. This, however, poses the question of how the associations govern themselves. Although the question is plainly relevant in view of the emphasis placed upon the private association as an essential of democracy, it is sometimes suggested that examination of the private association as a form of government is improper, probably because of the fear that such inquiry is a preliminary to suggestions for state regulation. But it can also be objected that the private association is not the same as the state and that the tests applied to public government are not applicable to the government of the private association.

Certainly state and private association are different, but the differences are hard to define. Both are to some extent based on territorial lines. The state, if it is a constitutional state, has, like the private association, limited ends. Both state and association exercise some form of authority. Each makes rules or laws (not infrequently the term "laws" is used by private associations for their own rules). These rules are enforced with penalities of varying degrees of severity, but some organizations' penalties are more severe than many punishments of the states. Fines, suspension, and expulsion, all exacted by private associations, are serious matters where the associations involved control the right to practice a particular trade or profession. This is especially true where, as with medicine, a large investment of money and years in education, training, and experience are also involved. Perhaps (at least for devout communicants) the most awesome penalty of all, excommunication, is enforced by the church, a private association. Of course not all private associations exist in spheres of interest with such degrees of importance. Yet some do, and where they do the problem of authority is substantially the same as it is in the state.

This problem is considerably more far-reaching than conflict between leaders and led, or the prospect of tyrannical leaders, for it is also a problem of conflict among members. Such conflict is very conspicuous in the state and constitutes a major part of the substance of politics. But it is far less apparent in the private association. Much of the ethos of these associations revolves about the belief that there are no differences among members, or at least no important differences. This is the tradition of the *Gemeinschaft*, expressed in the very language with which many associations cloak their proceedings: brotherhood, solidarity, fellowship, and so on. The members are likened to the members of a family, in which the ties of blood relationship reduce all transitory causes of dispute to insignificance. The roots of this tradition are ancient, and it is not to be despised. But not all associations have this communal quality. The distinction between the community and the more mundane society with narrow ends is familiar. In the latter, presumably, cohesion is markedly less than in the former, but since it exists for ends on which all members are agreed, there is no problem of government as found in the state. Different arguments thus apply to different kinds of associations, but they arrive at the same conclusion: that the private association does not have the problem of government which the state exhibits.

Unfortunately for this conclusion, there are very genuine differences among the members of most associations, differences, for example, of age, opinion, taste, sex, religion. Some of these differences are trivial and do not represent conflicts, but others are important, some of them involving direct conflicts of both interest and belief. They occur even in the associations that lay claim to the quality of community, in some of which it would be difficult to claim that the tradition of community actually overrides the differences and the conflicts. In associations with narrow ends the absence of differences is also an illusion. In both types the problem of government does exist, and unless (as with hierarchical churches) there is a superior source of authority, there is also a problem of legitimacy.

Beyond all these factors, two considerations are stressed by the pluralists themselves. First, according to their argument, the state is but one of many forms of association. Accordingly, if it stands on the same ground as the other associations, and if its exercise of authority is open to question, so too is the exercise of authority in the other associations. Second, the pluralists correctly insist that the activities and ends of private associations are profoundly important. Some of them have moral purposes higher than the state's; the activities of some are in practice intrinsically more important than many state activities. Thus, while many associations have trivial aims, engage in activities of little general concern, and may be safely ignored, other associations are genuinely important to the large community. It is therefore unreasonable to assert that private associations are both important to the general polity and yet so unimportant that their political life may be ignored. Unless it can be established that problems of authority and government within private associations stand on different grounds from those of the state, examination of such problems in the private association is not only proper but necessary.

II.

The initial difficulty confronting any attempt to examine the government of private associations is their great number. In the United States, as we have seen, they exist by the thousands. Many are national, but regional, state, and local associations are beyond counting, not merely because of their multiplicity but because they appear and disappear with the luxuriance of tropical vegetation. Indeed, even those that have attained national scope have different degrees of vitality, some being exceedingly vigorous while others are clearly moribund. Moreover, many organizations are associations in name only. Some bear titles which suggest large memberships, but in any realistic sense they have no members at all. This is particularly true of numerous "associations" and "institutes'" with Washington offices which not infrequently consist of small rooms occupied by one or two individuals who may represent six or more organizations; the organizations may be little more than fictions used by individual lobbyist entrepreneurs. This is not to say that professional lobbyists do not necessarily represent genuine groups; some of the groups so represented are very real.

Still other organizations which maintain substantial office establishments and which claim many members are not membership organizations at all. In these, the so-called "members" are no more than subscribers to a cause or to a service carried on wholly by the office professionals. The "members" have no voice whatever in the determination of organizational policy or choice of officers, and there is no pretense that they do. The supporter (a better term here than "member") may receive reports and information, and sometimes even a membership card. Nevertheless, he is quite outside the organizational reality, and his only recourse if he disagrees with policy is to end his support—a condition that is often quite openly stated. However, the distinction between this and the situation in which safeguards are deliberately established to prevent a genuine membership from exercising influence on policy is in practice sometimes difficult to perceive. The motive for such safeguards is usually to prevent enemies of the association from joining it and disrupting it or diverting it from its avowed objectives— as, in somewhat analogous fashion, constitutional barriers are erected against the subversion of a state. But there is a very great difference of degree in that the purposes and policies that the private association seeks to defend are usually much more narrow and concrete.

The governments of still other associations present problems that fall outside the democratic tradition and can only be noted here. The outstanding example is the organization of the Catholic Church. Although this is an organization of extraordinary complexity with an involved political life of its own, it has no presumption of democracy within itself. The principle of authority in the Church is, accordingly, much clearer than in many other organizations: authority derives from God and extends downward on a hierarchical pattern. There is no problem of deriving authority from the will of the members and, so long as the faith of the communicants is maintained, the major problem of government is efficient administration. The same situation prevails in other hierarchical churches. The problem of government is, of course, more prominent in sects which emphasize the role of individual conscience in the interpretation of divine authority.

Perhaps the most difficult problem is presented by the corporation, probably the most important form of private government in America today. The evidence of its role in modern life is pervasive and inescapable. In a formal sense, however, the corporation is a creation of the state, and presumably what the state may create it may destroy — or regulate. Nevertheless, many have claimed in recent years that here is in fact a genuine private government. The corporation makes rules, it is argued, and is thus within the category. Moreover, in a realistic view, the part played by the state in the creation of corporations is minimal and unimportant. And, to understand the actual behavior of corporations, a political analysis must be added to the more traditional economic analysis.

These considerations have been very persuasively argued and they carry much force. Some of the major corporate units of American business exercise great power, and it is significant that business economists have been urging extended consideration of the corporation in explicitly political terms. Concepts such as legitimacy, authority, power, and constitutionalism have now entered deeply into the discussion of the modern business corporation. Nevertheless, this approach exposes a serious dilemma. On the one hand, the corporation is today an intrinsic part of the economy and society. It is the dominant way of doing business and of producing and distributing most of the goods by which men live and earn their living. Its organizations reach deep into the patterns of daily life for millions. At different points it stands in opposition to the spirit of the nation's historic antitrust policy, but that policy has, to a significant extent, begun to give way. The brute fact that the corporation exists cannot be wished away. On the other hand, the existence of the modern corporation does not accord with long-standing conceptions of political organization, and no theory exists by which it can be reconciled with such conceptions.

The difficulty is apparent as soon as the corporation is regarded as a political body, that is, as having power. So long as one can maintain a fiction that the corporation is solely an economic unit exercising no power within the market, the problem is to some degree disguised. Even so, the fiction does not touch the difficulty of assessing political life inside the corporation, and it is this internal aspect that discussions of the corporation increasingly emphasize. Both critics and defenders of the corporation make the point that it is an association of people. Whether it is a fellowship or a form of tyranny, however, it poses a problem of authority within itself. It possesses no claims, like the church's, to superior heavenly sanction. It can rely upon a theory of concession or delegation from the state, but to do so exposes it to the claims of external political control.

The traditional theory of corporate government—and it is of some interest that there is such a theory—is that stock ownership confers votes, which in turn control the choice of directors. In this sense, the government of the corporation has been derived from democratic theory. There was always a difficulty in that votes are attached to shares of stock rather than to individual human beings. This may have some precedent in the long-standing property-holding qualifications for the vote in the state, but the comparison is not really valid, since wealth is much more explicitly represented in the corporation than people. However, the theory at least was clear on one point: the constituency of the corporation's government consisted of the stockholders.

For some time (at least three decades) this theory has been untenable in the light of common knowledge about the realities of corporate life. The now-classic work of Berle and Means exploded the idea that ownership meant control in the large corporations of America. Their demonstration of the actual separation of these factors created a sensation, but the demonstration withstood attack and in any event only confirmed what many observers had long sensed. The sheer size of the significant American corporations and the minute fractions of total stockholdings that any one owner might possess made obsolete the idea of simple control by ownership (except in a very few corporations, notably the Ford Motor Company). The development of numerous legal devices and the control of the proxy machinery by management made a mockery of any belief that management could be readily challenged by any faction of the corporate citizenry. Proxy fights occurred during the period following World War II in somewhat greater numbers than Berle and Means expected, but they remained exceptional.

The question of control, once raised, provided a Pandora's box. As questioners sought to discover the reality of control, it became apparent that to a very large degree management was in control. By virtue of its possession of the proxy machinery, it was more likely to select the directors than the directors the management. Uneasily, many observers felt that they had passed through the looking glass. In one sense they found themselves in a Michelian world: organization was indeed conservative in that the leaders of the corporation carefully and effectively preserved their positions, and were, in fact, virtually self-perpetuating. The files, the membership list, the control of meetings—most of the devices Michels noted as accruing to the advantage of leadership in a membership organization—were in management's hands. Moreover, the presumed "members" were either apathetic about the exercise of their rights of self-governance or quite frankly determined not to exercise them. Indeed, at this point the reality of stockholder "membership" was so blatantly contrary to the formal theory of corporation government that the Michelian analysis collapsed by virtue of its success as explanation: the question arose whether the stockholders were indeed entitled to the control the formal theory gave them. In the eyes of some critics, the stockholder was not only incompetent and helpless in his role of "member"; he was also irresponsible and deserved the powerless state to which corporate reality had consigned him. In short, the stockholder could not be considered a member of the corporation at all.

This, however, was not the last of the questions unleashed by the initial query. Just who could be considered a "member"? What was the corporation's constituency? For a long time leaders of major corporations have toyed with these questions and have been tempted to proclaim that their responsibilities extend far beyond the welfare of mere stockholders. But then how far do they reach? To the customer? Certainly no corporate executive could be expected to exclude this group. To the employees? This is less simple, since the conflict of interest between stockholders and employees is rather obvious; moreover, too bold or aggressive an assertion of this responsibility might even arouse charges of unfair labor practices under the National Labor Relations Act, since it could be taken as an attack on unions. To the general public? But what is the general public? The trend of business thought has sometimes been to deny that this concept is meaningful when it is invoked by government.

A variety of motives were at work to release these questions. The muckrakers' attacks upon "the soulless corporation" invited the response that corporations had souls and were not merely machines for the enrichment of their owners. This was an especially tempting trap, and for a long time its dangers were not apparent; thus Judge Elbert Gary, first Chairman of United States Steel, insisted that his giant firm had not abused its power and had behaved responsibly, and the corporation's official historian even went so far as to assert that U.S. Steel *had* a soul. With Gary's passing, however, whether because the danger in the position had become apparent or for other reasons, the firm's defense reverted to the blander assertion that it had no power. Perhaps there was also a motivation arising from a realistic sense of the behavior of corporations. Certainly it cannot have been very satisfactory to believe that the good that corporate leaders were convinced they were doing in the world was sheer inadvertence. At any rate, it is now almost fashionable for industrial chieftains to consider themselves statesmen and to enlarge in public upon the responsibilities they feel toward stockholders, consumers, employees, and the public. A few crusaders continue to struggle for "shareholder democracy," but their efforts are futile, and they are generally regarded with indulgent amusement.

Although opinion may now be tending toward acceptance of the view that corporation leaders have just such a broad constituency, the questions still do not end. The really difficult ones remain: if, for example, there is a responsibility to a constituency that includes consumers, employees, and the public, how is it enforced? What are the means of accountability? These are very unpleasant questions indeed, and although the reply is seldom made loudly, it seems to be that corporation leaders are good men and make good decisions.

Obviously, this is a dangerous assertion. By what standards are they good? By what criteria can it be said that they do good? By what right do they claim to rule? What is this but an arrogation of power? Here are all the questions that must converge on power, and the questions have no answers. Richard Eells, a former corporate executive, has stated very justly that there is a constitutional crisis in the corporation. The problem, in fact, is so acute that some sympathy may be given to the critics who would rather turn their backs upon it and take refuge in an extreme positivism which rejects the baleful notion of power entirely. Unfortunately, however, the problem of legitimacy is not so easily induced to go away.

A number of points regarding the corporation are, then, quite clear. Power is one of its principal characteristics, exercised not merely over significant sectors of the economy, but over members of its own "family" as well. As might be expected, criticisms are not lacking that such power amounts to a form of tyranny. The Michelian theory of oligarchy in organization seems all too well substantiated by the corporation, however numerous the various pressure-group influences on it may be; in fact, the reality is so plain that to dispute the thesis of oligarchy is scarcely worth undertaking. Second, there is no available theory by which this power can be regarded as legitimate, and without some such conception there are no guidelines for rendering it legitimate. Probably the only available ground for exonerating the corporation's present form of rule is the fact that stockholders generally find a ready market for their shares when they are sufficiently dissatisfied to resign their membership. This view, however, rests upon the theory that shareholders are the only true constituency of the corporation, a theory that is today acceptable to few people. Until its constitutional crisis has been solved, then, the corporation cannot be used as a model of private government for analytical or any other purposes.

In many ways the corporation presents a peculiar problem, and is untypical of the many associations with which the United States is endowed. If corporations, churches, and the various organizations lacking membership in any realistic sense are excepted, the overwhelming number of the remainder are founded on a conception of authority which derives from the democratic ethos of the surrounding culture. In most, membership has a defined meaning, and the will of the membership provides the basis of authority.

Although genuine membership organizations of this sort are exceedingly numerous, they have similar characteristics and share the same problems, much of the similarity being the result of their mutual imitation of organizational form. Constitutions for new organizations are quite frequently simple copies of those of existing organizations, with only trivial changes of names and detail. This borrowing takes place even where the substantive interests of the organizations involved are very different; thus, for example, the constitution of the International Typographical Union was apparently based upon that of the Order of Odd Fellows. Beyond this, it is to be expected that experience gained with organization in one sphere should be applied in others. The general conception of government in membership organizations, for whatever reasons, appears to be much the same. To understand the character of this conception, then, it is useful to follow the example of Michels and examine its operation in the practice of the organizations most devoted to the ideal of democratic association.

III

In the United States, as in a number of other countries, the associations which have most vociferously dedicated themselves to an ideal of democratic organization are the trade unions. Although their claim to superiority in this regard may be contested by various other groups, the unions are on the whole the most conspicuous claimants, and it would be mistaken to doubt their fundamental sincerity. They were born of a profound desire to establish democracy in the daily working conditions of industrial life. Whatever the American labor movement's aberrations in predatory unionism, the institution of industrial democracy has undeniably been one of its fundamental objectives. Here, if anywhere in the nation, the democratic vision should be clear and practice enlightened. What, then, are the conceptions at work, and how have they evolved?

The source of authority in a trade union is the same as in a democratic state: the membership or the whole of the citizen body. In a small organization, such as a local, the membership (or a given portion of it defined as a quorum) meets and makes its own governing decisions. Ideally the presiding officer is no more than a moderator acting to preserve the conditions of orderly discussion and decision; the meeting itself is the sovereign body. Here is the ideal of the town meeting, of direct democracy. In a large organization, however, the meeting of the whole citizenry or membership cannot be approximated by these devices. The effective substitute is the convention, which has some similarities to a legislature, but also important differences. The delegates are not representatives in the same sense as are, say, members of Congress who meet continuously for extended periods. They are a much closer approximation to the town meeting of the citizenry.

Accordingly, the convention frequently passes not only resolutions stating policies and "laws" or "statutes," but also constitutional amendments. This latter practice is not universal among trade unions, but it is nonetheless widespread. It underlies the fact that the convention in session is generally regarded as the embodiment of the sovereign power of the general membership and not merely as an ordinary legislature. An incident in the 1944 convention of the United Mine Workers will illustrate. At this convention the union's president, John L. Lewis, received a personal telegram from the Secretary of the Interior. Lewis referred the telegram to the convention and a reply was sent to the Secretary in the convention's name. A second telegram addressed personally to Lewis arrived, and he then proposed the following reply before the assembled delegates:

> You do not seem to understand that our telegram to you was adopted by the unanimous vote of 2700 delegates elected by the mine workers of the nation in their home communities. This convention is the supreme authority of the Union. We are the employers of John Lewis and he is responsible to our orders. While this convention is in session we will answer his telegrams if we elect to do so. When we go home you can move in on him if you desire but watch your guard and protect your wind. We think he will go around you like a cooper around a barrel.

With but one dissenting vote the telegram was adopted by the convention as its own.

The fiction that union leadership is no more than the servant of the assembled membership was perhaps transparent in this instance. Nevertheless, the underlying theory was consistent with the temper of the reply. Moreover, the existence of the theory sometimes has important consequences. Thus during the steel crisis of 1952, which resulted in President Truman's seizure of the steel mills, Philip Murray, president of the Steelworkers, persuaded the union to pass a measure forbidding the union leadership to accept a truce plan without approval of a special convention. As a tactical measure it almost precipitated extreme action by the federal government and Murray and the union leadership had to repudiate it hastily.

While the convention is in session, then, the leadership in theory serves only as moderator. The leadership has no authority for independent action, and can only carry out the mandate of the collective decisions. To fulfill the many tasks facing it in a short span of time, the convention is compelled to rely on the work of temporary committees, but these too are merely the agents and servants of the larger body. This rationale also applies to the periods between convention sessions. In a great variety of provisions, from arrangements for election at conventions to requirements of ratification of officers' actions by the next convention, the pattern is made clear. From time to time, as in the examples given above, the fictional character of the pattern becomes apparent, but generally these instances are regarded as exceptional.

In theory, then, the union's executive body is a committee or group of officers of the whole membership as embodied in the convention. Although it may make a very real practical difference whether the officers are elected in convention or by referendum vote, the theoretical conception is not greatly different here. The officers are in theory definitely subordinate to the convention, a term which implies a body with constituent powers. The convention will usually dissolve at the end of its meeting. The president will often have power to summon a new convention, but its members then will be newly elected and possessed of a completely fresh mandate. Its authority, whatever the variations of practice, will be virtually unlimited, far greater than that of any legislature. And this authority in turn will serve to justify the leadership's exercise of power after the convention has been dissolved.

The officers, in fact, have very great power when the convention is not in session — real and authorized power, not normally considered as usurped. In some organizations the president's actions are specifically made subject to the approval of the executive board — of which he is of course the chairman. Some students have regarded this as a check on his power, but it is important to see that such a provision is intended less as a check on power than as a form of insurance that the will of the membership is carried out. Actually, however, such a provision is a very slight check in any sense upon presidential power. Whatever the facts, it is quite clear that the purpose is not the division of power.

In a larger sense, the evaluation of private government in terms of its checks and balances is beside the point. For, as with the checks on executive power, there is little conception of checks and balances as a system. The convention is not a legislature, and the executive is only an instrument of the general membership as represented in convention; the executive board is only an agent and the president is its continuing chairman. These bodies do not check each other, nor are they intended to. It is true that measures are taken in some unions for auditing funds (in which experience has been most disillusioning) and for the unseating of officers. But these devices are frequently weak and have appeared as grafts on a scheme of government to which they are intrinsically foreign. There is no *system* of checks and balances here.

If we look within the government of unions — and most other associations—for other important features of public government in the United States, we find additional important differences. The most striking is the absence of a bill of rights. In almost any union constitution it is possible to cull a list of membership duties which could stand as a "bill of obligations," but almost never a list of members' rights comparable in importance to those in the first amendments to the federal Constitution. Such enumerations of rights as are found are apt to be those not accorded to nonmembers; they are not the rights of members against the association or its government. On the other hand, the items of the "bill of obligations" are both numerous and inclusive. Thus, "conduct unbecoming a union man," "creating dissention," "slandering an officer," and "undermining the union" are frequently named as punishable offenses.

There are rudimentary guarantees for trials and appeals. They need to be viewed, however, against the common provision of penalties for members who seek redress of grievances against the associations in public courts of law. The public courts are generally unwilling to take jurisdiction over such issues where there is a system of internal appeals and the entire system has not yet run its course. Typically, the system calls for an original trial by a trial committee of the local organization; decision by the local; appeal to the president or executive council of the national organization; appeal to the convention, with action by a trial committee; and final decision rendered by majority vote of the convention. This system may in some stable situations permit the development of a body of case law and a rule of *stare decisis,* but it is hardly conducive to either.

A discussion of United States government, or that of any Western democracy, would be very unrealistic if it did not treat the party system. In union government, however, parties have almost no place; the practice of most unions is, indeed, antagonistic to parties. In some organizations, parties are in effect forbidden by constitutional rules against circulating partisan electioneering materials or participating in "outside" meetings relating to union affairs. Thus, the Constitution of the International Brotherhood of Electrical Workers makes the following offenses punishable by fine, suspension, or expulsion:

> Attending or participating in any gathering or meeting whatsoever, held outside meetings of a L. U. [local union], at which the affairs of the L. U. are discussed, or at which conclusions are arrived at regarding the business and the affairs of a L. U. or regarding L. U. officers or a candidate or candidates for L. U. office.
>
> Mailing, handing out, or posting cards, handbills, letters, marked ballots or political literature of any kind, or displaying streamers, banners, signs or anything else of a political nature, or being a party in any way to such being done in an effort to induce members to vote for or against any candidate or candidates for L. U. office, or candidates to conventions.

These provisions are somewhat more stringent than those in some other union constitutions, but the point of view is widely shared. Thus Philip Murray, one of the most justly revered of American labor leaders, warned the 1942 convention of the Steelworkers at its first meeting:

> I do not want—as a matter of fact, I shall fight any attempt that is made to have little back room caucuses while this convention is going on. There is going to be one convention in the city of Cleveland and it is going to be held in this hall. We are not going to permit sharp practices and petty politics to be played in the Steelworkers. So if any of the boys are thinking right now of midnight sessions in strange places in the city of Cleveland, just begin to forget about it right now. There is only going to be one convention. . . . That is the democratic way to do business. . . .

Statements in a similar spirit have been made by numerous other prominent labor leaders, and convey the orthodox doctrine. Some factionalism does occur in many unions, but it is generally deplored within them and tends to die out with the complete victory of some of the contenders. Only one private association of importance, the International Typographical Union, has an *institutionalized* system of parties. This organization, the subject of an intensive study, is so atypical that it only sharpens the impression of an almost universal distaste for disunity and division within other unions.

The amendment process of many unions is also quite different from that provided in the United States Constitution, and ordinarily much easier to operate. Practice is somewhat varied. Although some union constitutions may be amended only by a two thirds vote, sometimes in convention and sometimes by general referendum, it is not at all uncommon for amendment to be by majority vote in convention. The distinction between constitutional amendment, ordinary legislation, and specific decree therefore tends to be blurred in such associations, and is not especially clear in some of the others. The common attitude toward constitutional amendment was expressed many years ago by John Mitchell, then president of the United Mine Workers:

> The constitution of the trade union, moreover, has been evolved by and through the efforts of workingmen. The trade union is a government of workingmen, by workingmen, for workingmen and the framers of its constitution have been workingmen. Although the supreme law of the union was not formulated by highly paid constitutional lawyers, nevertheless, it represents in a clear and definite manner the ideals, purposes, and aims of the great majority of the members of the organization.
>
> The faithfulness with which trade union constitutions represent trade union sentiment is due to the elasticity of these constitutions. The government of trade unions is loose and flexible and neither constitutions nor by-laws are rigidly

fixed and immutable. The object of the leaders, as of the rank and file of trade unionists, has been to preserve the largest possible elasticity and freedom of movement to the ruling majority of the organization. In trade union management, there is no tyranny of the "dead hand." Even the most conservative unions are not bound by a blind, unthinking worship of an outgrown instrument, but adjust their form of government to the changing needs and exigencies of the times.

To a certain extent, therefore, the formal written constitution of a trade union is rather a statement of principles and a formulation of the present policy of the union than a hard and fast determination of its future laws. Trade union constitutions are easily changed.

When all the foregoing features of trade union government are considered they fit into a remarkably consistent pattern. They are all derived from the same central conception of politics, sometimes termed "majoritarian democracy." The term, however, is a somewhat misleading description of the political realities of these associations, for it suggests that a very high place is given to majority rule. In actual practice, something more than mere majority assent is sought. The common stress upon "not washing dirty linen in public" and the frequent decrying of factionalism embody a goal far closer to unanimity than simple majority rule.

Unity is seen as the price of staying organized. The fear of organizational disintegration is recurrently the decisive factor in the framing of governing institutions, and although this fear may often be the immediate motivation, the arrangements that emerge are consistent with a particular conception of democratic rule. Even more important than fear of disintegration, however, is the belief that such devices as checks and balances and constitutional limitations are both unnecessary and improper. The argument may be summarized briefly: If power is good, why limit it? If power is evil, why have it? Since the organization is the total of its membership and since its goals are the common goals of its members, limitation of its power is not only undemocratic but also irrational.

IV

This conception of government seems to be pervasive throughout the array of American labor organizations, but it is not peculiar to unions. How widespread it is among other types of association is impossible to say in the absence of any thorough study of the multitude of American associations, but even the most casual inspection suggests that it is common to many farm organizations, veterans' organizations, and numerous others. What, then, is its validity?

If such a conception were offered for the government of the United States it is probably safe to say that it would be rejected by most people. It is incompatible with the actual practice of government in any large democratic society we know of. Moreover, many people would also reject the conception even if institutions compatible with it could be put into effect. The question accordingly arises whether there are peculiar characteristics of private associations that justify their accepting it.

There is no simple answer to this question. The unions and other associations are exceedingly varied, but they do have a number of common traits, and it is necessary to examine these traits one by one.

Perhaps first among the general traits of private associations is that emphasized in the word private. The implications of the concept of privacy have never been thoroughly and systematically explored, but it is safe to say that it is fundamental to Western traditions of government. It is closely tied to the idea of constitutionalism, which implies limitations upon the sphere of public government. Most typically, the distinction between *public* and *private* relates to the state and the individual. In the present discussion, however, the tradition of real corporate personality as developed by a long line of pluralist thinkers from Althusius to the early Laski is involved. Most of the pluralists of earlier times combined a deep concern for individual rights with enthusiasm and concern for the corporate personality of the association. If there is irony in their position, it has become apparent only in fairly recent years.

A second distinctive characteristic of these associations is autonomy. Almost all assert a right to be self-determining and self-governing. This may take the form of an appeal to the historical origin of the association in a spontaneous meeting of like-minded individuals. But it is often asserted where such an origin cannot be claimed. Thus the claim of autonomy is hardly less strong among those unions of the old CIO which were the direct creations of organizing campaigns under leadership provided by older unions. The claim and its presumption of rightfulness within the context of American labor ideology was one of the difficulties the CIO encountered when, some years ago, it "tried" several of its component unions for Communist domination and then attempted to destroy them by establishing new organizations to take possession of the convicted organizations' jurisdictions. Autonomy here seemed to reside in the international union rather than the federation, and it was asserted quite as much against the federation as it recently has been asserted by the Teamsters against both federation and public government.

Traditionally the claim to autonomy has involved a hesitancy to utilize public aid, even where this aid could be demonstrated to offer much to the associations' constituencies. Thus, during the long discussion of the merits of unemployment insurance the official (albeit challenged) position of organized labor was that less social security with autonomy for labor's organizations was better than greater social security provided through the medium of public government. The argument that what government might give government might also take away was in part founded on good grounds; it was also a rationalization of the desire for undivided member loyalties. If there was a nice counterpart here to the claims of *laissez faire* from the business organizations, it was also true that in practice the more conservative and consistent position was that of organized labor. Even organized agriculture, traditionally more willing than either organized business or organized labor to resort to public government, has attempted at various times to act autonomously. The Society of Equity sponsored a plan for farmers to withhold their produce from the market until the Equity-declared prices were met. The National Farm Organization has more recently attempted the same tactic. Here was good, if simple, imitation of business practice. It was also an attempt to maintain autonomy. The farm organizations have sought a similar goal with their cooperatives.

An important corollary of autonomy is the association's claim of the right to formulate its own constituency. Nearly every association lays down conditions for membership, affecting both entrance and continued membership. The conditions of eligibility are usually quite explicit, and oaths or pledges are frequently required of new members. Candidates for membership, even when they are solicited by the organizations, must come as suppliants or at least applicants, the formal decision on acceptance being made by the association.

A third important trait of these associations is limited purpose. They do not purport to concern themselves with all aspects of their members' lives. Sometimes their purpose is stated quite specifically, as for example: "To establish through collective bargaining adequate wage standards, shorter hours of work and improvements in the conditions of employment for the workers in the industry," at other times the object may be quite vague. In either event, it is presumed that the association's objects do not encompass the entire range of the individual constituent's interests or preoccupations. He will have his own privacy, and he will, accordingly, have other loyalties. So a man may be a trade union member of a particular craft; but he may also be a church member, a Legionnaire, and a member of a team in the municipal bowling league, to say nothing of his place within his family or in a political party. The assumption is that no association will encroach on spheres of life other than its own.

A fourth trait, in considerable degree a corollary of some of the characteristics already listed, is homogeneity. Since the autonomous association selects its membership, and since its purposes are limited, within the scope of the association there will be only people of similar characteristics and like minds. Most important, there will be no conflicts of interest or grounds for legitimate conflict within the association; there is thus a presumptive absence of the basic political problem that other democratic societies of larger scope must resolve. If there is no conflict of interest or outlook, the only possible reasons for conflict will be error, personality, or something amounting to treason. The condition of homogeneity is precisely the solution Madison named in his famous argument in the Federalist Number 10, but felt compelled to reject as a solution to the problem of faction in the larger society.

A fifth distinguishing characteristic is the voluntary character of the association. So, although the association may determine its own membership, the individual member also makes a decision to join or not. Typically he must actively request admittance. He is not a member automatically—as he is a citizen by birth in a state—but by virtue of positive choice. Initiation and probationary status serve to emphasize the element of individual choice in joining. Equally important is the individual member's right to resign. Resignation is the individual's ultimate recourse and the element that finally distinguishes the private association from the public body.

The voluntary aspect of private associations has repeatedly been held to place them in a very special relationship to democracy, one often so special that it is described as a necessary condition of democracy. Such a view was cogently argued by the pluralists of several decades ago; more recent writers have repeated the argument forcefully. Thus, V. L. Allen has argued that so long as individuals are free to join and to leave societies of their own choice, the essence of democracy is present even if there is no machinery permitting the members to control the societies.

It should be apparent that these different characteristics of the private association to a very large degree overlap and rest upon each other. The meaning of privacy is impaired without autonomy. Homogeneity cannot be achieved without limitation of purposes, and voluntary choice underlies the entire arrangement. These, indeed, are all aspects of a single perception of the private association.

The conclusion at this point, then, must be that insofar as the conditions prescribed in this perception are met, the system of government that has been described earlier is proper and reconcilable with the goals and objectives to which we are committed in the governments of the United States and other liberal democracies.

V

However, a question remains: to what extent are the qualities so described actually found in existing unions and other private associations? How well, for example, have they maintained the distinction between "public" and "private"? Obviously, no precise answer in general terms is possible; it is apparent, nevertheless, that for many associations this particular distinction has been seriously blurred in recent years.

This is most apparent with labor unions. Until 1933, it could reasonably be argued that their private character was relatively unimpaired. The

American labor movement had rejected political means of action, that is to say, the use of public government. Not only had socialism been decisively defeated within the labor movement, but positive legislation, however mild, was mistrusted. This was most striking with regard to social insurance: not until 1932 did the AFL so much as commend unemployment insurance. The only legislation commanding strong official enthusiasm was directed against labor injunctions, that is, it was legislation designed to curb state intervention in labor disputes. Organized labor sought its goals through the medium of its own economic bargaining power. It would be difficult to imagine a more thoroughgoing observance of the distinction between what is private and what is public.

With the passage of the National Industrial Recovery Act and its Section 7-A, however, and more particularly with passage of the Wagner Act and labor's acceptance and utilization of the provisions assisting labor organization, organized labor departed radically from its previous position. This was not just a matter of legal theory. Since the law conferred exclusive bargaining rights upon a union which succeeded in winning a government-supervised election, that union acquired a substantial measure of public power—power that extended to individuals and minorities which had not voted for the union in the election. The process of NLRB-supervised elections has been widely resorted to by American unions. The surrender of privacy so entailed was not fully apparent, however, until the Taft-Hartley Act was passed, and became even more apparent with passage of the Landrum-Griffin Act, which explicitly provided for public intervention in the internal affairs of unions. Although some unions have indicated a willingness to revert to the situation existing before the passage of the Wagner Act, the element of privacy is not likely to be regained.

Different situations prevail with other associations; it is nevertheless apparent that for many a question remains whether their private character has been preserved. Often, for example, the exercise of licensing powers is delegated to "private" associations, even though the coercive power involved is that of a state. In the clearest case of this sort an association receives direct delegation; in other cases professional or trade associations are given the power to nominate personnel, virtually as a form of representation, to official licensing boards (bar associations, for example) and, on occasion, to policy-making boards. This is by no means unusual and is perhaps a growing trend.

A more perplexing question arises when a private association called into being by actions of government officials acquires the power to exert great influence over policy and administration, in the form either of membership on advisory boards of administrative agencies or of any exceedingly influential association's commanding the close attention of powerful congressional committees. Examples here are the American Farm Bureau Federation and the Chamber of Commerce of the United States, both of which had direct governmental encouragement in their formation. Obviously in such situations there is a shadowland between what is public and what is private. The years since the inception of the New Deal have seen much rationalization of this blurring, but clearly it is a concomitant of the growth of associational power during this period; clearly also, the blurring is incompatible with the previous conception of the private association.

These comments apply, too, to the private association's claim of autonomy. Labor unions, in taking an extreme position for *laissez faire* and freedom from social legislation, were defending their autonomy vis-à-vis government. In defending themselves from their own federations with which they have individually had occasional conflicts, however, the "international" unions are in a sense also defending their privacy. Not that this has been a matter of explicit discussion within the labor movement; but here, as with other matters of policy, labor's highly pragmatic leadership has behaved with a greater consistency than it has always been ready to acknowledge. The consequences of large units of organization do seem to have been visualized, however vaguely. If the locus of power within the labor movement is to be in the federations, the common form of action must be broad in character—almost necessarily a form of political action. Whether this takes the form of pressure for legislation, closely controlled administration, or political strikes, it weakens organized labor's claims to be uninhibited by governmental action. A similar set of considerations applies to the development of the American Farm Bureau Federation. Much of the early controversy about this association centered around the supposed differences between the county farm bureaus and the state and national federations. It is significant that the particular compromise effected also involved a compromise over the distribution of power between the local and federal units of the association. Here, to an even greater degree than later developed in the labor movement, the drift of the gravitational center toward the larger unit inside the association meant a drift toward political action.

As for the third trait of the private association, limited purpose, the practice of some of our more important associations has evidently also departed rather far from the conception sketched above. Some trade unions have sponsored educational plans; others have developed housing and recreational resources for the benefit of their members. The activities of the United Automobile Workers and the International Ladies Garment Workers are leading cases in point. Almost all unions have long-established systems of friendly benefits—pensions, insurance, and so on—which, however advantageous they may be to their members, also serve the purpose of strengthening the members' ties to the organizations. Agricultural organizations have from their very beginnings sought to solve many of the problems of rural life through subsidiary cooperatives. Many associations seek to demonstrate their civic responsibility by resolutions on matters of citizenship, Americanism, and foreign policy, and by gifts to colleges, scholarships, and other means.

The fourth trait of private associations, homogeneity, is in some ways the most important. A membership united in interests, beliefs, and tastes is itself a solution to the most troubling problem of government, and the possibility of achieving such an identity is in some measure the peculiar governmental advantage possessed by private associations. Every such association must and does achieve it in some degree, yet none can achieve it completely. In the concept of homogeneity, in fact, lies a latent inconsistency with the characteristic of limited purpose. A single interest may be shared, but the complexities of human nature are too great for a homogeneity that extends much beyond this. Even where the boundaries of the association are fixed to coincide with the number of people sharing the one interest, divergencies of interest will arise and persist within the association. Examples are the differences between young and old in a trade union with a pension system, between employed and unemployed in any union during a depression, between producers of different commodities in a farm organization, between large and small producers in a trade association. There are serious grounds for doubting a claim of extensive homogeneity in any association that rests on the obvious differences in taste, ability, and understanding among men. Associations characteristically exaggerate the homogeneity they achieve.

The fifth trait of associations, their voluntary character, is probably the main justification of their forms of government. Here, it is evident that the penalities for not belonging to an association differ greatly in incidence and degree, and the severity of the penalty is an index of the association's power. The penalty for not belonging to a particular trade union in some communities may be forfeiture of the right to practice a trade; it may be the same with the right to practice medicine. The penalty may be denial of the most effective means of access to publicly offered benefits, for example those administered by the Veterans Administration. When the right of resignation is accompanied by the availability of membership in competing organizations, the right is worth something. However, few trade unions are true rivals in any sense meaningful to their members; "dual unionism," as we have seen, is accounted a cardinal sin within the American labor movement. General farm organizations do compete in this manner, but their respective areas of strength are different. As for trade associations, it is clear that their fundamental rationalizing impulse is hostile to competition. Where their jurisdictions overlap and open warfare cannot quickly settle the boundary, consolidation or demarcation by agreement is soon accomplished. In fact, this pattern seems almost to be a law of behavior among our most significant private associations. The simple fact, then, is that often the private association is not voluntary.

The conclusions emerge that, first, the government of private associations is very commonly founded on a theory of absolute democracy; second, the validity of this theory rests on a series of assumptions about the peculiar characteristics of private associations; and third, these assumptions are seriously at odds with the facts about some of our most important "private" associations.

In assessing the significance of these conclusions it must be kept in mind that there are very great differences among the practices of different associations. These differences may be principally of degree, and yet be of great importance; thus although the governments of the United Mine Workers and, say, the League of Women Voters may have some similarities, to ignore the differences between them would be to produce a very false picture.

But if the existence of large differences of degree among private associations is recognized, how widely shared is the theory of government that has been outlined in the preceding pages? No precise answer to this question is possible, but it does appear probable that the theory is very widely shared. The International Typographical Union is the only association of significance that has been offered as a great exception to the rule of the "iron law of oligarchy." Virtually all others that have been made the subject of careful study have to some degree substantiated that "law." The examples of trade unions are particularly important, since these profess a special dedication to democratic methods, with institutions very generally framed on a strictly majoritarian pattern.

The reasons for the prevalence of this pattern of government in private associations are not easy to state. The reason most commonly offered is that most associations, certainly most trade unions, are in some degree warring institutions. According to this argument, such an organization needs to present a united front, and must not display internal disagreement, lest advantage be given to its opponents. The argument probably had some effect in persuading potential dissidents not to voice their dissent; it is not altogether obvious, however, that expression of internal opposition necessarily weakens the organization. Generally, trade unions have experienced most internal opposition at times when their most intense battles for organizational survival have been fought. In point of fact the times of peace are those in which tolerance of internal opposition declines. The usual argument seems to rest on an assumption that any internal opposition can end only in complete victory for one of the contending factions, the defeated would-be leaders going over to the external enemy. Actual illustrations of such occurrences can be given, but they hardly support the contention that it is a necessary result.

Strong distaste for anything less than unanimity seems to be one of the principal characteristics of private associations. Perhaps the most common response to disagreement when it does appear is to attempt to suppress it, either by appeals for unity or by more drastic means. Some associations do attempt to confront the problem in a different manner. One of the more interesting devices was the elaborate system of referenda utilized until the late 1950s by the Chamber of Commerce of the United States in formulating its own positions on matters of national policy. On subjects the Board of Directors deemed to be "national in character, timely in importance, and general in application to business and industry," committee reports were sought and presented in pamphlets submitted to the membership. The committee recommendations were balanced by statements drawn up by the Chamber's research department, of reasons opposing the recommended position. The machinery for insuring the integrity of the balloting was elaborate. A two-thirds majority vote was required to commit the organization. The procedure had some large deficiencies as a democratic device, most notably the absence of genuine debate on the measures considered. Nevertheless, it was remarkable how frequently measures were adopted by majority votes of more than 90 per cent. This record is reminiscent of plebiscites elsewhere and suggests that the function served by the referenda was to proclaim policy rather than make it. The nature of the referenda themselves and their phrasing, however, indicated that the desire for unanimity had much to do with the results. The positions taken were, by comparison with the positions taken by other business groups on the same subjects, moderate, and the language in which they were stated was moderate. This consequence of the drive for unanimity, however, is not common.

In general, the weight of available evidence on private associations is overwhelmingly on the side of Michels' "law" of oligarchy. Supporters of particular associations quite properly insist that there are significant differences among associations, differences which cannot always be seen merely by looking at constitutional provisions; the spirit and practice of some unions and other organizations are more democratic than their internal law requires. It could well be argued that the differences are more important than any general similarities that may be found among associations; some observers, in fact, seek to dismiss the question of democratic control of union governments as unimportant. It is claimed, for example, that the members of the Carpenters' Union may be quite aware of the undemocratic character of many of their union's practices, but are generally satisfied with the union nonetheless; the economic benefits it confers on its members outweigh any misgivings on other scores. Nevertheless, when all these different arguments have been made, the really general fact is the prevalence of oligarchy in private associations.

In one sense oligarchic rule is what might have been anticipated once private associations were regarded as forms of government, for every government is to a degree an oligarchy. But the difference between public and private government does not lie here. Public governments have a long tradition of grappling with the problem of controlling and limiting power. Few topics have so occupied political philosophers over so many centuries. There have been many attempts to solve the problem by trial and error; consequently, a large variety of devices for checking and limiting power exists in public systems. The entire tradition of constitutionalism is discernible in the governing institutions of any Western nation.

With private associations, however, this tradition has not applied, and there have been few attempts to develop institutional restraints on governmental power or to seek in any way to limit it. There would appear to be no intrinsic reasons why such restraints should not be developed. A few American trade unions (the UAW, the Upholsterers, and the Packinghouse Workers) have instituted a device of independent boards to review cases involving individual members and their unions. Some unions have managed to tolerate very lively factional disputes without major disaster; the Typographical Union, as we have noted, has even had a formal system of parties. Although these are relatively exceptional examples, they are sufficient to illustrate the possibility of constitutionalizing private governments. Experience, nevertheless, does appear to bear out the expectation deriving from the considerations set forth in the previous chapter that small political bodies limited in diversity of constituency are unlikely to develop constitutional patterns of internal politics.

The remarkable fact about private government, then, is not that it is oligarchic, but that it generally lacks the limitations that guard against tyranny and injustice to minorities and individuals. This lack, in turn, seems to be related to a deep and widespread illusion about the nature of politics in private associations. The illusion is that in any group homogeneity is ever complete or that unanimity is ever possible. Certainly a greater degree of homogeneity is possible in a private association than in a nation. Agreement within a private association can perhaps be more extensive and more concrete. Nevertheless, the difference is one of degree, and the problems of politics, of reconciling differences, and of limiting political power remain. The record of private associations in dealing with these problems gives little justification for the wishful view that the private association is the natural home of democracy.

Attitude
Consensus and
Conflict in an
Interest Group:
An Assessment
of Cohesion

Norman R. Luttbeg/Harmon Zeigler

In America, interest groups operate within the democratic frame of reference. Like all political organizations, they are accorded more legitimacy when they can show that they are representative of the attitudes and values of a particular segment of the population. Consequently, the leaders of interest groups frequently spend a great deal of time explaining just how democratic their organizations are. If one examines the testimony of interest group leaders at state and national legislative hearings, he is likely to find that much of it is begun with an introductory statement explaining that the leadership of the testifying group is merely the voice of the membership. The personal values of the interest group leader are played down, and his function as representative (as distinguished from delegate) is exaggerated.

On the other hand, relatively few political interest groups have systematic and formalized means of ascertaining the desires of members. We know that most of the devices used to solicit member opinion are not very effective. Truman has shown that the affairs of most interest groups are run on a day-to-day basis by a fraction of the total membership. The mass of the membership takes a relatively passive role with regard to the formation of public policies by the organization.[1]

Communication between leaders and followers is spasmodic and cannot provide efficient guidelines for the actions of leaders. Whether or not leadership of an organization seeks to become a manifestation of Michel's iron law of oligarchy, the realities of communication within an organization suggest that most of the communication undertaken by leaders will

[1] David B. Truman, *The Governmental Process* (New York: Alfred A. Knopf, Inc., 1951), pp. 129-139.

SOURCE: Norman R. Luttbeg and Harmon Zeigler, "Attitude Consensus and Conflict in an Interest Group: An Assessment of Cohesion," *American Political Science Review*, LX (September 1966), 655-666. Reprinted by permission.

be with other members of the leadership clique rather than with the larger body of followers in the group.

This situation is not necessarily dysfunctional for the organization. By many criteria the leader's decision is superior to that of the average member. Leaders have more time to give to matters of special concern to the organization. The information on which they make their decisions is likely to be more extensive than that of the average member, and they are likely to be more cognizant of the long-term impact of a particular decision. Unlike the average member, however, the leader's decision is complicated by his need to consider the extra-group and intra-group impact of his various alternative decisions and actions.

In the area of extra-group considerations, he must estimate the probable responses of other actors in the political process and the effect of these responses upon the chances of achieving a desired goal, assuming that he does not possess all capabilities of realizing this goal himself. Concerning intra-group considerations he must consider how the followers will respond to a decision. Will they be aware of it? Do they care about the alternatives, and if so, how will they respond to a decision which is contrary to their desires?

Even in the absence of efficient consultative mechanisms, leaders and followers exist in a functional relationship.[2] That is to say, leaders are limited by the followers' expressed or latent values and expectations. Regardless of the efficiency of corrective mechanisms and apart from how extensive the violation of the followers' values must be before the corrective mechanism comes into play, the leader's position is less secure if he fails to satisfy the followers. If another leader is vying with him for the followers' support, the implications of failing to satisfy the followers are even more threatening. In a political interest group, the functional relationship of leaders to followers is keyed to the necessity for cohesion as a weapon in extra-group competition. The actuality or at least the appearance of unity is essential.[3]

Assuming that the leader desires to maintain an extra-group competitive position, he will therefore undertake efforts toward the fostering of intragroup cohesion. In a voluntary organization, one of the prime requisites for this cohesion is the extent to which the membership is satisfied with the performance of leaders.[4] There are three ways in which a leader may satisfy the desires of an organization's membership. First, he may unconsciously act consistently with their desires. For example, he may decide

[2]William Haythorn, *et al.*, "The Effects of Varying Combinations of Authoritarian and Equalitarian Leaders and Followers," *Journal of Abnormal and Social Psychology,* 53 (September, 1956), 210-219.

[3]Truman, *op. cit.*, pp. 167-187.

[4]Herbert Simon, *Administrative Behavior* (New York: The Macmillan Co., 1957), pp. 110-122.

to act on the basis of his evaluation of extra-group factors in such a way that the membership will be entirely satisfied. Second, he may respond entirely in terms of his personal attitudes and beliefs and, because he so accurately reflects the attitudes of his membership, again satisfy their desires. Third, a leader may consciously seek to do what he believes the membership of the organization desires. His success in satisfying the membership by this effort is dependent upon the accuracy of his perceptions of their attitudes and expectations.

Research Design

In this paper we examine the latter two dynamics by which leaders can satisfy members. Our data were gathered from the membership of the Oregon Education Association. Three sets of information were collected: the beliefs and attitudes of the members of the Association, the beliefs and attitudes of the leaders of the leaders of the Association, and the perception of the attitudes of the members as held by the leaders. The analysis consists of comparing these three sets of information and noting changes in their interrelationships on different attitudes. The nature of the analysis is illustrated by Figure 1.

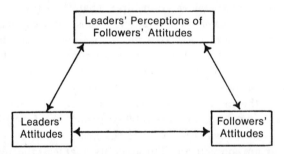

The sample of group members used in this study is a clustered stratified random sample of 803 high school teachers. This represents 14% of the high school teachers in Oregon.[5]

The sample of leaders includes all nine of the OEA's top administrative officials. These are the members of the executive staff, which is employed by the organization's Board of Trustees. Its official responsibility is to implement the policies of the Representative Council, which consists of 200 representatives elected by local teachers' organizations. The Representative Council is the official policy-making body of the Association. However, both the Representative Council, which meets only once a year, and

---

[5]Attitudes were assessed by personal interviews. There were 91 teachers in the original sample with whom interviews were not completed.

the Board of Trustees, which is supposed to deal with the specifics of the council's directives, are part-time functions. Thus, the permanent administrative staff is often forced to act in areas in which directives are vague or nonexistent. As is frequently the case in formal organizations, therefore, the permanent administrative staff has great flexibility and is a major delineator of policy.

In interviewing the leaders, we used a majority of the questions included in the teachers' interview schedule. Certain modifications in wording were made to allow for differences in organizational position. Leaders were first asked to answer the questions in terms of their own attitudes. They were then asked to take the point of view of the "average teacher" answering the same questions as they thought the "average teacher" would answer them. Only one of the leaders displayed any difficulty in assuming this attitude perspective; he had difficulty in keeping from answering questions in terms of what the teachers *should* believe rather than what he thought they actually *did* believe. The little difficulty the leaders experienced in answering these questions is evidence that the distinction between personal attitudes and the attitudes of the membership is a meaningful one for them.

These three sets of attitudes (teachers' attitudes, leaders' attitudes, and leaders' perceptions of teachers' attitudes) are studied in four attitudinal contexts. They are:

1. Mandates for organizational action,
2. Expectations and satisfaction with the direction of leadership behavior,
3. Abstract political values, and
4. Norms of teachers' political participation.

The mandates for organizational action consist of two parts: expectations of behavior on the part of leaders themselves and expectations of action undertaken by teachers' organizations. In both cases, the satisfaction of the members with a particular action is dependent upon a congruence of the attitudes of the leaders with the actual attitudes of the followers.

Attitudes related to satisfaction with the direction of leadership are concerned with three of the Oregon Education Association's most strenuous activities; efforts toward salary improvement, efforts to raise teacher standards and accreditation, and efforts toward the establishment of a state sales tax with the revenues going to the public schools.

Abstract political values describe a set of attitudes, many of which are clichés often used by persons to persuade others to accept their position. They represent the basic "truths" of both the conservative and liberal points of view. A leader perceiving the membership as adhering to conservative values is ascribing conservatism to the membership and at the same time indicating that he believes an argument for action based upon these values would draw support from the membership.

The attitudes dealing with teachers' political participating concerned a broad set of politically related activities which might be undertaken by teachers in the classroom or during leisure time. The leadership's ability to satisfy members in this regard will be reflected in their efforts or lack of efforts to support teachers in trouble in their local communities for various political activities and in the formal or informal articulation of a professional ethic with respect to these activities.

Although it would be possible to analyze these data using contingency tables, the existence of 50 attitude items and three comparisons for each item would tax the reader's ability to follow the analysis. A single measure which characterizes the relationship on each comparison of attitudes is therefore required. Although numerous measures of association and correlation were considered for this purpose, we settled upon Kendall's tau chi (τ_c).[6] This measure has its faults, the principal one being that its maximum value is dependent upon the marginals of the table. Our tables frequently have marginals of 803 and 9 (the N's of our two samples). Such great differences will yield a correlation of only .044 for a perfect relationship on a 2×2 table. Since we are more interested in finding a measure to characterize the comparison of attitude distributions of leaders and followers than in using the measure as a test of statistical significance, it was decided to rely upon a new measure, τ_c over τ_c maximum.

As we are using this measure in comparing the distribution of attitudes of leaders and followers, a high correlation would indicate a strong relationship between attitudes and the person holding them. That is to say, a high correlation would indicate that leaders hold attitudes different from those of the followers. The sign of the measure will indicate the direction of this difference. Notice that a correlation of .000 indicates that leaders share the attitudes of the followers or that the two sets of attitudes compared have the same distribution.

Some may inquire of the statistical significance of the findings. There

[6]Our data justify the use of ordinal measures of association, but there are several characteristics of our data and properties of various measures of association which complicate the choice of such a measure. First, on some of the items only two responses are possible while others are seven-point Likert scales. Thus any measure which is sensitive to the shape of the contingency table from which it is computed will decrease the comparability of the data across items. A measure which reached unity when only one cell is zero is also undesirable, as instances in which the leaders are in perfect agreement while the followers differ are common in our data. Such measures would be insensitive to the degree of followers' disagreement with the leaders. The final difficulty is that some measures are sensitive to the marginals of the contingency table. No measure was discovered which did not have at least one of the characteristics. See Hubert Blalock, *Social Statistics* (New York: McGraw-Hill Book Co., 1960), p. 323; and Leo A. Goodman and William H. Kruskal, "Measures of Association for Cross Classifications," *Journal of the American Statistical Association,* 49 (December, 1954), p. 750.

are two problems with the application of statistical significance tests to these data. First, one of the samples is not a sample at all but the universe of the administrative leaders of the Oregon Education Association. Thus, with no sampling error contributed by the leadership sample the comparing of leaders' and followers' attitudes does not necessitate as strong a relationship to achieve statistical significance as would be normally required. In the data comparing leaders' attitudes and their perceptions of followers' attitudes, clearly no statistical significance tests are applicable because the differences are real differences for the universe of leaders. Even if the leaders did constitute a sample, their small number places an unnecessarily strict requirement on the strength of the relationship necessary to achieve statistical significance.[7] In general, therefore, greater reliance is placed upon the consistency of a relationship within an attitude area rather than on the statistical significance of any one item. However, those single-item relationships which are significant are indicated by a small "s" in the tables (the Kruskal-Wallis h test is used to test statistical significance).

Findings

Leaders' perceptions of their roles. Before comparing the three sets of attitudes contained in this study, some discussion should be made of the leaders' perceptions of their roles within the organization. We refer here to the extent to which leaders believe they should act primarily in accordance with their own personal values rather than trying to reflect the desires of those whom they lead. We are asking whether leaders believe they should be delegates or representatives.[8]

Two questions were included in the leaders' interview schedule dealing with the problem of whose attitudes should be acted upon, those of the leaders or those of the followers. In one question the leaders were offered a brief dialogue between two persons, one arguing that a leader must do as the members wish and the other arguing that the leader must do what he personally believes to be correct. The leader was given the opportunity of selecting the argument which he found most satisfactory. Only one leader answered that the membership's desires should rule. Five answered that the leader should do what he personally believes to be right, although

[7] David Gold, "Some Problems in Generalizing Aggregate Associations," *American Behavioral Scientist,* 8 (December, 1964), p. 18.

[8] The terms "delegate" and "representative" are borrowed from the literature on the legislative process, where they are applied to the role perceptions of legislators. Heinz Eulau presents three legislative role orientations in John C. Wahlke, Heinz Eulau, William Buchanan, and LeRoy C. Ferguson, *The Legislative System* (New York: John Wiley and Sons, Inc., 1962), pp. 267-286. The "trustee" of Eulau's scheme has traditionally been described as a "delegate" while the "delegate" corresponds to "representative." These roles are the extremes, with "politico" falling somewhere between them.

they added the comment that they thought the problem would occur very infrequently. Three of the leaders said that if this problem could not be resolved the leader should resign.

The second question approached the problem from a slightly different angle and achieved very dissimilar results. The leaders were asked if they felt the organization should do pretty much what the average teacher wants, what the more influential teachers want, what the school administrators want, or what they themselves want. The "pretty much" phrase in the first alternative apparently was easier to accept than the wording in the other question, as five leaders chose this alternative. Two altered the second response to indicate that they believed they should do what the "more informed" teachers wanted while two indicated that they would prefer to do what they themselves thought best.

It would seem, therefore, that the leaders accept the maxim that they should do what the followers want, but they are also jealous of their autonomy to do what they think best. There appears to be a clear internalized conflict between the representative and delegate roles. Obviously the best of all possible worlds for the leaders would be perfect consensus between them and the members. In the absence of this consensus, they appear unable to reach a clear resolution of the conflict and to find a stable definition of their roles.

The leaders' acute awareness of the problem of communication with followers is indicated by a final question. Leaders were asked what policies of the Oregon Education Association they were most dissatisfied with. Seven volunteered the answer that the greatest problem was the OEA's failure to be true to the desires of its membership. Two of the leaders who gave this response explicitly criticized the administrative structure for not administering impartially the policy decisions of the Representative Council. It appears, therefore, that the representative nature of the organization is not only meaningful to leaders but is also potentially divisive of the leadership.

Expectations concerning organizational activity. The exact nature of this potential conflict within the organization will become clearer as we proceed to the analysis of the four attitude areas. We will first consider the mandates for organizational activity.

Table 1 presents the correlations for each of the attitude comparisons for each of the questions. In this, as in the tables which follow, the first column presents the objective attitudes, the "real world," and thus measures the extent of actual conflict. The second column shows the degree to which leaders are accurate in their perceptions of followers' attitudes, while the third column measures the extent of conflict as seen by the leaders. The negative sign of the correlation means that the bottom set of attitudes is more heavily weighted in the direction of believing that leaders of the organization *should* undertake a particular action. For example, in the first column a negative sign means that leaders believe more than the followers that they or the organization should undertake a given activity. In the second column the negative sign means that the leaders perceive the followers as being more in favor of undertaking a particular action than they actually are. The positive sign in the second column means that the followers are more in favor of undertaking a particular activity than the leaders believe them to be. A negative sign in the third column means that the leaders perceive the followers as more supportive of a particular activity than the leaders are. A positive sign in the third column indicates the reverse.

The table indicates that, with the single exception of eliminating from the OEA staff people believed to be politically extreme, the leaders are more inclined to favor the involvement of the organization in each of the actions presented. This is shown by the fact that in seven of the nine cases the signs of the first column are negative. The first three of these items are the more clearly "professional" of the set. They involve the traditional academic values of freedom of expression and the protection of teachers against hostile forces in the community. These are at best *quasi* political activities. Yet even here the followers are more restrained than the leaders. Note that on the question of eliminating political liberals from the OEA staff the followers are more in favor of such action than are the leaders. However, it is true that the greatest discrepancy between followers' and leaders' attitudes occur on those questions involving the more purely political aspects of the organization, such as endorsing political candidates, taking sides on public issues, and taking part in the electoral activities of school board members.

With regard to these political activities, the followers are much more restrained than they are concerning more purely educational activities. Granted that the distinction between quasi-political and political is arbitrary at best, the followers do appear to make it. Thus, they are much more inclined to support the activities of the OEA if it defends teachers against public attacks than they would be if the teachers' organization endorsed political candidates.

The glaring exception to the general reluctance of the teachers to support the OEA's political activities is on the question of lobbying. Here there is nearly perfect agreement between leaders and followers. Lobbying is perceived by teachers to be an absolutely legitimate function of the organization. Teachers, therefore, are making a distinction between legislative politics and electoral politics.[9] The Association is currently engaged in a vigorous lobbying program at the state legislative level. With regard to

[9] *Cf.* Gabriel Almond and Sidney Verba, *The Civic Culture* (Boston: Little, Brown, and Co., 1965), pp. 250-251.

TABLE 1.   Comparison of the Three Attitude Sets in the Area of Mandate for Actions by Leaders, Teachers' Organizations, and the OEA.

Questions	Sets of Attitudes Compared		
	Followers' Attitudes vs. Leaders' Attitudes	Followers' Attitudes vs. Leaders' Perception of Followers' Attitudes	Leaders' Attitudes vs. Leaders' Perception of Followers' Attitudes
Leaders should:			
1. Fight attacks on educational principles and methods.	−.134	−.134	.000
2. Fight against dismissal of teachers.	−.073	−.073	.000
3. Defend teachers from public attacks from getting involved in controversial issues.	−.059	−.059	.000
4. Eliminate from staff political liberals.	+.284	+.061	−.222
5. Give helping hand to school board members coming up for election.	−.317(s)	+.211	+.528
Teachers' organizations should:			
6. Endorse political candidates.	−.419(s)	+.184	+.603
7. Take sides on public issues.	−.404(s)	+.221	+.625
OEA should:			
8. Endorse candidates in school elections.	−.387(s)	+.058	+.444
9. Try to influence legislation.	.000	.000	.000

lobbying, it is interesting to notice that not only do the attitudes of the leaders and followers converge, but also the leaders perceive that the followers support the lobbying activities. This is indicated by the zero correlation in the second and third columns.

Notice also that with regard to the first three activities (fighting attacks on educational principles and methods, fighting against the dismissal of teachers, and defending teachers from public attacks) the leaders see *more* support among the teachers than actually exists. Since the leaders overestimate the enthusiasm of followers, they see a consensus which does not hold true in the "real world." Hence the perfect correlation in the third column between the leaders' attitudes and their perceptions of teachers' attitudes is based upon faulty perceptions. This is not true with regard to the consensus about lobbying.

It is in the more purely electoral activities of the organization that discrepancies occur. Notice that on questions five, six, seven, and eight, the negative signs of the first column become positive signs in the second column. This means that, whereas leaders are more likely to want to engage in the electoral activities than are followers, the leaders perceive the followers as far more hesitant than the followers actually are. Consequently, these electoral activities can be contrasted with the professional and lobbying activities. In these professional and lobbying activities, the third column indicates that the leaders see little or no discrepancy between their point of view and the point of view of the followers, whereas the correlations on items five, six, seven, and eight in the third column indicate that the leaders see a considerable conflict between their values and those of the followers. With regard to these political activities, the leaders are correct in perceiving conflict although conflict also exists in educational activities but is missed by the leaders.

At this point in its organizational history, the OEA is in fact more likely to engage in professional and lobbying activities than it is in electoral activities. It is these activities in which the leaders see the followers as being entirely supportive of the organization, although they are correct only with regard to lobbying. If the OEA were to increase its electoral activities, therefore, it would be engaging in practices which are less favored by the followers. However, the fact that the teachers are perceived as being more reluctant to support these activities than they actually are might result in the leaders engaging in these activities to a lesser extent than would be tolerated by the followers.

Evaluations of organizational performance. Turning from the extent to which leaders and followers are in agreement as to what the organization should do, we consider now the relationships between sets of attitudes concerning the extent of satisfaction with the actual behavior of the leaders of the organization. In Table 2 a negative sign indicates that the bottom set

TABLE 2. Comparison of the Three Attitude Sets in the Areas of Expectations and Satisfaction with Leaderships Actions.

Questions	Sets of Attitudes Compared		
	Followers' Attitudes vs. Leaders' Attitudes	*Followers' Attitudes vs. Leaders' Perception of Followers' Attitudes*	*Leaders' Attitudes vs. Leaders' Perception of Followers' Attitudes*
1. How important do you think has been the role played by the OEA in getting improved salaries and benefits?	+.556(s)	+.026	−.667
2. How about the Teachers' Union; how important do you think its role was in getting improved salaries and benefits?	−.297	−.098	+.185
3. Do you think the OEA is doing enough to improve teachers' salaries and benefits?	−.332	−.444	−.111
4. How about the Teachers' Union; is it doing enough in improving teachers' salaries and benefits?	−.396	−.396	.000
5. Do you think the OEA is doing enough in its support for higher teacher standards and accreditation to improve professional status?	−.016	−.016	.000
6. Do you think there should be a state sales tax with the revenue going to the schools?	+.253	+.364	+.111

of attitudes is less satisfied with the performance of the teachers' organization. A positive sign indicates that the bottom set is more satisfied.

In the first analysis, we found that the leaders consistently underestimate the followers' activism. In Table 2 we find a similar tendency with several notable exceptions. On the question of the importance of the OEA's role in getting improved salaries and benefits in the past, we find a great discrepancy between leaders' and followers' attitudes: the followers are inclined to give the OEA less credit than are the leaders. However, the second column shows that the leaders' perception is accurate. Hence, they perceive followers as exhibiting more dissatisfaction with past performance than the leaders do. Leaders, intimately involved in the successes and failures of the organization, see their role as more significant than do the more passive followers. Only about one-third of the followers think that the OEA was "very important" in securing past benefits, whereas all the leaders are of this opinion.

With regard to current performance a different situation exists. The leaders are more dissatisfied with the performance of the organization and its constant fight for better salaries. Once again, however, they perceive more dissatisfaction among the followers than actually exists. Although accurate in their perceptions of teacher satisfaction with past performance, leaders fail in their evaluation of current satisfaction. In fact, 56% of the followers indicated that they think the OEA is doing enough about salaries. This is not exactly an overwhelming vote of confidence, but it is apparent that more satisfaction exists in reality than is perceived by the OEA leadership.

In view of the current conflict between teachers' unions and professional organizations for the loyalties of teachers, it is interesting to note that the OEA leaders are more likely to denigrate the efforts of the teachers' union than are the teachers themselves. This is indicated by the negative sign of the correlations in column one considering the role of the union in past and present efforts toward salary increases. Again column two tells us that in both of these cases leaders perceive that followers are more dissatisfied with the union than they actually are. This distinction between past and present produces some curious results in the third column, showing the extent of conflict perceived by leaders. While they exaggerate the extent of dissatisfaction on the part of followers, perhaps projecting their own desires more than an objective evaluation would indicate, they recognize that the followers are more impressed with past union performance than they (the leaders) are. Yet they persist in seeing perfect agreement between themselves and teachers concerning current union performance, an agreement which does not exist. These distortions lead the leadership to assume a "what-have-you-done-for-me-lately" attitude somewhat along the lines of old fashioned bread and butter unionism. It seems likely that these perceptions will cause them to channel more of their resources into salary increase efforts at the risk of providing less satisfactory efforts in other areas. On the other hand this risk does not appear to be very great. For example, the leaders are extremely accurate in their perceptions of teacher satisfaction with regard to support for higher professional standards and accreditation. A consensus only slightly weaker than that regarding lobbying exists here.

The final item in the table dealing with the question of state sales tax enables us to return once again to lobbying. We may well ask "Lobbying for what?" The OEA has been strongly lobbying for a state sales tax with revenues going to the public schools, but only a slight majority (53%) of the teachers agree that a state sales tax should be enacted, while more than two-thirds of the leadership favor the tax. This is apparently an elite-derived effort enjoying only weak support from the followers. In this case, however, the leaders perceive far more support than actually exists. They actually believe that followers support this effort more than the leaders do, whereas the opposite is the case. Thus, although high consensus is achieved on the legitimacy of lobbying, leaders do not show a great capability of deciding how much effort should be devoted to the pursuit of certain policies by means of lobbying. The leaders want a sales tax, perceive the followers as wanting a sales tax, and pursue this effort vigorously. It is possible that if the efforts to achieve a sales tax are continued with increased intensity, membership support might be reduced beyond the bare majority it enjoys now, and intra-group conflict may result. If this happens the perceptual errors of the leaders could prove costly.

Abstract political values. Up to this point we have been considering the explicit programs of the Oregon Education Association, and the extent to which there is a congruence between leaders' and followers' values with regard to these programs. Members of organizations, however, may have values which are not directly translatable into explicit programs but which nevertheless color the relationship between leaders and followers. The overall ideological pattern of leaders and followers is, therefore, a component in determining the extent to which leaders represent the followers' values. It is this assumption which leads us to inquire about abstract political values. The items in Table 3 are offered as important in the leaders' evaluations as to what programs might appeal to the followers and also what the nature of appeals to the membership for support on a given issue might be. On the basis of their content, the items are separated into those indicating conservatism and those indicating liberalism. The first seven questions are the conservative questions, and the last six are the liberal questions. For each group, a negative sign indicates that the bottom set of attitudes shows greater acceptance of the item.

Looking at the first column, it can readily be seen that the leaders are

TABLE 3. Comparison of the Attitude Sets in the Area of Orthodox Values

Questions	Sets of Attitudes Compared		
	Followers' Attitudes vs. Leaders' Attitudes	Followers' Attitudes vs. Leaders' Perception of Followers' Attitudes	Leaders' Attitudes vs. Leaders' Perception of Followers' Attitudes
Conservative			
1. The American form of government may not be perfect, but it's the best type of government yet devised by man.	−.137	+.078	+.222
2. Democracy is considered the ideal form of government by most of the world.	−.160	−.658	−.407
3. Private enterprise could do better most of the things the government is now doing.	+.365	−.171	−.568
4. The participation of the federal government in local affairs leads to undesirable federal controls.	+.564(s)	−.389	−.926
5. Communism is a total evil.	+.142	−.466	−.630
6. People of most underdeveloped countries are by nature incapable of self-government.	+.303	−.226	−.506
7. Private enterprise is the only really workable system in the modern world capable of satisfying our economic needs.	+.257	−.182	−.469
Liberal			
8. Economic and social planning by government does not necessarily lead to dictatorship.	−.326	+.125	+.444
9. Man is the maker of his own society, such events as wars and depressions could be controlled by man.	−.122	+.161	+.259
10. The growth of large corporations make government regulation of business necessary.	−.190	+.088	+.309

11. We could increase spending for many government services without harming the nation's economy.	−.402	+.035	+.432
12. The federal government represents the needs of most people better than local government.	−.030	+.284	+.259
13. The government should increase its activities in matters of health, retirement, wages, and old-age benefits.	−.205	−.034	+.185

more likely to disagree with the conservative items and more likely to agree with the liberal items than are the followers. Furthermore, the high correlations in the third column show that the leaders believe that the followers differ greatly from them with regard to these items. Once again, however, the leaders' perceptions of teachers' attitudes tends to exaggerate the differences. In eleven of the thirteen cases, leaders perceive followers to be more conservative and less liberal than they actually are. Thus, although the OEA leaders are a biased section of the teachers with respect to their political and economic values, they tend to perceive their atypical posture as more extreme than it actually is. The discrepancy in perception is likely to influence the leaders to use more conservative appeals to the followers in the urging support of particular programs than would be called for by an accurate inventory of their values.

Combined with the bread and butter perception described previously, this perceived conservatism of teachers leads the leaders into the path of heavy emphasis on salaries and other basic issues while at the same time forcing them to restrict their activities in the realm of expansion of organizational activities. If the leadership seeks to venture into untried areas which are not specifically related to educational problems, it may be hesitant to begin for fear that the programs are too liberal for the membership.

Of course, as Krech and Crutchfield point out, the degree of association between cognitive attitudes and action-orientated attitudes is not necessarily great.[10] Thus, a person holding conservative beliefs does not automatically favor conservative actions by government. To ascertain the extent to which abstract values are translatable into immediate preferences for governmental action, we administered the items from the Survey Research

---

[10]David Krech and Richard Crutchfield, *Theory and Problems of Social Psychology* (New York: McGraw-Hill Book Co., 1948), p. 251.

Center's domestic attitude scale.[11] As in the abstract value index, the leaders proved to be much more liberal than the followers. Also, the leaders saw the followers as not being as liberal as they actually are. In this case, however, the leaders are not so greatly more liberal and they do not see the followers as so greatly more conservative than they actually are. The main thrust of the conservatism scale is identical to that of the abstract political value index, but the discrepancies are not as great. It may be, therefore, that the leaders are less in danger of under-cutting the cohesion of the organization should they lend its support to an explicit governmental program outside the realm of education related issues. The danger to cohesion may be not so much in the undertaking of new programs but in the appeal to followers on the basis of their perceived conservatism.

The political role of the teacher. Teachers, like the holders of any social position, have perceptions of what is permissible behavior by holders of their social position. Others who do not hold this position also have expectations. The interaction of these two expectations constitutes a role. Table 4 presents the comparisons between the three sets of attitudes with regard to norms of teachers political participation. A negative sign indicates that the bottom set of attitudes in the comparison favors teacher participation more than does the top set of attitudes.

Here we see a remarkably consistent pattern. Leaders are, in every case save one, more supportive of actions by teachers in these areas than are the teachers. This is even true of joining a teachers' union, but it is not true of striking to secure higher salaries and other benefits. In this latter case, the teachers are slightly more likely than leaders to be willing to undertake this activity and are much more likely to be willing to strike than leaders perceive them to be. This is the single example of followers being more "activist" than leaders to achieve liberal goals. In every other case, no matter what type of action is involved, leaders are more willing to take a risk, more willing to engage in controversial activity than are followers. When we examine the leaders' perception of followers' attitudes, we find once again the consistent pattern of underevaluation of the experimental nature of teachers. Leaders perceive teachers as being unlikely to engage in these activities whereas teachers themselves, although less anxious than leaders to take part in these activities, are more willing to do so than leaders believe them to be. Thus, the teachers are more willing to join teachers' unions, political party organizations, or racial organizations than leaders believe them to be.

[11]See Angus Campbell, *et al., The American Voter* (New York: John Wiley and Sons, 1960), pp. 194-198. V. O. Key gives the items used in this scale. See V. O. Key, Jr., *Public Opinion and American Democracy* (New York: Alfred A. Knopf, 1961), p. 561.

TABLE 4   Comparison of the Attitude Sets in the Area of the Norms of
Teachers' Political Participation.

Questions	Sets of Attitudes Compared		
	Followers' Attitudes vs. Leaders' Attitudes	Followers' Attitudes vs. Leaders' Perceptions of Followers' Attitudes	Leaders' Attitudes vs. Leaders' Perceptions of Followers' Attitudes
Teachers should if they want to:			
1. Join a teachers' union.	−.135	+.532(s)	+.667
2. Go on strike to secure higher salaries and other benefits.	+.067	+.317(s)	+.250
3. Join a political party organization.	−.036	+.186	+.222
4. Serve as party precinct worker in pre-election activities.	−.064	+.269	+.333
5. Publicly criticize local government officials.	−.268	+.510(s)	+.778
6. In a presidential election, outside school time, make speeches or give other services on the behalf of a candidate.	−.110	+.335(s)	+.444
7. Run for political office.	−.104	+.451(s)	+.556
8. In a presidential election, explain to class reasons for preferring one candidate.	−.055	+.279	+.333
9. Belong to the NAACP or CORE.	−.129	+.316(s)	+.444
10. Take part in a CORE or NAACP demonstration, such as public picketing.	−.112	+.460(s)	+.571
11. Allow an atheist to address the class.	−.126	+.430(s)	+.556
12. Argue in class against the censoring of literature by people who feel it is pornographic.	−.226	+.039	+.306
13. Speak out in class against the John Birch Society and groups like it.	−.153	+.180	+.333
14. Speak in favor of nationalizing the steel industry and the railroads.	−.249	+.307	+.556

15. Speak in class in favor of the Medicare program.	−.169	+.276	+.444
16. Speak in class in favor of the United Nations.	−.043	+.291	+.333
17. Allow the distribution of anticommunist literature put out by the National Association of Manufacturers.	−.254	+.191	+.444
18. Speak in class favorably about socialism.	−.105	+.229	+.333
19. Argue in class that labor unions should be more regulated or controlled by the government.	−.158	+.176	+.333
20. Allow the distribution of anticommunist literature put out by the John Birch Society.	−.443(s)	+.123	+.556

Conclusions

To summarize the findings of this analysis, the following points may be offered. As is true of most organizations, the leaders of the Oregon Education Association are more active than the followers. They are more liberal than the followers and they are more willing than the followers to expand the activities of the organization, but they consistently exaggerate the atypical nature of their position. They see the followers as being more conservative and restrained than they actually are. These discrepancies, both in perception and in actual attitudes, lead us to speculate as to how they came about. Is the relative activism of leaders a function of their social role, their organizational position, or their personality? It is certainly not feasible to argue that leadership positions somehow recruit more daring people. It is more feasible to seek explanations within the nature of the organization and the teaching profession. Consider, for example, the items dealing with political participation by teachers. Leaders would be subject to none of the pressures that teachers would feel from their community. Also, while teachers can recall relatively few cases in which the community made demands upon the school system for the dismissal of a teacher for engaging in controversial activity, those who can recall such incidents are of the opinion that the teachers' organization was ineffective in the defense of teachers. It is also true that the teachers look upon the local affiliates of the Oregon Education Association much more favorably than they look upon the state-wide organization which employs the leaders considered in this study. In arguing for organizational position as a funda-

mental contributor to differential perception, we draw added support from
the reaction of the leaders to the competition of the union. Leaders behave
in much the same fashion as political party leaders.[12] They are more emotionally committed to the organization than are the rank and file. Hence,
they find it difficult to comprehend the problems of teaching and the restrictions traditionally imposed upon teachers by the community.

It might be useful to know something about the leaders' backgrounds. All
have at one time been teachers and all have passed through some lower
administrative position before achieving their present status. Most have
taken graduate work, usually in educational administration. All earn in
excess of ten thousand dollars per year. Thus, although they do have a
teaching background, they are much more upwardly mobile than the average teacher and make more money. They are also substantially better
educated. The upper mobility of the leaders of the OEA can be gleaned
from the backgrounds of their fathers. Most of their fathers had less than
a high school education and held low status occupations. Thus holding a
position in the OEA marks more of a step up than does teaching. Perhaps,
therefore, the leaders consider themselves as more sophisticated and advanced than teachers.

When we consider the fact that serving as an OEA administrator is in a
sense moving beyond a teaching position, the explanation offered becomes
more plausible. Combine this with the fact that leaders have interaction
with a more heterogeneous environment and their perception of teachers
becomes even more understandable. Unlike the teachers, who interact
mostly with teachers, students, principals, and parents, the OEA administrative staff interacts with lobbyists, legislators, state officials, and national
educational officials.

As a final alternative to the explanation offered above, we considered
the possibility that, whereas the leaders incorrectly perceive the political
values and political role perceptions of teachers, they may base their reactions upon communication with a biased sample. There are, of course,
many different shades of opinion among teachers just as there are among
the general public. Is it true that the OEA leaders interact with a segment
of the teaching population which is more conservative and more restrained?
If this is true, then their perceptions of followers' attitudes might not be a
function of their social position but might be the result of an unrepresenta-
tive sample of opinion being communicated to them. However, our evidence indicates quite clearly that there is no relationship between political
conservatism and participation in organizational affairs. There is no evidence that the conservative teachers have any more interaction with OEA
leaders than do the liberal teachers. Also, those teachers who take a

---

[12]Herbert McClosky, "Consensus and Ideology in American Politics," [*American Political
Science*] *Review*, 58 (June, 1964), 361-382.

restrained view of the political role of the teacher are no more likely to communicate with OEA leaders than are those teachers who take a more expansionist view.[13] Thus, we can say that there is no weighting of communication which comes to the attention of OEA leaders in favor of conservationism and restraint.

Assuming, therefore, that being a leader in an organization contributes to a discrepancy between leaders' and followers' attitudes, we may inquire finally into the possibility of having a democratic interest group without frequent and carefully supervised consultative mechanisms. Can leaders be representative simply because they intuitively comprehend what is required of them? In considering this question, let us note that, with the exception of the last table, the discrepancy between leaders' attitudes and followers' attitudes is generally *greater* than the errors made by leaders in perceiving these attitudes. Thus, OEA leaders operating entirely upon their personal values would not be representative of the values of their followers. On the other hand, if they adopted a purely representative role, they would become more conservative and restrained than the teachers would prefer. Yet, with exception of the last set of attitudes, the error would be less than would be true if followers' wishes were ignored. That is to say, if they followed their understanding of followers' values, the resulting conservatism and restraint would be closer to the actual desires of teachers than would be true if leaders used their personal values as the sole criteria of judgment. "Virtual" representation in an interest group cannot serve as a substitute for actual representation, because the position of group leader contributes to the development of attitudes which differ from those of the followers.

Membership in Social Groupings

Angus Campbell/Philip Converse/Warren Miller/Donald Stokes

Of all the social groupings into which electorates may be divided, it is likely that the *social class* has drawn the most consistent attention from students of mass political behavior. In the first place, the notion of social

[13]It is true, however, that there is more interaction between leaders and small town teachers; these teachers are considerably more conservative and restrained than their big city counterparts.

SOURCE: From Angus Campbell, *et al., The American Voter* (New York: John Wiley and Sons, 1964), pp. 184-209. Reprinted by permission.

class provides an inclusive analytic concept. A "lower" class comes to have meaning because there is an "upper" class that serves as its foil; hence, analyses of social class come to deal with the total social structure at once.

Likewise, the concept of class is sufficiently general to permit wide application. Every nation has its minorities, but it is not always clear how specific subgroups, differing in composition and goals, may be compared from nation to nation. As for the social class, however, current evidence in sociology indicates that all societies are stratified into "upper" and "lower" layers as a result of unequal distribution of values and honors. In various times and places the characteristics of these layers have varied superficially, but the concept of class reduces such historical diversity to a set of minimum common elements, a reduction that is indispensable if we aspire to more powerful theory.

Class phenomena attract broad interest, too, because they represent a junction between the social, the economic, and the political order. The class, a social phenomenon, is yet defined in economic terms; and if class membership is conceived to have motivational significance, then the motives engaged are presumed to be economic. It is because of this economic aspect, furthermore, that the social class becomes linked with political strife. Political power signifies some potential for control of the economic system. If stratification arises from unequal distribution of rewards, there is likely to be competition between the classes for control of the allocation process.

Competition between upper- and lower-status groups appears to have been an element of some importance in political matters since the birth of the American republic. The precise nature of this role, however, is subject to scholarly debate, and our resources of data, particularly for the currents of mass behavior in the earlier elections, are meager or nonexistent. But we know that at the time our political system was designed, influential minds found in the "different sentiments and views" of the various classes "the most common and durable source of faction."[1] We know furthermore that the emergence of Jacksonian democracy—whatever its popular base—frightened gentlemen of the upper strata as a triumph of "mobocracy." And more recently, in the rise of trade unions and in the class-saturated political alignments formed in the wake of the Great Depression of the 1930's, the recurrent importance of social class in American politics is well documented.

We treat the social class apart from other social phenomena to some degree because of its popularity and its transitional position between the purely social and the purely economic. The most important consideration dictating separate treatment, however, lies in the nature of the social class itself. For whatever popularity the concept enjoys, its intellectual status

[1]*The Federalist, No. X.*

has remained controversial, even among sociologists. Nobody wishes to deny the reality of differences in status and privilege within the large social unit; yet the meaning that can be attributed these distinctions by the investigator is constantly subject to dispute. A large portion of social theory seems to presume that the social class is a self-conscious group striving toward recognized goals. This assumption is challenged by theorists who feel it tends to reify what is usually no more than an analytic construct imposed on the situation by the investigator. Status differences exist, and these differences are related to differences in attitudes and behavior. They do not, however, assure us that the social class has reality as a group, or that class "members" come to behave distinctively because they take the class as a reference point in decisions about behavior.

Thus the argument comes to rest on the nature of the class as a group. It is our thesis that the "group" reality of the social class is variable. Under certain circumstances, it is not difficult to conceptualize the social class as a "group." Under other circumstances, it is hard to see it as more than a vague demographic aggregate, arbitrarily marked off for purposes of analysis. When and to the degree that the social class is a group, we shall find our theory . . . quite applicable to it. But as the variable nature of the social class is one of its most intriguing characteristics, it requires separate discussion as a special and marginal case of the group phenomenon.

The Social Class as Political Group

The social class *per se* rarely becomes formalized as an organization. There is no official class leadership and no official class policy. Despite an absence of formal organization, leadership, or even informally accredited spokesmen, however, the social class may have reality as a group in the minds of many people. When the citizen being interviewed tells the investigator that he favors the Democratic Party "because it is the party of the common man, not the party of the big shots," it seems clear that he sees the society as divided into at least two camps representing conflicting interests, and that he feels he shares the interests of one of these camps. It is in this sense that the social class may have psychological reality as a group.

Identification: A "Subjective Reality" of Groups. The social class transcends the simple "demographic aggregate" to the degree that individuals in the population identify with a social class. When there is a "*we* feeling" directed toward other members of the class grouping as a whole, rather than purely toward other union members or other businessmen, then the class may influence behavior in the sense of our previous discussion of group influence.

Stratification refers to the differentiation of the population as a result of the unequal distribution of social values and honors. The product of stratification is a set of *social strata*. The social class, on the other hand, refers to a grouping of people who feel a sense of identification and shared interest as a result of membership in a common stratum of the society. The psychological unity tokens a degree of functional cohesiveness that the term *stratum* does not connote. Thus at base the psychological circumstances of identification determine whether a class exists. Social strata, the molds in which social classes may form, seem present in all societies. But the class itself emerges and disappears over a period of time. An adequate approach to the problem of social class in politics involves consideration of the conditions under which a sense of class identification develops in the social stratum.

Status Polarization

However helpful the distinction between "stratum" and "class," it should not mislead us into thinking that a society may properly be described in such "either-or" terms. It is desirable to think of different states of a society as differences in degree, rather than in kind, between such "ideal types" or qualitative stages. We shall attempt to approach the problem quantitatively rather than qualitatively. We shall refer to the condition of active discord between social strata as *status polarization*. We shall think of this polarization entirely as a matter of degree; a society may be more or less polarized, at any point in time. We cannot specify a degree of polarization beyond which a stratum becomes a class; the simple dichotomy is inadequate to express differences along the underlying continuum of polarization which we posit. But when the status groups of a society are sharply polarized, we shall assume that the entities that past theorists have labeled "classes" are present; and when a society is "depolarized," we shall presume that the concept of social strata is more appropriate.

Status polarization, then, refers to the degree to which upper and lower status groups in a society have taken up mutually antagonistic value positions. Polarization is by definition a group-level concept. A single element cannot polarize; the term has meaning only as a description of concurrent motion of two or more elements—in our case, status groups. We can say in a general way that *variation in the status polarization of a society reflects variation in the intensity and extent of class identification among its members.* When polarization is high, most of the citizenry must have perceived a conflict of interests between strata and have taken on class identifications with fair intensity. When polarization is low, either few people are identifying, or extant identifications are weak, or both.

Since polarization is bound up with divergences in values and interests, the concept is linked not only with status groups but with specific areas of conflict as well. We will find it useful to think of the degree of polarization as varying, not only over time, but from sphere to sphere within a social system as well. Under certain conditions, for example, there may be more status polarization visible in the economic sphere than in the political sphere. Generally speaking, we may hypothesize that polarization emerges first in connection with economic values, and that beyond a certain degree of intensity it will spread to other areas. As it becomes manifest in values less immediately bound up with economic interest, a more salient and generalized antagonism exists between class groups.

Finally, it is important to consider that the course of events depends not simply upon the intensity that polarization attains in sensitive spheres of the social system; it is also important to ascertain how constituent class identifications are distributed in the population. Polarization may become so intense within subgroups of a society that violence occurs, even when the vast bulk of the society is indifferent to the interests at stake. For the purposes of understanding the broad flow of events, then, we shall consider first the degree of polarization within the bounds of the larger society. A theory of the social context of political behavior must undertake to specify (1) the conditions in the total society that serve to thrust status polarization into the political order; and (2) the conditions that act to increase or limit polarization within that order.

Determining Social Class

The ambiguous nature of the class as a group poses important problems. Who "really" belongs to which class? In the groups discussed . . . we had little difficulty separating nominal members of the group from nonmembers. Similarly, in a caste society the location of an individual in the hierarchy of strata is quite clear. But in the United States and other modern democracies, the persistent or extreme formalization of social differences is absent. The distance that once separated serf from master has been filled in with a variety of roles and occupations that defy simple class assignment. Furthermore, there are strong American cultural values that inveigh against recognition of class differences. No other group that we have considered is begrudged the very reality of its existence in this manner.

These ambiguities have implications in two directions. First, if numerous individuals in the society are located in positions that are relatively indeterminate with respect to class lines, must we not expect a considerable attenuation of the role that class can play in political behavior? Secondly, if status is frequently ambiguous, how do we assign individuals to a social class for purposes of analysis? The first problem is an empirical matter; the second is methodological.

The two common solutions to the problem of assigning individuals to status groupings reflect some of the controversies over class phenomena that we have discussed. On the one hand, there are those whom Richard Centers[2] has called the "objectivists," who define class operationally according to some objective criterion like income, occupation, or education. This practice distinguishes what we have called social strata.

The opposing "subjectivists" look for evidence of psychological identification with a particular class as a criterion of membership. Centers, as an exponent of the subjectivist view, devised a relatively satisfactory method of getting individuals to locate their own position in class terms. He asked a national sample in 1945: "If you were asked to use one of these four names for your social class, which would you say you belonged in: the middle class, lower class, working class, or upper class?" Analysis revealed that the responses gave meaningful insights into patterns of behavior. With regard to political variables, for example, people who chose to designate themselves as working class were more frequently Democratic in their voting and party affiliation and chose more "radical" alternatives on a number of issue questions dealing with the role of government in the economy. Middle-class identifiers were more likely to be Republican and "conservative" in their politico-economic attitudes.

The study also showed that although occupation appeared to be the primary determinant of subjective class, identification of this sort was not always congruent with objective role in the social structure. For example, about one quarter of the people interviewed were either blue-collar workers who identified with the middle class, or white-collar people identifying with the working class. Nor was there any tendency for people who "misidentified" in this way to claim a higher status; in fact, members of the white-collar stratum designated themselves as "working class" more frequently than manual laborers chose the "middle class."

But the simple fact of choice between alternative class names posed by an interviewer may be only a pale shadow of the concept of "identification" that we have linked with status polarization and the development of a class group from a stratum. Only 2 per cent of Centers' sample responded that they did not know what class they were in or said that they did not believe in social classes. It does not necessarily follow that 98 per cent of Americans are "class conscious," except in a restricted sense of the term.

Class Consciousness, Class Identification and Self-Assignment. One demonstration of the weakness of the Centers question as a means of assessing class consciousness comes from our own data. In asking the Centers question in 1956 we preceded it with this query.

---

[2]Richard Centers, *The Psychology of Social Classes* (Princeton University Press, Princeton, N. J., 1949).

There's quite a bit of talk these days about different social classes. Most people say they belong either to the middle class or to the working class. Do you ever think of yourself as being in one of these classes?

Respondents who replied affirmatively were then asked "Which one?," whereas those who responded negatively were asked which class they would choose if they had to make a choice. About 4 per cent of the sample indicated that they usually thought of themselves as belonging in some other class, like an upper or lower class, or that they did not know to which class they belonged. But one out of every three respondents indicated that he never thought of himself as being in one of the classes mentioned, yet was subsequently willing to choose one of the class names.

This in itself is no conclusive finding; we might simply be encountering evasiveness. But we find further that people confessing awareness of their social class actually think and behave differently on political matters than do those individuals who say initially that they are unaware. For example, within the aware group in 1956, working-class identifiers tended to divide their presidential vote 14 per cent more Democratic than did middle-class identifiers. Among the "unaware" group, however, this class-related difference nearly fades from sight: the unaware working class are only 2 per cent more Democratic than the unaware middle class. It is hard to consider that these unaware individuals participate in any "consciousness of class." Yet they comprise one-third of the national population.

The distinction in voting behavior between the aware and the unaware gives results conceptually parallel to those . . . where a full identification variable was present. That is, where we feel there can be no identification — among the unaware — there is no significant tendency to behave in group-relevant ways. Among the aware, such a tendency is present. Thus the class is another case of a social grouping that may be fitted to the model for influence . . . .

Our Operational Treatment of Class. As tools for the ensuing discussion, we shall determine the class membership of the individual in part by his subjective location in the status hierarchy, as modified with the "awareness" distinction. We also have at our disposal a full battery of objective indicators of class, such as occupation, education, and income. Of the objective criteria, occupation tends to predict political attitudes and voting most efficiently, and we shall generally turn to it when we wish a measure of this type. Subjective class by itself shows relationships with political attitudes and behavior that are of about the same magnitude as those that emerge when occupation alone is used. The addition of the "awareness" variant to the subjective measure, as shown previously, makes the predictive value of the subjective measure stronger than that of occupation.

We shall also need a set of operations to measure the political manifestations of status polarization. For this purpose we shall employ coefficients of correlation that represent the *strength* of relationship between class indicators and political attitudes or behavior. The size of such coefficients will increase as lines of class cleavage swing more and more closely into alignment with broad divisions of political opinion. In a state of complete political depolarization, knowledge of a person's social status tells us nothing about his political attitudes or behavior. In other words, there is no relationship (i.e., zero correlation coefficient) between status and the political variables. Whatever compound of past experience and current attitudes is leading to aggregate differences in political partisanship, it is likely to be independent of the concurrent fact of social stratification. The role of social class is at its lowest ebb. In the state of perfect polarization, to know a person's class is to know his political ideals and allegiances, automatically and without margin for error (1.00 correlation coefficient). The social classes have become solidary and mutually antagonistic. The correlation coefficient, reflecting such differences in the state of the group, provides us with a convenient metric for graphing trends.

Short-term Fluctuation in Status Polarization

The extensive modern literature on social class and political behavior has shown persistently that individuals of higher status (subjectively or objectively) tend to give "conservative" responses on questions of economic policy and tend as well to vote Republican; individuals of lower status tend to respond more "radically" and vote Democratic. This simple finding has assured us that social class has some bearing on the way in which the individual behaves politically. It has also served theorists as evidence of the importance of the economic motive in political behavior. But there is much that it does not tell us. In the first place, it is a static generalization. It does not allow us to anticipate variation in class voting from election to election. It casts no light upon the waxing and waning of class-based political discord. Secondly, the relationships on which the generalization is based are quite modest ones. If it is evidence of an economic motive in political behavior, we might wonder why it is so weak, rather than marvel that it appears at all.

We find marked short-term variation in the clarity of status voting in this country over the past score of years. If we take some measure of status— any of the common indicators will do—and examine the strength of relationship between this measure and the vote for President, using national survey data collected over the four past presidential elections, we find that the relationship has been positive over this time. That is, lower-status groups have continually favored the Democratic Party, and higher-status the Republican Party; but at some times this fact is quite prominent and at other times the association is almost trivial. Instead of a static disposition toward leftist or rightist voting according to one's class, the role of social class in political behavior is a dynamic one. It is this phenomenon we have chosen to conceptualize as status polarization; and our aim is to specify conditions under which it fluctuates.

The fact that status polarization of the vote has varied so widely in only a dozen years might suggest that it is unduly influenced by superficial aspects of the immediate political situation, such as the pairing of two competing personalities in a given presidential race or the campaign themes chosen for emphasis in a certain year by the parties. A variety of supporting data lend assurance that this is not the case. While the trend line of coefficients for the presidential vote from 1944 through 1956 covers a considerable range, it does not oscillate wildly. Instead, it declines from 1948 in an orderly and almost linear fashion. The 1952 observation (0.25) falls very close to the midpoint of the range defined by the 1948 (0.44) and 1956 (0.12) observations.

Moreover, comparable coefficients for the congressional vote in 1952 (0.26), 1954 (0.20), and 1956 (0.10) show precisely the same orderly downward trend. The 1954 observation is of particular interest here, in addition to the fact that it represents an independent sampling of the adult population. It might be argued that the 1952 or 1956 points fall as they do because of the candidacy of Eisenhower or Stevenson. Yet in 1954 neither name was on the ballot, and the observation for that election takes its proper place in the declining polarization trend. Furthermore, since congressional races involve a plethora of candidate pairings, it is hard to attribute this variation in polarization to peculiar candidate pairings.

Finally, we encounter evidence of precisely the same trend in status polarization over this period when we depart from matters of parties and elections entirely. For example, we may relate status not simply to one or another partisan choice, but to economic issue responses . . . . Typically, lower-status persons tend to select "liberal" alternatives, whereas those of higher status give "conservative" responses. But the clarity of such class differences varies over time also. Unfortunately, we do not have a standard battery of issue items applied to the population periodically since 1944. Nevertheless, highly comparable questions posed in 1945 and 1956 show a depolarization quite like that of the vote over the same period.[4]

Evidence of this order leads to the conclusion that the broad lines of

---

[4]The polarization coefficient (calculated in both cases for White males, using occupation status) was 0.37 in 1945; in 1956 it was 0.17. Downward trends of very similar slope were found for three other questions having to do with government welfare activity and the role of government in areas traditionally restricted to private enterprise. See Philip E. Converse, "The Shifting Role of Class in Political Attitudes and Behavior," *Readings in Social Psychology*, Eleanor Maccoby, Theodore Newcomb, and Eugene Hartley, ed., 3rd edition (Henry Holt and Co., New York, 1958), pp. 388-399.

change in vote polarization are rooted in events that transcend the immediate circumstances of any particular election. Even if such fluctuations depended entirely on events within the political order, they would be of interest. But the fact that they seem to reflect broader conditions in the society adds greatly to their fascination. At a minimum, we would suppose that change of this scope must depend on a configuration of social and economic events, with their psychological derivatives; and, where we observe signs of polarization in the electoral process, additional factors arising from the political system must condition the phenomenon as well.

The Conditions of Status Polarization: Key Psychological Terms

We may distinguish two major dimensions of variability at a psychological level that provide crucial insight into the polarization phenomenon. Ultimately, we may trace these differences to broader social, economic, and political conditions; at the outset, however, they have interest as more than "intervening states."

Class Awareness and Identification. In our theoretical discussion we have suggested the importance of clear class identifications in the development of status polarization. We have also shown that the third of the population unaware of its class makes no contribution to the status polarization of the vote and hence, by default, serves to depress it. The same contrasts between the aware and the unaware seem to emerge wherever class differences are visible in partisanship or economic attitudes. Thus, for example, people who associate themselves with the "working class" and are aware of this location are 19 per cent more Democratic in their party identification than the aware "middle class"; the comparable difference among unaware people is 10 per cent. Similarly, on an issue attitude like the question of government guarantees of full employment, the aware working-class people give 22 per cent more frequent "liberal" responses than the middle-class aware; among the unaware this class difference fades to 14 per cent. The fact that there is some residual class differentiation of attitudes and behavior among the unaware may be readily traced to social influence in primary groups, where attitudes "appropriate" to the individual's class may be taken on without recognition of their class relevance.

It follows that signs of status polarization in a society are limited by the proportion of the population unaware of their social class. If we can determine the conditions under which persons come to think of themselves as class members, we should arrive at clues that will help us reconstruct some of the sources of variation in polarization over time. It is harder to specify these conditions than might be imagined. Awareness of class . . . shows little tendency to vary systematically with common sociological divisions of the population. Men and women, the educated and the uneducated, the various occupational strata, and the major ethnic and racial subdivisions of the population all show about the same two thirds rate of "awareness" that characterizes the nation as a whole.

Nevertheless, there are two points at which class awareness does show revealing variation. One involves differences in awareness across age grades in the population, and the other involves the rural-urban continuum. The first leads to consideration of past economic history, whereas the second sheds light upon the role of broader social patterns in the polarization phenomenon. We shall consider the evidence for each later in the chapter.

Levels of Conceptualization. We have observed that correlations between status and political behavior are normally rather low. [We suspect] this is not primarily because people are disinterested in their social class location but because they fail to translate class interest into political terms. In some cases this may spring from confusion over relevant alternatives; more often it probably reflects ignorance of the fact that political alternatives are relevant at all, even among those "aware" of their social class.

If these surmises are correct we would expect that signs of class voting would be clearest among the most sophisticated and would tend to diminish as we proceed to those whose view of politics is simpler or more fragmentary. Indeed, persons whom we classified as ideologues or near-ideologues who were at the same time aware of their social class contributed very disproportionately to the slight degree of status polarization that characterized the 1956 election. At other levels class voting is barely visible save as we "purify" our groups by removing those persons unaware of their social class. Once again we see that the people who organize their political behavior in the manner often assumed by sophisticated investigators are those who are most similar to such analysts in political concept formation. The familiar picture of the democratic process as a clearing house for conflict of class interest becomes increasingly inappropriate as we move to layers of the electorate more remote from the informed observer. If the role of social class in mass political behavior is less potent than we are frequently led to believe, these discrepancies in sophistication appear to be largely responsible. If we wish to deal with social class in its traditional garb in politics, we are dealing with a fairly restricted and sophisticated portion of the population.

Earlier we showed that this kind of sophistication was strongly dependent upon education and political involvement. The education component is fixed early in life and remains constant. Hence it does not seem helpful in accounting for fluctuations in polarization. Rather, the fact that there are poorly educated persons in all societies poses a fundamental limiting condition on status polarization in politics. But political involvement is more responsive to external conditions. Of course it can be doubted that isolated bursts of political enthusiasm on the part of the individual provide much real sophistication. Yet, we may imagine that some events external to the political order can drive persons to an enduring interest in politics.

It is feasible to examine differences in class voting within degrees of political involvement. The more involved the individual is in politics, the more likely he is to cast his vote according to class lines. In this case we have the benefit of comparable data for the 1952 election, which provide some insight as to what goes on when polarization varies over time. Differences in the class behavior of the involved were much sharper relative to the uninvolved at the high levels of polarization in 1952 than we find them to be in 1956. The suggestion is that the decline in polarization between 1952 and 1956 sprang from changes in behavior among the more sophisticated. In a time of depolarization, the behavior of the involved voter becomes less and less distinct from that of the apathetic, *with respect to the class axis.* This statement does not mean that the sophisticated lose interest in politics when class interests are not clearly perceived. Other axes of political dispute may engage the attention of the politically alert. The relationship between involvement and class voting may simply be a special case of a more general phenomenon: whatever the current major dimensions of political conflict, they are reflected less clearly where involvement is lower.

We have seen that individuals highly involved in 1956 had shifted their attention from the class dimension in some degree since 1952. We can imagine that elections may be sharply contested when status polarization is absent. Conversely, and for much the same reasons, elections may show high levels of status polarization in conjunction with low overall levels of voter interest. The 1948 election, marking a low point in vote turnout for its era, is a case in point. An examination of aggregate statistics suggests that turnout dropped off most radically in those areas where we typically observe little or no status polarization: in the South the decrement in the vote was very marked, and it was disproportionate in rural areas of the North as well. Not all of the decline, however, can be accounted for in this manner; it remains visible even in the large Northern industrial states where polarization tends to focus. It is as though most of the forces that propelled citizens to the polls in 1944 and 1952—including dramatic personalities and the whole quadrant of foreign issues—had dropped from sight, leaving only one force, the increasing polarization of socio-economic attitudes, active in an opposing direction. Where these attitudes had some significance, the decline in turnout was not large; but where they enjoyed little leverage, the failure of the citizenry to participate became striking. If we were to ignore the dependence of involvement on other sources as well as socio-economic concern, these aspects of the 1948 election would remain incomprehensible.

In short, when external conditions warrant, status polarization occurs in politics primarily among those who are sophisticated and for whom class position is salient. We have introduced these two intervening psychological dimensions separately because as an empirical matter they are independent of one another. That is, knowledge of a respondent's level of conceptualization of politics does not help us predict whether he will report awareness of his class location. At all levels of conceptualization the probability of class voting increases if there is some sensitivity to social class location, although these differences are not large save among the sophisticated. But political sophistication and class awareness vary independently.

With these facts in mind, we may turn to some of the broader external conditions that enhance and inhibit the development of status polarization in the political system. Both class awareness and the involvement component of sophistication will provide useful clues to the impact of these conditions as we proceed.

The Economic Background of Status Polarization

In view of the economic axis of class feeling we would readily assume that status polarization should increase in time of depression and decrease in periods of prosperity. The most striking feature of the polarization trend in the recent past has been the steady and rapid depolarization between 1948 and 1956. This decline occurred in a postwar period when the nation was enjoying a striking ascent to prosperity and a consequent release from the pressing economic concerns that had characterized the Depression. Therefore, the basic outlines of variation in polarization fit our preconceptions of changes in the economic state of the union.

Although class awareness shows little variation across most sociological divisions of the electorate, there are differences in the proportion who express awareness as a function of age. These differences are far from striking in their magnitude but are nonetheless intriguing. When we deal with age we cannot be sure that patterns that make historical sense are not due instead to the phenomena of the life cycle. Across a fair portion of the age continuum we find rising awareness with increasing years, but there is a large drop after 60. Perhaps awareness builds up through the active working lives of people in a particular age grade, to fade out rapidly after retirement. But there are significant irregularities here that seem to betray the overlay of historical events. The age group in which awareness is most prevalent includes those individuals who were in their twenties and thirties during the depths of the Great Depression, a generation long assumed to have been strongly affected by economic events. Although people who were over 60 in 1956 also experienced the Depression, they tended more often to be vocationally established, and may have resisted some of the new definitions of social reality in class terms that appealed to a younger age cohort.

This interpretation is bolstered by the fact that this "Depression generation" is also prominent in its status voting. People falling in this cohort contributed disproportionately to the high levels of vote polarization recorded in the 1948 and 1952 elections. But by 1956, these orientations had become scarcely visible. We cannot say that the decline in polarization between 1948 and 1956 depended entirely on changing patterns of behavior within this group. Status voting falls away within other age strata as well. But it is this portion of the electorate that showed the greatest relative depolarization and that best illustrates the fading of the effects of the Depression.

We may also trace out the progressive obliteration of past disaster by surveying changes in the proximal attitudes of this "Depression generation" from election to election. We have pointed out elsewhere that a concern over issues of domestic policy is a striking accompaniment of status voting.[5] In 1952, respondents of the critical age category reacted to the election in terms of domestic issues with a frequency significantly greater than that of any other age cohort. By 1956, however, these persons were no more likely to bring up domestic issues in their spontaneous evaluations of the political scene than were people of other ages. There was a major decline in references to prosperity and depression between 1952 and 1956; it appears the rate of decline was highest within this critical group. It is in this sense that involved people who had contributed to high levels of polarization in 1948 and 1952 increasingly turned their attention to other axes of political dispute by 1956. What we may be observing are the declining effects of the Great Depression of the 1930's rather than other economic perturbations that have occurred in the interim.

The postwar period surveyed here had its high prosperity marred by two economic troughs, in 1949 and 1953-1954. The second of these two disturbances is more interesting from the point of view of our data, as it very nearly coincided with the 1954 congressional election. Although recovery was apparent by the time voters went to the polls in November of that year, much of the campaign had been conducted under the threat of serious collapse, a situation exploited by Democrats attempting to regain control of Congress. Yet the polarization coefficient referring to the congressional vote in this election seems to suggest that polarization was declining steadily throughout this period. Pending the slow accumulation of further data, then, we conclude that although economic distress is a prime mover in enhancing the role of social class in politics, it must constitute a severe and prolonged trauma before its effects are felt.

[5]Converse, *Ibid.*

The Role of War in Status Polarization. We have linked the decline of status polarization in politics between 1948 and 1956 to increasing prosperity and fading memories of the Great Depression of the 1930's. But the economic state of the nation cannot be seen to determine the level of polarization completely. If the progress of polarization after 1936 involved only the receding spectre of depression, we should expect it to show a constant decline within our recorded history. Between 1944 and 1948 the general trend of the economy was upward, and the Depression was more remote by four years. Yet the polarization of the presidential vote shows an increase between these elections. How may we account for this discrepancy?

If we compare the behavior of voters whose concern over domestic issues outweighs their interest in foreign policy with those for whom the reverse is true, it is clear that higher rates of status voting attach to the domestic issue group. Among voters concerned primarily with foreign issues, such tendencies are almost invisible.[6]

It appears plausible therefore that much of the discrepancy could be understood in terms of an interplay between war and depression. Polarization tendencies carrying over from the Great Depression may have been dampened as a result of the national crisis posed by the Second World War, rebounding upward after that conflict was concluded. The temporary lull in foreign threat from 1945 to 1950, along with the outbreak of "postponed" strikes in major industries, the struggle in Congress to place legislative controls on the activities of labor unions, and the development of first anxieties over an "inevitable" postwar depression, all must have contributed to a rise in the relative salience of domestic issues that had lain dormant during the war. After the 1948 peak of polarization, however, the renewal of the threat of global war and the outbreak of hostilities in Korea may have acted, in concert with increasing prosperity, to depress the level of status polarization once again.

Political Manifestations of Status Polarization

Economic attitudes of class relevance were showing much the same increase and decline of polarization in the period from 1944 to 1956 that were registered in partisan choice at the presidential and congressional level in this period. Hence we contend that the primary lines of fluctuation in polarization in this era had to do with events in the economic rather than the political order. Nonetheless, it would be unwise to assume that the trend of status polarization in politics has remained unmodified by the context of parties and candidates within which voters have arrived at poli-

[6]*Ibid.*

tical decision. In fact, we can isolate a number of circumstances of these years that would appear, on theoretical grounds, to have facilitated the prevailing direction of polarization change.

The Role of the Candidates. We have presented data that suggest that the major lines of change in vote polarization from 1944 to 1956 were not dependent upon the personalities of the five presidential candidates in this era. Nonetheless, two observations may be made concerning the role of candidates in the political polarization phenomenon. First, since the personalities associated with these four elections have been types that, in a *post hoc* vein, lead us to expect in each instance the specific change in polarization that has actually been observed, we cannot disengage the candidates from the polarization phenomenon. It may be that each pairing of candidates during this period has facilitated the existing motion of polarization, so that the magnitude of variation was larger than otherwise might have occurred. That is, had Eisenhower run for the presidency in 1948, there might have been a crest of polarization, but one somewhat less marked than that which the Dewey-Truman contest evoked. Conversely, had Truman run in 1952, the decline in polarization of the presidential vote might have been less sharp.

Secondly, it is hard even conceptually to disassociate the man from the times. Each pairing of presidential candidates seemed to fit the tenor of its times. Yet to what degree are the salient features of these personalities a direct product of the times in which they operated? Roosevelt the wartime leader presented a different image from the Roosevelt who lashed out at "economic royalists." Clearly these changes depended less on the man than upon external events well beyond his control. Harry Truman was not responsible for the timing of the Taft-Hartley Act; if Eisenhower had run in 1948 could he have maintained the same class neutrality with this issue prominent? On the other hand, Truman was delighted to make the most of the Taft-Hartley furor, and another man might have kept it from becoming such a focal point for the campaign. In short, we cannot hope to determine here whether the times make the man, or the man the times. We suspect that a good deal of the aura of each election, and the connotations that have come to surround the protagonists of each race, have been determined by the context in which they were destined to operate. But we would not gainsay the capacity of these personalities to muffle or amplify the class divisions of the moment.

The Role of the Political Parties. The role of the parties in modifying the level of status polarization in politics may be analyzed from a number of vantage points. But we may immediately propose that unless the parties differentiate themselves in matters of policy relevant to class interest, we have little reason to expect partisan preference to reflect whatever polarization exists in other spheres of the social system.

In reality, both a perceptual and an institutional condition must be fulfilled for partisan behavior to manifest status polarization. The class-oriented voter, to act in accord with his class position, must perceive that differences exist between the parties that are relevant to class interests. Individuals who fail to arrive at such perceptions are much less likely to engage in class voting. However attentive the class-oriented voter may be, the differences that he *can* perceive are limited by the divergence that actually exists between the positions of competing parties.

There are some important circumstances in which party differentiation on class matters is not likely to be clear. Circumstances may arise in which status polarization outside the political order is inadequately reflected in matters of political partisanship. This pattern of events is most likely to characterize a period of rising polarization in a political system bound to traditional parties. If status polarization continues to mount, we would expect either that (1) new parties will break through institutional barriers, or that (2) events will force the existing parties to a clearer class alignment.

It would be ill-advised, however, to dwell upon the lag in party policies without noting as well the lag that is evident in the public response to the parties. There is reason to believe that in a system of long-standing parties it is the rare exception that any large proportion of the public departs from the existing parties in search of new policy positions. Usually calamity that is sufficient to make any broad segment of the public demand new answers is at the same time sufficient to stimulate change in the policies of even traditional "patronage" parties. And under such circumstances, enduring loyalties to the existing parties tend to maintain the traditional system.

The Role of Party Identification. For the period of declining polarization that we have observed we can trace out the conserving influence of party identification. The individual's identification with his party comes to have a force autonomous of the events which established the initial loyalty. Thus a person drawn to the Democratic Party on economic grounds during the 1930's is likely to retain this allegiance after economic problems have become less salient. When status polarization is declining, its manifestation in current voting behavior should be less marked than that witnessed by distributions of party identification between classes.

We have been measuring party identification only since 1952, a fact that leaves a limited time series for comparison. But numerous pieces of evidence support our deductions. For example, among non-Southern voters, polarization of the vote fell from 0.29 to 0.13 between 1952 and 1956; the polarization of party identification over the same period declined from 0.28 to 0.21.[7] Thus the relationship between status and party identification

[7]It should be pointed out that some portion of this change is accounted for not by individuals shifting their party allegiance but by normal turnover of personnel in the electorate due to

varied in the same direction as that between status and vote, but less sharply, supporting the hypothesis.

When forces act to change partisan alignments in the electorate the bonds of party allegiance constitute an inertia that is only slowly overcome. If this statement is true, then we would expect inertia to be marked among those who identify most strongly. In the face of pressure toward political change, Independents and weak identifiers will succumb most readily. Therefore, the marks of the past should be most visible among strong party identifiers. With regard to class, we have developed the thesis that status voting patterns established in the 1930's have been eroding since that time. Status voting should then be most prevalent among the strongly identified and least clear for people toward the "independent" end of the identification continuum. This configuration of relationships emerges handsomely from our 1952 materials and appears substantially intact in 1956 as well. In this era, the probability of status voting was much higher among strong partisans than among weak or independent people.

One further datum is relevant at this point. The South, as so frequently happens in political analysis, presents class patterns that are often anomalies. Generally speaking, polarization is lower in the South than in other regions of the nation; many of the materials presented in this chapter for the entire nation show sharper patterns when the South is excluded from consideration. Between 1952 and 1956, however, when levels were declining elsewhere, there was an actual increase in polarization in the South, from a coefficient not much above zero to a point of clear significance in 1956.[8] Coupled with this rise, we find status voting more prevalent among *weak* party identifiers than among strong in the South in 1952, and a residual difference, no longer strong enough for statistical significance, in the same direction in 1956. In other words, patterns characterizing the regions outside the South in a period of rapid depolarization are reversed in the South, where there seems instead to be a mild increase in polarization.

This pattern of findings in the South is of particular interest as it lends weight to our interpretation of the association between status voting and strength of party identification. With polarization rising in the South, status voting within identification categories shows a gradient the reverse of that which we find where polarization is declining. This fact supports the "lag" interpretation. At the same time in the South there is no reversal of the relationship between involvement and status voting: in both 1952 and 1956 Southerners who voted most according to class lines were the most involved. Hence different interpretations of the type given for the two patterns seem warranted.

---

mortality in the older cohorts and new voters of the younger generation.

[8]This trend may reflect growing industrialization and urbanization in the South, processes that are likely in the long run to blur traditional differences in political behavior generally.

We feel confident, then, in viewing party identification as a conserving influence in mass political behavior. This influence is particularly clear when changes in polarization outside the political order create forces toward change within that order. When polarization is receding and no major conflicts of another nature arise to realign the parties on a different axis, the strength of party allegiances may maintain polarization in political partisanship above that which we would otherwise predict.

Status Polarization and Social Structure

Broad features of social structure have a bearing on the *potential* for status polarization. We can locate several properties of the American social system that appear to condition the polarization potential of the nation in this way.

Urbanization. Although class awareness shows little tendency to follow common sociological divisions of the population, one such correlate emerges with some clarity. Contact with modern urban life increases the likelihood of class awareness. The level of awareness is highest in the central cities of large metropolitan areas and declines steadily through smaller cities to a low among people living in sparsely settled areas. It is particularly low among people in farm occupations. Furthermore, the probability that an individual thinks of himself as a class member shows some variation according to the amount of his life that he has spent in urban areas where ideas of social class are abroad. Among people who reside in large metropolises, those who have lived in such urban concentrations all of their lives are more likely to be aware of class than metropolitan people who grew up on farms.

The migration of populations to urban areas tends to stimulate perceptions of social class, and it follows that urbanization is likely to increase the potential for status polarization in a society.

Class Identification and the Problem of Status Ambiguity. If a class location is ambiguous, we would expect less clarity in class-relevant behavior and, as a consequence, a reduced potential of the social group for status polarization.

In discussing operational definitions of class and status we noted that some students use objective criteria, whereas others depend upon the subject's self-assignment. Of the several objective indices of status, occupation tends to generate the strongest relationships with political variables, and up to this point we have often used it as a measure of status. But a sub-

---

[9]We shall use occupation as our objective criterion of "misidentification." We use the term "misidentification" only with some hesitation. We do not intend to imply that the misidentifier is either dishonest or suffers distorted perceptions. At the outset, the term need be no more than a denotation of an analytic category.

stantial proportion of individuals assign themselves to a class other than that to which they would be assigned by the sociologist employing occupation as a criterion. Blue-collar workers of varying skill can and do identify with the middle class, whereas white-collar persons frequently identify with the "working" class. It is these people "misidentifying" across class lines who are symptomatic of status ambiguity in the culture.[9] Therefore it is among this group we must look for evidence of political behavior that is, from a class point of view, indeterminate.

Such behavior is readily demonstrable, as data compiled by Richard Centers have shown. Figure 1 compares the prevalence of recognizable class voting among individuals whose subjective class matches their occupation with class voting found among misidentifiers. This comparison is drawn separately within the three levels of political involvement employed previously. In each case, it is clear that most of the evidence for class voting within each group is contributed by voters whose class identification is congruent with occupation. As expected, tendencies toward class voting are indistinct among misidentifiers. Blue-collar workers who say they are middle class do not vote in a manner that is very distinct from that of white-collar, working-class identifiers.

Our initial presumption is that class voting is blurred among misidentifiers because such persons behave under cross-pressures. The individual has reason to identify with one class, but the occupational milieu in which he operates from day to day consists primarily of members of the "opposing" class. The class with which he sympathizes has one set of political norms, but his active social group, to the degree it is class-oriented, has opposing norms.

The addition of the involvement distinction communicates further information. If misidentifiers behave under cross-pressures, then the pressure that tends to carry the day varies systematically according to degree of involvement in the political process (Fig. 1). We find that while the involved misidentifier more often than not follows his class identification in preference to his occupational milieu, the situation is reversed among the most apathetic third of the population. Differences in behavior lead us to suspect that either of two conditions obtains among the politically apathetic: (1) the choice of a class location is relatively meaningless in itself; or (2) this choice is not endowed with any of its traditional political meaning. In either case the behavioral result is the same: the pressure stemming from class identification is weak relative to that stemming from the actual social group, and partisan choice, to the degree that it shows traces of class influence at all, reflects occupation primarily.[10]

---

[10]Although the negative correlation among the misidentifying apathetic is not strong, a similar correlation of almost the same magnitude emerges when the same table is drawn from

Earlier we introduced a method for determining whether or not the field of proximal attitudes is actually conflicted where sociological cross-pressures are suspected. If we apply this technique to test the hypothesis that behind the indeterminate class behavior of misidentifiers lies actual

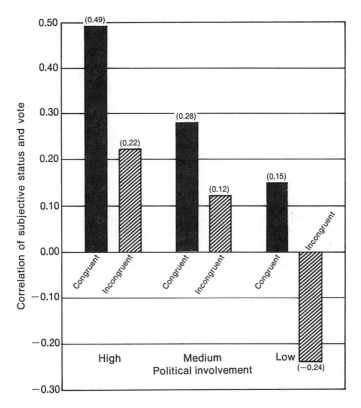

Figure 1. Status voting; political involvement and types of class identification, 1952. The solid bars include persons whose subjective class location is congruent with occupation, that is, blue-collar people choosing the "working class" and white-collar people of "middle class" identification. The shaded bars include blue-collar workers identifying with the "middle class" and white-collar, "working class" individuals.

conflict in political attitudes, we find that where there is some political involvement, class misidentification is associated with greater inconsistency of the field of proximal attitudes. But where involvement is low, there is no significant difference between congruent persons and those who misidentify in choice of social class location. Therefore, the assumption seems warranted that among politically involved types the relatively in-

1956 data. The 1956 graph duplicates the 1952 findings, although all coefficients are lower, reflecting the overall decline in status polarization of the vote.

determinate class behavior of misidentifiers is linked with actual psychological conflict.

Class misidentification leads to cross-pressures and thereby restrains the level of polarization in a society. It follows that the more frequent class misidentification is within a society, the lower is the potential of that society for status polarization. If the proportion of misidentifiers is an important datum in assessing the polarization potential of a society, then any characteristics of the social structure that promote misidentification serve at the same time to limit that potential. On the basis of current data it is possible to suggest a number of such characteristics.

First, it appears that the degree of misidentification in a society depends on the way in which its population is distributed along a status continuum. If we analyze the proportion of misidentifiers within successive groups along any of our objective status dimensions, we find that the rate of misidentification is low at the extremes (about 15 or 20 per cent) and rises symmetrically to a peak (approaching 50 per cent) at the center of the continuum. In other words, the closer an individual is located to a hypothetical dividing line between the two major classes by virtue of his objective situation, the more likely he is to locate himself psychologically on the other side of that line.

The caste society, with its sharply delineated strata, would have relatively few if any marginal people of ambiguous status. As we move from the caste extreme toward societies without gulfs defining status layers, however, the proportion of the population that occupies marginal locations increases. We would presume that as a result, the rate of misidentification increases as well, and the potential of the society for status polarization is consequently reduced. The United States, with its relatively swollen ranks of intermediate statuses—highly skilled labor and clerical workers—falls toward the extreme of the continuum. Other things equal—including the important elements of expectation and aspiration—it would seem that the United States has less potential for polarization than nations with other types of status structure.

We may also link the rate of social mobility in a society with the nature of its polarization potential. We find that when proximity to a hypothetical dividing line between classes is held constant, misidentification is more likely where the individual has, in times past, had some kind of contact with the opposing class milieu. For example, within each category of white-collar occupations, individuals of lower educational background are more likely to identify with the working class than are comparable people of high education. Similarly, blue-collar people of relatively high education are more likely to identify with the middle class. These situations are symptoms of mobility: a person's educational background, whatever his current status position, tends to reflect the status of his father's occupation. When education appears discrepant with current occupation, it is usually the case that the individual's current status differs from that of the family in which he was reared. When upward or downward mobility of this sort occurs, we tend to find what we classify as misidentification, and signs of conflict in political behavior where class is concerned.

Within societies in which movement of individuals upward or downward in the status hierarchy is rare, the possibility of misidentification arising from this source is minimized, and the potential of the society for status polarization is consequently increased. At the other extreme, the "open-class" society characterized by a high rate of social mobility maintains some ceiling on polarization potential by keeping its members' class identification, as it were, "off balance."

Class Interests and Social Groupings

If we are to understand the finer grain of political events, it becomes important to assess not only the degree of status polarization that characterizes the society as a whole, but also the *distribution* of class interest in the population. There may be only a small portion of the population infused with class feeling; yet if these few are organized into cohesive groups, their activity may become disproportionately significant.

We have treated the union as a cohesive interest group with certain mechanisms for member influence. We assume that influence is exerted through the business community in much the same way. We are interested here not in the mode of influence but in the content of that influence as it relates to social class and politics.

Class awareness is somewhat higher among union members than among nonunion members of the same status level. Political involvement runs much stronger among union members than among comparable nonunion people. As far as business is concerned we find no unusual report of class awareness. But businessmen at all levels of income are much more strongly involved in politics than their status or educational background would lead us to expect. This unusual heightening of involvement among union members in the lower half of the status hierarchy and the business community in the upper reaches is of a piece with our earlier findings concerning political involvement and class voting, for these groups show strong status polarization in their political behavior as well. This combination of circumstances lends support to our assumption that perception of an economic stake in politics leads to involvement, rather than the reverse. People do not as a rule come to choose business or unionized occupations in order to implement prior political involvement. Rather, the exceptional involvement seems to rise from the occupational situation and its intrinsic conflict of economic interest.

Another striking demonstration of the way in which the labor union contributes to maintenance of polarization is its apparent effect on the class identifications of its membership. Union members are in general more likely to maintain their identifications with the working class than are other people of similar occupation status. Furthermore, this tendency toward "proper" class identification increases as a function of identification with the union. And when union members are involved, "misidentification" fails to appear in some of the peculiar combinations of life situations where we have come to expect it. For example, all other data suggest that workers of lower status who receive unusually high wages should also show a higher rate of misidentification with the middle class than is true of low-income, low-occupation types. Instead, this group shows only a slight increase in misidentification. But we find at the same time that this group contains a surprising proportion of union members: the labor union clearly brings its membership financial rewards not available to others of the same occupational status. When we examine *nonunion* people in this situation separately, we *do* find the expected large proportion of misidentifiers; but *union members* receiving wages normally associated with higher occupation strata *maintain their identification with the working class.* The labor union is dedicated to the promotion of such wage mobility; it must exert further influence on the membership to avoid dissolving its support in the process. Maintenance of appropriate class identification despite mobility is one challenge that the labor movement appears to meet.

Thus we find that groups somewhat more formal than the social class can, when class interests are incorporated as group goals, serve to heighten status polarization. Since the labor and management groupings are current points of heightened class sensitivity within the total society, they bear particularly close attention. At the same time we should not underestimate the significance of a polarization measure that encompasses the total society and thereby places such contestants in proper social perspective. The larger, more indifferent portion of the community serves to hold expression of tension within socially acceptable bounds. Summary measures of polarization in the total society ignore pockets of ferment in the social structure. Further information as to the distribution of class concerns in the social structure is necessary in order to understand more localized events. Nonetheless, such summary measures do reflect as well the restraining forces constituted by the majority of peripherally involved. Thus yeast and leaven are represented in proportions that are dictated by the total social scene. It is likely that such an assessment best anticipates the direction of large-scale social and political events.

Part Three

Group
Impact
on Governmental
Policy

G ROUPS differ in the degree to which they influence governmental policy.[1] To a large extent the variation in influence is related to the type of goals sought by the groups. In general, groups which seek to reinforce the views and interests of governmental officials are more likely to achieve their goals than groups which aim at changing the views and at affecting the interests of governmental officials.[2] Another major factor involved in the likelihood of success in achieving group goals is the location of the group in the social structure.

Group Impact: Tactics and Strategic Location

The group's position in the social structure is strongly related to the group's access to powerful political institutions,[3] which in turn is related to the type of tactics the group can successfully employ, and the scope of goals it is likely to achieve.[4] The selections by Edelman and Gamson in Part I detailed the manner in which social structure affects different sets of individuals forming organized groups. In this part the selections focus on the governmental impact of organized groups.

In the first selection Michael Lipsky reviews tactics employed by rela-

[1]The selections in this part concentrate on group efforts to directly affect governmental policy. From a broader perspective group efforts indirectly affecting governmental policies through control over the kind of issues taken to the public arena may be more important in explaining the public policy process than direct group efforts. For an excellent statement of this view, see Peter Bachrach and Morton Baratz, "Decisions and Nondecisions: An Analytical Framework," *American Political Science Review*, LVII (March 1963), pp. 632-642; and for some examples of decisions which indirectly have major impact on governmental policy, see Andrew Hacker, "Power to do What?" in *The Bias of Pluralism*, ed. William Connolly (New York: Atherton, 1969), pp. 67-80.

[2]David Truman, *The Governmental Process* (New York: Alfred Knopf, 1951), pp. 336-343, comes to this conclusion in his analysis of overlapping group memberships of legislators.

[3]This is frequently referred to a group's strategic location in society by Truman which he relates to general access (pp. 262-270), access to communication structures and public opinion (pp. 248-260), access in electioneering (pp. 290-293), access to government (pp. 265-268, 339-340), and access to potential allies (pp. 362-368).

[4]One of the critical features of social structure is to give a group established access to particular decision-making points which in turn can give the group a defensive advantage in preserving the status quo via the tactic of keeping the public involved in the decisions relatively small. Truman, pp. 353-362, and generally Chapter 12.

tively powerless groups in the United States. He deals with groups which have moved past the stage of an aggregate of like-minded individuals to the study of groups with minimal cohesion and organization. Relatively powerless groups are groups which lack conventional political resources such as stable access to decision-making points in political institutions. Lipsky notes that the use of protest activities is a frequent tactic of the relatively powerless groups such as minority and low income groups in America. Protest is a tactic within the system[5] which aims at (1) gaining access to the target group, (i.e., the authorities) for the purpose of communicating the group's discontent and demands, *and* (2) activating reference publics to whom the authorities are sensitive. The protest frequently enables relatively powerless groups to gain access to the mass media which in turn gives the group access to reference publics. If enlisted, this support can be converted into a temporary political resource to be used in bargaining with the authorities. Lipsky notes that protest tactics are more likely to produce symbolic rather than tangible response by the authorities, hence in the long run, protest tactics can increase alienation and rejection of conventional political channels among the constituents of the protest leaders.

The tactics of groups with enough political resources to maintain stable access to decision-making points within political institutions are different in kind and aim from the tactics of relatively powerless groups. In the first place the emphasis shifts from gaining access which primarily involves the achievement of political visibility to maintaining access which primarily involves the maintenance of reciprocal benefits. Secondly, emphasis shifts from pressure to influence. Finally, the focus shifts from protest leader to lobbyist.

In the second selection Lester Milbrath presents findings on the relative preference of tactics by lobbyist.[6] In general lobbyists prefer to use tactics of subtle influence rather than high pressure techniques such as political reprisal at the polls or bribery. Most lobbyists favor face-to-face conversations for the communication of facts and the arguments which support them, but limit such presentations to really important matters because of the limited time resources of most officials. Lobbyists also communicate their views through intermediaries, preferring contact of decision-makers by constituents who have a power relationship to the official. Tactics such as entertaining or campaign aid are generally viewed as much less important in maintaining access for lobbyists than mutuality of interest and confidence between lobbyist and official. The importance of mutual interest in main-

[5]The line between what is within or outside the system is not absolute and varies with differences in political cultures. For an interesting collection of articles dealing with protest activities ranging from riot to revolution, see *American Behavioral Scientist,* ıI (March-April, 1968).

[6]For a study of the reciprocal attitudes of legislators and lobbyists at the state level, see Harmon Zeigler and Michael Baer, *Lobbying* (Belmont, Calif.: Wadsworth, 1969).

taining access and influencing officials is reflected in the high rating by
both lobbyists and legislators for the tactic of collaboration between groups
sharing a common interest.

While the relationship between lobbyist and official can be viewed as a
communication process, Heinz Eulau in the next selection cautions against
an interpretation that ignores or places too little emphasis on the power
aspects of the relationship. He points out that groups use lobbyists for purposes of influence and that if the groups are not receiving benefits they are
not likely to continue paying lobbyists. The absence of high pressure sales-
manship is not equivalent to the absence of influence.

Group Impact: Structure of Political Systems

In his study of the impact of interest groups on selected aspects of state
politics, Lewis Froman initiates systematic measurement of the influence of
interest groups.[7] States are divided into strong, moderate, and weak interest group systems. Assuming that interest groups seek special privileges
which will be reflected in governmental structure, he predicted that the
strength of the pressure system would be related to the length and detail
of the constitutions and the mode of selecting officials. Analysis of state
data confirmed his hypotheses.

Other findings that Froman presents raise an important question. The
findings that party competition and socio-economic level within the state
are negatively related to strength of the interest group system tends to
contradict findings at the societal level. At the societal level socio-economic
development is related to both party competition and industrialization, and
the concurrence of all three factors is positively associated with pluralistic
democracy, which compared to other political systems has greater numbers
of interest groups.[8] Froman's findings at the state level and the findings at
the societal level raise the question of the relationship between the number
of interest groups in the system and the relative strength of the impact of
the interest system on governmental structure.

The selection by Samuel Beer permits us to take a tentative look at that
question. Beer compares the interest group systems of the United States and

[7]For similar efforts at measuring the effect of party competition, see Charles Cnudde and
Donald McCrone, "Party Competition and Welfare Policies in the American States" and Ira
Sharkansky and Richard Hofferbert, "Dimensions of State Politics, Economics and Public
Policy," *American Political Science Review*, LXIII (September 1969), 858-879.

[8]See the Kornhauser selection (pages 5-25) and the Almond and Verba selection (pages
25-44) for a review of some of these relationships. Also keep these relationships in mind when
reading the Castles' selection (pages 273-288). For additional materials, see Seymour Lipset,
Political Man (Garden City, N. Y.: Doubleday Anchor Books, 1960), Chapter 2; and the critical
restatement of the relationship by Harry Echstein, "A Theory of Stable Democracy," *Reader
in Political Sociology*, ed. Frank Lindenfeld (New York: Funk & Wagnalls, 1968), pp. 116-128.

England. This comparison, in effect, controls industrialization, socio-economic level, and party competition, thus leaving the relationship between numbers and impact of interest group systems relatively free of influence from these major variables. Beer's analysis indicates that the impact of the interest group system on the government is likely to remain similar regardless of the number of groups in the system. He points to a reciprocal influence between concentration in the interest group system and collectivation in other political institutions such as party, government, and the electorate. Thus, an interest system composed of many groups may have as much impact on a decentralized governmental system as the impact of a concentrated interest system on a centralized political system.

The Froman and Beer selections indicate the difficulty in trying to measure the influence of groups. On the one hand we can visualize groups influencing the governmental structure, and on the other hand we can visualize governmental structure influencing the next wave of inputs by interest groups. The reciprocal influence of interest group systems and governmental structure can be clarified to some extent by distinguishing situations of influence between the politically-organized from situations of political influence of the organized over the unorganized.[9]

The totalitarian regime represents the archtype of influence by the politically organized over the unorganized. In the ideal type the politically organized represent a monolithic bloc which controls all bases of power in the society. In such a society there is only one influence—the influence of the controlling party.

In the selection by Joel Schwartz and William Keech the conditions of group influence in a totalitarian oriented society are explored. So long as the society retains the pure totalitarizn form, group influence is impossible. Group influence is only initially possible when the ruling elite is divided on policy.[10] The likelihood of group influence is increased when the issue is technical, the leadership is collective, the use of terror is reduced, and the society is dependent on technical expertise.

The study of group impact on governmental policy in totalitarian societies is by definition the study of group influence on relatively narrow manifest conflicts. To a large degree the conflicts in the Anglo-American democracies are also narrow in scope.[11] In both types of societies large-scale manifest ideological conflicts are absent. At least in this sense both

---

[9]For a review of the power relationships between the politically organized and unorganized in a democratic society, see the selections by Edelman and Gamson (pages 44-60 and 60-75).

[10]For another study concurring that a divided elite is a necessary prerequisite to group influence in a totalitarian society, see Roman Kolkowicz, "Interest Groups in Soviet Politics: The Case of the Military," *Comparative Politics*, II (April 1970), 445-472.

[11]See, for example, Theodore Lowi, "American Business, Public Policy, Case Studies and Political Theory," *World Politics*, XVI (July 1964), 677-715; and T. Alexander Smith, "Toward a Comparative Theory of the Policy Process," *Comparative Politics*, I (July 1969), 498-515.

totalitarian societies and Anglo-American democracies enjoy a relatively
high degree of consensus[12] in comparison to societies such as France and
Italy where manifest ideological conflict constitutes a major characteristic
of the political culture. It is likely in societies with major ideological cleavages that the importance of similarity of interest in gaining access and obtaining influence in government is exaggerated. Thus compared to high
consensus nations, low consensus nations are more likely to have an emphasis on loyalty rather than technical expertise in access and influence relationships between groups and government.

In the last selection Joseph LaPalombara reviews the impact of various
Italian groups on government. In the relationships between various interest groups and legislators, similarity of interest is important in terms of
external access to the legislature. In a fair number of cases virtual unity of
interest is achieved by major groups with mass followings which obtain
direct internal access to the legislature by electing their own leaders to
that body. LaPalombara also notes the importance of similarity in interest
in developing access and maintaining stable patterns of influence in Italian
bureaucracies. A *clientela* relationship exists if an interest group is seen as
the natural representative of a given social sector by an administrative agency. *Parentela* refers to a relationship between an interest group and the
bureaucracy which is essentially based on political kinship. These findings
suggest a reinforcing pattern in which ideological cleavages encourage
loyalty-oriented political patterns which in turn tend to maintain the cleavages.

Finally the assessment of the impact of groups on governmental policy
must take into account the degree and rate of cultural change in the particular society under study. In traditional authoritarian regimes such as
Spain the *status quo* oriented ruling class, which is typically composed of
large landowners, the military and the church, may tolerate a plurality of
groups so long as they remain apolitical in function.[13] In rapidly changing
societies led by a modernizing elite, the traditional group structures may
be the objects of penetration and change by the central authorities.[14] In this

---

[12]Generally consensus is a concept which refers to a latent agreement on basic values and/or
rules. In this sense the consensus of a democracy differs from that of totalitarian society in
terms of the source of consensus. William Connolly, *Political Science and Ideology* (New York:
Atherton, 1967), Chapter 2, argues a similar point in terms of elitism and pluralism. The evidence on latent consensus has grown rapidly in recent years with the advent of the large scale
survey research operation. For a recent article citing most of the relevant literature and offering a very interesting interpretation of the research findings, see Michael Mann, "The Social
Cohesion of Liberal Democracy," *American Sociological Review*, XXXV (June 1970), 423-439.

[13]Juan Linz, "An Authoritarian Regime: Spain," *Reader in Political Sociology*, ed. Frank
Lindenfeld (New York: Funk & Wagnalls, 1968), pp. 129-148.

[14]See, for example, the discussion of "mending and smashing" of traditional social structures
in attempts to economically develop the third world in Irving Louis Horowitz, *The Three
Worlds of Development* (New York: Oxford University Press, 1966), Chapter 7.

case, group impact may be best measured by resistance to change rather than by success in initiating change in governmental policy.

Estimates of the impact of groups on government must involve a number of factors. In the course of making these estimates the student of group politics should ask the following questions. What is the group's location in the social structure? What resources are available to various groups? What kinds of tactics are likely to be effective in what kinds of situations? What is the relationship between group interests and the interests expressed in existing governmental policy? To what degree is the political system concentrated and centralized? To what degree is the political culture marked by consensus or dissensus? What is the rate and scope of social and cultural change in the society under study? What are the differences between the politically organized and unorganized sectors of the society? And finally, to what extent are the significant groups external to the society under study?[15]

[15]There are two aspects of the question on the impact of external groups on governmental policy. In the first place there is the traditional one of imperialism where a powerful nation economically penetrates a weak nation (see Horowitz, pp. 188-190 and David Mermelstein, ed., *Economics* [New York: Random House, 1970] , pp. 417-441). Secondly, there is the question of whether subgroups, such as "hawks," in one nation influence the behavior of their counterparts in other nations (see Murray Edelman, "Escalation and Ritualization of Political Conflict," *American Behavioral Scientist,* XIII (November-December 1969), 231-246.

Protest as a Political Resource

Michael Lipsky

The frequent resort to protest activity by relatively powerless groups in recent American politics suggests that protest represents an important aspect of minority group and low income group politics.[1] At the same time that Negro civil rights strategists have recognized the problem of using protest as a meaningful political instrument,[2] groups associated with the "war on poverty" have increasingly received publicity for protest activity. Saul Alinsky's Industrial Areas Foundation, for example, continues to receive invitations to help organize low income communities because of its

[1]"Relatively powerless groups" may be defined as those groups which, relatively speaking, are lacking in conventional political resources. For the purposes of community studies, Robert Dahl has compiled a useful comprehensive list. See Dahl, "The Analysis of Influence in Local Communities," *Social Science and Community Action,* Charles R. Adrian, ed. (East Lansing, Michigan, 1960), p. 32. The difficulty in studying such groups is that relative powerlessness only becomes apparent under certain conditions. Extremely powerless groups not only lack political resources, but are also characterized by a minimal sense of political efficacy, upon which in part successful political organization depends. For reviews of the literature linking orientations of political efficacy to socioeconomic status, see Robert Lane, *Political Life* (New York, 1959), ch. 16; and Lester Milbrath, *Political Participation* (Chicago, 1965), ch. 5. Further, to the extent that group cohesion is recognized as a necessary requisite for organized political action, then extremely powerless groups, lacking cohesion, will not even appear for observation. Hence the necessity of selecting for intensive study a protest movement where there can be some confidence that observable processes and results can be analyzed. Thus, if one conceives of a continuum on which political groups are placed according to their relative command of resources, the focus of this essay is on those groups which are near, but not at, the pole of powerlessness.

[2]See, e.g., Bayard Rustin, "From Protest to Politics: The Future of the Civil Rights Movement," *Commentary* (February 1965), 25-31; and Stokely Carmichael, "Toward Black Liberation," *The Massachusetts Review* (Autumn 1966).

SOURCE: Michael Lipsky, "Protest as a Political Resource," *American Political Science Review,* LXII (December 1968), 1144-1158. Reprinted by permission. [Author's Note: This article is an attempt to develop and explore the implications of a conceptual scheme for analyzing protest activity. It is based upon my studies of protest organizations in New York City, Washington, D. C., Chicago, San Francisco, and Mississippi, as well as extensive examination of written accounts of protest among low-income and Negro civil rights groups. I am grateful to Kenneth Dolbeare, Murray Edelman, and Rodney Stiefbold for their insightful comments on an earlier draft. This paper was developed while the author was a Staff Associate of the Institute for Research on Poverty at the University of Wisconsin. I appreciate the assistance obtained during various phases of my research from the Rabinowitz Foundation, the New York State Legislative Internship Program, and the Brookings Institution.]

ability to mobilize poor people around the tactic of protest.[3] The riots which dominated urban affairs in the summer of 1967 appear not to have diminished the dependence of some groups on protest as a mode of political activity.

This article provides a theoretical perspective on protest activity as a political resource. The discussion is concentrated on the limitations inherent in protest which occur because of the need of protest leaders to appeal to four constituencies at the same time. As the concept of protest is developed here, it will be argued that protest leaders must nurture and sustain an organization comprised of people with whom they may or may not share common values. They must articulate goals and choose strategies so as to maximize their public exposure through communications media. They must maximize the impact of third parties in the political conflict. Finally, they must try to maximize chances of success among those capable of granting goals. The tensions inherent in manipulating these four constituencies at the same time form the basis of this discussion of protest as a political process. It is intended to place aspects of the civil rights movement in a framework which suggests links between protest organizations and the general political processes in which such organizations operate.

I. "Protest" Conceptualized

Protest activity as it has been adopted by elements of the civil rights movement and others has not been studied extensively by social scientists. Some of the most suggestive writings have been done as case studies of protest movements in single southern cities.[4] These works generally lack a framework or theoretical focus which would encourage generalization from the cases. More systematic efforts have been attempted in approaching the dynamics of biracial committees in the South,[5] and comprehensively assessing the efficacy of Negro political involvement in Durham, N.C. and Philadelphia, Pa.[6] In their excellent assessment of Negro politics in the South, Matthews and Prothro have presented a thorough profile of Sou-

---

[3]On Alinsky's philosophy of community organization, see his *Reveille for Radicals* (Chicago, 1945); and Charles Silberman, *Crisis in Black and White* (New York, 1964), Chapter 10.

[4]See, e.g., Jack L. Walker, "Protest and Negotiation: A Case Study of Negro Leadership in Atlanta, Georgia," *Midwest Journal of Political Science*, 7 (May 1963), 99-124; Jack L. Walker, *Sit-Ins in Atlanta: A Study in the Negro Protest*, Eagleton Institute Case Studies, No. 34 (New York, 1964); John Ehle, *The Free Men* (New York, 1965) [Chapel Hill]; Daniel C. Thompson, *The Negro Leadership Class* (Englewood Cliffs, N. J., 1963) [New Orleans]; M. Elaine Burgess, *Negro Leadership in a Southern City* (Chapel Hill, N. C., 1962) [Durham].

[5]Lewis Killian and Charles Grigg, *Racial Crisis in America: Leadership in Conflict* (Englewood Cliffs, N. J., 1964).

[6]William Keech, "The Negro Vote as a Political Resource: The Case of Durham," (unpublished Ph.D. Dissertation, University of Wisconsin, 1966); John H. Strange, "The Negro in Philadelphia Politics 1963-65," (unpublished Ph.D. Dissertation, Princeton University, 1966).

thern Negro students and their participation in civil rights activities.[7]
Protest is also discussed in passing in recent explorations of the social-
psychological dimensions of Negro ghetto politics[8] and the still highly suggestive, although pre-1960's, work on Negro political leadership by James
Q. Wilson.[9] These and other less systematic works on contemporary Negro
politics,[10] for all of their intuitive insights and valuable documentation,
offer no theoretical formulations which encourage conceptualization about
the interaction between recent Negro political activity and the political
process.

Heretofore the best attempt to place Negro protest activity in a framework
which would generate additional insights has been that of James Q. Wilson.[11] Wilson has suggested that protest activity be conceived as a problem
of bargaining in which the basic problem is that Negro groups lack political
resources to exchange. Wilson called this "the problem of the powerless."[12]

While many of Wilson's insights remain valid, his approach is limited in
applicability because it defines protest in terms of mass action or response
and as utilizing exclusively negative inducements in the bargaining process.
Negative inducements are defined as inducements which are not absolutely
preferred but are preferred over alternative possibilities.[13] Yet it might be
argued that protest designed to appeal to groups which oppose suffering
and exploitation, for example, might be offering positive inducements in
bargaining. A few Negro students sitting at a lunch counter might be engaged in what would be called protest, and by their actions might be trying
to appeal to other groups in the system with positive inducements. Additionally, Wilson's concentration on Negro civic action, and his exclusive
interest in exploring the protest process to explain Negro civic action,
tend to obscure comparison with protest activity which does not necessarily
arise within the Negro community.

Assuming a somewhat different focus, protest activity is defined as a mode
of political action oriented toward objection to one or more policies or conditions, characterized by showmanship or display of an unconventional
nature, and undertaken to obtain rewards from political or economic sys-

---

[7]Donald Matthews and James Prothro, *Negroes and the New Southern Politics* (New York,
1966). Considerable insight on these data is provided in John Orbell, "Protest Participation
among Southern Negro College Students," [*American Political Science*] *Review,* 61 (June 1967),
446-456.

[8]Kenneth Clark, *Dark Ghetto* (New York, 1965).

[9]*Negro Politics* (New York, 1960).

[10]A complete list would be voluminous. See, e.g., Nat Hentoff, *The New Equality* (New
York, 1964); Arthur Waskow, *From Race Riot to Sit-in* (New York, 1966).

[11]"The Strategy of Protest: Problems of Negro Civic Action," *Journal of Conflict Resolution,*
3 (September 1961), 291-303. The reader will recognize the author's debt to this highly suggestive article, not least Wilson's recognition of the utility of the bargaining framework for examining protest activity.

[12]*Ibid.,* p. 291.

[13]*Ibid.,* p. 291-292.

tems while working within the systems . The "problem of the powerless" in protest activity is to activate "third parties" to enter the implicit or explicit bargaining arena in ways favorable to the protesters. This is one of the few ways in which they can "create" bargaining resources. It is intuitively unconvincing to suggest that fifteen people sitting uninvited in the Mayor's office have the power to move City Hall. A better formulation would suggest that the people sitting in may be able to appeal to a wider public to which the city administration is sensitive. Thus in successful protest activity the *reference publics* of protest *targets* may be conceived as explicitly or implicitly reacting to protest in such a way that target groups or individuals respond in ways favorable to the protesters.[14]

It should be emphasized that the focus here is on protest by relatively powerless groups. Illustrations can be summoned, for example, of activity designated as "protest" involving high status pressure groups or hundreds of thousands of people. While such instances may share some of the characteristics of protest activity, they may not represent examples of developing political resources by relatively powerless groups because the protesting groups may already command political resources by virtue of status, numbers or cohesion.

It is appropriate also to distinguish between the relatively restricted use of the concept of protest adopted here and closely related political strategies which are often designated as "protest" in popular usage. Where groups already possess sufficient resources with which to bargain, as in the case of some economic boycotts and labor strikes, they may be said to engage in "direct confrontation."[15] Similarly, protest which represents efforts to "activate reference publics" should be distinguished from "alliance formation," where third parties are induced to join the conflict, but where the value orientations of third parties are sufficiently similar to those of the protesting group that concerted or coordinated action is possible. Alliance formation is particularly desirable for relatively powerless groups if they seek to join the decision-making process as participants.

The distinction between activating reference publics and alliance formation is made on the assumption that where goal orientations among protest groups and the reference publics of target groups are similar, the polit-

---

[14]See E. E. Schattschneider's discussion of expanding the scope of the conflict, *The Semisovereign People* (New York, 1960). Another way in which bargaining resources may be "created" is to increase the relative cohesion of groups, or to increase the perception of group solidarity as a precondition to greater cohesion. This appears to be the primary goal of political activity which is generally designated "community organization." Negro activists appear to recognize the utility of this strategy in their advocacy of "black power." In some instances protest activity may be designed in part to accomplish this goal in addition to activating reference publics.

[15]For an example of "direct confrontation," one might study the three-month Negro boycott of white merchants in Natchez, Miss., which resulted in capitulation to boycott demands by city government leaders. See *The New York Times,* December 4, 1965, p. 1.

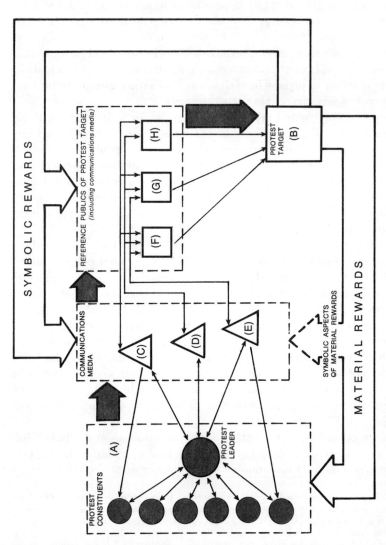

Figure 1. Schematic representation of the process of protest by relatively powerless groups.

ical dynamics of petitioning target groups are different than when such goal orientations are relatively divergent. Clearly the more similar the goal orientations, the greater the likelihood of protest success, other things being equal. This discussion is intended to highlight, however, those instances where goal orientations of reference publics depart significantly, in direction or intensity, from the goals of protest groups.

Say that to protest some situation, A would like to enter a bargaining situation with B. But A has nothing B wants, and thus cannot bargain. A then attempts to create political resources by activating other groups to enter the conflict. A then organizes to take action against B with respect to certain goals. *Information concerning these goals must be conveyed through communications media* (C, D, and E) to F, G, and H, which are B's *reference publics*. In response to the reactions of F, G, and H, or in anticipation of their reactions, B responds, *in some way,* to the protesters' demands. This formulation requires the conceptualization of protest activity when undertaken to create bargaining resources as a political process which requires communication and is characterized by a multiplicity of constituencies for protest leadership.

A schematic representation of the process of protest as utilized by relatively powerless groups is presented in Figure 1. In contrast to a simplistic pressure group model which would posit a direct relationship between pressure group and pressured, the following discussion is guided by the assumption (derived from observation) that protest is a highly indirect process in which communications media and the reference publics of protest targets play critical roles. It is also a process characterized by reciprocal relations, in which protest leaders frame strategies according to their perception of the needs of (many) other actors.

In this view protest constituents limit the options of protest leaders at the same time that the protest leader influences their perception of the strategies and rhetoric which they will support. Protest activity is filtered through the communications media in influencing the perceptions of the reference publics of protest targets. To the extent that the influence of reference publics is supportive of protest goals, target groups will dispense symbolic or material rewards. Material rewards are communicated directly to protest constituents. Symbolic rewards are communicated in part to protest constituents, but primarily are communicated to the reference publics of target groups, who provide the major stimuli for public policy pronouncements.

The study of protest as adopted by relatively powerless groups should provide insights into the structure and behavior of groups involved in civil rights politics and associated with the "war on poverty." It should direct attention toward the ways in which administrative agencies respond to "crises." Additionally, the study of protest as a political resource should influence some general conceptualizations of American political pluralism. Robert Dahl, for example, describes the "normal American political process" as

> one in which there is a high probability that an active and legitimate group in the population can make itself heard effectively at some crucial stage in the process of decision.[16]

Although he agrees that control over decisions is unevenly divided in the population, Dahl writes:

> When I say that a group is heard "effectively" I mean more than the simple fact that it makes a noise; I mean that one or more officials are not only ready to listen to the noise, but expect to suffer in some significant way if they do not placate the group, its leaders, or its most vociferous members. To satisfy the group may require one or more of a great variety of actions by the responsive leader: pressure for substantive policies, appointments, graft, respect, expression of the appropriate emotions, or the right combination of reciprocal noises.[17]

These statements, which in some ways resemble David Truman's discussion of the power of "potential groups,"[18] can be illuminated by the study of protest activity in three ways. First, what are the probabilities that relatively powerless groups can make themselves heard effectively? In what ways will such groups be heard or "steadily appeased"?[19] Concentration on the process of protest activity may reveal the extent to which, and the conditions under which, relatively powerless groups are likely to prove effective. Protest undertaken to obstruct policy decisions, for example, may enjoy greater success probabilities than protest undertaken in an effort to evoke constructive policy innovations.[20]

Second, does it make sense to suggest that all groups which make noises will receive responses from public officials? Perhaps the groups which make noises do not have to be satisfied at all, but it is other groups which receive assurances or recognition. Third, what are the probabilities that groups which make noises will receive tangible rewards, rather than symbolic assurances?[21] Dahl lumps these rewards together in the same paragraph, but dispensation of tangible rewards clearly has a different impact upon groups

[16]*A Preface to Democratic Theory* (Chicago, 1956), pp. 145-146.
[17]*Ibid.*
[18]*The Governmental Process* (New York, 1951), p. 104.
[19]See Dahl, *A Preface to Democratic Theory*, p. 146.
[20]Observations that all groups can influence public policy at some stage of the political process are frequently made about the role of "veto groups" in American politics. See *Ibid.*, pp. 104 ff. See also David Reisman, *The Lonely Crowd* (New Haven, 1950), pp. 211 ff., for an earlier discussion of veto-group politics. Yet protest should be evaluated when it is adopted to obtain assertive as well as defensive goals.
[21]See Murray Edelman, *The Symbolic Uses of Politics* (Urbana, Ill., 1964), Chapter 2.

than the dispensation of symbolic rewards. Dahl is undoubtedly correct when he suggests that the relative fluidity of American politics is a critical characteristic of the American political system.[22] But he is less precise and less convincing when it comes to analyzing the extent to which the system is indeed responsive to the relatively powerless groups of the "average citizen."[23]

The following sections are an attempt to demonstrate the utility of the conceptualization of the protest process presented above. This will be done by exploring the problems encountered and the strains generated by protest leaders in interacting with four constituencies. It will be useful to concentrate attention on the maintenance and enhancement needs not only of the large formal organizations which dominate city politics,[24] but also of the ad hoc protest groups which engage them in civic controversy. It will also prove rewarding to examine the role requirements of individuals in leadership positions as they perceive the problems of constituency manipulation. In concluding remarks some implications of the study of protest for the pluralist description of American politics will be suggested.[25]

II. Protest Leadership and Organizational Base

The organizational maintenance needs of relatively powerless, low income, ad hoc protest groups center around the tension generated by the need for leadership to offer symbolic and intangible inducements to protest participation when immediate, material rewards cannot be anticipated, and the need to provide at least the promise of material rewards. Protest leaders must try to evoke responses from other actors in the political process, at the same time that they pay attention to participant organizational needs. Thus relatively deprived groups in the political system not only receive symbolic reassurance while material rewards from the system are

---

[22]See Dahl, *Who Governs?* (New Haven, 1961), pp. 305 ff.

[23]In a recent formulation, Dahl reiterates the theme of wide dispersion of influence. "More than other systems, [democracies] . . . try to disperse influence widely to their citizens by means of the suffrage, elections, freedom of speech, press, and assembly, the right of opponents to criticize the conduct of government, the right to organize political parties, and in other ways." *Pluralist Democracy in the United States* (Chicago, 1967), p. 373. Here, however, he concentrates more on the availability of options to all groups in the system, rather than on the relative probabilities that all groups in fact have access to the political process. See pp. 372 ff.

[24]See Edward Banfield, *Political Influence* (New York, 1961), p. 263. The analysis of organizational incentive structure which heavily influences Banfield's formulation is Chester Barnard, *The Functions of the Executive* (Cambridge, Mass., 1938).

[25]In the following attempt to develop the implications of this conceptualization of protest activity, I have drawn upon extensive field observations and bibliographical research. Undoubtedly, however, individual assertions, while representing my best judgment concerning the available evidence, in the future may require modification as the result of further empirical research.

withheld,[26] but protest leaders have a stake in perpetuating the notion that relatively powerless groups retain political efficacy despite what in many cases is obvious evidence to the contrary.

The tension embraced by protest leaders over the nature of inducements toward protest participation accounts in part for the style adopted and goals selected by protest leaders. Groups which seek psychological gratification from politics, but cannot or do not anticipate material political rewards, may be attracted to militant protest leaders. To these groups, angry rhetoric may prove a desirable quality in the short run. Where groups depend upon the political system for tangible benefits, or where participation in the system provides intangible benefits, moderate leadership is likely to prevail. Wilson has observed similar tendencies among Negro leaders of large, formal organizations.[27] It is no less true for leadership of protest groups. Groups whose members derive tangible satisfactions from political participation will not condone leaders who are stubborn in compromise or appear to question the foundations of the system. This coincides with Truman's observation:

> Violation of the "rules of the game" normally will weaken a group's cohesion, reduce its status in the community, and expose it to the claims of other groups.[28]

On the other hand, the cohesion of relatively powerless groups may be strengthened by militant, ideological leadership which questions the rules of the game and challenges their legitimacy.

Cohesion is particularly important when protest leaders bargain directly with target groups. In that situation, leaders' ability to control protest constituents and guarantee their behavior represents a bargaining strength.[29] For this reason Wilson stressed the bargaining difficulties of Negro leaders who cannot guarantee constituent behavior, and pointed out the significance of the strategy of projecting the image of group solidarity when the reality of cohesion is a fiction.[30] Cohesion is less significant at other times. Divided leadership may prove productive by bargaining in tandem,[31] or by minimizing strain among groups in the protest process. Further, community divisions may prove less detrimental to protest aims

---

[26]As Edelman suggests, cited previously.

[27]*Negro Politics*, p. 290.

[28]*The Governmental Process*, p. 513.

[29]But cf. Thomas Schelling's discussion of "binding oneself," *The Strategy of Conflict* (Cambridge, Mass., 1960), pp. 22 ff.

[30]"The Strategy of Protest," p. 297.

[31]This is suggested by Wilson, "The Strategy of Protest," p. 298; St. Clair Drake and Horace Cayton, *Black Metropolis* (New York, 1962, rev. ed.), p. 731; Walker, "Protest and Negotiation," p. 122. Authors who argue that divided leadership is dysfunctional have been Clark, p. 156; and Tilman Cothran, "The Negro Protest Against Segregation in the South," *The Annals*, 357 (January, 1965), p. 72.

when strong third parties have entered the dispute originally generated by protest organizations.

The intangible rewards of assuming certain postures toward the political system may not be sufficient to sustain an organizational base. It may be necessary to renew constantly the intangible rewards of participation. And to the extent that people participate in order to achieve tangible benefits, their interest in a protest organization may depend upon the organization's relative material success. Protest leaders may have to tailor their style to present participants with tangible successes, or with the appearance of success. Leaders may have to define the issues with concern for increasing their ability to sustain organizations. The potential for protest among protest group members may have to be manipulated by leadership if the group is to be sustained.[32]

The participants in protest organizations limit the flexibility of protest leadership. This obtains for two reasons. They restrict public actions by leaders who must continue to solicit active participant support, and they place restraints on the kinds of activities which can be considered appropriate for protest purposes. Poor participants cannot commonly be asked to engage in protest requiring air transportation. Participants may have anxieties related to their environment or historical situation which discourages engagement in some activities. They may be afraid of job losses, beatings by the police, or summary evictions. Negro protest in the Deep South has been inhibited by realistic expectations of retribution.[33] Protests over slum housing conditions are undermined by tenants who expect landlord retaliation for engaging in tenant organizing activity.[34] Political or ethical mores may conflict with a proposed course of action, diminishing participation.[35]

[32]This observation is confirmed by a student of the Southern civil rights movement:

Negroes demand of protest leaders constant progress. The combination of long-standing discontent and a new-found belief in the possibility of change produces a constant state of tension and aggressiveness in the Negro community. But this discontent is vague and diffuse, not specific; the masses do not define the issues around which action shall revolve. This the leader must do.

Lewis Killian, "Leadership in the Desegregation Crises: An Institutional Analysis," in Muzafer Sherif (ed.), *Intergroup Relations and Leadership* (New York; 1962), p. 159.

[33]Significantly, southern Negro students who actively participated in the early phases of the sit-in movement "tended to be unusually optimistic about race relations and tolerant of whites [when compared with inactive Negro students]. They not only *were* better off, objectively speaking, than other Negroes but *felt better off.*" Matthews and Prothro, *op cit.*, p. 424.

[34]This is particularly the case in cities such as Washington, D. C., where landlord-tenant laws offer little protection against retaliatory eviction. See, e.g., Robert Schoshinski, "Remedies of the Indigent Tenant: Proposal for Change," *Georgetown Law Journal*, 54 (Winter, 1966), 541 ff.

[35]Wilson regarded this as a chief reason for lack of protest activity in 1961. He wrote: ". . . some of the goals now being sought by Negroes are least applicable to those groups of Negroes most suited to protest action. Protest action involving such tactics as mass meetings, picketing,

On the other hand, to the extent that fears are real, or that the larger community perceives protest participants as subject to these fears, protest may actually be strengthened. Communications media and potential allies will consider more soberly the complaints of people who are understood to be placing themselves in jeopardy. When young children and their parents made the arduous bus trip from Mississippi to Washington, D.C. to protest the jeopardizing of Head Start funds, the courage and expense represented by their effort created a respect and visibility for their position which might not have been achieved by local protest efforts.[36]

Protest activity may be undertaken by organizations with established relationship patterns, behavior norms, and role expectations. These organizations are likely to have greater access to other groups in the political system, and a demonstrated capacity to maintain themselves. Other protest groups, however, may be ad hoc arrangements without demonstrated internal or external relationship patterns. These groups will have different organizational problems, in response to which it is necessary to engage in different kinds of protest activity.

The scarcity of organizational resources also places limits upon the ability of relatively powerless groups to maintain the foundations upon which protest organizations develop. Relatively powerless groups, to engage in political activity of any kind, must command at least some resources. This is not tautological. Referring again to a continuum on which political groups are placed according to their relative command of resources, one may draw a line somewhere along the continuum representing a "threshold of civic group political participation." Clearly some groups along the continuum will possess some political resources (enough, say, to emerge for inspection) but not enough to exercise influence in civic affairs. Relatively powerless groups, to be influential, must cross the "threshold" to engage in politics. Although the availability of group resources is a critical consideration at all stages of the protest process, it is particularly important in explaining why some groups seem to "surface" with sufficient strength to command attention. The following discussion of some critical organizational resources should illuminate this point.

Skilled professionals frequently must be available to protest organizations. Lawyers, for example, play extremely important roles in enabling protest groups to utilize the judicial process and avail themselves of adequate preparation of court cases. Organizational reputation may depend upon a combination of ability to threaten the conventional political system and of exercising statutory rights in court. Availability of lawyers depends upon ability to pay fees and/or the attractiveness to lawyers of participation in protest

---

boycotts, and strikes rarely find enthusiastic participants among upper-income and higher status individuals": "The Strategy of Protest," p. 296.

[36]See *The New York Times,* February 12, 1966, p. 56.

group activity. Volunteer professional assistance may not prove adequate. One night a week volunteered by an aspiring politician in a housing clinic cannot satisfy the needs of a chaotic political movement.[37] The need for skilled professionals is not restricted to lawyers. For example, a group seeking to protest an urban renewal policy might require the services of architects and city planners in order to present a viable alternative to a city proposal.

Financial resources not only purchase legal assistance, but enable relatively powerless groups to conduct minimum programs of political activities. To the extent that constituents are unable or unwilling to pay even small membership dues, then financing the cost of mimeographing flyers, purchasing supplies, maintaining telephone service, paying rent, and meeting a modest payroll become major organizational problems. And to the extent that group finances are supplied by outside individual contributions or government or foundation grants, the long-term options of the group are sharply constrained by the necessity of orienting group goals and tactics to anticipate the potential objections of financial supporters.

Some dependence upon even minimal financial resources can be waived if organizations evoke passionate support from constituents. Secretarial help and block organizers will come forward to work without compensation if they support the cause of neighborhood organizations or gain intangible benefits based upon association with the group. Protest organizations may also depend upon skilled non-professionals, such as college students, whose access to people and political and economic institutions often assist protest groups in cutting across income lines to seek support. Experience with ad hoc political groups, however, suggests that this assistance is sporadic and undependable. Transient assistance is particularly typical of skilled, educated, and employable volunteers whose abilities can be applied widely. The die-hards of ad hoc political groups are often those people who have no place else to go, nothing else to do.

Constituent support will be affected by the nature of the protest target and whether protest activity is directed toward defensive or assertive goals. Obstructing specific public policies may be easier than successfully recommending constructive policy changes. Orientations toward defensive goals may require less constituent energy, and less command over resources of money, expertise and status.[38]

---

[37]On housing clinic services provided by political clubs, see James Q. Wilson, *The Amateur Democrat: Club Politics in Three Cities* (Chicago, 1962), pp. 63-64, 176. On the need for lawyers among low income people, see, e.g., *The Extension of Legal Services to the Poor*. Conference Proceedings (Washington, D. C., n.d.), esp. pp. 51-60; and "Neighborhood Law Offices: The New Wave in Legal Services for the Poor," *Harvard Law Review*, 80 (February, 1967), 805-850.

[38]An illustration of low income group protest organization mobilized for veto purposes is provided by Dahl in "The Case of the Metal Houses." See *Who Governs?*, pp. 192 ff.

III. Protest Leadership and Communications Media

The communications media are extremely powerful in city politics. In granting or withholding publicity, in determining what information most people will have on most issues, and what alternatives they will consider in response to issues, the media truly, as Norton Long has put it, "set . . . the civic agenda."[39] To the extent that successful protest activity depends upon appealing to, and/or threatening, other groups in the community, the communications media set the limits of protest action. If protest tactics are not considered significant by the media, or if newspapers and television reporters or editors decide to overlook protest tactics, protest organizations will not succeed. Like the tree falling unheard in the forest, there is no protest unless protest is perceived and projected.

A number of writers have noticed that the success of protest activity seems directly related to the amount of publicity it receives outside the immediate arena in which protest takes place. This view has not been stated systematically, but hints can be found in many sources. In the literature on civil rights politics, the relevance of publicity represents one of the few hypotheses available concerning the dynamics of successful protest activity.[40]

When protest tactics do receive coverage in the communications media, the way in which they are presented will influence all other actors in the system, including the protesters themselves. Conformity to standards of newsworthiness in political style, and knowledge of the prejudices and desires of the individuals who determine media coverage in political skills, represent crucial determinants of leadership effectiveness.

The organizational behavior of newspapers can partly be understood by examining the maintenance and enhancement needs which direct them toward projects of civic betterment and impressions of accomplishment.[41] But insight may also be gained by analyzing the role requirements of reporters, editors, and others who determine newspaper policy. Reporters, for example, are frequently motivated by the desire to contribute to civic affairs by their "objective" reporting of significant events; by the premium they place on accuracy; and by the credit which they receive for sensationalism and "scoops."

These requirements may be difficult to accommodate at the same time.

---

[39]Norton Long, "The Local Community as an Ecology of Games," in Long, *The Polity,* Charles Press, ed. (Chicago, 1962), p. 153. See pp. 152-154. See also Roscoe C. Martin, Frank J. Munger, *et al., Decisions in Syracuse: A Metropolitan Action Study* (Garden City, N. Y., 1965) (originally published: 1961), pp. 326-327.

[40]See, e.g., Thompson, *op. cit.,* p. 134, and *passim;* Martin Oppenheimer, "The Southern Student Movement: Year I," *Journal of Negro Education,* 33 (Fall 1964), p. 397; Cothran, *op. cit.,* p. 72; Pauli Murray, "Protest Against the Legal Status of the Negro," *The Annals,* 357 (January 1965), p. 63; Allan P. Sindler, "Protest Against the Political Status of the Negroes," *The Annals,* 357 (January 1965), p. 50.

[41]See Banfield, *op. cit.,* p. 275.

Reporters demand newsworthiness of their subjects in the short run, but also require reliability and verifiability in the longer run. Factual accuracy may dampen newsworthiness. Sensationalism, attractive to some newspaper editors, may be inconsistent with reliable, verifiable narration of events. Newspapers at first may be attracted to sensationalism, and later demand verifiability in the interests of community harmony (and adherence to professional journalistic standards).

Most big city newspapers have reporters whose assignments permit them to cover aspects of city politics with some regularity. These reporters, whose "beats" may consist of "civil rights" or "poverty," sometimes develop close relationships with their news subjects. These relationships may develop symbiotic overtones because of the mutuality of interest between the reporter and the news subject. Reporters require fresh information on protest developments, while protest leaders have a vital interest in obtaining as much press coverage as possible.

Inflated reports of protest success may be understood in part by examining this relationship between reporter and protest leader. Both have role-oriented interests in projecting images of protest strength and threat. In circumstances of great excitement, when competition from other news media representatives is high, a reporter may find that he is less governed by the role requirement of verification and reliability than he is by his editor's demand for "scoops" and news with high audience appeal.[42]

On the other hand, the demands of the media may conflict with the needs of protest group maintenance. Consider the leader whose constituents are attracted solely by pragmatic statements not exceeding what they consider political "good taste." He is constrained from making militant demands which would isolate him from constituents. This constraint may cost him appeal in the press.[43] However, the leader whose organizing appeal requires militant rhetoric may obtain eager press coverage only to find that his inflammatory statements lead to alienation of potential allies and exclusion from the explicit bargaining process.[44]

News media do not report events in the same way. Television may select for broadcast only thirty seconds of a half-hour news conference. This cov-

---

[42]For a case study of the interaction between protest leaders and newspaper reporters, see Michael Lipsky, "Rent Strikes in New York City: Protest Politics and the Power of the Poor," (unpublished Ph.D. dissertation, Princeton University, 1967), pp. 139-49. Bernard Cohen has analyzed the impact of the press on foreign policy from the perspective of reporters' role requirements: see his *The Press and Foreign Policy* (Princeton, N. J., 1963), esp. chs. 2-3.

[43]An example of a protest conducted by middle-class women engaged in pragmatic protest over salvaging park space is provided in John B. Keeley, *Moses on the Green*, Inter-University Case Program, No. 45 (University, Ala., 1959).

[44]This was the complaint of Floyd McKissick, National Director of the Congress of Racial Equality, when he charged that ". . . there are only two kinds of statements a black man can make and expect that the white press will report. . . . First . . . is an attack on another black man. . . . The second is a statement that sounds radical, violent, extreme—the verbal equivalent of a riot. . . . [T]he Negro is being rewarded by the public media only if he turns on

erage will probably focus on immediate events, without background or explanatory material. Newspapers may give more complete accounts of the same event. The most complete account may appear in the weekly edition of a neighborhood or ethnic newspaper. Differential coverage by news media, and differential news media habits in the general population,[45] are significant factors in permitting protest leaders to juggle conflicting demands of groups in the protest process.

Similar tensions exist in the leader's relationships with protest targets. Ideological postures may gain press coverage and constituency approval, but may alienate target groups with whom it would be desirable to bargain explicitly. Exclusion from the councils of decision-making may have important consequences, since the results of target group deliberations may satisfy activated reference publics without responding to protest goals. If activated reference publics are required to increase the bargaining position of the protest group, protest efforts thereafter will have diminished chances of success.

IV. Protest Leadership and "Third Parties"

I have argued that the essence of political protest consists of activating third parties to participate in controversy in ways favorable to protest goals. In previous sections I have attempted to analyze some of the tensions which result from protest leaders' attempts to activate reference publics of protest targets at the same time that they must retain the interest and support of protest organization participants. This phenomenon is in evidence when Negro leaders, recognized as such by public officials, find their support eroded in the Negro community because they have engaged in explicit bargaining situations with politicians. Negro leaders are thus faced with the dilemma that when they behave like other ethnic group representatives they are faced with loss of support from those whose intense activism has been aroused in the Negro community, yet whose support is vital if they are to remain credible as leaders to public officials.

The tensions resulting from conflicting maintenance needs of protest organizations and activated third parties present difficulties for protest leaders. One way in which these tensions can be minimized is by dividing leadership responsibilities. If more than one group is engaged in protest activity, protest leaders can, in effect, divide up public roles so as to reduce

---

another Negro and uses his tongue as a switchblade, or only if he sounds outlandish, extremist or psychotic." Statement at the Convention of the American Society of Newspaper Editors, April 20, 1967, Washington, D. C., as reported in *The New York Times,* April 21, 1967, p. 22. See also the remarks of journalist Ted Poston, *ibid.,* April 26, 1965, p. 26.

[45]Matthews and Prothro found, for example, that in their south-wide Negro population sample, 38 per cent read Negro-oriented magazines and 17 per cent read newspapers written for Negroes. These media treat news of interest to Negroes more completely and sympathetically than do the general media. See pp. 248 ff.

as much as possible the gap between the implicit demands of different groups for appropriate rhetoric, and what in fact is said. Thus divided leadership may perform the latent function of minimizing tensions among elements in the protest process by permitting different groups to listen selectively to protest spokesmen.[46]

Another way in which strain among different groups can be minimized is through successful public relations. Minimization of strain may depend upon ambiguity of action or statement, deception, or upon effective intergroup communication. Failure to clarify meaning, or falsification, may increase protest effectiveness. Effective intragroup communication may increase the likelihood that protest constituents will "understand" that ambiguous or false public statements have "special meaning" and need not be taken seriously. The Machiavellian circle is complete when we observe that although lying may be prudent, the appearance of integrity and forthrightness is desirable for public relations, since these values are widely shared.

It has been observed that "[t]he militant displays an unwillingness to perform those administrative tasks which are necessary to operate an organization. Probably the skills of the agitator and the skills of the administrator . . . are not incompatible, but few men can do both well."[47] These skills may or may not be incompatible as personality traits, but they indeed represent conflicting role demands on protest leadership. When a protest leader exhausts time and energy conducting frequent press conferences, arranging for politicians and celebrities to appear at rallies, delivering speeches to sympathetic local groups, college symposia and other forums, constantly picketing for publicity and generally making "contacts," he is unable to pursue the direction of office routine, clerical tasks, research and analysis, and other chores.

The difficulties of delegating routine tasks are probably directly related to the skill levels and previous administrative experiences of group members. In addition, to the extent that involvement in protest organizations is a function of rewards received or expected by individuals because of the excitement or entertainment value of participation, then the difficulties of delegating routine, relatively uninteresting chores to group members will be increased. Yet attention to such details affects the perception of protest groups by organizations whose support or assistance may be desired in the future. These considerations add to the protest leader's problem of risking alienation of protest participants because of potentially unpopular cooperation with the "power structure."

In the protest paradigm developed here, "third parties" refers both to the reference publics of target groups and, more narrowly, to the interest groups whose regular interaction with protest targets tends to develop into patterns

---

[46]See footnote 31 above.
[47]Wilson, *Negro Politics,* p. 225.

of influence.[48] We have already discussed some of the problems associated with activating the reference publics of target groups. In discussing the constraints placed upon protest, attention may be focused upon the likelihood that groups seeking to create political resources through protest will be included in the explicit bargaining process with other pressure groups. For protest groups, these constraints are those which occur because of class and political style, status, and organizational resources.

The established civic groups most likely to be concerned with the problems raised by relatively powerless groups are those devoted to service in the public welfare and those "liberally" oriented groups whose potential constituents are either drawn from the same class as the protest groups (such as some trade unions), or whose potential constituents are attracted to policies which appear to serve the interest of the lower class or minority groups (such as some reform political clubs).[49] These civic groups have frequently cultivated clientele relationships with city agencies over long periods. Their efforts have been reciprocated by agency officials anxious to develop constituencies to support and defend agency administrative and budgetary policies. In addition, clientele groups are expected to endorse and legitimize agency aggrandizement. These relationships have been developed by agency officials and civic groups for mutual benefit, and cannot be destroyed, abridged or avoided without cost.

Protest groups may well be able to raise the saliency of issues on the civic agenda through utilization of communications media and successful appeals or threats to wider publics, but admission to policy-making councils is frequently barred because of the angry, militant rhetorical style adopted by protest leaders. People in power do not like to sit down with rogues. Protest leaders are likely to have phrased demands in ways unacceptable to lawyers and other civic activists whose cautious attitude toward public policy may reflect not only their good intentions but their concern for property rights, due process, pragmatic legislating or judicial precedent.

Relatively powerless groups lack participation of individuals with high status whose endorsement of specific proposals lend them increased legitimacy. Good causes may always attract the support of high status individuals. But such individuals' willingness to devote time to the promotion of specific proposals is less likely than the one-shot endorsements which these people distribute more readily.

Similarly, protest organizations often lack the resources on which entry into the policy-making process depends. These resources include maintenance of a staff with expertise and experience in the policy area. This exper-

[48]See Wallace Sayre and Herbert Kaufman, *Governing New York City* (New York, 1960), pp. 257 ff. Also see Banfield, *op. cit.,* p. 267.

[49]See Wilson, *The Amateur Democrats,* previously cited. These groups are most likely to be characterized by broad scope of political interest and frequent intervention in politics. See Sayre and Kaufman, *op. cit.,* p. 79.

tise may be in the areas of the law, planning and architecture, proposal writing, accounting, educational policy, federal grantsmanship or publicity. Combining experience with expertise is one way to create status in issue areas. The dispensing of information by interest groups has been widely noted as a major source of influence. Over time the experts develop status in their areas of competence somewhat independent of the influence which adheres to them as information-providers. Groups which cannot or do not engage lawyers to assist in proposing legislation, and do not engage in collecting reliable data, cannot participate in policy deliberations or consult in these matters. Protest oriented groups, whose primary talents are in dramatizing issues, cannot credibly attempt to present data considered "objective" or suggestions considered "responsible" by public officials. Few can be convincing as both advocate and arbiter at the same time.

V. Protest Leadership and Target Groups

The probability of protest success may be approached by examining the maintenance needs of organizations likely to be designated as target groups.[50] For the sake of clarity, and because protest activity increasingly is directed toward government, I shall refer in the following paragraphs exclusively to government agencies at the municipal level. The assumption is retained, however, that the following generalizations are applicable to other potential target groups.

Some of the constraints placed on protest leadership in influencing target groups have already been mentioned in preceding sections. The lack of status and resources that inhibit protest groups from participating in policy-making conferences, for example, also helps prevent explicit bargaining between protest leaders and city officials. The strain between rhetoric which appeals to protest participants and public statements to which communications media and "third parties" respond favorably also exists with reference to target groups.

Yet there is a distinguishing feature of the maintenance needs and strategies of city agencies which specifically constrains protest organizations. This is the agency director's need to protect "the jurisdiction and income of his

---

[50]Another approach, persuasively presented by Wilson, concentrates on protest success as a function of the relative unity and vulnerability of targets. See "The Strategy of Protest," pp. 293 ff. This insight helps explain, for example, why protest against housing segregation commonly takes the form of action directed against government (a unified target) rather than against individual homeowners (who present a dispersed target). One problem with this approach is that it tends to obscure the possibility that targets, as collections of individuals, may be divided in evaluation of and sympathy for protest demands. Indeed, city agency administrators under some circumstances act as partisans in protest conflicts. As such, they frequently appear ambivalent toward protest goals: sympathetic to the ends while concerned that the means employed in protest reflect negatively on their agencies.

organization [by] . . . [m]anipulation of the external environment."[51] In so doing he may satisfy his reference groups without responding to protest group demands. At least six tactics are available to protest targets who are motivated to respond in some way to protest activity but seek primarily to satisfy their reference publics. These tactics may be employed whether or not target groups are "sincere" in responding to protest demands.

1. Target groups may dispense symbolic satisfactions. Appearances of activity and commitment to problems substitute for, or supplement, resource allocation and policy innovations which would constitute tangible responses to protest activity. If symbolic responses supplement tangible pay-offs, they are frequently coincidental, rather than intimately linked, to projection of response by protest targets. Typical in city politics of the symbolic response is the ribbon cutting, street corner ceremony or the walking tour press conference. These occasions are utilized not only to build agency constituencies,[52] but to satisfy agency reference publics that attention is being directed to problems of civic concern. In this sense publicist tactics may be seen as defensive maneuvers. Symbolic aspects of the actions of public officials can also be recognized in the commissioning of expensive studies and the rhetorical flourishes with which "massive attacks," "comprehensive programs," and "coordinated planning" are frequently promoted.

City agencies establish distinct apparatus and procedures for dealing with crises which may be provoked by protest groups. Housing-related departments in New York City may be cited for illustration. It is usually the case in these agencies that the Commissioner or a chief deputy, a press secretary and one or two other officials devote whatever time is necessary to collect information, determine policy and respond quickly to reports of "crises." This is functional for tenants, who, if they can generate enough concern, may be able to obtain shortcuts through lengthy agency procedures. It is also functional for officials who want to project images of action rather than merely receiving complaints. Concentrating attention of the maintenance needs of city politicians during protest crises suggests that pronouncements of public officials serve purposes independent of their dedication to alleviation of slum conditions.[53]

Independent of dispensation of tangible benefits to protest groups, public officials continue to respond primarily to their own reference publics. Murray Edelman has suggested that:

[51]Sayre and Kaufman, *op. cit.*, p. 253.

[52]See *ibid.*, pp. 253 ff.

[53]See Lipsky, *op. cit.*, Chs. 5-6. The appearance of responsiveness may be given by city officials *in anticipation* of protest activity. This seems to have been the strategy of Mayor Richard Daley in his reaction to the announcement of Martin Luther King's plans to focus civil rights efforts on Chicago. See *The New York Times*, February 1, 1966, p. 11.

> Tangible resources and benefits are frequently not distributed to unorganized political group interests as promised in regulatory statutes and the propaganda attending their enactment.[54]

His analysis may be supplemented by suggesting that symbolic dispensations may not only serve to reassure unorganized political group interests, but may also contribute to reducing the anxiety level of organized interests and wider publics which are only tangentially involved in the issues.

2. Target groups may dispense token material satisfactions. When city agencies respond, with much publicity, to cases brought to their attention representing examples of the needs dramatized by protest organizations, they may appear to respond to protest demands while in fact only responding on a case basis, instead of a general basis. For the protesters served by agencies in this fashion it is of considerable advantage that agencies can be influenced by protest action. Yet it should not be ignored that in handling the "crises" cases, public officials give the appearance of response to their reference publics, while mitigating demands for an expensive, complex *general* assault on problems represented by the cases to which responses are given. Token responses, whether or not accompanied by more general responses, are particularly attractive to reporters and television news directors, who are able to dramatize individual cases convincingly, but who may be unable to "capture" the essence of general deprivation or of general efforts to alleviate conditions of deprivation.

3. Target groups may organize and innovate internally in order to blunt the impetus of protest efforts. This tactic is closely related to No. 2 (above). If target groups can act constructively in the worst cases, they will then be able to pre-empt protest efforts by responding to the cases which best dramatize protest demands. Alternatively, they may designate all efforts which jeopardize agency reputations as "worst" cases, and devote extensive resources to these cases. In some ways extraordinary city efforts are precisely consistent with protest goals. At the same time extraordinary efforts in the most heavily dramatized cases or the most extreme cases effectively wear down the "cutting-edges" of protest efforts.

Many New York City agencies develop informal "crisis" arrangements not only to project publicity, as previously indicated, but to mobilize energies toward solving "crises" cases. They may also develop policy innovations which allow them to respond more quickly to "crisis" situations. These innovations may be important to some city residents, for whom the problems of dealing with city bureaucracies can prove insurmountable. It might be said, indeed, that the goals of protest are to influence city agencies to han-

[54]See Edelman, *op. cit.,* p. 23.

dle every case with the same resources that characterize their dispatch of "crisis" cases.[55]

But such policies would demand major revenue inputs. This kind of qualitative policy change is difficult to achieve. Meanwhile, internal real-location of resources only means that routine services must be neglected so that the "crisis" programs can be enhanced. If all cases are expedited, as in a typical "crisis" response, then none can be. Thus for purposes of general solutions, "crisis" resolving can be self-defeating unless accompanied by significantly greater resource allocation. It is not self-defeating, however, to the extent that the organizational goals of city agencies are to serve a clientele while minimizing negative publicity concerning agency vigilance and responsiveness.

4. Target groups may appear to be constrained in their ability to grant protest goals.[56] This may be directed toward making the protesters appear to be unreasonable in their demands, or to be well-meaning individuals who "just don't understand how complex running a city really is." Target groups may extend sympathy but claim that they lack resources, a mandate from constituents, and/or authority to respond to protest demands. Target groups may also evade protest demands by arguing that "If-I-give-it-to-you-I-have-to-give-it-to-everyone."

The tactic of appearing constrained is particularly effective with established civic groups because there is an undeniable element of truth to it. Everyone knows that cities are financially undernourished. Established civic groups expend great energies lobbying for higher levels of funding for their pet city agencies. Thus they recognize the validity of this constraint when posed by city officials. But it is not inconsistent to point out that funds for specific, relatively inexpensive programs, or for the expansion of existing programs, can often be found if pressure is increased. While constraints on city government flexibility may be extensive, they are not absolute. Protest targets nonetheless attempt to diminish the impact of protest demands by claiming relative impotence.

5. Target groups may use their extensive resources to discredit protest leaders and organizations. Utilizing their excellent access to the press, public officials may state or imply that leaders are unreliable, ineffective as leaders ("they don't really have the people behind them"), guilty of criminal behavior, potentially guilty of such behavior, or are some shade of "left-wing." Any of these allegations may serve to diminish the appeal of protest groups to potentially sympathetic third parties. City officials, in their frequent social and informal business interaction with leaders of established civic groups, may also communicate derogatory information concerning protest groups. Discrediting of protest groups may be undertaken

[55]See Lipsky, *op. cit.*, pp. 156, 249 ff.
[56]On the strategy of appearing constrained, see Schelling, *op. cit.*, pp. 22 ff.

by some city officials while others appear (perhaps authentically) to remain sympathetic to protest demands. These tactics may be engaged in by public officials whether or not there is any validity to the allegations.

6. Target groups may postpone action. The effect of postponement, if accompanied by symbolic assurances, is to remove immediate pressure and delay specific commitments to a future date. This familiar tactic is particularly effective in dealing with protest groups because of their inherent instability. Protest groups are usually comprised of individuals whose intense political activity cannot be sustained except in rare circumstances. Further, to the extent that protest depends upon activating reference publics through strategies which have some "shock" value, it becomes increasingly difficult to activate these groups. Additionally, protest activity is inherently unstable because of the strains placed upon protest leaders who must attempt to manage four constituencies (as described herein).

The most frequent method of postponing action is to commit a subject to "study." For the many reasons elaborated in these paragraphs, it is not likely that ad hoc protest groups will be around to review the recommendations which emerge from study. The greater the expertise and the greater the status of the group making the study, the less will protest groups be able to influence whatever policy emerges. Protest groups lack the skills and resource personnel to challenge expert recommendations effectively.

Sometimes surveys and special research are undertaken in part to evade immediate pressures. Sometimes not. Research efforts are particularly necessary to secure the support of established civic groups, which place high priority on orderly procedure and policy emerging from independent analysis. Yet it must be recognized that postponing policy commitments has a distinct impact on the nature of the pressures focused on policy-makers.

IV. Conclusion

In this analysis I have agreed with James Q. Wilson that protest is correctly conceived as a strategy utilized by relatively powerless groups in order to increase their bargaining ability. As such, I have argued, it is successful to the extent that the reference publics of protest targets can be activated to enter the conflict in ways favorable to protest goals. I have suggested a model of the protest process which may assist in ordering data and indicating the salience for research of a number of aspects of protest. These include the critical role of communications media, the differential impact of material and symbolic rewards on "feedback" in protest activity, and the reciprocal relationships of actors in the protest process.

An estimation of the limits to protest efficacy, I have argued further, can be gained by recognizing the problems encountered by protest leaders who somehow must balance the conflicting maintenance needs of four groups in the protest process. This approach transcends a focus devoted primarily to characterization of group goals and targets, by suggesting that even in an environment which is relatively favorable to specific protest goals, the tensions which must be embraced by protest leadership may ultimately overwhelm protest activity.

At the outset of this essay, it was held that conceptualizing the American political system as "slack" or "fluid," in the manner of Robert Dahl, appears inadequate because of (1) a vagueness centering on the likelihood that any group can make itself heard; (2) a possible confusion as to which groups tend to receive satisfaction from the rewards dispensed by public officials; and (3) a lumping together as equally relevant rewards which are tangible and those which are symbolic. To the extent that protest is engaged in by relatively powerless groups which must create resources with which to bargain, the analysis here suggests a number of reservations concerning the pluralist conceptualization of the "fluidity" of the American political system.

Relatively powerless groups cannot use protest with a high probability of success. They lack organizational resources, by definition. But even to create bargaining resources through activating third parties, some resources are necessary to sustain organization. More importantly, relatively powerless protest groups are constrained by the unresolvable conflicts which are forced upon protest leaders who must appeal simultaneously to four constituencies which place upon them antithetical demands.

When public officials recognize the legitimacy of protest activity, they may not direct public policy toward protest groups at all. Rather, public officials are likely to aim responses at the reference publics from which they originally take their cues. Edelman has suggested that regulatory policy in practice often consists of reassuring mass publics while at the same time dispensing specific, tangible values to narrow interest groups. It is suggested here that symbolic reassurances are dispensed as much to wide, potentially concerned publics which are not directly affected by regulatory policy, as they are to wide publics comprised of the down-trodden and the deprived, in whose name policy is often written.

Complementing Edelman, it is proposed here that in the process of protest symbolic reassurances are dispensed in large measure because these are the public policy outcomes and actions desired by the constituencies to which public officials are most responsive. Satisfying these wider publics, city officials can avoid pressures toward other policies placed upon them by protest organizations.

Not only should there be some doubt as to which groups receive the symbolic recognitions which Dahl describes, but in failing to distinguish between the kinds of rewards dispensed to groups in the political system, Dahl avoids a fundamental question. It is literally fundamental because the kinds of rewards which can be obtained from politics, one might hypothesize, will have an impact upon the realistic appraisal of the efficacy of political activity. If among the groups least capable of organizing for political activity there is a history of organizing for protest, and if that activity, once engaged in, is rewarded primarily by the dispensation of symbolic gestures without perceptible changes in material conditions, then rational behavior might lead to expressions of apathy and lack of interest in politics or a rejection of conventional political channels as a meaningful arena of activity. In this sense this discussion of protest politics is consistent with Kenneth Clark's observations that the image of power, unaccompanied by material and observable rewards, leads to impressions of helplessness and reinforces political apathy in the ghetto.[57]

Recent commentary by political sceintists and others regarding riots in American cities seems to focus in part on the extent to which relatively deprived groups may seek redress of legitimate grievances. Future research should continue assessment of the relationship between riots and the conditions under which access to the political system has been limited. In such research assessment of the ways in which access to public officials is obtained by relatively powerless groups through the protest process might be one important research focus.

The instability of protest activity outlined in this article also should inform contemporary political strategies. If the arguments presented here are persuasive, civil rights leaders who insist that protest activity is a shallow foundation on which to seek long-term, concrete gains may be judged essentially correct. But the arguments concerning the fickleness of the white liberal, or the ease of changing discriminatory laws relative to changing discriminatory institutions, only in part explain the instability of protest movements. An explanation which derives its strength from analysis of the political process suggests concentration on the problems of managing protest constituencies. Accordingly, Alinsky is probably on the soundest ground when he prescribes protest for the purpose of building organization. Ultimately, relatively powerless groups in most instances cannot depend upon activating other actors in the political process. Long-run success will depend upon the acquisition of stable political resources which do not rely for their use on third parties.

[57]Clark, *op. cit.*, pp. 154 ff.

Lobbying as a
Communication
Process

Lester W. Milbrath

Lobbyists and their activities have traditionally been of interest to political scientists because they play a role in the governmental decision process. But just what is that role? Or, to put the question in a more researchable fashion, what kind of model can the analyst apply to their activities which will provide the most accurate perspective on their role? The answer to this question must be derived from the larger frame of reference of the over-all governmental decision process.

Social scientists have approached the analysis of governmental decision making from several different perspectives. For example, some analysts have approached it from the perspective of the role of groups in the process.[1] Others have done research which seemed to indicate that governmental decisions are made by a select power elite,[2] although the elite theory has been challenged by other scholars.[3] One could catalog additional perspectives on the process, some of which are very provocative,[4] but that is not the purpose of this paper. The purpose, rather, is to present an alternative perspective on the process which may provide some new insights and also lead to a communication model for analyzing the lobbying aspects of the process.

The perspective on the lobbying process reported here is gained from a sample survey of Washington lobbyists. The study focused primarily on lobbyists as individuals who comprise a political skill group rather than

[1]The two outstanding examples probably are: Arthur F. Bentley, *The Process of Government,* Chicago, University of Chicago Press, 1908, and David B. Truman, *The Governmental Process,* New York, Knopf, 1951.

[2]Some leading examples here are: Floyd Hunter, *Community Power Structure,* Chapel Hill, University of North Carolina Press, 1953, and his recent *Top Leadership U.S.A.,* Chapel Hill, University of North Carolina Press, 1959, C. Wright Mills, *The Power Elite,* New York, Oxford, 1956, and Ferdinand Lundberg, *America's Sixty Families,* New York, Vanguard, 1937.

[3]See Robert A. Dahl, "A Critique of the Ruling Elite Model," *American Political Science Review,* Vol. 52, 1958, pp. 463-469.

[4]As a result of some recent studies of community politics, Norton Long has suggested that community decision making can be analyzed with a game theory model. His concept is that political decision making results from the interactive forces of a variety of games being played in any given community. The players in one game may be the pawns in another game or may

SOURCE: Lester W. Milbrath, "Lobbying as a Communication Process," *The Public Opinion Quarterly,* XXIV (Spring 1960), 37-53. Reprinted by permission.

on the nature and power of the groups which they represent, as most other studies of lobbying have done. The universe from which the sample was selected included all the individuals with Washington addresses who registered as lobbyists with the Clerk of the House and Secretary of the Senate during the first two quarters of 1956 (the most recent period prior to the field-work phase of the study). One hundred and fourteen names were randomly selected from the total universe of 614; I succeeded in interviewing 101 of these individuals. These interviews were supplemented by interviews with 38 people in Congress, in order to get the perspective of the recipient of lobbying.

The confidential interviews averaged about two hours in length and covered such topics as the occupational history of the respondent; how he happened to get into lobbying; how well he likes the role he plays; what his political background was; what his socio-economic background was; how he relates to his employer; what role he plays in relation to the government; what tactics and techniques he uses and prefers for communicating with governmental decision makers; and how he evaluates the lobbying process and the role he plays in it. Finally, each respondent was asked to fill out a short personality test.[5]

Under the American system of government, certain individuals, occupying certain governmental offices, are charged by the Constitution with making decisions which in effect lay down the policies for the country and which have the force of governmental authority and finality behind them. I am thinking mainly here of the President, the members of the Supreme Court, and the members of Congress. The charge has been made that the decisions pronounced by these persons essentially are not their own, but rather they are merely parroting the decisions made by individuals and groups upon whom they are dependent for support. In one sense, close attention to the desires of supporters is considered laudable in a representative democracy. On the other hand, we are distressed if it seems that the decision maker is following the desires of some special interest and ignoring the general welfare.

Although students of politics have been making educated guesses for some time about the propensity for decision makers to follow either the general welfare or someone's special welfare, a clear-cut discernment of the influence of such factors as pressure-group activity or political money

---

use players in other games as pawns in their own game. The remarkable thing is that community decisions result from the diverging activities and purposes of the games being played. See his "The Local Community as an Ecology of Games," *American Journal of Sociology*, Vol. 64, 1958, pp. 251-261. Although extensive research would be required for verification, the evidence suggests that national decision making may also be the result of an ecology of games.

[5]The purposes of the study were broader than the analytical scheme presented in this paper: thus data were gathered on several topics that do not fit into a communication model.

upon governmental decision makers can come only from detailed examination of the decision processes of these individuals. Unhappily, it is an extraordinarily difficult research problem to ascertain the bases for judgment made by these decision makers. Even if the researcher had free access to decision makers within a context of mutual trust and thirst for truth, it is highly unlikely that these persons could plumb their unconscious and dredge up all the factors that entered into any given decision. Detailed examination of the psychological processes of a decision maker concerning a given decision would probably, at least at this stage of social science, get bogged down in a mass of unanalyzable detail. Thus, it is not my purpose to present an analytical scheme for assessing the influence of lobbying on the governmental decision process.

My purpose, rather, is to build upon our general knowledge of decision making to construct a framework showing how lobbying fits into, or plays a role in, the over-all governmental decision process. In decision-making theory, an almost universally accepted concept is that a decision maker must have access to ideas, arguments, information, and so forth, before these factors can figure in his decision. Another concept of decision making suggests, however, that mere accessibility is not enough. Every person has a set of predispositions that derive from a variety of sources, such as conditioned learning experiences, which includes the whole of a person's background as well as the internalized role constraints of his present situation, physiological needs, and inherited physical characteristics and capabilities. These personal predispositions are enduring rather than transitory and condition the behavior of people on a long-term basis, so that we say everyone has a personality. We recognize this when we apply to people such adjectives as liberal, conservative, manipulative, submissive, sociable, cynical, and so forth.

The important thing about predispositions, for our analysis, is that they provide a perceptual screen for each individual. Some stimuli are allowed to pass through the screen, while others are stopped. It is a well-known phenomenon that different people viewing the same event may perceive it quite differently. The chairmen of our respective political parties almost invariably arrive at a different interpretation of the factors creating the outcome of an election. Anyone reading Congressional hearings extensively must arrive at the conclusion that most members of Congress hear what they want to hear from a witness. The process by which selected stimuli are allowed to pass through the perceptual screen can be referred to as "receptivity."

Anyone wishing to influence the decision of a governmental official, then, must be concerned not only with getting the information to him but also with the problem of presenting it so that the decision maker will be receptive. The only effective communications are those which get through the perceptual screen. In fact, there is no other way to influence govern-mental decisions short of remaking the personalities of decision makers or replacing them with other persons. The lobbying process, then, is essentially a communication process, and the task of the lobbyist is to figure out how he can handle communications most effectively in order to get through to decision makers.

Although many lobbyists did not use communication terminology, it was clear that most conceived of their job as one of communication. As the interviews progressed, it seemed that lobbyist communications tended to fall in three categories: facts, arguments, and power. As merchants of information, lobbyists generally have a factual base for their message; especially they provide facts about how a contemplated action will affect the group represented. Because of the constraints of the relationship be-tween lobbyist and decision maker (to be discussed later), most lobbyists take particular pains never to present anything but accurate facts.

Lobbyists do not depend on facts alone; almost invariably the facts are accompanied by a set of arguments concerning the rightness, wisdom, or justice of the proposed action. Most lobbyists readily admit that these arguments usually present only one side of an issue, but they justify this on the ground that the decision maker knows the source and is likely to get arguments on the other side from opposing groups. Some lobbyists try to take a posture of objectivity by presenting arguments on both sides of the question, although generally they are also careful that the balance lie in their favor.

Much more difficult and subtle is the task of communicating power. While we recognize that for some officials re-election is not paramount, the majority of elective officials show great respect for power at the polls. In its rawest form, this power can be communicated by defeating an incum-bent and substituting a new official who, presumably, will act favorably toward the concerns of the group which put him over. Most lobby groups do not have this much power to throw around and, furthermore, it is a rather crude and expensive way to communicate, especially since some competing group or coalition is likely to press vigorously in opposition.

Most lobbyists try to communicate power without going to the trouble and expense of defeating someone at the polls. The accent is on subtlety, because an overt threat to defeat an official at the next election unless he "goes along" may serve only to stiffen his resistance. A forthright offer of campaign money to a cooperating decision maker might be used to smear the donor rather than accomplish its intended purpose. The much-publi-cized contribution to Senator Case of South Dakota from a natural gas lobbyist in early 1956 is an example. Even such a tactic as publicizing the voting records of incumbent members of Congress is looked upon as fool-hardy by many lobbyists and resented by many members. Lobbyists prefer to approach officials through constituents, stimulate letter writing, put on a public relations campaign, and collaborate with other groups, as more subtle devices for communicating power.

In addition to its threatening aspects, power can be used in a supportive or positive way. A legislator may be assured of enthusiastic support at the next election by a large membership group as a reward for promotion of a policy that the group wanted. Power has another facet too: it is not only a relationship about which information can be communicated, but it is also a strong factor influencing decision makers to keep open channels of communication to groups which hold power. Officials keep open channels of communication for other affective reasons also, such as good will, rapport, rewards for service or favors, and so forth, but political power is a factor they may ignore only at considerable peril.

The lobbyists in this sample were asked to evaluate a series of tactics and techniques for communicating with decision makers. These tactics can be divided into three broad categories for analytical purposes: (1) techniques for direct personal communication between the lobbyist and decision maker, (2) techniques for communication through intermediaries, and (3) techniques for keeping channels of communication open. Although these materials have not yet been exhaustively analyzed, the analysis is far enough along to make possible some general comparisons.

Direct Personal Communication

One assumption behind the practice of sending to the capital personal envoys of groups is that direct personal communication is more effective than written communication in gaining access and is more likely to reach the decision maker when he is in a receptive frame of mind.[6] The presence of a personal envoy at the capital normally tends to give one group a competitive advantage over another without an envoy. As a result, an ever-increasing number of groups have sent such envoys. Now, however, there are such a great number and variety of lobbyists competing for the limited time and attention of the decision makers that the Washington atmosphere has been characterized by some observers as filled with hustle and noise. One result of this competition is that lobbying resources are being diverted from direct communication toward communication through intermediaries who are believed to have better access. Indeed, there are many instances of successful lobbyists who have little or no direct contact with governmental decision makers. Seventy-five per cent of the lobbyists spent less than 10 per cent of their time calling on members of Congress and no more

[6]Groups also send personal envoys to perform liaison functions. Many groups are worried that they will be taken advantage of unless they have someone on the scene to check on governmental activities.

than another 10 per cent calling on staff assistants to decision makers.

Personal presentation of arguments. Despite this shift toward communication through intermediaries, lobbyists tend to believe that their most effective tactic is the personal presentation of their case to the office-holder, provided they can get in to see him or get him on the phone.[7] Out of the 101 lobbyists interviewed, 65 chose this technique as the one they prefer and generally follow. It is curious that lobbyists spend such a small part of their time calling on members of Congress or their staffs if this tactic is considered so effective. There are several reasons for this. Preparations for these presentations must be careful and thus consume some time in addition to all the other tasks of lobbyists. (About three-fourth of the lobbyists spend more than 40 per cent of their time in the office.) Another factor is that lobbying is only one of the responsibilities of most people who register. In addition to lobbying, they may be executives of their organization; act as a liaison between their organization and the executive department of government; carry on a law practice with a variety of clients, many of whom do not have legislative problems; and so forth. But perhaps the most important reason is that lobbyists must be careful not to "carry their pitcher to the well too often," as one Congressman put it. Most lobbyists perceive that they must save up their good will and access for a time when they want to see the decision maker about something really important. One lobbyist expressed it this way: "I figure I am doing them a favor by not inviting them out to dinner and by not calling on them until I really need something."

All the lobbyists were asked to rate the fourteen communication tactics discussed in this paper on a general scale running from 0 for not effective at all to 10 for very effective. These tactics were evaluated primarily as devices for communicating with legislators; however, several are also applicable to communications with decision makers in the executive branch. The scale was presented visually in this form: 0___1___2___3___4___5___ 6___7___8___9___10, and the techniques to be rated were listed underneath it. Fifty-eight of the lobbyists rated personal presentation of arguments at 10 (or very effective), and the mean score for the entire group was 8.43. . . . This technique rated higher than any other. When mean ratings are broken down by the type of organization the lobbyist represents, and then ranked . . . we discover that personal presentation of arguments is given first rank by all except the representatives of farm groups, church

---

[7]Because of heavy time pressures on officials, it is often necessary for the lobbyist to present his case to the staff assistant of the decision maker rather than to the decision maker himself. This is technically communication through an intermediary rather than direct communication; however, most assistants are very close to their bosses and, therefore, for the analytical purposes of this paper, no distinction will be made between communications to staff and communications to the decision maker personally.

and humanitarian groups, and foreign governments or firms, and even here arguments usually ranked very high.

The personal presentations discussed here are generally oral and incorporate both facts and arguments. Most members of Congress prefer that this statement be very brief and merely summarize the main points. Many lobbyists follow the practice of leaving a short written summary behind for future reference and thus save the decision maker, or his staff, the trouble of taking notes. Most people in Congress report that they prefer that personal presentations be informative, unbiased, clear, short, sincere, and unaccompanied by pressure. The threat implied in pressure is painful, and persons who use it will be shunned when they try to gain access in the future. Members of Congress are also skeptical of lobbyists who play the role of advocate without personal conviction about the arguments they present. Members frequently probe for personal conviction and drastically discount the presentations of those who are mere advocates. Lobby groups guard against this by "sidelining" a lobbyist who does not share a particular policy position with the group he represents.

Presenting research results. The lobbyists were also asked to rate the presentation of research results. Most of them conceived of this as an integral part of arguments and had difficulty evaluating it separately. On the other hand, some lobbyists made little effort to bolster their arguments with research, either because they felt that their problem was not amenable to research or because they felt the research would not be respected. The representatives of large labor organizations and large trade associations ranked research considerably below arguments. Farm representatives, on the other hand, ranked research above arguments. *Post hoc* reasoning suggests that large labor and trade have sufficient membership to rate tactics related to politics (collaboration with other groups, constituent contact, letters, etc.) above research. Farm representatives with large memberships also rate these tactics highly, but they still place research above arguments. There is a deep-seated respect for research in the farming industry, and it may be that this colored their response to this tactic.

If one breaks down these mean ratings by the relation of the lobbyist to his employer . . . one sees, interestingly, that legislative relations staff persons, who are generally in closer contact with Congress than those in other roles, place less than average emphasis on research. They place greater emphasis on collaboration, constituent contact, hearings, letters, and so forth. . . . Research has an over-all mean rating of 7.4, slightly lower than for arguments, but still higher than the rating for other techniques.

Testifying at hearings. In contrast with presentation of one's case to a single person, most lobbyists rated testifying at hearings somewhat lower. Only 24 gave it a rating of 10, and the mean for the entire group was 6.55. The rank orders . . . disclose that hearings are ranked up close to arguments and research by most groups. They are about on a par with collaboration and constituent contact. . . . Interestingly, the mean rating of hearings by corporations was only 4.7, lower than that of any other group; yet the rank order was 3 (above all other techniques except arguments and research), so one might surmise that corporation representatives have a generally more pessimistic view of most of the remaining techniques than do the people representing other kinds of organization.

Since hearings are formal procedures available to nearly anyone wanting to get his point of view before Congress and require only a single presentation, why is it that they are not the clearly preferred technique? Most lobbyists perceive that members of Congress give sporadic attention, at best, to hearing testimony. Furthermore, they are aware that many members of committees have already made up their minds before the hearings begin and there is little the lobbyist can say that will influence them. Another factor is that many hearings are held when only one member of the committee is present, to say nothing of the absence from hearings of all the other members of the House who are not on the committee. Although printed hearing records are available to members of Congress (also to the public), the average member does not have the time to read them. Despite the limitations of this means of communication, most lobbyists dare not forego an invitation to go on record favoring or opposing a particular course of action. There is always the possibility that some decision maker will read their testimony; it is an opportunity for some free publicity; and it is a useful way for the lobbyist to demonstrate to the membership that he is earning his salary. In other words, most lobbyists feel they are expected to testify, or have someone from their group testify, and therefore they nearly always do.

Communication Through Intermediaries

Although lobbying connotes personal representation before government, a far-reaching effort to influence policy making must include communication with decision makers through intermediaries. The intermediaries chosen almost invariably have some special relationship to the decision maker, either a constituent relationship or a close personal relationship. Constituents can be urged to communicate with government in two basic ways. Voting is an indirect but very effective medium of communication. Even if an endorsed candidate does not win, a strong showing of votes indicates the desires and power potential or a large bloc of the incumbent's constituents. The second type of communication is the conventional written or oral message transmitted from the citizen to people in government. Communications through intermediaries are, like the personal presentations of the lobbyist, also designed to communicate facts, arguments, and power. They are especially instrumental in communicating power.

Contact by constituent and friend. If the lobbyist believes that he will have difficulty getting an appointment with an elected official, or that the official will listen with a closed ear, he may attempt to communicate through a constituent whom he thinks the official respects. The constituent may be asked to phone the officeholder and set up an appointment for the lobbyist or he may be asked to present the case himself. Sometimes the constituent hastens to Washington and spends a few days calling on his representatives.[9]

The constituent is generally preferred over other intermediaries such as close friends of the decision maker. This is because many lobbyists feel the power relationship between constituent and officeholder more adequately ensures receptiveness to the communication. . . . The representatives of large membership groups with potential political power (big labor, farm, big trade, church and humanitarian) give constituent contact a much higher rating than friend contact; whereas the representatives of other groups give them more equal ratings. It is reflected . . . where the highest ratings for constituent contact are given by legislative relations people whose jobs take them into closest contact with Congress. The over-all picture is . . . where we see that 24 lobbyists gave a rating of 10 to contact by a constituent, whereas only 5 rated contact by a friend that highly. The mean rating for contact by a constituent was 5.9, and for a friend it was only 3.76. The difference in evaluation introduced by the political-power variable is also reflected in the greater variance shown for the constituent contact rating than for the friend contact rating.

Letter and telegram campaigns. A time-honored lobbying technique is the stimulation of a mass letter-writing and telegram campaign from constituents to their representatives. Most people in Congress are skilled at spotting form letters or telegrams which are inspired by some organization. They are likely to ignore or discount such a campaign on the ground that it does not accurately represent sentiment in the constituency; on the other hand, if the letters come in a deluge, they must pay attention because of the political weight they represent. Some members may move to counteract the campaign by sending out a mailing to the constituents in an attempt to inform them about the member's position, or they may request an opposing organization to turn out an equal or greater number of letters on the other side, leaving the representative free to vote as he chooses. Lobbyists are aware of these barriers to letters, and the mass campaign is not as

[9]It should also be recognized that constituents are speaking on their own behalves as well as acting as intermediaries between lobbyist and decision maker; thus the designation of communications from constituents as communications through an intermediary is true only from the perspective of the professional lobbyist. In practice, lobbyist and constituent frequently make joint calls on decision makers.

widely used as it once was. Those who do use a letter or telegram campaign are generally careful to instruct their people to write each communication individually, speaking their personal thoughts on the subject. The lobbyist's calculation is that the representative will heed such a communication as a true reflection of sentiment.

There was a good deal of variation in the way lobbyists evaluated letter campaigns. . . . 20 gave it a 0 and 7 gave it a 10. Big labor and big farm lobbyists gave it higher rankings than other lobbyists did. . . . This suggests that organizations with a mass membership enabling them to turn out thousands of letters are more likely to believe that the tactic is effective. Corporation representatives and lobbyists for foreign governments or firms, with no mass membership behind them, ranked letters below the average. . . . Those more intimately associated with a given organization (officers and staff) tended to rank letters higher than those in a more peripheral relationship (lawyers, "PR" men, etc.).

Public relations campaigns. A very expensive and indirect method of communication is the public relations campaign. The supposition is that if enough people favor the viewpoint of the organization sponsoring the campaign, this viewpoint, and the power behind it, will be communicated in various ways to Congress and the Administration. It is also hoped that the campaign will have some long-range effects on the voting behavior of the public and thus find policy expression through the selection of governmental decision makers. Since the effects of a PR campaign are so diffuse and delayed, they are extraordinarily difficult to measure. This is reflected in the wide variance in the lobbyists' ratings: 17 gave it a rating of 10 and 21 gave it a rating of 0. . . .

The over-all mean rating for PR campaigns was 5.55, slightly higher than for letter campaigns, yet the pattern of response was very similar to that for letter campaigns. Mass-membership farm and labor lobbyists gave it the highest ratings, while church and humanitarian and foreign government or firm lobbyists gave it the lowest. Lawyers gave it a lower rating than did those closely tied into an organization, while officers of organizations gave it the highest rating. It is interesting that some lobbyists felt that the tactic had utility even though they were not sure their message was getting through to the public, not to mention getting from the public back to the decision makers. They reasoned that the decision makers are quite likely to conclude that the campaign is very persuasive and convincing many people how they should vote. Therefore, the decision maker may possibly alter his behavior in the desired way in anticipation of the reaction from his constituents, without receiving communication from many of them.

Publicizing voting records. Like the public relations campaign, the publicizing of voting records is a device for stimulating communications from the people to their representatives. (Both tactics are also used to generate political power, which has utility for keeping open channels of communication to decision makers.) Organizations which have considerable power at the polls (labor, farm, and large citizens' organizations) believe that the method is moderately efficacious . . . while lobbyists from nearly all the other groups rate the method as almost worthless. In fact, many lobbyists actually view the method as dangerous, since a member of Congress whose voting record has been reported unfavorably is likely to resent it and may close the door to them in the future. Many lobbyists and members of Congress felt that voting records are misleading, because they do not accurately assess the over-all performance of a member.

Opening Communication Channels

We noted above that it was just as important to the lobbyist to keep his channels of communication to decision makers open as it was to transmit the communications themselves. Lobbyists give a lot of attention to this problem and guide their behavior so as to create and maintain the open channel. There is a recognized *quid pro quo* relationship between lobbyist and decision maker. The lobbyist can provide information and perform certain chores that the decision maker desires. Several of the people in Congress that I interviewed reported that they lined up lobby groups as reinforcements to strengthen their side in policy battles. This practice is so prevalent that it is difficult to discover who is using whom in most instances. The *quid pro quo* for providing services that the decision maker wants is that he will lend a sympathetic ear when the lobbyist has a problem he wants to present. Mutual confidence is the lubrication which ensures the smooth working of this relationship. The official decision maker has the upper hand, however, in that he alone has the power to pass out the policy rewards that the lobbyist wants and can turn to many alternative sources for the services he wants. Access and a confidential relationship with officials are so crucial to the task of the lobbyist that most astute lobbyists would not consider jeopardizing them in any way. Many decision makers use their superior position to guide their relationships with lobbyists and will specify the conditions under which lobbyists are welcome. If the lobbyist does not conform to these expectations, the decision maker will discard him and turn to someone on whom he can depend. Interestingly, many lobbyists welcome these prescriptions for access because they give structure to a highly unstructured role and give them security in job performance.

One specific result of this relationship is that very little inaccurate information is presented by lobbyists to public officials. The harried decision maker frequently utilizes information provided by lobbyists, sometimes without double-checking, in speeches or other public communications. If the information should later prove to be false, or biased to the point of serious distortion, the decision maker is publicly embarassed and is likely to retaliate by cutting off further access sought by the delinquent lobbyist. Another facet of this relationship is that lobbyists generally are scrupulously careful not to disclose things which are told to them in confidence by a decision maker; the cost of disclosure would be the cutting off of access.

Entertaining and parties. One of the popular conceptions of the lobbying process is that most lobbyists depend on entertainment and parties to keep open the channels of communication to decision makers. The assumption here is that the official will be grateful for the favor and, therefore, will be receptive to the communications of the lobbyist. Almost the reverse is true. Officials feel they must attend a certain number of "required" social events and this, coupled with other responsibilities, places them under such time pressure that an evening spent at home with the family seems like a gift. Under such conditions, an invitation by a lobbyist to "do the town" is anything but welcome. Lobbyists are aware that entertainment is an imposition, and it is used very little as a device to keep the channels of communication open.

Nearly all the lobbyists rated both techniques very low. . . . Forty-seven gave a rating of 0 to entertainment, and the mean for the group was 1.59. Interestingly, officers of organizations, who generally have more prestige than the average lobbyist and a less restricted expense account, gave entertainment a higher rating than did those in other roles, but even here the mean was only 2.8. . . . Giving a party was felt to have even less utility; 56 rated it 0 and the mean was only 1.24. Only foreign governments or firms and church and humanitarian representatives ranked it much above next to the last place. . . .

Direct bribery. Contrary to another popular conception, lobbyists have no faith whatsoever in bribery as a device for keeping channels open. Only one lobbyist rated bribery any higher than 0 and he did so with the comment, "If this assumes that the member of Congress is bribable, in that case I'd say 10. There is no surer way to get him to come along with your point of view." But even he was aware that nearly all members of Congress are not open to bribes. A few lobbyists claimed to know of bribes that had been passed, but in every instance their knowledge was second- or third-hand. One Congressman reported that a bribe had been offered him in the guise of a campaign contribution, but, as a result, he reported it to the Justice Department and voted against the lobbyist.

Most lobbyists recognize that the method is not effective and will not have anything to do with it.[10] Most believed that nearly all members of Congress are unbribable. Also, most viewed it as a dangerous gamble, since it could well turn a member of Congress against the donor instead of producing the desired good will. An official whose ideological rudder is so vacillating that he can be bribed can also be bribed by the other side and does not constitute a very safe investment. Another controlling factor here, according to respondents, is that keeping a bribe secret is an exceedingly difficult task in a "rumor factory" like Washington.

Contributing political money and campaign work. Since nearly all elected officials have a profound respect for political power, the lobbyist who represents a group with power at the polls finds there is a distinct advantage in keeping channels of communication open to these officials. The tactics of publicizing voting records and conducting public relations campaigns, discussed above, have some utility in producing political power. But what do lobbyists think of direct political actions, such as having members of their groups contribute political money or do volunteer work in the campaign? Both tactics were generally rated quite low, but campaign work, with a mean of 2.28, usually was ranked higher than political money (mean 1.88). The higher mean for campaign work can be traced, in part, to the higher rating given to this tactic than to money by the representatives of small labor organizations. . . .

Collaboration with other groups. The tactic of collaborating with other groups in planning strategy and making presentations is difficult to categorize, since it has aspects of direct communication, communication through intermediaries, and keeping communication channels open. The tactic is generally highly prized (over-all mean of 6.16), although there was considerable variance in the ratings. . . . Those whose lobbyist roles are closest to a given organization (executive, officer, staff) rate it higher than do lawyers and Washington representatives who generally represent more than one group. In fact, full-time legislative relations persons give it the highest ranking, even above presentation of arguments.

Several factors enter into an evaluation of collaboration. From the lobbyist point of view, it distributes the work load so that it is possible to communicate with more people on more issues. This is especially helpful for those groups with a wide range of policy interests. Lobbyists with common interests meet regularly to discuss strategy and exchange information. Not only does collaboration increase the volume and skill of communication, but it also communicates the enhanced power, in terms of numbers of

[10]It should be noted that some use is made of small gifts and favors by lobbyists; these are given more to the staffs of decision makers than to decision makers themselves, because staff members also have considerable control over access. It is very difficult conceptually to draw firm lines between bribes, campaign contributions, gifts, and favors. Rather than explore such a conceptual tangle in this paper, suffice it to say that the remarks in this section refer primarily to direct bribery.

committed persons, that lies behind a policy position. The member of Congress also welcomes joint presentations, because it means a saving of work and tension for him. Congress spends endless hours resolving controversies, and it is a welcome relief to have a controversy settled before it reaches that body.[11] Legislators are so relieved not to have to take a position favoring one group over another that any proposal which carries the backing of most potentially antagonistic groups will almost always be approved.

Summary

The most adequate explanation of the impact of the lobbying process on governmental decision making would come from a detailed examination of all the influences or pressures producing the behavior of decision makers. The social scientist is not equipped conceptually or methodologically at this stage to handle such a research problem. On the other hand, he can make some headway in analyzing the lobbying process by viewing it as a communication process. Communication is not necessarily complete when stimuli have been presented by a lobbyist; he must also attempt to gauge the receptivity of the decision maker and, hopefully, get the message through to him. A communication model does not explain all the variables involved in any given decision, but it does include all the variables involved in the lobbying process. The lobbyist has finished his job when he has communicated in the most effective way possible. He cannot control the workings of the decision maker's mind unless he can remake his personality or, alternatively, get him thrown out of office and replaced by another person. Not only does a communication model encompass the lobby process, but it is also the simplest explanation which accounts for the known evidence.

In general, lobbyists favor face-to-face conversations for the communication of facts and the arguments which support them. However, competition for the limited attention of decision makers in recent years has forced lobbyists more and more to seek access through intermediaries, especially the constituents of elected officials who have a power relationship to the decision maker. In order to ensure receptivity, lobbyists also attempt in other ways to communicate subtly the political power behind their groups. Preservation of open communication channels to decision makers is of such prime importance to lobbyists that the possible cutting off of access can be used as a sanction forcing lobbyists to behave in ways that the decision makers find desirable.

[11]Corroborating evidence from Vermont is reported in Oliver Garceau and Corinne Silverman, "A Pressure Group and the Pressured," *American Political Science Review,* Vol. 48, 1954, pp. 672-691.

Lobbyists:
The Wasted
Profession

Heinz Eulau

What would politics in America be like without lobbies and lobbyists? A silly and fanciful question, the realist will say. Why not take for granted what is so self-evident? What is to be gained from being absurd? Lobbies are as obviously part of the political landscape as parties are. No parties, no politics; no lobbies, no politics.

Of course. American politics, as we know it, could probably not function without lobbies. The tricky item is "as we know it." But just what do we know about lobbying? . . . Yet most talk about politics ends up just there: American politics is inconceivable without interest groups, and interest groups are inconceivable without lobbying. Without lobbying, interest groups could not perform the function of interest articulation that is required for the maintenance of the American political system as we know it—a tautological discovery. . . .

●   ●   ●

These reflections are occasioned by the publication . . . of *The Washington Lobbyists.*[1] Before the publication of this book, information on lobbying came largely from three sources: the not altogether unprejudiced investigations of Congress,[2] the not altogether dispassionate revelations of journalists,[3] and the not altogether coherent studies of political scientists.[4] . . .

What recommends Milbrath's book as a peg for cerebration beyond its

[1]Lester W. Milbrath, *The Washington Lobbyists,* Chicago, Rand McNally & Company, 1963, 431 pp., $6.

[2]See *Final Report,* U. S. Senate, Special Committee to Investigate Political Activities, Lobbying and Campaign Contributions, Government Printing Office, May 31, 1957. This report of the McClellan Committee can serve as a guide to past congressional investigations of lobbying.

[3]Among the best known are Kenneth G. Crawford, *The Pressure Boys: The Inside Story of Lobbying in America,* New York, Messner, 1939, and Karl Schriftgiesser, *The Lobbyists: The Art and Business of Influencing Lawmakers,* Boston, Little, Brown, 1951.

[4]The best and fullest bibliography may be found in Milbrath, *op. cit.,* pp. 399-421. A critical survey is Samuel J. Eldersveld, "American Interest Groups: A Survey of Research and Some Implications for Theory and Method," in Henry W. Ehrmann, editor, *Interest Groups on Four Continents,* Pittsburgh, University of Pittsburgh Press, 1958, pp. 173-196.

SOURCE: From Heinz Eulau, "Lobbyists: The Wasted Profession," *The Public Opinion Quarterly,* XXVIII (Spring 1964), 27-38. Reprinted by permission.

own limits is that it points up the limitations of the traditional studies of interest-group politics. These studies, descriptive rather than systematically explanatory or theoretical, and focused on institutions or organizations rather than on individual actors, commonly take the form of case studies— sometimes of a particular group or set of groups in a particular political system or culture, sometimes of a particular decision or cluster of decisions, and sometimes of group activity in general in a particular system.[5] Milbrath's book represents, therefore, a new departure. Once again, as it was first in the study of electoral politics and more recently in the study of legislative politics, the sample survey turns out to be an innovating tool in the study of a political phenomenon.

The Washington Lobbyists is, above all, a book about lobbyists—who they are, whom they represent, how they work, what they seek, and how they try to influence the governmental decision-making process. To find these things out, Milbrath interviewed 101 lobbyists who came from a random sample of 114 lobbyists drawn from the list of 614 persons with a Washington address who had registered during the first two quarters of 1956 under the Federal Regulation of Lobbying Act of 1946. In addition, to assess the evidence about lobbying provided by the lobbyists themselves and to penetrate somewhat more fully the interactional process of lobbying, interviews were conducted with thirty-eight "significant others" in Congress—Senators, Representatives, chiefs of committee staffs, and staff assistants. The material provided by these interviews represents the richest source of information now available about lobbying and lobbyists.

•   •   •

Milbrath also attempts a new theoretical departure in the study of what has conventionally been called "pressure politics"—whether a successful departure I will postpone for later discussion. The point to be made here simply is that in self-consciously theorizing about the lobbying process, Milbrath at least *tries* not to commit the *faux pas* of taking for granted whatever is to be discovered and tested. This, it seems to me, has been the error of many who have written on group politics, from Arthur F. Bentley to E. E. Schattschneider.[6] The result of the error has been lack of a cumulative research tradition. Bentley took a stance toward the group process with which nobody seemed to be able to disagree, precisely because it seemed so realistic, yet which was insufficient to generate careful, microscopic research that could disprove or support his propositions. For to say,

[5]I am indebted in this connection to an unpublished working paper on pressure groups by Professor John C. Wahlke of the State University of New York at Buffalo, who first made me aware of the flaws of the literature on interest groups.

[6]Arthur F. Bentley, *The Process of Government,* Chicago, University of Chicago Press, 1908; E. E. Schattschneider, *The Semi-sovereign People,* New York, Holt, Rinehart & Winston, 1961.

as Bentley did, that politics is nothing more and nothing less than the activities and relationships of social groups, whose unending interactions constitute the political order, represents a realism that only points to a seamless web. The metaphor is mine, not Bentley's, but I think it symbolizes the approach that has been dominant ever since. If one makes the assumption—whether explicitly or implicitly—of the social process as a seamless web, research, if any, is not likely to lead anywhere.

In fact, when, in the twenties and early thirties, scholars began to pay empirical attention to interest-group politics, their descriptive case studies or global generalizations did not acknowledge any indebtedness to Bentley, and there is no internal evidence in their writings that they were aware of Bentley's sometimes subtle theoretical formulations.[7] Interest groups and their activities were simply taken for granted.

When, in due time, the attempt at closing the gap was made—for example by Herring in more or less impressionistic fashion, or by Bailey in the form of an empirical case study—the political process appears yet again as a seamless web. Herring defined the policy-making process as "a working union of interests, ideas, institutions, and individuals."[8] Bailey, in what I believe is still the best case study of legislative policy making, tried to bring order out of the chaos of Herring's four interacting I's in a particular historical context in relation to a particular economic issue.[9] But his "attempt to make a vector analysis of legislative policy-making"—the vectors presumably being the four I's—did not really come off. Vector analysis, whatever it was meant to mean, yielded to minute description and suggestive interpretation. No hypotheses were formulated about just how the four I's interact, and the solution of the problem was left to the reader's imagination. . . .

●   ●   ●

. . . It is pertinent to compare the approach of the muckrakers, much preoccupied with interest groups, with that of the group theorists, for their modes of analysis, in spite of different predispositions, are much alike. The muckraking view (which also influenced a good deal of the early literature in political science) was that "special interests" are a threat to democracy and the "public interest." The view of the "realistic" group

---

[7] I have in mind studies such as Peter H. Odegard, *Pressure Politics: The Story of the Antisaloon League,* Boulder, University of Colorado Press, 1928; E. Pendleton Herring, *Group Representation before Congress,* Baltimore, The John Hopkins University Press, 1929; Harwood L. Childs, *Labor and Capital in National Politics,* Columbus, Ohio State University Press, 1930; or E. E. Schattschneider, *Politics, Pressures and the Tariff,* New York, Prentice-Hall, 1935.

[8] E. Pendleton Herring, *The Politics of Democracy,* New York, Rinehart, 1940, p. 421.

[9] Stephen K. Bailey, *Congress Makes a Law: The Story behind the Employment Act of 1946,* New York, Columbia University Press, 1950, p. x.

theorists was that interest groups are legitimate channels of private demand making on government, and that "pressure," so-called, is a "natural" phenomenon. The "public interest," therefore, can never be more, or less, than the product, however computed—through aggregation, combat, or compromise—of private pressures as potent as the "forces" that fascinated a Newton. Truman had called a halt to this analogical naïveté:

> The politician-legislator is not equivalent to the steel ball in a pinball game, bumping passively from post to post down an inclined plane. He is a human being involved in a variety of relationships with other human beings. In his role as legislator his accessibility to various groups is affected by the whole series of relationships that define him as a person.[15]

Interestingly, Truman's injunction paid off in the study of legislative politics, though not in the study of interest-group politics. As behavioral research penetrated the study of legislative institutions by studying legislators, it became increasingly clear that he was right. Garceau and Silverman,[16] Matthews,[17] and Wahlke and his associates[18] came to disenchant the proponents of the view that the universe of politics is a multiverse of quasi-mechanical forces.

Milbrath's interviews with lobbyists and with some of the targets of their activities—Congressmen and congressional staffers—open up new theoretical possibilities. I am by no means satisfied that his formulations do his material justice. I am saying only that his theorizing is in the right direction, because, on reading what lobbyists and others told him and what he did statistically with what they told him, one gets a more human view of the lobbying process than the mechanical metaphor of "pressure" can ever possibly convey. We are back, again, in the world of *social* relations, out of a world of mechanical relations. Lobbyists no longer appear to be the kind of superman—shady or not—that the image of power associated with the mechanical model seemed to impart. And the world of social relations, as Einstein once suggested, is much more difficult to study than the world of physical relations.

To handle the relations in which he is interested—between lobbyists and their clienteles, between lobbyists and officials, between lobbyists and lobbyists—Milbrath introduces a model of government as a communication system. Lobbying conceived as communication seems to meet the requirements of a science that purports to explain human behavior. Never-

[15]Truman, *The Governmental Process*, pp. 332-333.

[16]Oliver Garceau and Corinne Silverman, "A Pressure Group and the Pressured: A Case Report," *American Political Science Review*, Vol. 48, September 1954, pp. 672-691.

[17]Donald R. Matthews, *U. S. Senators and Their World*, Chapel Hill, University of North Carolina Press, 1960, pp. 176-196.

[18]John C. Wahlke, Heinz Eulau, William Buchanan, and LeRoy C. Ferguson, *The Legislative System: Explorations in Legislative Behavior*, New York, Wiley, 1962, pp. 311-342.

theless, I do not find the communication model very persuasive as a tool
for explaining lobbying. If the mechanical model of "pressure politics"
is much too strong to accommodate the realities of lobbying, the communication model is too weak. This is not to say that the communication model
does not make for more researchable questions than the mechanical model,
nor that it does not "fit" at least some aspects of interest-group politics.
It seems to be "weak" in the sense that it does not tell us much more than
what the data, in their stark nakedness and unclothed by conceptual garment, can tell us. In fact, as I have suggested already, I find the raw data
more palatable than the uses to which they were put.

"Communication" is so built into all social relations that a communication model does not really explain a highly specific social process like
lobbying. In the end, all social relations are communication: learning is
communication, praying is communication, loving is communication, selling is communication. And lobbying is communication. Just because lobbying, like everything else human beings do, involves communication (in the
concrete sense of exchanging verbal or nonverbal symbols whose meaning
is mutually understood), it does not follow that a model of communication
is the best tool to explain lobbying, as it does not follow that, because
selling involves communication, a communication model contributes much
to explaining what goes on in the market place.

•   •   •

. . . Three things should be pointed out. First, Milbrath overstates his
case when he writes: "Communication is the only means of influencing or
changing a perception; the lobbying process, therefore, is totally a communication process" (p. 185). Second, the theoretical underpinnings presumably derived from communication theory are not utilized very extensively in the *analysis* of the research findings. They are used for purposes
of global interpretation, when convenient, rather than for specific explanation. And, third, the analysis of the data is permeated by concepts
derived, more or less explicitly, from other theoretical formulations. In
fact, concepts derived from role analysis and personality theory are more
prominent in the data analysis than concepts derived from communication
theory. . . .

If lobbying as a political process was Milbrath's central concern, I think
he could have made better use of his data by addressing himself at the
very outset, rather than at the end of his book, to the critical problems of
the impact of lobbying on governmental decisions. . . .

How does Milbrath deal with the questions that arise in this connection?
First of all, he deals with them not in terms of the roles and functions of
lobbyists, but in terms of the responses that are given by the recipients of
lobby communications. In other words, the focus of evidence shifts from

lobbying to its context, and it is the context that circumscribes the lobbying function. One would have expected that the proof of influence or lack of it would consist in demonstrating the degree to which lobbying as a political activity affects the context. For, presumably, without lobbying the context would be different. Let me illustrate this by way of some propositions that I derive from Milbrath's discussion. The effectiveness of lobbying varies with (1) the decision maker's degree of freedom from those expectations of his constituents that define his role; (2) the decision maker's personal convictions about an issue; (3) the degree of conformity that a legislative working majority can achieve through discipline or compromise; (4) the degree of need a decision maker has for information about some problem; (5) the degree to which informal relations within the decision-making group make for mutual respect and trust (6) the degree to which decision makers rely for advice on staff assistants. If these hypotheses are valid, it appears that there is relatively little room for lobbying to be effective. The task of research would be to measure, if measurement were possible, the contribution lobbying makes to whatever variance in decision-making behavior is yet to be accounted for.

What do we learn about the contribution that lobbying makes? Here the research focus shifts back to the lobbyists themselves, who were asked how often their views had been solicited. We learn that "no more than 10 per cent of the lobbyists achieve this [i.e. solicitation of their views] with even one official; only 9 per cent are consulted frequently on a wide range of policy issues. There is no evidence . . . that lobbying messages are widely sought after by decision-makers" (p. 340). And so it goes. Milbrath suggests that lobbyists "do have a kind of nuisance impact," and there are situations—as when legislation is specialized and affects only a small segment of the population—in which lobbyists may be more effective. But "on broad political issues commanding considerable public attention, the major determinant is the desire of the public. Lobbyists can do very little to affect the outcome, though they may influence the details of a bill or the specific language of small sections" (p. 343). Finally, Milbrath rejects the contention that lobbyists are most influential in closely contested decisions. He feels that it is rather superficial to give lobbyists credit for the outcome if they have switched a few votes in a close contest: "It ignores all the factors that originally made the contest close, the influences that created the firm stands of the persons lined up on both sides of the issue" (p. 345). This conclusion is surprising indeed. For it appears that lobbyists cannot even be credited with a small contribution to the total variance in decision making. One wonders what the shouting was all about.

Yet, having come to these conclusions, Milbrath does not bury the corpse. Instead, he addresses himself to something he calls "the balance of power in lobbying." And he comes up with the old mechanistic model:

An important factor attenuating the impact of lobbying on governmental decisions is the fact that nearly every vigorous push in one direction stimulates an
opponent or coalition of opponents to push in the opposite direction. This
natural self-balancing factor comes into play so often that it almost amounts to
a law [p. 345].

I find it rather incredible, after all that has been said about the contribution lobbying makes, that presumably lobbying tends toward zero, except on details, on specialized matters, or where it involves only a small
clientele. . . .

. . . The point is that I do not find any indication of what the communication model contributes to our understanding of lobby impact on decision
making, and I miss any reference to the model in this central matter. It is
as if all that has been presented in the bulk of the book is for naught.
There we learned about the relative effectiveness of direct and indirect
communication tactics, about attempts to locate key people, about the
uses of research, about hearings and testimony, about collaborative relations between lobbyists and decision makers, about the use of intermediaries such as constituents or friends, about lobby-inspired letter and
telegram campaigns, about publicizing voting records, and so on. Why,
one wonders, do interest groups expend so much time, money, and effort
to influence the decision-making process if the payoff of lobbying is so
minimal?

Milbrath's answer is largely a *non sequitur.* He invokes Eckstein, who,
in the postscript of his fine study of the British Medical Association, had
raised certain questions of a "structural-functional" sort. Eckstein's questions referred to pressure groups, but Milbrath considers them relevant to
lobbies. Eckstein had asked "What contributions do pressure groups make
to the political system as a whole, and do these contributions tend to make
the system more or less viable (stable, effective)? Are their consequences
'dysfunctional' or 'eufunctional' for the larger systems in which they 'operate?"[20]

•   •   •

. . . Milbrath does not ask: If lobbies are not quite what they are made
out to be, and the evidence suggests they are not, what alternate structures
are there for performing the functions that lobbying presumably performs?
Only the discovery of functionally equivalent, though structurally different, units of action is likely to satisfy our thirst for "explanation." I
am not sure if the structural-functional approach makes for explanation,
as explanation is commonly understood in science. But it surely makes for

[20]Harry Eckstein, *Pressure Group Politics: The Case of The British Medical Association,*
Stanford, Calif., Stanford University Press, 1960, p. 152.

some interesting and possibly fruitful research questions. At least it does not take for granted whatever it is that should be discovered. . . .

Some Effects
of Interest Group
Strength
in State Politics

Lewis A. Froman, Jr.

The literature on interest groups is, by and large, either heavily abstract and theoretical or highly concrete and descriptive. There are, on the one hand, several attempts to provide a theoretical framework for the study of interest groups, the major foci being either "the group basis of politics"[1] or "mass society."[2] On the other hand are numerous case-studies which describe in some detail, either for a particular policy[3] or for a particular interest group,[4] relevant political activities which lead to inferred conclusions about the impact that such groups have on the issue or issues. What we lack, and what is needed to raise the study of interest groups to the level of empirically-based generalization, are studies which collect data and generalize about interest groups using multiple units of analysis.

●   ●   ●

[1]See, for example, David B. Truman, *The Governmental Process* (New York: Knopf, 1951), Chapters 2 and 3; Earl Latham, *The Group Basis of Politics* (Ithaca: Cornell University Press, 1952), Chapter 1; E. E. Schattschneider, *The Semisovereign People* (New York: Holt, Rinehart & Winston, 1960); and Harmon Zeigler, *Interest Groups in American Society* (Englewood Cliffs: Prentice-Hall, 1964), Chapters 1-3. There is also a voluminous journal literature discussing the pros and cons of "the group approach." See, for example, Stanley Rothman, "Systematic Political Theory: Observations on the Group Approach," [*American Political Science*] *Review,* 54 (March, 1960), 14-33.

[2]See William Kornhauser, *The Politics of Mass Society* (New York: Free Press, 1959).

[3]See Raymond A. Bauer, Ithiel de Sola Pool, and Lewis Anthony Dexter, *American Business And Public Policy* (New York: Atherton, 1963) for a policy case study which also develops very interesting and useful theory.

[4]See R. Joseph Monsen, Jr., and Mark W. Cannon, *The Makers of Public Policy* (New York: McGraw-Hill, 1965) for a number of discussions of particular interest groups and their activities.

SOURCE: Lewis A. Froman, Jr., "Some Effects of Interest Group Strength in State Politics," *American Political Science Review,* LX (December 1966), 952-962. Reprinted by permission.

I think there are two major reasons why the literature on interest groups lacks a comparative base. First, many of the concepts which are employed in theories about interest groups are difficult to operationalize for data collection. Such concepts as "cohesion," "access," "resources," etc., represent complex phenomena and would involve a good deal of effort to apply rigorously and empirically. Take, for example, the interesting proposition that, *ceteris paribus,* "interest groups with high cohesion are more effective than interest groups with low cohesion." Clearly this is an important assertion which attempts to explain why some interest groups may have more influence than others. How such a proposition might be tested is, unfortunately, also clear. Simply take a sample of interest groups, devise measures of group cohesion and political effectiveness, collect the data on both measures, and see whether the proposition is confirmed or invalidated.

Second, it is usually very difficult and expensive to collect data on a wide variety of groups which might then be used for purposes of generalization. Such data is not generally available, and what is available is often incomplete, inaccurate, or both. Even to collect such relatively simple data as group size often presents serious problems in compiling membership lists, deciding who is a member and who isn't, perhaps identifying those who feel some allegiance to the group but who may participate in the activities of the group only minimally, and other equally knotty problems. To attempt to determine, across groups, what difference a particular independent variable (such as cohesion, group size, leadership ability, etc.) may have in the distribution of political outcomes raises formidable data problems indeed.

This paper will suggest how a comparative base for generalization about the activity of interest groups may be developed. I will attempt to answer the question: Do political systems that vary in the strength of their interest groups also vary in a systematic way with regard to certain structural and output variables within their respective political systems? That is, can we explain certain differences in political systems by knowing something about the strength of interest groups within the system? The data to be employed will be for forty-eight state governments within the United States.[5] It is by now a truism to assert that states may provide a convenient laboratory to test certain propositions about politics. The number of states, the fact that they are all part of a larger political system (and hence share many things in common) while at the same time providing a certain amount of diversity make the states a useful data source in which to generalize and test political hypotheses.

---

[5]Alaska and Hawaii are excluded.

The First Set of Dependent Variables

Political scientists have long been interested in questions regarding constitutions and constitution-making. . . .

What will concern us here is how state constitutions differ in certain respects from one another, and how these differences might be explained. There are, of course, a large number of possible differences in state constitutions. State constitutions may vary, for example, in the kinds of governments they establish (unicameral vs. bicameral legislatures, a large number of elected executive officials vs. a large number of appointed officials, elected vs. appointed judiciaries, etc.). State constitutions may also vary in the detail in which they cover various aspects of government, and in the discretion which they give to public officials to carry out certain functions. They may also vary in the specific content which they give to questions of public policy (labor practices, regulation of utilities, transportation problems, etc.).

The differences among state constitutions which are of most interest to us here have to do with how specific and comprehensive they are, how easy or difficult they are to amend, how often proposals are made to amend the constitution, and how often the respective constitutions are in fact changed. More specifically, there are four dependent variables in which we will be primarily interested.[6]

1. *Length of Constitution.* State constitutions vary greatly in their length. We are not, however, interested in length of constitutions in and of itself but rather assume that the longer the constitution the greater the range of activity it attempts to cover and the more specific and detailed it is in its provisions. Length of constitution, then, will be used as an indirect measure of extent of coverage and specificity.

2. *Number of Amendments Proposed.* What we are interested in here is the number of official proposals which have been made to amend the respective state constitutions. The measure to be employed will control for age of constitution by taking the number of proposed changes for each state and dividing by the number of years the constitution has been operative.

3. *Number of Amendments Adopted.* This measure is similar to the previous one except that amendments actually adopted rather than simply proposed is the unit employed. Age of constitution is again appropriately controlled.

4. *Percentage of Amendments Adopted.* This is the ratio of amendments

[6]Data from *The Book of the States,* 1964-1965 (Chicago: The Council of State Governments, 1964), pp. 12-15.

adopted to amendments proposed for each state and is expressed in a simple percentage.

TABLE 1.   Median and Range for States on the Four Dependent Variables

	Median	Range
Length of Constitution (No. of words)	15,000	4,840—227,000
Number of Amendments Proposed Per Year	1.35	.31—12.63
Number of Amendments Adopted Per Year	.65	.10—9.98
Percentage of Amendments Adopted	58%	23%—94%

Source: *The Book of the States, 1964-1965* (Chicago: The Council of State Governments, 1964), p. 12.

Table 1 gives some indication of how the states vary on these four measures.

As can be seen from Table 1, there is a wide diversity among states with respect to these four variables. Now, assuming that constitutions are one of the mechanisms through which advantages and disadvantages are distributed in a political system, we would expect that differences in length of constitutions and the frequency with which they are amended would help us to understand, in some measure, how responsive states are to demands made by groups within the political system.

The Independent Variable

The role of interest groups in political systems is an extremely important, and hotly contested, open question. At one level we can talk of the functions which most interest groups, or interest groups collectively, perform in political systems. David Truman, Robert Dahl, William Kornhauser, and V. O. Key, Jr., for example, suggest that, among other functions, intèrest groups:[7]

1. channel communications to decision-makers,
2. help structure alternative policy choices,
3. act as buffers between the government and the people,
4. help check demands made by others,
5. provide for functional representation,
6. compartmentalize access to decision-makers,
7. lead to a system of minorities rule,
8. provide people with an emotional outlet.

[7]David B. Truman, *op. cit.;* Robert A. Dahl, *A Preface to Democratic Theory* (Chicago: University of Chicago Press, 1956); William Kornhauser, *op. cit.;* and V. O. Key, Jr., *Politics, Parties, and Pressure Groups* (New York: Crowell, 1964), 5th ed.

This kind of analysis helps us to understand how interest groups in general fit in with other aspects of a society and polity. What we are interested in here, however, is a somewhat different question. It would be useful to know whether variations in interest group strength make a difference with respect to structural and output variables of political systems. More specifically, do interest groups vary in strength from state to state, and if so, might this variation help to explain why certain other variables also vary?

The major question of this section, then, is how may states be classified according to strength of interest groups? The answer, "obviously," is that some measure of "strength" must be developed by which the states may be ranked. This task would, equally obviously, be an exceedingly difficult, expensive, and time-consuming enterprise.

It is possible, however, to employ a probably less valid and less reliable technique to measure interest group strength. The Committee on American Legislatures of the American Political Science Association sent questionnaires to political scientists located in the various states asking them to judge whether interest groups in their respective states were strong, moderately strong, or weak.[8] On the basis of the responses to this questionnaire the Committee then classified state interest groups into the three categories.

Judgmental measures are not unique with this study. Several psychological measures, for example, rely on this technique (rating scales of various kinds).[9] Seymour Martin Lipset's seminal piece on social requisites of democracy also relies heavily on a judgmental measure of whether countries are democratic and stable.[10] A recent comparative study of polyarchy also employs ratings on several variables.[11]

•   •   •

On the basis of this classification of state interest group systems into strong, moderate, and weak, Harmon Zeigler, in a very useful study, relates this classification to other variables which help to show why states are likely to vary in strength of interest groups, and how such variation is related to political party structure and legislative cohesion. Zeigler finds that states with stronger interest groups are also more likely to be (1) one-party states, (2) states which have legislative parties with weak cohesion,

[8]Belle Zeller (ed.), *American State Legislatures* (New York: Crowell, 1964), Chapter 12, especially Table 9, pp. 190-191.
[9]See, for examples, Claire Selltiz, Marie Jahoda, Morton Deutsch, and Stuart W. Cook, *Research Methods in Social Relations* (New York: Holt, Rinehart and Winston, 1961).
[10]Seymour Martin Lipset, "Some Social Requisites of Democracy," [*American Political Science*] *Review*, 53 (March 1959), 69-105.
[11]Deane E. Neubauer, *On The Theory of Polyarchy: An Empirical Study of Democracy in Ten Countries* (Ph.D. thesis, Yale University, 1966).

(3) less urban, (4) less wealthy, and (5) less industrial. Table 2 presents these findings from Zeigler's study.

What we will do now is to employ the Committee's classification of state interest group systems and see whether this classification helps us to explain variations among the states in the four dependent variables previously described.[12]

Theory, Hypotheses, and Findings

Why would one expect strength of interest groups and certain aspects of state constitutions to be related to one another, and what would be the expected relationships?

The answer to the first part of the question, the theory underlying the expected associations, is that where interest groups are stronger one manifestation of this greater strength as compared with weaker interest group systems would be a larger number of requests for, and the actual giving of special privileges and advantages. This distribution of special advantages would be predicted to show up in a political system in a number of ways. For example, we might hypothesize that in states with stronger interest groups the latter would have relatively greater success with state legislatures in receiving legal protection and encouragement for their activities. It would also not be unreasonable to suppose that states with stronger interest groups would differ with respect to the ways in which laws are administered and adjudicated. It would be interesting, for example, to observe if such states also differ in the manner in which the administrative personnel are recruited and appointed and, consequently, in the decisions which are reached concerning various regulations and distributions within

[12]A note of caution, however, should undoubtedly be entered here. The measurement of "strength" of interest groups being employed may probably best be construed to mean strength of interest groups *vis-a-vis* the state legislature. At least this is the sense in which it appears that the Committee defined strength. It is certainly the case that interest groups could vary in strength in a number of different ways. For example, size of membership, or number of groups may, under certain conditions, be appropriate measures of strength. As strength of interest groups is being used here it will be defined primarily in terms of legislative activity.

In addition, the results of this study must be interpreted cautiously since the time periods in which the independent and several of the dependent variables were measured are not coterminous. Strength of interest groups was measured by the Zeller Committee in 1954. Length of constitution and difficulty of amending the constitution (a variable to be introduced later in this paper) correspond to this time period, but the three variables having to do with amendments (number proposed, number adopted, and percentage of amendments adopted) are measured to the date when each state's current constitution was adopted. In several cases this reflects many years. It is therefore necessary, in three of the propositions, to make the assumption that strength of interest groups in states is a relatively stable phenomenon. Although there is not much evidence to support or deny the validity of this assumption, it does not appear unduly unrealistic to make it. Changes in governments, barring revolutions, are likely to take place slowly. If this is the case it does offer a certain plausibility to the assumption.

TABLE 2. The Strength of Pressure Groups in Varying Political and Economic Situations

	Types of Pressure System*		
Social Conditions	Strong**	Moderate†	Weak‡
Party Competition	(24 states)	(14 states)	(7 states)
One-party	33.3%	0%	0%
Modified One-Party	37.5%	42.8%	0%
Two-Party	29.1%	57.1%	100.0%
Cohesion of Parties in Legislature			
Weak Cohesion	75.0%	14.2%	0%
Moderate Cohesion	12.5%	35.7%	14.2%
Strong Cohesion	12.5%	50.0%	85.7%
Socio-Economic Variables			
Urban	58.6%	65.1%	73.3%
Per Capita Income	$1900	$2335	$2450
Industrialization Index	88.8	92.8	94.0

*Alaska, Hawaii, Idaho, New Hampshire, and North Dakota are not classified or included.
**Alabama, Arizona, Arkansas, California, Florida, Georgia, Iowa, Kentucky, Louisiana, Maine, Michigan, Minnesota, Mississippi, Montana, Nebraska, New Mexico, North Carolina, Oklahoma, Oregon, South Carolina, Tennessee, Texas, Washington, Wisconsin.
†Delaware, Illinois, Kansas, Maryland, Massachusetts, Nevada, New York, Ohio, Pennsylvania, South Dakota, Utah, Vermont, Virginia, West Virginia.
‡Colorado, Connecticut, Indiana, Missouri, New Jersey, Rhode Island, Wyoming.
Source: Harmon Zeigler, "Interest Groups in the States," in Herbert Jacob and Kenneth N. Vines (eds.), *Politics in the American States* (Boston: Little, Brown, 1965), p. 114.

the political system. An investigation of part of this hypothesis will appear near the end of this paper.

We would also, however, expect there to be a relationship between strength of interest groups and state constitutions. If we assume that constitutions essentially lay out important ground rules by which the game of politics will be played, and that they may place certain restrictions or give certain dispensations to the players involved in the game, then we would expect variations in state constitutions to be intimately related to variations in other aspects of political systems. Generally, we would expect state constitutions in states which have stronger interest groups to reflect, in certain systematic ways, a greater amount of interest group activity than do the constitutions in states with weaker interest groups. More specifically, we would hypothesize the following relationships:

1. The stronger the interest groups, the greater the length of state constitutions.

This hypothesis follows in that states with stronger interest groups would be predicted to make greater efforts to achieve special advantage through constitutional provisions which refer to their activities. These efforts would result in longer and more detailed constitutions than in states with weaker interest groups. Table 3 presents data which tests this hypothesis.

As can be seen from Table 3, the twenty-four states which are classified as strong-interest-group states have constitutions which average 33,233 words in length; the fourteen states which are classified as moderate in interest group strength have constitutions which average 17,985 in length; and the seven states which are classified as weak in interest group strength have constitutions which average 14,828 in length.

2. The stronger the interest groups, the greater the number of proposed amendments.

If the theory we have suggested is correct, then we would expect states with strong interest groups to have more proposals for constitutional changes than states with moderately strong interest groups which, in turn, would have more proposals for changes than would states with weak interest groups. This hypothesis would reflect a greater number of attempts to gain some special constitutional status.

The data from Table 3 confirm this hypothesis. The average number of proposed amendments per year in states with strong interest groups is 2.97, in states with moderate interest groups 1.14, and in states with weak interest groups .68.

3. The stronger the interest groups, the greater the number of amendments which are adopted.

As with proposed amendments, we would expect stronger interest group states to have a larger number of changes in the constitution than in states with less strong interest groups.

TABLE 3.   Relationships Between Strength of Interest Groups and Three
Dependent Variables

Strength of Interest Groups	Average Length of Constitution	N*	Average No. of Proposed Amendments per year	N**	Average No. of Adopted Amendments per year	N†
Strong	33,233	24	2.97	19	1.58	22
Moderate	17,985	14	1.14	12	.76	14
Weak	14,828	7	.68	5	.41	7

*Alaska and Hawaii are excluded from this and the following tables. In addition, Idaho, New Hampshire, and North Dakota were not classified by strength of interest groups.

**Arkansas, Colorado, Connecticut, Delaware, Iowa, Michigan, North Carolina, Utah, and Washington are excluded for lack of data.

†Michigan and North Carolina are excluded for lack of data.

Sources: *The Book of the States, 1964-1965* (Chicago: The Council of State Governments, 1964), pp. 12-15, and Harmon Zeigler, "Interest Groups in the States," in Herbert Jacob and Kenneth N. Vines, eds., *Politics in the American States* (Boston: Little, Brown, 1965), p. 114.

From Table 3 we can see that the data confirm the hypothesis. Strong-interest-group states have an average of 1.58 amendments adopted per year, moderate states an average of .76, weak-interest-group states an average of .41.

Additional support for this hypothesis, and for the theory being proposed here, is the following. We would also expect states with longer constitutions to have a greater number of changes in their constitutions. This follows if we assume, as we have been doing, that longer constitutions indicate a larger range of activities provided for in the constitution, and a greater specificity and detail. The greater constitutional comprehensiveness in states with longer constitutions would also suggest a greater need to revise the constitution as economic, social, and political changes occur. Hence we would predict that the longer the constitution, the greater the number of amendments. Table 4 provides data on this point.

TABLE 4. Relationship Between Length of Constitution and Number of Constitutional Amendments Adopted

Length of Constitution	Average No. of Adopted Amendments per year	N*
Less than 10,000 words	.27	7
10,000—19,999	.67	18
20,000—29,999	.78	12
30,000 & over	3.04	9

*Michigan and North Carolina are excluded for lack of data.
Source: *The Book of the States, 1964-1965* (Chicago: The Council of States Government, 1964), pp. 12-15.

As Table 4 indicates, the average number of amendments adopted per year increases as the average length of the constitution increases.

Since states with stronger interest groups tend to have longer constitutions (Table 3), and since states with longer constitutions tend to have a greater number of amendments (Table 4), hypothesis three, the stronger the interest group, the greater the number of amendments which are adopted, is directly derivable from these other hypotheses. The fact that this three-step chain of hypotheses is true at all three steps lends additional validity to the general theory being proposed here. It is also interesting to note that both strength of interest groups and length of constitution have an independent effect on the number of amendments adopted. When each is held constant the relationship with the other and number of amendments adopted is attenuated, but still present.

4. States with moderately strong interest groups will have the highest percentage of amendments adopted.

This hypothesis, although not immediately obvious, follows from the following argument. To this point our data indicate a positive relationship between strength of interest groups and both number of amendments proposed and number of amendments adopted. It is clear, however, that it is easier to propose an amendment than to get an amendment adopted. States with strong interest groups, then, would be expected to have a larger number of amendments proposed and a larger number of amendments adopted, but since it is easier to propose amendments than to have them ratified, their rate of success would not be expected to be the largest among the states.

Similarly, states with weak interest groups have the fewest number of amendments proposed and the fewest number of amendments adopted. But, again, since it is easier to propose than to adopt, weak interest group states would not have the highest rate of success. This reasoning would predict that states with moderately strong interest groups would have the highest ratio of amendments adopted to amendments proposed. Table 5 provides data on this hypothesis.

As Table 5 indicates, it is the states with moderately strong interest groups that have the highest percentage of amendments which are proposed adopted. States with strong interest groups have a ratio of adopted amendments to proposed amendments of 54.8%, states with moderate interest groups 62.8%, and states with weak interest groups 52.6%. Those states with the weakest interest groups have the lowest rate of success, but those states with the strongest interest groups do not have the highest rate of success. Indeed, their rate of success is much closer to weak interest group states than to moderately strong ones.

A Possible Alternative Explanation

Before accepting the above theory and hypotheses relating strength of interest groups to variations in state constitutions, it might be useful to explore a possible alternative explanation.

States also differ considerably in the extent to which it is easy or difficult to amend their constitutions. Some states, for example, require a two-thirds or three-fifths majority of the legislature and/or passage by two successive legislatures to propose and ratify constitutional amendments. All states but one also require a popular referendum after legislative action, but require differing majorities in the referendum. In addition, states also differ on whether they allow constitutional amendments to be pro-

posed by initiative, and have different ways of calling together and proposing amendments in constitutional conventions.[13]

Given these widely varying practices in states, an index of difficulty
of proposing and ratifying constitutional amendments was constructed.
This index is derived from the three major ways in which the constitution

TABLE 5.   Relationship Between Strength of Interest Groups and Percentage of
Proposed Amendments Adopted

Strength of Interest Groups	Average % of Amendments Adopted	N*
Strong	54.8%	19
Moderate	62.8%	12
Weak	52.6%	5

*See footnote 3, Table 3.
Source: See Table 3.

may be amended and therefore reflects: (1) legislative difficulty, (2)
presence or absence of the initiative, and (3) constitutional convention
difficulty in proposing and ratifying constitutional amendments. One
point was given to each state if a majority greater than a simple majority
is required in the legislature, one point if approval by two sessions is
needed, and one point if ratification by a majority vote in the election
rather than a majority vote on the amendment is required. Additionally,
one point is given if there are no initiative procedures in the state. With
regard to constitutional conventions, one point is given if greater than a
majority in the legislature is required to call a constitutional convention,
one point if approval is needed by two sessions of the legislature, one point
if a referendum on whether there should be a constitutional convention is
necessary, one point if a majority in the election rather than a majority on
the proposition is required, one point if after the constitutional convention ratification of the amendment is required (one-half point is given if
no provision is in the constitution for a referendum ratifying the amendment but the legislature may determine if a referendum is necessary), and
one point if ratification requires a majority in the election rather than a
majority on the amendment.

This index of difficulty of amending the constitution, then, can vary from
0 to 10. The median score was 4, the range from 1 to 9. Fifteen states had
scores of 3.5 or less, sixteen had scores from 4 to 5, and fifteen had scores
from 5.5 to 9.

[13]For descriptions of the differing state systems see *The Book of the States, op. cit.,* pp. 13-15.

Given this wide range in difficulty in amending state constitutions, we would expect that such variation might have an impact on the number of amendments which are adopted by the states. More specifically, we would hypothesize that the greater the difficulty in amending the constitution, the fewer the number of amendments which will be adopted. Table 6 provides the data to test this hypothesis.

Table 6 only partially confirms the hypothesis. Those states with the most difficult procedures to amend the constitution do have fewer amendments adopted, but the states with the easiest procedures do not have the greatest number of amendments adopted.

TABLE 6.   Relationship Between Difficulty in Amending the Constitution and Average Number of Amendments Adopted Per Year

Score on Difficulty of Amending Constitution	Average No. of Adopted Amendments Per Year	N*
Less than 3.5	1.29	15
4-5	1.32	16
5.5-9	.66	15

*Michigan and North Carolina are excluded for lack of data.
Source: See Table 4.

This partial explanation of why states vary in the number of changes in their constitutions may be further explained, however, by variation in states in strength of interest groups. Consistent with our theory, it may be proposed that states would be expected to vary in ease or difficulty in amending their constitutions by strength of interest groups. That is, we would expect the following hypothesis to be true: the stronger the interest groups, the less the difficulty in amending the constitution. Table 7 presents data on this hypothesis.

The data from Table 7 confirm the relationship between strength of interest groups and difficulty of amending the constitution. States with strong interest groups have a difficulty score of 4.21, states with moderately strong interest groups have a score of 5.00, and states with weak interest groups have a difficulty score of 5.65. Hence we may say that even though the number of changes in the constitution is related to difficulty of amending the constitution as well as strength of interest groups, the reason why this additional explanation is at least partially true is because strength of interest groups is also related to difficulty of amending the constitution.

One further piece of data will also help to confirm the theory being proposed here. Since states with strong interest groups have longer constitutions (Table 3), and since strong interest group states also have constitutions which are easier to amend (Table 3), we would also expect there to be a relationship between length of constitution and ease of amendment. More specifically we would hypothesize the greater the length of the constitution, the less the difficulty in amending the constitution. Table 8 provides data on this hypothesis.

TABLE 7.   Relationship Between Strength of Interest Groups and Difficulty of Amending the Constitution

Strength of Interest Groups	Average Difficulty of Amending the Constitution	N
Strong	4.21	24
Moderate	5.00	14
Weak	5.65	7

Sources: See footnote 3, Table 3.

As can be seen from the Table, this hypothesis is for the most part confirmed. The states with the shortest constitutions have the most difficult amending procedures, and the states with the longest constitutions have the easiest amending procedures, although the two sets of states in the middle do not fall in the predicted order.

Summing up this section, then, there is a partial relationship between the difficulty of amending the constitution and the number of changes made in the constitution. However, this relationship can be accounted for by the fact that there is also a relationship between strength of interest groups and ease of amending the constitution. The alternative explanation, then, may be rejected and the original explanation retained. Strength of interest

TABLE 8.   Relationship Between Length of Constitution and Difficulty of Amending State Constitution

Length of Constitution	Average Difficulty of Amending the Constitution	N*
Less than 10,000 words	6.29	7
10,000-19,999	4.58	18
20,000-29,999	4.71	12
30,000 & over	4.11	9

*Michigan and North Carolina are excluded for lack of data.
Source: See Table 4.

group seems to be a major factor in explaining why states vary with regard to certain constitutional practices.

The Second Set of Dependent Variables

In the previous sections our concern was with the effect of strength of interest groups on some general features of state constitutions. In this section the focus will shift slightly to a combined constitutional-legislative variable, the method of selection of state officials. States differ widely in the number of office-holders who are appointed as opposed to elected to office. We will be concerned, in the following, with an explanation of this variation.

A priori one might predict that states with stronger interest groups would be *either* more likely or less likely to have a larger number of elected as opposed to appointed officials. The major political variable in either prediction is the ability of interest groups to influence the selection of personnel. Those who would predict that interest groups will have more influence if governmental officials are appointed rather than elected would suggest that interest groups would prefer the politics of dealing with the governor and, in some instances, the legislature, to the uncertainties of electoral politics. If this hypothesis is combined with the already-established hypothesis that strength of interest groups is related to political outcomes then this group would predict that states with stronger interest groups would have a greater number of appointed rather than elected officials.

On the other hand one could, with equal logic, agree that interest groups do want to maintain influence over the selection of governmental personnel but that such influence can better be established if personnel are elected rather than appointed. A governor is likely to be responsive to a wide variety of state interests. In some cases he may be a member of a political party which is less responsive to the concerns of certain interest groups. Gubernatorial appointment combined with legislative confirmation would provide some check on the governor, but interest groups, on balance, might be better able to influence the selection of personnel of such persons were elected in what, for minor positions, would be relatively low turnout elections rather than take a chance with governors. Proponents of this view would deduce an opposite conclusion from that previously advanced: stronger interest group states would have a larger number of elected rather than appointed officials.

How does one choose between these competing theories? Since the logic of each produced contradictory conclusions we might test those conclusions. Although this does not produce a direct test of the competing theories it does provide an indirect test, since the conclusions drawn from each are

TABLE 9. Relationship Between Strength of Interest Groups and Four Dependent Variables

Strength of Interest Groups	Average No. of State Elected Officials	Average No. of State Agencies With Elected Officials	% of Elected State Public Utility Commissions	% of Elected State State Courts of Last Resort	N
Strong	19.54	9.17	50%	79%	24
Moderate	14.64	7.14	7%	57%	14
Weak	7.71	5.86	0%	43%	7

Source: *The Book of the States, 1964-1965* (Chicago: The Council of State Governments, 1964).

clearly contrary to each other. Evidence on these derivative hypotheses may support one theory as opposed to the other.

The relationship between interest group strength and selection of governmental officials will be tested in four different ways. First, what is the relationship between interest group strength and the total number of state officials who are elected? Second, what is the relationship of interest group strength and the number of state agencies with elected officials? This relationship will give us some idea of the range of offices which are subject to election.

Each of these variables gives an indication of the overall elective-appointive system within and among states. But what about specific instances? Third, then, what is the relationship between strength of interest groups and the selection of state public utility commissions? Fourth, what is the relationship of strength of interest groups with the selection of judges on state courts of last resort? Table 9 provides data to test these four relationships.

From Table 9 it is clear, in each instance, that states with strong interest groups rely more heavily on election of state officials than do states with weaker interest groups. The stronger the interest groups the greater the number of elected officials, the greater the number of state agencies with elected officials, the greater the likelihood that public utility commissions will be elected, and the greater the probability that judges on state courts of last resort will be elected.

The data, then, lend support to the second of the alternative theories. States with stronger interest groups are better able to isolate governmental agencies and officials from executive or legislative influence than are states with weaker interest groups, and are more likely to have agencies of government which are independent from the governor and legislature.

One further bit of evidence lends additional support to this conclusion. Given the evidence that elections rather than appointments are related to strong interest groups, it may also be inferred that those states with strong interest groups would have shorter terms of office than those states with weaker interest groups. This would provide additional control by interest groups by making governmental officials run for office more frequently and hence be less independent from outside influence. Table 10 provides data on terms of office of judges of state courts of last resort.

The data in Table 10 confirm this hypothesis. Length of term for judges on state courts of last resort decreases as strength of interest groups increases.

Summary and Conclusions

We began our discussion by suggesting that the literature on interest groups, generally speaking, lacks studies which attempt to test generalizations about interest group activity. The emphasis on theory and/or case studies we attributed to two factors: (1) difficulty in operationalizing theoretical concepts, and (2) difficulty and expense in collecting data for many interest groups or on many policies.

This study attempts to test several propositions about the relationship between strength of interest groups and variations among states with regard to structural and output variables centering on the constitution and the election of state officials. A theory was developed which explained why state governments would have such wide variations in their constitutions and the political processes surrounding them. More specifically the following hypotheses about strength of interest groups were tested and confirmed:

1. The stronger the interest groups, the greater the length of the state constitutions.
2. The stronger the interest groups, the greater the number of proposed amendments.
3. The stronger the interest groups, the greater the number of amendments which are adopted.
4. States with moderately strong interest groups will have the highest percentage of amendments adopted.
5. The stronger the interest groups, the less the difficulty in amending the constitution.
6. The stronger the interest groups, the greater the number of state elected officials.
7. The stronger the interest groups, the greater the number of state agencies with elected officials.
8. The stronger the interest groups, the greater the likelihood that state public utility commissions will be elected.
9. The stronger the interest groups, the greater the probability that judges on state courts of last resort will be elected.
10. The stronger the interest groups, the shorter will be the terms of office of judges on state courts of last resort.

In addition, the following subsidiary hypotheses were also tested.

11. The longer the constitution, the greater the number of amendments which are adopted.
12. The longer the constitution, the less the difficulty in amending the constitution.
13. The greater the difficulty in amending the constitution, the fewer

the number of amendments which will be adopted (partially confirmed).

TABLE 10.   Relationship Between Strength of Interest Groups and Average Length
of Term of Judges on State Courts of Last Resort

Strength of Interest Groups	Average Length of Term	N
Strong	7.58	24
Moderate	11.21	14
Weak	13.43	7

Source: *The Book of the States, 1964-1965* (Chicago: The Council of State Governments, 1964).

All of these hypotheses confirm the theory which has been proposed here. Variation in strength of interest groups does have an impact on political systems. It was expected that states with stronger interest groups would be characterized by attempts by those groups to gain special advantages. Since constitutions are one of the vehicles through which advantages and disadvantages are distributed in political systems, these attempts would have an effect on the length of the constitution, the amending procedures within states, and the number of changes which are made. Since the selection of governmental personnel is also of primary concern to interest groups, it would be expected that differences in selection procedures would also vary by interest group strength. The data presented in this paper lend credence to these suppositions.

Statistical Appendix

A political scientist must, with some data projects, give attention to the possible conflict between data analysis sophistication and general readability. In the text I have attempted to present the findings in the simplest way possible consistent with accuracy and at least minimum precision. However, there are techniques of data analysis which provide more powerful data manipulation. One of these techniques, appropriate for this analysis, is multiple regression analysis. This statistical appendix will present the findings in terms of correlation coefficients, holding some variables constant where appropriate.

Two points, however, should be made immediately. First, the results of the multiple regression analysis are entirely consistent with the findings already reported. The interpretation of the data also remains the same. Second, the entire analysis was performed in two steps, one with all of the states (in most cases this is forty-five states), and the second with the eleven former Confederate states dropped from the analysis. It has been found consistently that in many respects southern states differ from northern states. However, the propositions reported here are true whether one includes or excludes the southern states.

The correlation coefficients for the propositions listed in the summary, in the same numerical order, are as follows (correlations in parentheses exclude the southern states):

1. .36 (.34), 2. .40 (.33), 3. .30 (.25), 4. curvilinear, 5. —.30 (—.31), 6. .26 (.27), 7. .52 (.45), 8. .41 (.45), 9. .32 (.31), 10. —.43 (—.42), 11. .53 (.53), 12. —.24 (—.24), 13. —.12 (—.17) (partial relationship reported).

In addition, the relationship between interest group strength and number of constitutional amendments adopted, with length of constitution held constant is .19. Similarly, the relationship between interest group strength and number of constitutional amendments adopted, with difficulty of amending the constitution held constant, is .24.

The relationship between strength of interest groups and number of state elected officials is not affected by population size.

Group Representation in Britain and the United States
Samuel H. Beer

We usually think of Great Britain as a country of strong parties and weak pressure groups; the United States as a country of weak parties and strong pressure groups. I wish to suggest some contrary views: that not only are British parties strong, but so also are British pressure groups; that in comparison both American parties and pressure groups are weak. The terms "strong" and "weak" cry out to be defined. The meanings I give them derive from a historical development—the rise of "collectivism"—that has similarly affected both parties and pressure groups.

What are the consequences for policy? Strong parties can more readily resist pressure groups. They can also more readily yield them what they want. On the other hand, the dispersion of power may simply produce a self-defeating war of all against all in which even the special interests suffer. Centralized power at least creates the possibility of deliberate and orderly solutions.

SOURCE: Samuel H. Beer, "Group Representation in Britain and the United States," *The Annals of the American Academy of Political and Social Science*, CCCXIX (September 1958), 130-140. Reprinted by permission.

The Collectivist Economy

The virtue of centralized power is worth examining if for no other reason than that the opposite doctrine holds so high a place in liberal democratic thought. Liberals and Radicals in both Britain and America have applied the doctrine of dispersed power to both the economy and the polity. In the Smithian model of the economy, for instance, the wealth of the nation and the satisfaction of consumers' wants will be maximized if the market is free. No unit, not even government, is to exercise "market power." Once power is removed, rational and voluntary exchange will result and along with it other desirable consequences in the allocation of resources and the satisfaction of the consumer.

Very similar is the Liberal-Radical model of the polity. Remove Burke's "established" aristocracy and all other agents of power that had historically guided the political process; reduce society to its individual, rational atoms; then, power removed, reason will reign. A free, competitive marketplace of ideas, automatic and self-regulating like the marketplace of the laissez-faire economy, will test the truth of opinions. Upon opinions so tested, popular government will base public policy.

In both the British and American economies in the nineteenth century, the market conditions required by the self-regulating model did actually exist in very great degree. And in both, to no inconsiderable extent, these conditions still exist. But in the past two generations or so, certain structural changes have taken place—reaching a further point of development in Britain than in the United States—that depart radically from this model. These developments, which we may call "collectivism," can be summarized under four headings. One is the tendency to a concentration of economic power among a few large buyers or sellers in a particular industry or complex of industries. Along with the increase in size of units has gone a change in internal structure that is referred to by terms such as bureaucracy and managerialism. Moreover, where such large units have grown up, they tend to deal with one another by a process of "bargaining"—or perhaps it is better to say, "collective bargaining." Finally, while bargaining tends to be confined to the relations of producers—whether business firms or trade unions—in their dealings with the mass of ultimate consumers, large units have learned to shape, even to create, the very "wants" that presumably they have come into existence to satisfy.

Collectivist Parties

In the polity as in the economy, there have been similar tendencies toward collectivism. By this I do not mean the increase in government intervention—the rise of the welfare state and the controlled economy. I mean rather that in the political structure have occurred certain changes analogous to those changes in economic structure summarized above. Starting from these contrasting models of the polity, the self-regulating and the collectivist, we may compare the distribution of power in Britain and the United States. It would appear that, as economic collectivism has proceeded farther in Britain than in the United States, so also has political collectivism.

We may look first at the relative number of units and their internal structure. Examined in the light of these criteria, both British parties and pressure groups present striking contrasts with the American models. While in both polities there are two major parties, the loose and sprawling parties of American politics make the British appear highly concentrated. In the American party, power is dispersed among many units — for example, personal followings or state and local machines — with the result that only occasionally and for limited purposes, such as nominating a Presidential candidate, does the national party act as a unit. In terms of density — that is, the per cent of eligibles organized as party members — American parties exceed British. But if we apply a measure of intensity, such as payment of dues, it is clear that British parties have mobilized the electorate far more highly than have American. In the British party, moreover, this membership is brought together for unified action by an elaborate and effective system of articulation, in particular active representative bodies extending from bottom to top and a bureaucratic staff running from top to bottom. There are still semiautonomous centers within the party that a perfected merger would obliterate. But to an American, a British party is a highly unified social body, remarkably well equipped for co-ordinated action: we think, for instance, of the fact that all candidates must be approved by a central-party agency and that they will all run on the same platform. No doubt, the most striking expression of this power of united action is the extent of party voting in the House of Commons. Judged even by Lowell's strict criteria, party voting has been on the increase for a hundred years and today reaches nearly one hundred per cent.[1]

Along with such concentration, and perhaps making it possible, goes a high measure of political homogeneity. (I do not mean social homogeneity, for, measured by nonpolitical criteria, the British are a very heterogeneous people.) This political homogeneity in the electorate as a whole is reflected in what students of voting behavior call the "nationalizing" of British politics. When political opinion moves, it moves in unison throughout the country: in a general election the "swing" from one party to the other is

[1]Lowell counted as a party vote a division in which at least 90 per cent of one party voted in favor and at least 90 per cent of the other party voted against. A. L. Lowell, "The Influence of Party upon Legislation in England and America," *Annual Report of the American Historical Association for 1901*, Vol. 1 (Washington, 1902), pp. 319-542.

much the same in every constituency. In the United States, as Schattschneider and Paul David have shown, voting has also tended in this direction.[2] Sectionalism and the number of one-party states are on the decline. But—as 1956 illustrates—nothing like the uniformity of swing in British voting has been reached.

In spite of mass membership and representative bodies, however, the internal structure of the British party gives great power to central party leaders—far more, of course, than that possessed by American leaders. It is rather as if the Congressional caucus of post-Federalist days had been imposed upon the Jacksonian party system. In both British parties, as R. T. McKenzie has shown, the leaders of the parliamentary party, and especially the Leader, are dominant.[3] That is a loose description and needs must be, since the Leader's power is complex and certainly far from dictatorial. He must continually practice "the art of management," appeasing a dissident faction, finding a formula, keeping up party morale. Indeed, he is a "manager"—a modern-day manager committed to party principle, of course, but by his function compelled above all to think of the continuation of the organization.

Collectivist Pressure Groups

Turning from parties to pressure groups, we find that in Britain as in the United States, the center of the stage is occupied by organizations based on the great economic interest groups of modern society, especially the big three of business, labor, and agriculture. Given the nature of public policy, which affects these interests so often and so intimately, pressure groups claiming to speak for them are bound in turn to influence policy making more frequently and on the whole more effectively than pressure groups of other types.

In Britain as well as the United States, in addition to such "self-oriented" pressure groups, we must also deal with what S. E. Finer calls "promotional" groups.[4] Among the former we may classify such organization as the Federation of British Industries, the Trades Union Congress, the National Farmers Union, the British Medical Association, the National Union of Teachers, the British Legion, the National and Local Government Officers' Association. The "promotional" groups include the Howard League for

---

[2] E. E. Schattschneider, "The United States: The Functional Approach to Party Government," in Sigmund Neumann (Ed.), *Modern Political Parties* (Chicago: University of Chicago Press, 1956), pp. 194-215; Paul David, "Intensity of Inter-Party Competition and the Problem of Party Realignment," a paper presented at the meeting of the American Political Science Association, September 5-7, 1957.

[3] R. T. McKenzie, *British Political Parties* (New York: St. Martin's Press, 1955), *passim.*

[4] S. E. Finer, *Anonymous Empire: A Study of the Lobby in Great Britain* (London: Pall Mall Press, 1958), p. 3.

Penal Reform, the National Council for Civil Liberties, the Peace Pledge Union, the Campaign for the Limitation of Secret Police Powers. As compared with the self-oriented groups, writes Finer, the latter "do not represent 'interests' in the same sense at all. They represent a cause, not a social or economic 'stake' in society." [5]

Such a broad distinction in the character of goals tends to have important consequences for structure and behavior. The promotional group, for instance, tends to be open to all like-minded persons, while the self-oriented group has, so to speak, a fixed clientele. By and large the self-oriented group can more readily extract money and work from its members on a continuing and regularized basis. It may also be less subject to splintering and more capable of continuous, unified action. At least in part for such reasons, the more powerful pressure groups of the British polity are self-oriented groups, based on a vocational interest, bureaucratic in structure, and continuing over a long period of time. While some form of group politics has long flourished in the British as in other polities, this modern, collectivist type has emerged only in recent generations. [6] There is some sense in saying that one line of development in the history of British pressure groups has been from the promotional to the self-oriented, vocational type. Possibly a similar development has taken place in the United States, although here the third party has often played the role of the promotional group in Britain. We might also find that the promotional group remains a more important feature of the American polity than of the British.

FARM, LABOR, AND BUSINESS ORGANIZATIONS

Concentration and bureaucracy characterize British pressure groups as well as parties. Hardly without exception the big vocational pressure groups in Britain have a higher index of density and concentration. There, for instance, the National Farmers Union is the only significant organization of farmers and includes 90 per cent of its potential membership. In the United States, of course, only a fraction—no more than 30 per cent—of all farmers are organized and these are divided among three main groups and various minor ones. While absolute numbers are much smaller in Britain, we must remember that British agriculture is highly diversified as to crops, size of farms, and location. Yet through the NFU British farmers speak with one voice to a degree rarely achieved by farmers in the United States. No doubt this is true because to no small extent the organization is run from the top. In Bedford Square is a large and able bureaucracy and at its head stands one of the ablest managers in modern Britain. Sir

---

[5] *Ibid.*

[6] S. H. Beer, "The Representation of Interests in British Government: Historical Background," *American Political Science Review*, Vol. 51, No. 3 (September 1957), pp. 635-45; "Pressure Groups and Parties in Britain," *American Political Science Review*, Vol. 50, No. 1, (March 1956), p. 4.

James Turner—sometimes known as the "Sacred Bull of British Agriculture."

In the field of trade unions, just a little less than half the total working force has been organized, while in the United States the figure is around a quarter. To one peak organization, the TUC, nearly all unions are affiliated and it has been the undisputed spokesman for organized labor for generations. Its permanent secretary, even when Walter Citrine held the post, has never occupied the position of, say, a Gompers. The heads of the Big Three,[7] however, have as prominent a political role as our Reuther, Meany, and Lewis. The British labor leaders of this generation are more likely to have worked their way up the bureaucratic ladder by long and able management than to have emerged from heroic struggles for the right to organize or for better contracts. Contrary to popular impression and in strong contrast with American experience, the strike has almost ceased to be an instrument of labor-management relations in Britain since as far back as 1932.[8] If by bureaucracy, however, we mean fulltime paid staff, then British unions generally are far less well endowed than American. The reluctance of the rank and file to pay dues sufficient to employ such staff—and to pay substantial salaries to any permanent official—seriously handicaps British unions.[9]

In the field of business, in Britain as in the United States the basic unit of political action is the trade association. Comparison is made a little easier if we consider only national manufacturing trade associations.[10] Of these there are 1,300 in Britain and some 950 in the United States. Density is high: a sample survey showed that 90 per cent of larger firms and 76 per cent of smaller firms in Britain belong to such associations. Concentration among manufacturing trade associations is considerably greater in Britain. The peak association is the Federation of British Industries (FBI) which represents, through its affiliated trade associations and directly through member firms, some 85 per cent of all manufacturing concerns employing ten or more workers.[11] In the United States, on the other hand, the National Association of Manufacturers has never represented more than 6 per cent of all manufacturing concerns.[12] If the same base as that used for the FBI

[7]The Transport and General Workers' Union; the National Union of General and Municipal Workers; the Amalgamated Engineering Union—which among them include 30 per cent of all unionists affiliated to the TUC.

[8]Hugh A. Clegg, "Strikes," *Political Quarterly*, Vol. 27, No. 1 (January-March 1956), pp. 31-35.

[9]John A. Mack, "Trade Union Leadership," *Political Quarterly*, Vol. 27, No. 1 (January-March 1956), p. 77.

[10]Data on British associations are from P.E.P., *Industrial Trade Associations; Activities and Organization* (London, 1957).

[11]S. E. Finer, "The Federation of British Industries," *Political Studies*, Vol. 4, No. 1 (February 1956), p. 62.

[12]R. W. Gable, "N.A.M.: Influential Lobby or Kiss of Death?," *Journal of Politics*, Vol. 15 (May 1953), p. 257.

were taken, however, there is reason to think that the NAM figure would be more like 20 per cent to 25 per cent. The contrast would still be striking.

Bargaining in the Polity

Let us turn to the modes of interaction of these massive unit actors, in particular the political party and the pressure group.

What we have called bargaining is a principal trait of the relationships of large producers in the collectivist economy. Its essence is that each of the negotiating units is highly dependent on the other as a seller or as a buyer. In a free market, on the other hand, each seller can turn to other buyers and each buyer to other sellers and none have significant market power. In bargaining, however, each unit has substantial market power; hence, the ultimate decision is made as a result of negotiations in which each gauges his offers in the light of expectations about the possible offers of the other.[13]

A similar kind of decision making occurs where a party enjoys large power over the authority of government, while a pressure group with which it deals enjoys similar power over something — such as votes — that the party wants. Such a situation is very different from one in which government authority is dispersed among many elected office-holder and voting power among an unorganized electorate. In the latter situation, there is a kind of bidding for votes on one side and for promises or policies on the other that has a limited, but real, analogy with the economic free market. Where the centralized party in office confronts the massively organized pressure group, decisions are made quite differently. Indeed, some who have sat in on the Annual Price Review between the National Farmers Union in Britain and the Ministry of Agriculture have reported that the proceedings and the way in which a settlement is reached resemble nothing so much as collective bargaining. For both the farmers and the ministry there is a range of outcomes that would be better than no agreement at all. Each opponent pretty well knows what this range is. No wonder it has sometimes taken four months for a decision to be reached!

Consultation with interests is a feature of all modern Western democratic governments. Some years ago Leiserson, writing of representative advisory committees, traced their origin to "the delegation of discretionary rule-making powers under legislative standards to administrative agencies executing various types of social legislation."[14] Leierson's statement, broadened somewhat, is a generalization valid for not only American, but also for Wes-

---

[13]See Thomas C. Schelling, "An Essay on Bargaining," *American Economic Review*, Vol. 45, No. 3 (June 1956), pp. 281-83.

[14]Avery Leiserson, *Administrative Regulation: A Study in Representation of Interests* (Chicago: University of Chicago Press, 1942), p. 162.

tern European government: increasing government intervention for such purposes as social reform, economic stability, and national defense has led to the grant of rule-making power to administrative agencies and to increasing participation of interested groups in decision making at that level.

Different stages in this development, however, can be distinguished, depending upon how far the scope of policy has been expanded and the polity has become collectivist. The extent to which power has been mobilized and unified on each side — on the side of the party in power and on the side of the pressure group with which it deals — will determine whether bargaining predominates in the relationship. In the United States, we find administrative consultation on a vast scale both in Washington and in the state capitals. In Britain, a more collectivist polity, the situation is better described as "quasi-corporatism."

It is against the background of this power pattern that we must examine the emphasis that British pressure groups give to the various points in the process of decision making. The formal structure of authority — British parliamentary government as compared with the American separation of powers — will play its role. But we must recall that a hundred years ago Britain also had parliamentary government, yet pressure groups then gave far more attention to the legislature than they do now.

Administrative Consultation

In each polity we may distinguish four main phases of policy making: at elections, in the legislature, within the party, and at the administrative level. British pressure groups exert their major influence at the administrative level, taking this to include both ministerial and official contacts. Perhaps their second most important point of influence is within the party. In contrast American pressure groups, by and large, concentrate on the first two points: the electorate and the legislature.

There are, of course, many variations within these two broad patterns. A very important difference may result from the character of the power base of a group. There is a kind of power — and this is particularly important in Britain — that is created by the expansion of policy itself. "The greater the degree of detailed and technical control the government seeks to exert over industrial and commercial interests," E. P. Herring wrote, "the greater must be their degree of consent and active participation in the very process of regulation, if regulation is to be effective or successful."[15] This generalization, I should think, holds for most Western democracies and surely for Britain. There, certain types of control exercised in recent years — price control, materials allocation, tariffs, import control, and the

[15]E. Pendleton Herring, *Public Administration and the Public Interest* (New York: McGraw-Hill Book Co., 1936), p. 192.

encouragement of exports and productivity are only some of the more striking examples—simply could not be enforced effectively without the substantial cooperation of the groups concerned. The group's technical advice is often well-nigh indispensable. But co-operation—something more than grudging consent to "the law"—is a further necessity. Our farm programs with their referenda and farmer-elected committees recognize this necessity. But in Britain the far wider scope of regulation and planning—even after the various "bonfires of controls"—gives this power factor far greater weight.

A few examples: The farmers—meaning in effect the NFU—are represented on a set of local committees that have had important administrative duties under various agricultural programs, and the chance that the NFU might encourage these farmer representatives to withdraw from the committees has been a force in the annual price reviews. When the Conservatives in denationalizing part of the transport industry in 1946 dismantled the government haulage (that is, trucking) system, a standby scheme was organized by the industry itself. The Labour government's limitation of advertising expenditure was policed by the organized advertisers, and its important anti-inflationary effort to restrain both dividends and wage increases was carried out—and with remarkable success—on a voluntary basis by organized business and labor.

Neither the British nor the American system of consultation between government and pressure groups has been fully described.[15a] Some rough impressions, modestly intended, may be in order. In both countries the central device is the representative advisory committee. British examples range from high level bodies such as the Economic Planning Board, the National Joint Advisory Council of the Ministry of Labour, the National Production Advisory Council on Industry, on which the relevant peak organizations, the FBI, BEC and TUC, are represented, to the multitude of advisory committees of the main economic departments to which trade associations send representatives. The latter are connected with the system of "sponsoring" departments which grew up during and after World War II and which means today that every industry and every branch of it, no matter how small, has a sponsoring department or section of one, somewhere in the government machine. Apart from such committees, although often around them, a regular system of informal consultation has grown up. Private and public bureaucrats continually call one another on the telephone or meet for luncheon and discuss a problem on a first-name basis. Often several departments and several groups are concerned.

[15a]For a brief sketch of important aspects of American practice see *Consultation with Industry*. Historical Reports on Defense Production, Report No. 19. A History of the Office of Industry Advisory Committees of the N.P.A. (Washington, D. C.: U. S. Dept. of Commerce, 1953).

... The number of advisory committees associated with government departments at the center—and in addition to many more at the local or regional level—runs into the hundreds. One major set established by statute are in the Department of Agriculture—for instance, the Commodity Stabilization Committees. Of the remainder, the vast majority it seems are associated principally with the defense effort—procurement, development, standards, stockpiling, and so on—and consists of industry advisory committees. In comparison with similar British industry advisory committees, the American appear to depend less on trade associations, the result at least in part of the Defense Production Act of 1950 that requires that nonmembers as well as members of trade associations be included. The peak associations—the NAM and United States Chamber of Commerce—also play a much less prominent role than their British counterparts not being represented, as such, on even the Business Advisory Council. Certainly trade unions are not called in for advice so frequently or on so broad a front in the United States as in Britain. The TUC alone, for instance, is represented on some 60 committees touching all aspects of social and economic problems.

Of the broad character of the power relationship we can speak with confidence: the American executive possesses far less actual power than the British. Quite apart from the degree of delegated powers in this country, the political independence of Congress and the exercise of administrative oversight by Congressional Committees mean that the group interested in influencing policy must give great attention to the legislature. Some years ago Blaisdell found that pressure groups, while concerned with the administration, focused their attention principally upon Congress.[17] Broadly this must still be the case, although it would be interesting to know how far the defense effort may have shifted the balance.

Pressure on Parties

At the Democratic National Convention in 1956 the number of trade-union officials sitting as delegates ran into the hundreds, while at the Republican convention there was no more than a scattering. Generally, however, in both national and state parties in the United States, the connection of pressure groups and parties is less close than in Britain. We do not have the formal affiliation of the trade union movement with one party. But the more important difference arises from the fact that American parties are so poorly unified that they do not provide an effective channel for influencing the use of government authority. In Britain, on the other hand, the

[17]Donald C. Blaisdell, *Economic Power and Political Pressures*, Monograph 26, T.N.E.C., Investigation of Concentration of Economic Power, 76th Congress, 3rd Session (Washington, 1941), pp. 57 and 70.

party ranks second—although perhaps a poor second—to the administration as an object of pressure.

Where the power is, there the pressure will be applied. Where we see the pressure being applied, therefore, we shall probably find the seat of power. Judged by this rule, the central organs of the British party, especially the parliamentary party, are far more powerful than the party's representative assemblies. Pressure groups do not openly descend on a British party conference as they do on the platform hearings of an American party convention. Their representatives, however, may be present and spokesmen for various special interests—farmers, trade unionists, veterans, teachers, old-age pensioners, advertising men with a concern for commercial broadcasting—will take up a good deal of time at a party conference.

The important point of influence, however, is the parliamentary party—its regular, full meetings and its specialized committees—and to a lesser extent the party's central office. We are familiar with the way leaders of the Labour party while in power or in opposition will frequently consult with the trade unions on pending decisions. There is also an active alignment, if not formal affiliation, of organized business with the Conservatives. During the passage of the bill nationalizing transport in 1946-47, for instance, the Conservative opposition tabled several hundred amendments. Where had they come from? In practice the party's Parliamentary Secretariat—a body of party employees, not MP's—acted as intermediary between the transport committee of the parliamentary party and the various pressure groups, especially the General Council of British Shipping, the Dock and Harbors Association, and a joint committee of the Federation of British Industries, National Union of Manufacturers, and the Association of British Chambers of Commerce.[18]

Inseparable from these channels of influence is one of the, to an American, most curious phenomena of British politics. He is the "interested MP" —that is, the member who is connected with an outside interest group by direct personal involvement, such as occupation or ownership of property, or by membership or office holding in an outside organization speaking for an interest group. Today and for generations the House of Commons through the personal involvement of its members has represented a far wider range of interests than has the American Congress, notoriously inhabited by lawyers.

In Britain such personal involvement was a principal way in which interest groups of the nineteenth century made themselves heard in government. Of more importance in today's collectivist polity is the member connected with an outside organization. The MP's sponsored and subsidized by

[18]Finer, *op. cit.* (note 3 *supra*), pp. 67-68. For other examples of pressure group activity in the House of Commons see J. D. Stewart, *British Pressure Groups: Their Role in Relation to the House of Commons* (Oxford: Oxford University Press, 1958).

the trade unions are the best-known examples. But there is also a host of others: a joint Honorary Secretary of the Association of British Chambers of Commerce, the Chairman of the Howard League for Penal Reform, a Director of the Society of Motor Manufacturers and Traders, the President of the British Legion, the Secretary of the National Tyre Distributors Association—there seems to be hardly a member who fails to note some such connection in his biography in the *Times' House of Commons.* Perhaps some Congressmen also have similar connections. Amid their wide membership in churches, fraternal organizations, and "patriotic" groups as recorded in the *Congressional Directory,* however, they fail to mention them.

Perhaps, as S. E. Finer has suggested, the absence of such interested members from the Congress is one reason why American pressure groups must make up the deficiency by hiring lobbyists in such large numbers. For the interested MP is an active lobbyist within the legislature. His principal role is played within the parliamentary party, but his activity in the House itself is more observable. He may speak openly as the representative of a group, as the President of the British Legion often does in forwarding the Legion's campaign to increase disability pensions.[19] He is more likely to be effective at the amendment stage of a finance or other bill when, briefed by his association, he suggests changes, which perhaps at the same time are being urged on the Minister and civil servants by officers or staff of the pressure group.

Influencing Public Opinion

Herring long ago observed how American pressure groups direct great attention to influencing public opinion: not only to win support for some immediate objective, but also to build up generally favorable attitudes. This he found to be a trait of the "new" lobby, and it is not irrelevant that this technique arose along with the development of modern mass-advertising methods and media. A major difference in Britain is that the big vocational pressure groups rarely mount such public campaigns. In the nineteenth century, this was not so. Beginning late in the century, however, this propagandist function seems more and more to have passed to political parties. Today and for many years now, the parties, in contrast with the pressure groups, have virtually monopolized communication with the voters as such—that is with the general public as distinguished from communication by a pressure group with its clientele.

This differentiation of function in political communication has gone very much farther in Britain than in the United States. A striking feature of nearly all the vocational pressure groups there is the extent to which they

---

[19]J. H. Millett, "British Interest Group Tactics: A Case Study," *Political Science Quarterly* (March 1957).

urge their demands simply and frankly as special interests. There is a significant contrast, I think, with American pressure groups which tend to base their claims on some large principle of social philosophy or national policy—as, for example, in the vast public-relations program of the NAM.

Yet the public campaign has sometimes been used by the big pressure groups of British politics and its use may be on the increase. Examples are the antinationalization campaign launched by the Road Haulage Association in 1946-47; Tate and Lyle's famous "Mr. Cube" campaign against the nationalization of sugar refining in 1949-50; and in general the growing use of Aims of Industry, a public-relations agency founded to defend and advocate free enterprise. Lesser efforts have been pressed by the National Union of Teachers and the British Legion. If this practice grows greatly, one might well expect it to weaken the position of the parties.

Such a development—which I do not expect—could have great consequences for the British polity. For without in any degree being cynical, one must acknowledge the large part played by British parties in creating the present political homogeneity of the British electorate—the national market for their brand-name goods. The British party battle is continuous and highly organized and so also is the stream of propaganda directed at the voter. Through it the party voter is strengthened, if not created, and the tight party majority in the legislature prepared. Even more important, the framework of public thinking about policy, the voter's sense of the alternatives, is fixed from above. Popular sovereignty in the polity has been qualified by the same means that have qualified consumers' sovereignty in the economy.

In this Americans are not likely to find much cause for self-congratulation. We will hardly say that we are more free of political propaganda. As in other aspects of the American power pattern, the difference is that the centers from which this weighty influence emanates are far more dispersed and unco-ordinated. Is this necessarily to our advantage? Some words of E. P. Herring's suggest an answer:

> A democracy inclines toward chaos rather than toward order. The representative principle, if logically followed, leads to infinite diversity rather than ultimate unity. . . . Since the "voice of the people" is a pleasant fancy and not a present fact, the impulse for positive political action must be deliberately imposed at some strategic point, if democracy is to succeed as a form of government.[20]

[20]Herring, *op. cit.* (note 15 *supra*), p. 377.

Group Influence
and the Policy
Process
in the Soviet
Union

Joel J. Schwartz / William R. Keech

It has become widely recognized that Soviet officials do not formulate
public policy in a vacuum, and that, indeed, their deliberations take into
account in some fashion the needs and demands of various elements of
the society. Further, it has been observed that social groups of various
types play a noticeable, if only rudimentary role in articulating interests
to the top of the hierarchy. In fact one author has gone so far as to assert
that communist policy-making results from a "parallelogram of conflicting
forces and interests."[1] While such viewpoints are now far more widely
accepted than in the early fifties, relatively little effort has been devoted
to illustrating or illuminating how Soviet public policy in general or even
a given Soviet policy can be importantly affected by group activity.

We propose here to make a contribution in that direction. Using the
Educational Reform Act of 1958 as an exemplary case, we intend to show
how and through what process groups can affect policy outcomes, and by
identifying circumstances under which this takes place to generate some
hypotheses about when such influence is most likely to recur. In their
excellent analysis of Soviet policy formation, Professors Brzezinski and
Huntington identify what they call "policy groups," which come closest
of any nongovernmental groups to participating in policy formation. These
groups, such as the military, industrial managers, agricultural experts
and state bureaucrats

> whose scope of activity is directly dependent on the allocation of national re-
> sources and which are directly affected by any shift in the institutional distri-
> bution of power, . . . advocate to the political leadership certain courses of action;
> they have their own professional or specialized newspapers which, at times and

[1] H. Gordon Skilling, "Interest Groups and Communist Politics," *World Politics,* 18 (April
1966), p. 449.

SOURCE: Joel J. Schwartz and William R. Keech, "Group Influence and the Policy Process in
the Soviet Union," *American Political Science Review,* LXII (September 1968), 840-850. Reprinted by permission.

subject to over-all Party control, can become important vehicles for expressing specific points of view.[2]

In this article we will investigate an instance wherein such groups seemed to influence policy with the result of virtually scuttling one of Khrushchev's own major proposals.

• • •

The first major section of the paper will describe the situation we use as a basis for our speculative analysis about the Soviet decision making process. The second will attempt to explain why things happened as they did, and the third will report some hypotheses about when such phenomena are likely to recur.

I. Debate over the 1958 Act

A prominent feature of post-Stalin Russia has been the nationwide discussion of certain legislative proposals. This does not constitute a totally new innovation in the Soviet Union. During the preceding period such important laws as the constitution of 1936 received nationwide discussion before enactment. A few differences, however, deserve mention. First, the frequency of these discussions has substantially increased. Second and more important, the impact of these discussions on the proposed legislation has in some instances been far more than peripheral. This especially applies to the debate which surrounded the Educational Reform Act of 1958. A closer look at this debate will afford us an opportunity to consider how the opinion of various "publics" can influence the policy process.

There can be little doubt about whose initiative lay behind the proposed reform. At the thirteenth Komsomol Congress in April of 1958, First Party Secretary Khrushchev severely criticized the existing school system and demanded fundamental changes.[3] This attack seems to have been motivated by three problems facing Soviet society in the mid-fifties, the cause of which Khrushchev linked to the existing school system.

First, the Soviet press had unceasingly criticized the denigrative attitudes of the younger generation toward physical labor.[4] In the opinion of the First Secretary, the undue emphasis upon classical academic training and the neglect of the polytechnical side of education were largely responsible for this attitude.

[2]Zbigniew Brzezinski and Samuel P. Huntington, *Political Power: U.S.A./U.S.S.R.* (New York, 1963), p. 196.

[3]Khrushchev's statement can be found in XIII *S"ezd vsesoiuznogo leninskogo kommunisticheskogosouiza molodezhi: stenograficheskii otchet* (Moscow 1959), pp. 278-282.

[4]See, for example, L. Bueva, "Tvorcheskii trud- osnova kommunisticheskogo vospitaniia molodezhi," *Kommunist,* Vol. 37, No. 3 (February 1961), p. 53; and also *Komsomol'skaia pravda,* March 2, 1956; February 10, 1957.

Second, competition for admission to higher education had reached an excessive degree and this likewise had caused great concern among political leaders.[5] The competition itself has largely been a by-product of changes in the economic and educational systems.

Prior to 1950 the rapid growth of the economy and the underdeveloped secondary educational facilities maintained the demand for skilled technical cadres at a higher level than the supply. Throughout this period the number of available places in higher education exceeded the number of secondary school graduates. The post war years, however, witnessed a remarkable acceleration of secondary school facilities and enrollment. In 1949, out of a total enrollment of thirty-three million pupils only about one million were in grades eight to ten. Four years later the number of pupils in secondary education had risen to four and one half million.[6] Now the annual supply of secondary school graduates greatly exceeded the number of vacancies in higher education. Since the Soviet regime, for reasons of its own, was unwilling to widen the availability of higher education, the gates of universities were closed to millions of youth regardless of their educational attainment.

An inevitable consequence has been the intensification of competition for the available number of places.[7] The pressures for admission became abnormally high because of the wide-spread notion that a college degree represents the key to individual advancement and entrance into the new class of Soviet intelligentsia. Consequently, those high school graduates initially denied admission refused to accept their fate. Instead of entering the labor force, many of them became perennial college candidates. Very often they applied to schools whose area of specialization was of no genuine interest to them. But in the absence of alternatives they would often enter an agricultural institute just to be able "to study somewhere."[8] Here again Khrushchev charged that the educational system had bred such attitudes. By allowing students to continue their education uninterruptedly and by stressing almost exclusively academic material, the schools naturally generated the expectation that the path to life lay solely through higher education.

The third problem involved the increasing stratification of Soviet society. The notion that higher education was the key to membership in

[5]See XIII *S"ezd op. cit.,* p. 280. See also S. Pavlov, "Sovetskaia molodezh' v bor'be za kommunizm," *Kommunist,* Vol. 36, No. 4 (March 1960), p. 63.

[6]Nicholas DeWitt, *Education and Professional Employment in the USSR* (Washington 1961), p. 140.

[7]In his speech to the XIII Komsomol Congress, Khrushchev noted that "last year higher educational institutions were able to accept 400,000 new students, half of them for full time study.—. However, at least 700,000 secondary school graduates failed to gain admission last year to higher or technical schools and between 1953-1956 about 2,200,000 failed to gain admission" *XIII S"ezd, op. cit.,* p. 278.

[8]*Ibid,* p. 282.

the "new class" had a firm basis in fact. Yet these educational channels for upward social and political mobility were being drastically constricted as a consequence of their preemption by the incumbent political and bureaucratic elites. Khrushchev himself admitted that in the competition for admission to college the influence of parents often proved more important than the merit of the candidates. He further stated that only thirty to forty per cent of the enrolled students in higher education institutions came from worker and peasant backgrounds.[9] The differential access to a prime source of mobility gravely concerned the First Secretary. Both the content and tenor of his statements clearly indicate that Khrushchev sought to eliminated privilege and inequality from the Soviet educational system.[10]

Finally we should mention an additional factor which *may* have influenced the reform movement. At the time of the debate some western scholars argued that the specifics of Khrushchev's proposals owed much to the serious labor shortage the Soviet economy was about to experience.[11] The argument may be briefly summarized as follows. Because of severe war losses and a declining birth rate in the post war period the Soviet Union would have one-third fewer people entering the labor force during the late fifties and early sixties than normally would have been the case. Consequently the ambitious economic growth program could be achieved only if the vast majority of young people were channelled into the active labor force instead of higher education. It is important to note, however, that the Soviet press never cited a labor deficit as cause for the reform. Other evidence also casts doubt upon the validity of this thesis.[12]

While there is room for disagreement as to what problems motivated the reform, there is no ambiguity regarding Khrushchev's proposals for dealing with them. In September of 1958, the party secretary published his "thesis" on school reorganization.[13] He suggested that continuous academic education be abolished and that all students be required to combine work with study. In effect this meant phasing out the ten year school which at that time constituted a complete secondary education. After finishing a seven or eight year primary school, said Khrushchev, every young person should enter the labor force. Those who wished to prepare themselves for higher education could continue their studies in evening and correspondence schools. Successful students would receive two or three days released time from work to facilitate studying.

---

[9]*Pravda*, September 21, 1958.

[10]XIII *S"ezd, op. cit.*, p. 280.

[11]See, for example, DeWitt, *op. cit.*, p. 15.

[12]For a refutation of the labor deficit thesis see "Facts and Figures," *Bulletin of Radio Free Europe*, September 22, 1958.

[13]See *Pravda*, September 21, 1958.

The substitution of part time work and study for full time education in secondary day schools had, from Khrushchev's point of view, two advantages. First, it would instill in the younger generation a respectful attitude toward physical labor. Second, it would equalize access to higher education. The secondary day schools had become the province of children from the urban intelligentsia. Evening and correspondence schools, on the other hand, recruited most of their students from worker and peasant families. The difference in the quality of education offered by these two divisions gave the day school graduate an obvious advantage. By fusing the two channels into one undifferentiated system, Khrushchev hoped to eliminate the class bias in Soviet education. The road to a higher education would be the same for all irrespective of the positions or jobs which the parents held in society.

Study in higher educational institutions was also to be put on a part time basis. The student would acquire the first two or three years of his college education through evening or correspondence courses. Thereafter he could complete his training on a full time schedule. Moreover, no individual was to be granted admission to higher education unless he had already worked full time after completing secondary school. Once again we see Khrushchev's determination to deemphasize the purely academic side of education and to enhance the importance of work experience.

If we compare Khrushchev's September Memorandum with the actual law adopted in December 1958 we find that the two differ not only in detail but in basic principle.[14] To begin with, the old secondary day school was preserved more or less intact both in form and content. Khrushchev's demand that work be combined with study had received token satisfaction by increasing the number of hours devoted to polytechnical training *within* the schools. But the quantity and quality of academic subjects had in no way been sacrificed. The law established an eleven year day school to replace the old ten year day school system. The addition of another year permitted greater emphasis upon labor training without simultaneously diluting the quality of academic education. Indeed, the number of hours devoted to purely academic subjects proved to be *exactly the same* under the new system as it had been under the old.[15]

The maintenance of continuous secondary full time education must be seen as a rebuff to Khrushchev's demands. When the new law went into effect, it became apparent that nearly all the former ten year schools would

---

[14]For a text of the law see *Spravochnik partiinogo rabotnika* (Moscow 1959), pp. 517-533.

[15]For an analysis of this point see an article by Klaus Mehnert in *Die Welt*, July 18, 1959.

[16]The actual law left this point unclear but later developments indicated that just as many children—about a third of the total—would attend full time high schools as had been the case before the reform. See Thomas Bernstein "Soviet Educational Reform," (M. A. Thesis, Columbia University, 1962), p. 111, and articles in *The New York Times*, September 2, 1959; *Wall Street Journal*, June 29, 1960.

continue to operate as part of the new eleven year system. Some figures also suggest that the number of students enrolled in the new system was comparable in size to the two senior grades of the old ten year school.[16] It is true that Khrushchev recognized in his memorandum the need for *some* full time day schools. But he envisaged that they would operate only during a transitional period and he expected their number to be sharply reduced right from the beginning of the reform.

While the eleven year system might have satisfied the demand that work be combined with study, it could not possibly have achieved Khrushchev's other expressed purpose—the elimination of privilege and inequality. The perpetuation of a bifurcated full time and part time school system insured that inequality would persist. Nevertheless the disadvantages faced by the evening and correspondence student might have significantly diminished had the law incorporated Khrushchev's suggestion regarding released time for study. Yet in this area as well important modifications were made. The reorganization decree left this question open and subsequent legislation resulted in a far less liberal policy.[17] Under these circumstances the vast majority of college students would continue to come from the full time secondary schools and an inevitable by-product would be the continuation of class bias in higher education.

The provision for admission to and study in higher educational institutions likewise markedly deviated from Khrushchev's suggestions. Instead of *absolutely* requiring full time work before admission, the law merely stipulated that *priority* would be granted those with the record of employment or military service. But precedence for people with production experience already existed before the reorganization of the school system. Thus the wording of the law gave only formal recognition to an on-going practice. It cannot be interpreted as a "concession" to the demands made by Khrushchev in his memorandum.

His insistence upon part time study during the first few college years appears to have been more successfully realized. At least the law accepted it in principle. However, even here some important alterations occurred. The law explicitly exempted from this requirement all students in difficult theoretical disciplines. Similarly, the requirement would be inoperative in both non-technical higher educational institutions and in arts faculties at universities since "factory work for students cannot in these cases be connected with their future job."[18]

---

[17]Instead of the two to three days released time from work as suggested by Khrushchev, students in evening schools received only one additional free day for study. See A. I. Shebanova, "O l'gotakh dlia lits sovmeshchaiushchikh rabotu s obucheniem," *Sovetskoe gosudarstvo i pravo* Vol. 20 (November 1960), pp. 99-102.

[18]This point was made by the Soviet Minister of higher education and was reflected in the final law. See V. P. Eliutin, "Soveshchanie rabotnikov vysshei shkoly," *Vestnik vysshei shkoly*, Vol. 16, No. 10 (October 1958), p. 9.

Generally speaking, the education reform failed to implement the most important goals and purposes which Khrushchev had articulated in his memorandum. What factors can account for the observable disparity between the September proposal and the December law? To answer that question we must look briefly at the discussion which ensued during this period of time. The content of that debate clearly revealed that different societal groups, or at least some members of them, opposed Khrushchev's reform.

Teachers and administrators identified with the ten year school obviously wished to preserve and protect their institutional bailiwicks. But a frontal assault on the First Secretary's ideas would not have been good politics. Instead they opposed the reform more deviously. Essentially they argued that to prepare youth for manual labor it was not necessary to send them after the eighth grade to factories or farms. A much better way would be to bring the factories and farms into the schools by setting up first class workshops. Under these conditions it would be possible to teach pupils the same skills they could learn by entering the labor force. To substantiate their case the proponents of this approach assumed the initiative even *before* the appearance of Khrushchev's September memorandum. Prior to the opening of the school year in 1958, Y. I. Afanasenko, Minister of Education for the Russian Republic, announced that the number of schools giving training in industrial and agricultural skills would double. He further announced that the Russian Republic had begun to experiment with extending secondary schools from ten to eleven years. Under the extended program students would spend half of their time at school and the other half at jobs on farms, in factories, or at construction sites. He mentioned that fifty schools with this program had operated the last year and this number would increase to two hundred this year. Here, in embryonic form, was the eleven year school system that became law in December of 1958. Thus, through word and deed, those occupational groups associated with full time secondary education sought to protect the organization they had built with effort and care.[19]

Other groups opposed to the reform included higher educational and scientific personnel. Their arguments were perhaps more telling. They warned that it would be impossible under the new system to ensure the supply of highly qualified cadres for economic and societal growth. How can we, they asked, perfect and advance scientific knowledge when new entrants to higher educational schools would have only eight years of regular schooling behind them and who, in the following years, would have forgotten the little they had once learned. Several prominent educators and scientists went so far as to assert that a hiatus between incomplete and

[19]*Literaturnaia gazeta*, August 30, 1958.

complete secondary school as well as between complete secondary school and higher education would result in irreparable damage to the state. For creative work in scientific research often manifests itself when the individual has reached his mid-twenties and the acquisition of theoretical knowledge on a large scale demands uninterrupted study.[20]

The warning of experts reinforced grave doubts raised by many parents. The basic argument of the latter was that a shortened basic school program would adversely affect the physical and intellectual maturation of adolescents. Furthermore, it was said that channeling young people into production at an early age does not give them a chance to adequately choose a skill which best suits them.[21] While both of these points had merit, parental views were somewhat suspect because other motives could be readily discerned. As Khrushchev himself pointed out, many parents were determined that their children receive opportunities for maximum education. They saw his plans as a threat to that opportunity and responded by attacking it. To the extent that pedagogical experts echoed parental concerns, as some did, they served as a linkage between public opinion and political decision makers. By articulating the interests of an amorphous group in technical terms, the experts transformed their claims into a politically relevant issue.

A few words must also be said about the attitudes of factory managers. Although their opposition did not find explicit expression in the debate, their behavior left few doubts as to where they stood on the issue. Long before the question of reform had arisen, managers had displayed a reluctance to hire and train juvenile workers. Under the new arrangements they would become responsible for all sorts of educational functions for which the factory was ill prepared. Moreover, the large influx of school children and the necessity to train them would inevitably divert managers from their own duties of production and plan fulfillment. In light of this fact it is not surprising that the reform act failed to implement Khrushchev's suggestions regarding released time from work. That would have greatly complicated the managers' task and we can assume that their views were transmitted to the proper authorities.[22]

At this point, our task is to account for the role of groups in forming educational policy in this instance by interpreting a number of facts. The objective facts we must work from are, in summary, that Khrushchev made

[20]For examples of such arguments see *Literaturnia gazeta,* June 26, 1958; December 20, 1958; *Pravda,* September 24, 1958; October 17, 1958; November 19, 1958. K Ia Kondrat'ev and P.A. Shi'lov" O nekotorykh voprosakh universitetskogo obrazovaniia," *Vestnik vysshei shkoly,* Vol. 16, No. 10 (October 1958), pp. 17-23.

[21]See *Pravda,* November 30, 1958; December 2, 1958; *Literaturnaia gazeta,* December 20, 1958.

[22]For a scathing criticism of managerial attitudes toward juvenile workers see the lead editorial in *Pravda,* September 25, 1957.

a far-reaching proposal to deal with a number of educational problems facing the regime, and that the substance of the proposal was radically modified. The major proponent of the reform was obviously Khrushchev himself. The most important—indeed the only—opponents of the changes we can identify are the social groups cited above.

Here we should note that if one quantifies the number of articles which appeared during the debate, the oppositional point of view is clearly a minority. It is quite possible that a "war of memoranda" may have been raging behind the scenes and that during this exchange the minority position was in fact the majority point of view.[23] Whatever may have been the case, it is undeniable that the oppositional arguments were closer to the form of the finally enacted law.

There are several possible interpretations which would explain the outcome of the educational reform debate. One might argue, for example, that the disparity between the September memorandum and the December law resulted from Khrushchev changing his mind. Once the technocratic elites had pointed out the potentially dangerous consequences inherent in Khrushchev's proposals, the First Secretary simply revised his original position. There is no way, of course, to verify or falsify this interpretation. Since we have no knowledge of Khrushchev's preference schedule or to whom he would most likely listen, we must allow for the possibility that anyone who had a position and stated it prior to the outcome might have influenced Khrushchev. If we accept this interpretation, however, we must resolve certain questions which detract from its credibility.

When Khrushchev spoke to the Komsomol Congress in April, 1958, he stated that the Party Central Committee had, *for some time*, been discussing the improvement of public education. Presumably, experts had been consulted during the course of such discussions. We might also presume that Khrushchev sounded out experts between April and September when he was preparing a detailed proposal for educational reform. In light of this, it seems unlikely that Khrushchev changed his mind because he heard convincing arguments which had not been made in the far longer period which preceded publication of his memorandum.

It is also important to recall that Khrushchev clearly identified himself personally with the issue of educational reform. He placed his public

[23]There is some evidence that the opposition was far greater than one would gather from simply reading the official press. For example, relatively few parental criticisms found their way into print. But during 1963-64 when the first author of this paper was conducting interviews in the Soviet Union, it was learned that a very large number of urban middle class parents had strongly criticized Khrushchev's proposals at "PTA" meetings held during the reform debate period. Similarly, Professor William Johnson of the University of Pittsburgh told the same author that opposition among educational officials was far more widespread than the official press revealed. Professor Johnson was in the Soviet Union at the time of the debate and is known to have extensive contacts with Soviet educators.

prestige squarely upon the line. As Richard Neustadt has pointed out, chief executives cannot afford to make indiscriminate public pronouncements. If they are sensitive to the prerequisites of power and influence, they must carefully weigh the consequences which flow from what, when and how they say things.[24] All the evidence we have on Khrushchev's career suggests that he was highly sensitive to the requisites of power and influence. Thus not only did the First Secretary have ample opportunity to consult expert opinion on the educational question, but he also had a vested political interest in doing so before publicly stating his position.

Our own inclination then is to discount, though not categorically reject, the possibility that Khrushchev simply changed his mind between September and December. An alternative interpretation is that bureaucratic groups prevailed over the First Secretary and forced him to act against his will.[25] To accept this, however, would demand a rewriting of the literature on political power and resources in the Soviet Union that we think is neither necessary nor appropriate. It is quite easy on the other hand to imagine more important actors prevailing over Khrushchev with the social groups associating themselves spuriously, so to speak, with the stronger actors. In suggesting this interpretation we must argue inferentially because the only direct evidence we have about opposition to the proposal relates to the groups. In the section below we will attempt to account for what happened and to assess the role of the social groups in it.

II. The Role of Social Groups in Shaping the Act

Brzezinski and Huntington express the orthodox interpretation in arguing that the key political resource in the Soviet Union is control of the party organization, and that such control can be shared only at the top.

> Thus, insofar as there are limits on the power of the top leader in the Soviet Union, they stem from his sharing control of the *apparat* with a small number of colleagues . . . the principal limits on the power of the Soviet leader are inside the Kremlin.[26]

We agree, and we feel that those colleagues were crucially important in defeating Khrushchev's proposal. But the opposition of the groups identified above was not coincidental. We submit that the groups were mobilized after the dispute was left unresolved at the top.

Such an argument forces us to take sides in a dispute among Soviet scholars about whether or not there is conflict within the Soviet leadership

[24]Richard Neustadt, *Presidential Power* (New York, 1964).
[25]For an analysis of the reform with this type of implication see David Burg, "Some thoughts on the Soviet educational reform," *Bulletin*, 6 (March 1959), 32-36.
[26]Brzezinski and Huntington, *op. cit.*, p. 145.

at times other than succession crises. It is the position of the "conflict" school that policy issues such as those on agriculture, heavy industry, consumer goods, foreign affairs, Stalinism, economic reorganization and education are continuous sources of dispute among the top leadership. When one issue is resolved, another is likely to take its place. We think there is strong evidence for this viewpoint, which became more compelling than ever with Khrushchev's political demise in October, 1964.[27]

In this specific case, Khrushchev stated in April, 1958, that the Party Central Committee was presently engaged in preparing a resolution on the improvement of public education.[28] But the September "theses" proved to be simply a note by Khrushchev with the "approval" of the Central Committee, instead of a formal resolution by that august body. This suggests that Khrushchev's educational reform was a highly personal document which lacked support among a substantial element of the top political leadership. Esoteric evidence to support this thesis is provided by the unusual silence of the top political leadership during the educational reform debate. Khrushchev appears to have been the only Praesidium member to have played a significant role in the reform discussions and to have clearly and publicly expressed his attitudes. Sidney Ploss has argued that in the context of Soviet politics the silence of leaders on a topical issue must be construed as disagreement with the expressed viewpoint of their colleagues.[29] It is also significant that major amendments to Khrushchev's plan were reflected in the Central Committee resolution on education reform which was finally issued on November 16, 1958.[30]

If, as we have argued, the important conflict was on the top leadership level, and if the persons on that level have the power to determine policy outcomes, what role did the social groups play? The answer hangs on the nature of conflict among the leaders. It is well known that such conflict involves elements of power struggle and elements of dispute over policy alternatives.[31] Sometimes these elements operate independently of one another; more often they intertwine. Since Khrushchev had decisively defeated his rivals for power in 1957, we can assume that in the case of the education reforms of 1958 the elements of power struggle were less important than at almost any time since Stalin's death, and that the elements of unadulterated policy dispute were correspondingly more important. Indeed, it is unlikely that Khrushchev would have survived such a defeat as this had this policy dispute involved much power struggle.

[27]See for example, Carl A. Linden, *Khrushchev and the Soviet Leadership 1957-1964* (Baltimore, 1966).

[28]See *XIII S"ezd, op. cit.,* p. 282.

[29]See *Conflict and Decision-Making in Soviet Russia* (Princeton 1965), p. 17-18.

[30]For an analysis of these amendments see Rudolph Schlesinger, "The Educational Reform," *Soviet Studies,* 10 (April 1959), 432-444.

[31]See Brzezinski and Huntington, *op. cit.,* pp. 267, 269-283, 295-300.

Insofar as this was really a policy dispute, it involved numerous problem-solving considerations, as we emphasized above. The problems and policy positions associated with them involved a number of questions of judgment about what courses of action would solve the problem, and what the consequences of such action would have for other goals of the regime. It is here that the groups play an important role. Numerous groups have recognized expertise about what problems are in their own area. The ten year school personnel had an authoritative position for a judgment that students could get work experience without radically changing the school organization and curriculum. The scientific community had good claim to special insight into the needs of training scientists. Parents may be viewed as having some legitimate judgment about the needs of adolescents, although this is less apparently expertise. One student of the reform debate has argued that

> The most important factors responsible for the change in Khrushchev's original proposals probably were the arguments of experts—the function of expert opinion was to point out to the leadership the possibly harmful consequences to Soviet society of the literal adoption of Khrushchev's original plans.[32]

It is hard to identify any concrete resource other than their own recognized expertise which the groups might have used in the dispute. Neither money, votes nor popularity were relevant to its resolution. Only the expert judgment was clearly relevant. The only reasonable alternative would seem to be that the regime may have accorded the positions of these groups a certain legitimacy just because they were group preferences, much as an American public official might yield to a constituent's demand simply because he views it as legitimate and because he may view his job as one of servicing such demands when they are legitimate and do not conflict with other goals. We have no reason to believe that Soviet officials view their jobs this way. Communist ideology, unlike democratic ideology, supplies its own policy goals, rather than depending on public expressions of preference to define them. Besides, we have already seen that the goals of these groups conflicted with the goals of none other than the First Secretary of the Communist Party. It does not seem apparent that insofar as groups influenced the outcome of this issue it was through the communication of their expert judgments to people at the top of the hierarchy who *were* in a position to influence outcomes. The expertise became a resource to be used in making a case that more harm than good would result from the proposed reform.[33] We contend that in the Soviet Union policy issues

---

[32]Bernstein, *op. cit.*, p. 119. See also Brzezinski and Huntington, p. 214.

[33]In this instance, many political leaders may have been especially inclined to "believe" these arguments. As primary members of the new class, Communist Party cadres had good

are often decided on the basis of such debates. If such is the case the arguments of persons who are recognized as being knowledgeable can be an important resource for the proponent or opponent of a policy proposal.[34]

One can see elements of ambiguity in this interpretation of the role of these groups as articulators of expert judgment. It may appear, for example, that the ten year school personnel are looking out for themselves when they oppose changes in their institution. The position of the parents seems even more transparent. There may even have been some self-interest involved in the position of the scientists. The point is that there is no objective way for either Soviet leaders or American scholars to clearly separate the elements of self-interest from those of expert predictions of dire consequences. We would argue that in western democracies as well there is often an almost indecipherable mixture of preference and prediction in policy debate. For example, social welfare policies in the United States are commonly defended in terms of the prospects of contraction and recession if welfare funds are not fed into the economy. The very ambiguity between preference and prediction may serve to enhance the prospects of group influence through the pressing of interests with the support of expert judgments. The congruence of one's interests with one's predictions is probably less important than the persuasiveness of the predictions and the acknowledged expertness of predictors, no matter whose interests they seem to support.

This almost inevitable mixture of self-interest and expertise provides a channel through which groups in the Soviet Union *may* influence policy when higher powers seek their judgment. We do not know how common this occurrence is, but we are confident that expertise is not used in this way to resolve all policy disputes. We will devote the remainder of this paper to an assessment of conditions leading to such a state, and to hypotheses about when to expect it. Our first set of hypotheses deal with what conditions within the current post-Stalin regime will be associated with such group influence. The second set will attempt to identify what it is about post-Stalinist Russia that makes this possible in contrast with the Stalin era.

---

reason to support the educational *status quo*. They were among the chief beneficiaries of the existing system. Their children enjoyed advantageous access to full-time secondary and higher education. There is no question that such cadres hoped to perpetuate the provision of such education for their children. Khrushchev's proposals surely must have caused consternation among party cadres which other top party leaders would readily have been conscious of. In this respect the party itself was probably an important constituent pressure group which reinforced the doubts Khrushchev's colleagues had about the wisdom of his proposals.

[34]For a view of government as problem solving and adapting to environments in which communications play a crucial role, see Karl W. Deutsch, *The Nerves of Government* (New York 1963).

III. Some Hypotheses

Leadership conflict has already been cited as an important factor in leading top officials to look to group expertise. It is more than conceivable that monolithic leadership would itself seek expert advice, but we expect that it would do so more surreptitiously than through semi-public debate. More importantly, it could ignore the advice when it chose to rather than in effect being reversed by it. Under conditions of leadership conflict, unresolved disputes may lead some of the participants to broaden the scope of conflict by involving policy groups who might shift the balance. The dynamic involved may be something like the following. There is a split, for example, among the Politbureau, wherein the First Secretary is about to prevail. Holders of the minority position may react to their imminent defeat by contacting their sympathizers among the "policy groups" and urging them to state their position on the issue in their specialized publications, in hopes that the balance of power will shift in their favor when more actors are involved. Broadening the scope of conflict may change the outcome.[35]

> We hypothesize that the more and greater the disputes on the top policy making level, the more likely it is that policy groups will be involved and listened to.

Brzezinski and Huntington point out that policy-makers are "more responsive to the demands or aspirations of groups" during a struggle for power, which would seem to bear out our point.[36] They use Khrushchev's struggle as an example but they themselves point out elsewhere that victors in power struggles often reverse themselves and adopt the policies advocated by their opponent.[37] This pattern would seem to reduce the long term impact of group influence in a power struggle. Our own example is of an unreversed policy decided in a period when the heat of the struggle for power had diminished, whether it had completely died or not. Indeed the absence of a threat to his power may well have made Khrushchev more willing to yield. Brzezinski and Huntington say that while policy is the means to power in succession struggles,

> In stable dictatorial conditions, however, the leader may sometimes exercise power in matters that do not affect the security of his position. Then, as with the

---

[35]See Ploss, *op. cit.*, pp. 61, 84, 286, for other examples and a discussion of changes in the scope of conflict in the Soviet Union. See also E. E. Schattschneider, *The Semisovereign People* (New York 1960), for a discussion of the impact of other kinds of changes in patterns of conflict in the United States.

[36]*Op. cit.*, p. 198.

[37]*Ibid.*, pp. 193, 240-252.

education reform of 1958, he can tolerate substantial amendments to his original proposal.[38]

It may be, then, that conditions of tranquility lend themselves more effectively to more or less permanent and far-reaching group influence than do power struggles. Leaders are probably more eager to solicit the support of groups when they are trying to secure power or ward off threats to their position, but group influence may be more permanent and real outside of power struggles. We are not prepared to predict that group influence over policy will be greater under power struggles or more ordinary policy conflicts, but we are prepared to argue that under either of these conditions of leadership conflict group influence will be greater than when leadership is relatively monolithic. Such an hypothesis is at the core of our whole argument.

Bauer, Inkeles and Kluckhohn observe that the failure of a policy may lead the Politburo to adopt an approach that they recently opposed.[39] Our example does not directly support this observation, although of course it does not conflict with it, but the important point suggested by it is that the nature of the issue may be an important variable. Pursuing the rationale for our argument of group influence in the educational reforms it is apparent that the problematic character of the issue and the fact that the consequences of a shift were not known with certainty made the judgment of policy groups more important than they would have been otherwise. The obvious implication of this is that the more problematic the consequences of a given course of action the more likely it is that groups would be involved.

A related point that is derived from interest groups politics in western democracies is that groups are likely to be more influential in policy outcomes when the issue is narrow and technical than when the issue is broad and general.[40] In democratic polities, this is partly because other publics are less likely to be paying any attention or to care when the issue is technical. Thus the field is left relatively open for the interested group. A further rationale would be pertinent in the Soviet Union. It is not so much that other actors are or are not concerned; it is rather that technical advice and opinions are at a premium on technical issues.

We hypothesize that the more problematic and technical the issue, the more dependent on expert judgment elites will be. Consequently they will be more likely to consult policy groups, who will thereby be more influential on such issues.

[38]*Ibid.*, p. 270.
[39]Raymond A. Bauer, Alex Inkeles and Clyde Kluckhohn, *How the Soviet System Works* (New York 1956), p. 98.
[40]See Harry Eckstein, *Pressure Group Politics* (Stanford, 1960).

While we hope that the above hypotheses help account for conditions varying *within* the current post-Stalinist regime which we associated with such group influence as we have illustrated, we do not argue that such influence ever occurred in the Stalin era. We know of no such prominent examples. In this final section we will identify several underlying conditions which in part distinguish the two eras and make groups more important in policy formation, or at least potentially so, in the present.

One important change is that the rigid dictatorial one-man rule of the Stalin period has given way to collective leadership. While there may be one dominant leader, his power is shared among several key figures at the apex of the political structure. Under conditions of a diffused power structure, group influence is far more likely.[41] When power is exercised in an autocratic manner, groups must gain the ear of the all-powerful leader if they are to influence the policy process. During a period of collective leadership the access routes to points of decision making become more numerous. Indeed, the very nature of collective leadership may make political leaders more responsive to group demands.

Carl Linden has argued that the transition from autocracy to oligarchy brings with it a constant struggle for political primacy at the very top. Since no individual is automatically assured of predominant power he must secure that position by winning and holding the support of a combination of societal groupings. His actual or potential rivals, on the other hand, can build their own constituency coalitions by identifying with those elements discontented with an incumbent leader's policy. The politics of leadership struggle then intertwines with the politics of group conflict. It is this interdependence which facilitates group influence on the policy process.[42]

We hypothesize that the larger and more collective the top leadership, the greater the prospects for the sort of disputes that can lead to the involvement of social groups in policy formation.

The attitudes of those leaders and their methods of social control will also have an important bearing on the prospects for group influence. Under a system of terror individuals are frightened into silent submissiveness and live in an atomized state. Unaware that others share common attitudes, grievances and interests, the terrorized citizen accepts his lot and does

[41]Dispersion of decision making can assume a "personalized" as well as an institutional form. Instead of separation of powers between executive legislative, and judicial groups one may find a separation of powers between leaders at the top of an outwardly monolithic political structure. See Ploss *op. cit.*, p. 286. On the relationship between group influence and a diffusion of power see Harry Eckstein, "Group Theory and the Comparative Study of Pressure Groups," *Comparative Politics* edited by Harry Eckstein and David Apter (New York 1963), p. 396.

[42]*Op. cit.*, pp. 20-21.

not attempt to influence the behavior of decision makers.[43] Only when terror subsides does this condition of "pluralistic ignorance" end and the opportunity for interest articulation emerge. For now communication, both through the formal mass media and through informal personal interaction, assumes a more candid and realistic nature. Under these new conditions the communication process itself facilitates group influence. It serves to generate widespread awareness of commonly shared attitudes which in turn becomes a powerful factor inducing groups to influence policy outcomes in their favor.

The leashing of terror enhances the prospect for group influence in other ways as well. David Easton points out that not all societal claims and demands are converted into policy outputs. Only those which become public issues have this possibility.[44] In any polity this requires the patronage and support of some political authority figure. In a system where terror is no longer all-pervasive individuals may be far more likely to risk identification with unresolved issues since the consequences of poor choices are far less serious. At best it may mean that one's power position remains static. At worst it may mean a diminution in political power and perhaps even demotion. But it does not mean internment or execution as it so often did during the Stalinist period. The individual has lost a political battle but not necessarily the war. He remains on the scene with the possibility of recouping his losses and rising once again to top political positions.

> We hypothesize that groups will be influential as technocratic spokesmen only when terror subsides and the regime accords them legitimacy of expression of their point of view.

The kind of expert judgment involved in the interest articulation we have described is a function of the nature of the society. Harry Eckstein has noted that modernization increases the significance of groups in the political process.[45] We suggest that the modernization of Russia positively relates to potential group influence in several ways. First, it introduces a functional specialization and differentiation into the society which in turn generates a diffusion of interests competing with one another to write the laws of society to their advantage. During the early stages of Soviet rule the party preempts interest articulation not only because it wants to but also, to some degree, because it has to. The society which the Bolsheviks inherited was largely composed of an undifferentiated mass of peasants who had traditionally played a politically passive role. Thus the task of identifying and articulating interests fell to the party by default.

[43]This condition of "pluralistic ignorance" is discussed in Bauer and others, *op. cit.,* p. 263.
[44]David Easton "The Analysis of Political Systems," *Comparative Politics: Notes and Readings,* edited by Roy C. Macridis and Bernard E. Brown (Homewood 1964), pp. 94-95.
[45]"Group Theory and the Comparative Study of Pressure Groups," *Comparative Politics, op. cit.,* p. 395.

This is not to say that at the time of Bolshevik ascendancy there were no functionally specialized groups with political experience in the protection of their interests. They existed but they were far fewer and far less significant than in the present period. Furthermore, those groups tended to be stigmatized by their identification with the old regime. Thus any demands put forth by them lacked an essential ingredient for success—the presumption of legitimacy. The *a priori* belief of the party that such individuals were disloyal deprived them of any political currency which could be used in the process of trading support for recognition of their demands.

The modernization of Russia has fundamentally altered this situation. Not only has it generated a complex economic and social pluralism but it also has provided new cadres to staff these skilled groups.[46] Those who possess scarce technical capabilities are far more likely to exert influence today than in the past. Such technocrats are products of the new system (the new Soviet man) and their loyalty is not impugned. Consequently, their attempts to influence the political process is perceived in legitimized rather than counterrevolutionary terms. The arguments of scientific, educational, and managerial experts may have been motivated by selfish concerns. But, as we noted earlier these arguments were made in the context of what would best serve the interests of the Soviet Union. Given the fact that these experts are the products of the Soviet period, their counsel cannot be ignored on the grounds that the purveyors of such ideas are politically suspect. The handicap which afflicted old specialists simply does not operate in the contemporary period.

Stalin's transformation of Russia insured the increased importance of groups in the policy process in yet another way, although the full impact of this development had to await the dictator's death. It was during the thirties and forties that the politicization of society reached totalitarian dimensions. As politics came to predominate in all areas of life individuals realized that the protection of their interests could be achieved only by gaining access to and influencing the political structure. Unlike western political systems where many issues are resolved in the private sector of the society, the struggle over who gets what when and how in the Soviet Union takes place entirely within the public domain.[47] Thus individuals and groups

[46]For an interesting suggestive article on the growth of pluralism in Russian society see Henry L. Roberts, "The Succession to Khrushchev in Perspective," *Proceedings of the Academy of Political Science*, 28 (April 1965), 2-12.

[47]We are identifying here a difference of degree. As Eckstein notes, pressure groups have become very active and significant in the postwar political systems of Britain, France, etc., for similar reasons. "One rather obvious reason for this development is the growth of the social service state—of positive government regulating, planning, directing, or entirely drawing into itself all sorts of social activities. This trend has given social groups a greater stake in politics and therefore mobilized them to a much greater extent while making government increasingly dependent on the collaboration and advice, technical or otherwise, of the groups," *Comparative Politics, op. cit.*, p. 395.

are perforce compelled to focus their attention and pressure on the decision-making process if they hope to maintain or improve their status.

The fourth contribution of modernization stems from the fact that a complex technological society requires stable occupational group membership. As we have already suggested the behavior of managers, teachers, educators and scientists was motivated in part by their desire to protect interests derived from their occupational roles. Such a phenomenon occurs, however, only when individuals have an opportunity to firmly anchor themselves in one occupational role so that it becomes for them an important reference group. This connotes, in turn, an absence of the recurring purge so characteristic of the Stalinist period. Stalin purposefully removed leading strata of important groups lest they become too closely identified with the interests of those groups and more specifically lest they use the economic, social and political resources inherent in those groups for the purpose of delimiting the decision making power of the leader.

Now this is a very costly procedure and one that a developed society cannot afford to engage in for very long. Managers, teachers, scientists and other specialists are not created overnight and their summary purge means not only a loss of experienced and skilled personnel but also the forfeiture of scarce economic resources invested in their education and training. As Soviet society has become more complex and sophisticated this type of gross economic waste proved intolerable. We do not imply, of course, that high ranking Soviet personnel are no longer removed from their positions. The official press is full of accounts concerning the removal of such personnel. We do argue, however, that "the purge" today significantly differs from its Stalinist predecessor. At present leading occupational strata are not removed in the wholesale manner reminiscent of the thirties and forties. More importantly their removal is seldom if ever accompanied by internment or execution. Most often they seem to be demoted to a less prestigious and influential job but within the same area of expertise.

> We hypothesize that the more modern the society, the more dependent it is on technical expertise, which in turn improves the prospects that groups may influence policy when higher powers seek their judgment.[48]

We have attempted in this article to illustrate that under some circumstances social groups can influence policy formation in the Soviet Union. We have specified those circumstances as clearly as we could, providing hypotheses according to which we expect group influence to vary. If our analysis is sound and valid, we hope that it may provide some guidelines

[48]See S. N. Eisenstadt, *The Political Systems of Empires* (New York 1963), for a suggestive analysis of the role of skill groups in historical bureaucratic empires.

for further research on group influence in the comparative study of Communist political systems.[49] Indeed, we hope that some parts of our analysis may be relevant to the study of the role of groups in policy formation in non-communist political systems as well.

[49]See Robert C. Tucker, "On the Study of Comparative Communism," *World Politics,* 19 (January 1967), 242-257.

Interest Groups in Italian Politics

Joseph LaPalombara

The Italian Political Culture

INTEREST ARTICULATION

. . . In the terminology of Gabriel Almond, Italian interest groups can be fruitfully divided into institutional, nonassociational, anomic, and associational types. The first of these—the *institutional groups*—are structures established primarily for purposes other than interest articulation. They would include the Catholic Church, the bureaucracy (including the armed services), the political parties (which should, theoretically, primarily aggregate interests), and the various formal institutions of government. In all societies, for part of the time, such structures are likely to become involved in direct-interest articulation, either on behalf of themselves or of other groups in whose interest these institutions behave. However, where the incidence of direct-interest articulation becomes exceedingly heavy, we can agree with Almond that such behavior makes for poor boundary maintenance between the polity and the society.

Italy is clearly characterized by poor boundary maintenance. Although specialized structures for interest articulation exist, they are forced to compete with a heavy incidence of institutional interest-group behavior. The Catholic Church, for example, intervenes in the political process directly, as well as through the intermediary of its organized secondary associations. Priests campaign—and therefore articulate interests—from the pulpit and in the confessionals. Members of the clergy call on the ministries, even if the halls of the bureaucracy are not as crowded with black-robed messen-

SOURCE: From Joseph LaPalombara, "Bureaucratic Intervention: Clientela," in *Interest Groups in Italian Politics* (Princeton: Princeton University Press, 1964), pp. 252-305. Copyright © by Princeton University Press. Reprinted by permission. Footnotes have been deleted.

gers as some Italians suggest. Bishops, following a pattern that dates back
several centuries, intervene directly in the political affairs of the diocese.
Although this study does not present very much data on the political process at the local and provincial level, I am convinced that an adequate understanding of the interest-group phenomenon would require more information on the manner in which clergy and others seek to intervene in the
decisions of prefects, provincial assemblies, mayors, chambers of commerce,
field administrative agencies, and other decentralized formal institutions
of government.

It is necessary to do more than recognize that other institutions such as
the legislature, armed forces, and other sectors of the bureaucracy intervene
in the political process in order to articulate expediency rather than princi-
pled interest. This phenomenon in Italy is not unlike that which we would
expect to find in most western countries. It can occur with even greater
impact and intensity in some of the less-developed countries, where the
bureaucracy is overpowering, and associational interest groups are not
well developed and are often nothing more than the mere instrumentalities
of the bureaucracy itself.

Similarly, there are also evident in the Italian political process *nonassociational* and *anomic* interest groups that make intermittent demands on
government. A typical nonassociational group might be a regional conference called to discuss the problems of the development of the South, or of
civil liberties and their observance. Such conferences, which are fairly frequent in Italy, often recruit participants from a wide variety of formally
organized groups. They are, however, essentially *ad hoc* affairs, out of
which may emerge certain political policy resolutions or actual communications to governmental bodies demanding or requesting action. In many
cases, the meetings are organized by a fairly cohesive, even associational
interest group. Thus the labor unions, as part of their over-all strategy,
will sponsor economic conferences or study groups to which a wide variety
of citizens—representing other groups, the bureaucracy, the legislature and
cabinet, journalism, and the universities—are invited as participants and
performers. The hope is that greater prestige and authority will be lent to
the sponsoring group's demands as a result of the broad and presumably
expert and neutral participation in the formulation and appraisal of the
demands themselves. Two loosely structured groups of intellectuals—those
organized around the prestigious weekly newspaper *Il Mondo* and the
equally important monthly journal *Il Mulino*—are particularly active in
sponsoring study conferences of the type described. The results of these en-
counters are not only reported in the journals involved but often published
as single volumes. Through this strategy, the intellectuals hope to have an
impact on such varied policy matters as education, civil liberties, foreign

policy, motion pictures, and television, even the formation of particular coalitions in the legislature.

Among the other nonassociational interests that might be cited we would include those that reflect the demands of particular geographic regions or linguistic groups. Where, as in Sicily, there is a highly developed system of regional government under the decentralizing provisions of the Constitution, the communication of regional demands is highly structured and flows regularly to Rome through formal governmental channels. On the other hand, where the nonassociational interest group has a linguistic base, such as the German-speaking Italians who live in the South Tyrol, the communication of demands is not as structured and tends to be more intermittent. The same intermittency is characteristic of families, single industrial firms, and minority religious groups, which from time to time, depending on the problems that confront them, seek to communicate demands for policy or administrative action to government at the local or central level. As one would expect in a society of great structural differentiation, the incidence of this type of demand communication is apparently not as high as in the less developed societies, where secondary associations have not taken firm hold. As a matter of fact, where a felt interest exists in Italy, there has been, since the War, an increased tendency to devise some associational pattern whereby the interest might be systematically articulated and communicated.

Italy is also a country that has experienced a great deal of *anomic interest group* behavior. In a strict sense, the articulation of interests by anomic groups—riots, demonstrations, revolutions—should be spontaneous. As a matter of practice, most such occurrences in Italy are the premeditated work of political parties or voluntary associations. Pregnant women, for example, do not spontaneously appear lying prone on roads leading from Montecatini sulphur mines in order to keep trucks from passing. Mutilated veterans who converge on Rome en masse to protest pension policies do not get there because, as if by magic, they all decided that a demonstration before the ministry might have some influence. Italians do not spontaneously riot to protest alleged germ warfare in Korea or the establishment of NATO missile bases on Italian soil. With rare exceptions even the desperate peasants who forcibly occupy land, or the workers who refuse to leave factories, take such anomic action because of the leadership provided by more than one group. There are, of course, some marginal cases. It is not clear, for example, that all the riots that broke out in 1959 at ceremonies to commemorate the Resistance Movement were carefully organized by neo-Fascist and Monarchist organizations. Similarly, some of the demonstrations that occurred when the issue of Trieste reached explosive proportions evidently bordered on complete spontaneity in the sense that people were reacting to information communicated by the mass media. But when students stone

embassies, protest demonstrations are held over the execution of the Rosen-
bergs, or roughnecks invade political meetings indoors or in the public
piazzas, it is reasonably certain that some organizational propelling force
lies behind them.

It is difficult to be sure that anomic interest-group behavior is largely
the result of the ineffectiveness of political parties and voluntary associations as interest articulators and aggregators. One is led to that easy conclusion because such behavior is primarily fostered by parties and groups
of the political extremes who do not have great influence over governmental policy. It is obvious, for example, that the Communist and Neo-Fascist
parties accord the riot and the demonstration a high priority in their arsenal
of political tactics. The use of these and other means of articulating interests even for political matters that are considerably far removed from
matters of immediate domestic concern has been very well documented in
the postwar years.

Yet it would be a mistake to overlook the fact that such behavior is deeply ingrained in Italian history and culture, and that many groups from time
to time have had recourse to violence. While Italy is not in the same category as many Latin American republics that seem unable to handle any
political affairs except through anomic means, neither is she close to the
traditions of Anglo-American democracy, where anomic behavior is a genuinely rare occurrence. The point is that in a fragmented, nonbargaining
political culture such as Italy's, characterized as it is by ideological rigidities and absolute value rationality, all these qualities are transferred to the
competing groups. Out of this kind of interaction emerge certain patterns
of violence that are expressions of fragmentation, as well as unbelievably
strong instruments for reinforcing the fragmentation itself.

To a considerable extent, the extreme consequences of anomic behavior
are held in check by the existence of thousands of *associational interest
groups.* . . .

Legislative Interaction

LOBBYING

•   •   •

. . . [N]othing prevents business groups, or any other group, from engaging in lobbying activities as another means of interaction with the legislative
process. By lobbying is meant informal or formal contacts with members
of the legislature designed to elicit their cooperation in support of or in
opposition to a particular legislative proposal. The essence of lobbying as
I am using the term is contact, direct or indirect, with a lawmaker in order
to persuade him to act in a particular way in regard to a legislative issue.

What the legislator is asked to do might include introducing a bill or offering amendments, talking to colleagues, making speeches in legislative committees or party or parliamentary group caucuses, presenting evidence for or against a proposal, engaging in dilatory or delaying tactics, making public pronouncements concerning an issue, coordinating support for or opposition to a bill, voting for or against a bill, or abstaining from voting. This listing does not exhaust what a lawmaker may be asked to do for a group, but it covers the major actions that might be taken. Representations of group leaders to the legislators may range all the way from abject pleas to threats of sanctions; inducements, explicit or implied, may vary between the expressed gratitude of the group to promises of economic and electoral support. It is important to understand that the act of lobbying involves a two-sided relationship between, on the one hand, an interest group that makes demands, and, on the other hand, a legislator who is formally in a position to satisfy the demands that are communicated.

A great many respondents comment on the pervasiveness of lobbying activity in Italy, and data from interviews suggest that this represents the most frequent type of interaction between groups and lawmakers. One member of Parliament comments that one should not be misled by the widespread belief that the United States experiences more lobbying than does Italy. He notes that the arm-chair scholars often assume that the combination of centralized legislative control under a parliamentary system and the existence of highly disciplined parties reduces the efficacy and attractiveness of legislative lobbying. This is largely myth, says the respondent. He adds that there are probably as many interest groups in Italy as in any country in the world and that many of them are continually in touch with the lawmakers. As far as trying to maximize the effectiveness one can have in the legislature is concerned, our respondent remarks: "Obviously, if the pressure group leaders can reach the party leadership, so much the better. But this does not mean that the groups ignore the individual deputy. In fact, pressure groups often send whole delegations to talk with various members of Parliament for purposes not necessarily of influencing a single vote but of encouraging the single deputy to represent the position of the pressure group in the meetings of the parliamentary group."

• • •

If, as certainly seems to be the case, Italian deputies can deviate from the party line in the legislature to some degree, and if they can represent the views of groups to their party leaders, it is obvious that interest-group approaches to them can pay some rewards. However, it is also necessary to understand that not all points of access in the legislature are of equal attraction to groups seeking to articulate interest. As we noted earlier, the European Federalist Movement found it convenient to concentrate its earlier activities on De Gasperi, who was at the apex both of his party and of the legislature, Representatives of *Il Mulino* and other such groups also indicate that they attempt where possible to gain the attention and support not of the average legislator but of someone — in the majority or minority — who is viewed as holding more than average power. Thus, for example, a leader of the *Il Mondo* group says that they rely heavily on Ugo La Malfa, long a prestigious, brilliant, and articulate Republican leader who entered the Fanfani government as Minister of the Budget in 1962. Confindustria, Catholic Action, and other conservative groups tend to rely very heavily on someone like Giulio Andreotti, a Christian Democratic notable with an immense electoral following at Rome who has held ministerial positions in several governments. . . .

Similarly, we are told by a leader of the Italian Banking Association that a complete hierarchy of relationships prevails between the group, on the one hand, and the legislature, on the other. At the top level, there are maintained contacts between the top leadership of the association and the top leaders of the government. When matters not of crucial import may be at issue, lesser association leaders will contact individual numbers of Parliament. . . .

Not all groups, however, are able so readily to choose the points at which legislative intervention will occur. For clearly depicted in our interviews is the existence of the fragmented and isolative nature of group-governmental relationships. . . . The Italian Association of Building Constructors (A.N.C.E.) tells us that it must rely primarily on Giovanni Malagodi (P.L.I.), Giovanni Spagnolli (D.C.), and Mario Dosi (D.C.), "who are good friends and very reliable." The Italian Banking Association deliberately singles out the bankers in the legislature because "The association feels that it can approach these individuals and in most instances obtain a sympathetic hearing for a proposal that the association wishes to make." The Italian Stockbrokers Association had a stalwart supporter in Senator Teresio Guglielmone (D.C.). The Italian Union of Labor, largely because it is considerably handicapped in the public administrative arena, concentrates its efforts in the legislature and relies on the sympathetic attitudes of Ugo La Malfa (P.R.I.), Guido Ceccherine (P.S.D.I.), and Cino Macrelli (P.R.I. Mixed). The Italian Confederation of Professionals and Artists, which strongly eschews political involvement, tends to restrict its legislative contacts to deputies and senators of the political right because of the particular ideological coloration of one of its top leaders. As far as industrial groups in general go, one political party leader put it this way: "All major industries have their hand-picked deputies. These deputies are rewarded either by consultantships or by patronage in the sense that the deputy is given an opportunity to reward his electoral helpers by finding them jobs in the industries with which they are identified."

Only two of the group leaders interviewed made a point of stressing that they attempt to lobby with lawmakers of decidedly different ideological leanings. One of these represents *Confapi* (National Confederation of Small Industries), which is in open competition with Confindustria for the membership allegiance of small and medium-size business firms. The organization, which claims to include 15,000 of such industries in its ranks, deals with their trade-union, economic, personnel, credit, fiscal, and other problems. In so doing, and notwithstanding its avowed apolitical nature, the *Confapi* often drafts legislative proposals and attempts to have them introduced in Parliament. A leader of the confederation stresses that it seeks the widest possible political support and, for this reason, attempts to maintain contacts with legislators representing widely different political parties.

The other group that maintains a relatively broad approach to the legislature is the Italian General Association of Entertainment (A.G.I.S.), a federation encompassing a number of other associations organized at both the national and the local levels. The Association itself cuts across ideological lines, including in its midst the Catholic Association of Motion Picture Distributors. A central function of the group is that of safeguarding in every way possible the common interest of theater owners, motion picture distributors, comedians, circus owners, impresarios, and others who make up its membership. In so doing, this apolitical group nevertheless finds it necessary frequently to intervene in the legislature and, at the time of the interview, in the Undersecretariat for Entertainment, which was then located in the Office of the Presidency of the Council of Ministers. As far as the legislature itself is concerned, there has apparently existed for some years a parliamentary "center for entertainment," with which the association maintains close relations. Although the strongest support for A.G.I.S. is said to come primarily from Socialist and Neo-Fascist deputies, the "center" includes deputies from many parties. Among those specifically named by our respondent were Giulio Andreotti (D.C.), Iaures Busoni (P.S.I.), Giuseppe Clabrò (M.S.I.), Bruno Corbi (P.C.I.), Guiseppe Brusasca (D.C.), Guido Mazzoli (P.S.I.), and Lucianni Viviani (P.C.I.). Needless to say, basic legislative support for an interest group including such disparate ideological positions as these deputies represent is most unusual. It is largely a function of the mixed ideological character of A.G.I.S. and of the fact that the association is not likely to raise issues of major national import.

Where the area of interest of a group is closely linked to major social, political, and economic policies, and where interest groups themselves fall into different ideological categories, the groups tend to find in the legislature supporters who share their values and who can give aid that is consistent with their own ideologies. Although this pattern is probably true to some degree whenever there are groups and lawmakers interacting, it seems to be true on a much larger scale in an isolative culture such as Italy's. Where the rigid conflicts and antagonisms that characterize the groups are transferred in turn into the legislature, it makes much more difficult for that body the task of fulfilling its function as an interest-aggregating mechanism.

I am noting here exclusively a form of contact—lobbying—which may be viewed as *external* to the legislature. That is, this process involves the establishment of a particular kind of rapport between a group seeking access and one or more members of the legislature who have no open or official connection with the group itself as leaders, members, employees, consultants, and the like. As we shall note in the next section, there also exists in Italy an *internal* form of access of certain groups to the legislative process, and this fact quite radically changes the group's prospects of influencing the making of public policy. . . .

•   •   •

DIRECT REPRESENTATION

To some degree, as far as the legislative rule-making arena is concerned, all of the various kinds of *external* intervention pale alongside the tendency of some major groups to achieve direct *internal* access to the Parliament. There are some interest groups that succeed in electing their own leaders to the legislature and, in some instances, these lawmakers openly organize as a parliamentary group demanding formal recognition. For obvious reasons, this strategy or style of intervention seems to be available primarily to the larger groups with mass followings. When such groups achieve this degree of participation in the legislative process, to continue, as some do, to call themselves "apolitical" implies either extraordinary ingenuousness or self-delusion of striking magnitude.

In order to achieve direct representation, the interest group is compelled to effect very close ties with one of the established political parties—or to establish its own party. An interesting example of the latter type occurred in 1958 when the *Comunità* groups, associated with and headed by the now deceased Adriano Olivetti, organized as a political party. The result of this effort was disappointing; only Adriano Olivetti, a brilliant and humane person with strong misgivings about personal involvement in the legislature, was elected. Many leaders of the *Comunità* movement, skeptical about the strategy from the beginning, would rather not repeat the experience and would return instead to the kinds of interaction with government that prevailed prior to Olivetti's daring attempt at a quantum political jump.

The major interest groups with direct representation are Italian Catholic Action, the Direct Cultivators, some of the auxiliary political party organizations, the Christian Association of Italian Workers (A.C.L.I.), and the Christian Democratic (C.I.S.L) and Communist-Socialist (C.G.I.L.) trade-union confederations. Because of some overlapping, it is difficult to know exactly how many Catholic Action leaders are in the legislature. For the moment, it will suffice to observe that the number is considerable and that Catholic Action has tried deliberately to place them where they are. Nor is Catholic Action the only agency through which organized Catholicism finds representation in the legislature. If one wanted to, of course, the entire Christian Democratic contingent might be viewed in this way. Such a characterization, while it makes sense at a very broad level of abstraction, is both excessive and possibly misleading when one stops to consider the many ideological faces of organized Catholicism as well as the fact that Christian Democracy itself is a brokerage party consisting of a number of groups that are in conflict with each other.

Bureaucratic Intervention: Clientela

• • •

My purpose [next] is to examine aspects of the structure of interest-group interaction with the national bureaucracy in Italy. Just as we noted regarding legislative intervention, the process whereby Italian groups relate to the bureaucracy is not open and fluid. Rather, one can detect that the situation is highly structured and somewhat rigid, and that within it one can discern certain broad types of access and influence, at least as these types are perceived and articulated by bureaucrats, group leaders, and others who have some knowledge of the administrative process. I have called the first of these types *clientela,* referring to a clientelistic relationship between groups and the bureaucracy. The second relationship is called *parentela* and implies a process of group interaction with the bureaucracy which is essentially based on political kinship. Although no group will manifest exclusively one of these types in pure, unblemished form, they are analytically separable and will be treated separately. The analysis itself should also lead to some observations and insights regarding how far Italy's bureaucracy deviates from Weberian requisites or democratic norms, or, to put it in terms of the basic conceptualization worked out earlier, how "traditional," "transitional," or "modern" this particular aspect of Italy's political system might be.

THE MEANING OF CLIENTELA

The process whereby groups exert influence over organs of the state is *structured* rather than *fluid.* It is necessary to emphasize the point, in order to avoid the perilous naïvete about the political process that tends to grow up in democratic countries—or that is held by some advocates of the democratic process. The notion of structured influence is an overriding

generalization. It is meant to suggest, among other things, that the existence of the structured pattern itself will make it both easier to understand the interest group phenomenon and more difficult to manipulate or
modify (or restructure) the patterns of access and influence. This is not to
imply a static social mechanism; it means that formulas that aim to change
the nature of group interaction with government will have to take account
of the degree to which the patterns themselves have become institutionalized.

. . . What often pass for the basic rules of the game of politics are in fact
the values that are strongly held by only a sector of the society—the sector
with access. Laws of property and contract are typical manifestations of this.
But so are the formal and informal institutionalized patterns of government.
It is perfectly obvious, as we shall see in details as we proceed, that those
groups in Italian society which aim . . . at the basic transformation of the
society (and, incidentally, which do not play by the rules) are to a considerable degree disadvantaged. This would be so if the advantaged groups
were able to claim no more than that particular interest-group tactics tend
to undermine the basic stability of the system.

What I call the *clientela* relationship between interest groups and the
bureaucracy illustrates and helps us to understand the notion of structured
access. Briefly put, the *clientela* relationship exists when an interest
group, for whatever reasons, succeeds in becoming, in the eyes of a given
administrative agency, the natural expression and representative of a given
social sector which, in turn, constitutes the natural target or reference
point for the activity of the administrative agency. . .

. . . [T]he administrative agencies dealing with economic affairs maintain natural-logical relationships with economic and industrial groups of
the country. These groups tend to provide the ministries with special
studies, memoranda, a mass of data which is useful, even essential, in the
making of administrative policy. A good example, cutting across several
agencies, would be the C.I.P.—the Interministerial Committee on Prices on
which several economic groups are formally represented. This Committee,
which fixes prices on everything from newspapers to fuel and power, must
necessarily maintain on-going contacts with the very groups that are likely
to be the objects of its regulative activities. It would not be conceivable that
the Committee could long operate with any effectiveness if this intimate
nexus were nonexistent.

. . . Thus, one might possibly view the various branches of Italian public administration as the feudal holdings of the various major groups of
the society. The administrators, in each of these feudal sectors, tend to be
about as rigid in their attitudes as the groups of which they are the expression and representatives. This may also be true of the ministers themselves,

and, to the extent that it is, the possibilities of the Cabinet serving to counteract this advantage are thereby and to that degree limited.

• • •

. . . [E]ach administrative agency, in its efforts to survive and to expand in the struggle with other administrative units, will seek to develop a very close and intimate *clientela* relationship for purposes of having the group or groups apply pressure on government of the *agency's* behalf. Typical of such pressures are those applied in the *sottogoverno* on the Bureau of the Budget. . . . Thus. . . it is not unusual for Confindustria, say, to make an approach to the Budget Bureau on behalf of the Ministry of Industry and Commerce or, more typically, on behalf of some specific directorate-general within the ministry. The same thing, to a lesser extent, is true of trade unions that intervene on behalf of some segment of the Ministry of Labor and Social Security, or the Direct Cultivators who front for the Ministry of Agriculture. The point to bear in mind is that the *clientela* relationship is established and thrives because *both* sides to the relationship can and do derive certain clear-cut advantages from it.

• • •

It is widely perceived and understood both inside and outside the bureaucracy that Confindustria has for several decades maintained a clientelistic relationship to the Ministry of Industry and Commerce. One leader of the Confederation speaks of the many friends it has in the Ministry and points out that over the years the latter has come to understand how fully it is dependent on the good will and the cooperation of the Confederation. The Ministry as a matter of practice prefers to deal with it. So much is this the case that whenever a member association or an individual firm makes a direct approach to the Ministry, the latter will immediately contact Confindustria in order to assure itself that the Confederation is aware of and has no objection to what might otherwise be interpreted as an attempt to intervene in the administrative process over the head of the peak association. Confindustria's leader remarks: "From these friends we can expect a loyal attempt to keep the Confederation completely informed regarding attempts on the part of single member associations or individual plants to engage in the kind of activity with the public administration that might be damaging to the industrial sector as a whole. . . . A combination of the personal friendships we have plus the inevitable dependence of the ministry on our facilities means that, over a period of time, our relations with the Ministry have been more than cordial. We continue to maintain extremely cordial relations with these people."

• • •

We saw above how, in the *clientela* relationship, the interest groups are sometimes used to press the interests of particular ministries or agencies in other administrative sectors (and, presumably, before the legislature as well). It must be noted that this service is often reciprocal in the sense that the Ministry may and usually does press the interests of its clientele groups in both the rule-making and rule-applying spheres of the political system. To some extent, then, the situation we are describing implies that an interest group tends to become the clientele of a single ministry and does not distribute its energies throughout the hierarchy of the public administration. This is evidently true of Confindustria, one of whose leaders points out that although the Confederation *sometimes* approaches, say, the Ministry of Labor and Social Security, this method is an exception rather than the rule. Speaking of this latter agency, he remarks: "When we go to the ministry we expect to be treated as equals. However, the ministry with which we have the best rapport is not the Ministry of Labor but the Ministry of Industry. Whenever we are trying to advance a point in the labor field, we inform the Ministry of Industry and Commerce, the Ministry of Finance, and the Presidency of the Council of Ministers."

Thus, although Confindustria will interact, even on a daily basis, with several or many of the ministries and other administrative agencies, its first and basic contact is with the Ministry of Industry and Commerce, which is viewed as an advocate of the Confederation's demands. To a much more limited degree, it may be that similar advocacy, as two of our bureaucrats claim, is manifested by the Ministry of Labor and Social Security on behalf of (some of) the trade unions. However, for historical as well as for some of the sociological reasons outlined earlier in this chapter, no other interest group in Italy appears to have been as successful as Confindustria in establishing a *clientela* relationship. . . .

•   •   •

Bureaucratic Intervention: Parentela

. . . A *parentela* relationship is the second major pattern of interest-group intervention in the bureaucracy. In its strict Italian sense, *parentela* means consanguinity, lineage, or kinship. A *parentela* is a member of one's family and in Italian culture is entitled thereby to special consideration. In the traditional South, whence most of Italy's bureaucrats are recruited, ties of *parentela* are particularly strong, implying the kinds of rights and obligations that are generally associated with pre-industrial societies.

As used here, *parentela* involves a relatively close and integral relationship between certain associational interest groups, on the one hand, and the politically dominant Christian Democratic Party (D.C.), on the other. It is this relationship between group and party—and not strictly between group and bureaucracy—which is of interest to us. The generalized proposition we shall explore is that where *parentela* exists, and where certain other related conditions are met, interest groups that enjoy the relationship can exercise considerable influence over a bureaucracy quite apart from any consideration of *clientela*.

•   •   •

. . . When viewing the pressure activities of a group like Catholic Action, it is necessary to recognize that its mode of intervention—its style—will differ qualitatively from that manifested by Confindustria or other groups that we would depict as enjoying primarily a *clientela* relationship. This respondent speaks of Catholic Action as a mass movement, displaying immense electoral prowess and generally inclined to approach policy-makers in the name of goodness and morality, rather than openly on behalf of the interests of its membership.

•   •   •

Thus one of the top career officials in the Ministry of the Treasury flatly—even if somewhat simplistically—asserts that "the only groups that count in Italian public administration, as long as the Christian Democrats hold governmental power, are the Catholic groups. The Catholics, because they have direct access to the ministries, are likely to get anything they wish from the ministries. Other groups, such as the left-wing parties and trade unions, are not as fortunate. They are compelled to come to the ministry hat in hand. They are not in a position to make telephone calls to the ministers. They are not in a position to have administrative decisions made in their favor as a result of political interference from the apex of the administrative organization."

•   •   •

Catholic Action is not the only group concerning which *parentela* assertions are made. Others include the Coltivatori Diretti and the Italian Confederation of Workers Unions (C.I.S.L.), which also enjoy positions of considerable, even if limited, prominence with the D.C. . . .

The benefits deriving to C.I.S.L. from its *parentela* relationship are also mentioned by leaders of Confindustria. One of them says that "the industrialists are outraged over the power of the Christian Democratic trade unions to compel agencies of public administration to behave in a certain way." As an example, he cites the case of the National Productivity Committee which, according to the respondent, told all of those Italian industrial plants asking for productivity subsidies that no money would be forthcoming unless the shop committees [which have important labor representation functions] in their plants were staffed with a majority of C.I.S.L.

members and unless the industrialists, in addition, refused to deal at all with C.G.I.L.

This kind of denunciation is what one has come to expect from the political left and from groups with which Christian Democratic organizations such as C.I.S.L. are in acknowledged conflict. Greater credence must be lent to the claim, however, when the information is offered by an industrial leader who is at odds with all of the unions and who cannot be supposed to want to increase the power in industrial firms of the Socialists or Communists. The point underlined by our respondent is really that the industrialists detect a pattern of cooperation—even collusion—between Christian Democratic interest groups and the Italian bureaucracy which the industrialists might find extremely damaging in the long run. In terms of the conceptualization I have been developing, it is apparent that some of Confindustria's leaders—indeed, most of them—understand that the *clientela* relationship they have established with the bureaucracy is severely challenged, possibly basically jeopardized, by the *parentela* relationship that C.I.S.L. and other Catholic groups have cemented with the Christian Democratic Party.

•   •   •

No one will doubt that leading families and large economic concentrations exercise some, even considerable, influence over the legislative and administrative processes in Italy. But as one of our trade-union respondents observes, it is critical to recognize that economic power is now divided between the traditional Liberals and a segment of Christian Democracy. As we shall note later, it is far from clear that these two groups are in collusion. Indeed, events of recent years, including a monumental 1962 decision to nationalize the powerful electric power industry, suggest that leaders of Confindustria are perfectly right in viewing at least the left-wing of Christian Democracy as a serious threat. Recognizing that Confindustria has been subjected to political adversity since 1953, one of our respondents aptly remarks: ". . . groups such as Confindustria and other associations which had previously been able to operate effectively outside Christian Democracy are today required, if they are to have any weight at all in the making of governmental policy, to insert themselves in some way inside the D.C. and to achieve some control over the making of laws and their application through the agency of the dominant party."

This argument suggests that if Confindustria wishes to continue to maximize its political effectiveness, it must achieve a *parentela* relationship to the Christian Democratic Party as well as a *clientela* relationship to the bureaucracy. For many reasons . . . movement in this direction is fraught with all sorts of difficulties, both external and internal to Confindustria. In any event, under the most favorable of circumstances, it is most unlikely that

Confindustria, in the foreseeable future, will be able to effect the type of *parentela* to the D.C., and consequent impact on the bureaucracy, that is true of C.I.S.L. . . .

•　　•　　•

Part Four

Theoretical
Implications
on Trends
of Future Studies
in Group Politics

T

HERE is little debate over the question of whether group politics can be under certain circumstances a significant aspect of a political system. The serious questions today are what extent and under what conditions do group politics play a significant role in specified political systems. Earlier views by Bentley,[1] Truman[2] and Latham[3] which asserted that virtually all politics can be explained in terms of groups have been qualified by various critics.[4] At least in part the theoretical significance of these broad definitions of group politics is contradicted by their strong tendency to pragmatically define political groups narrowly.[5]

In practice group politics is equated with the political role of trade, labor, professional, and civic associations such as the Chamber of Commerce, the AFL-CIO, the American Medical Association, and the League of Women Voters respectively. This narrow definition excludes political parties,[6] class politics,[7] and public opinion as major foci of group politics. The restriction of group politics to a focus on the political role of highly specialized associations has major theoretical implications.

[1]Arthur Bentley, *The Process of Government*, rev. ed. (Evanston, Ill.: Principia Press, 1935), esp. p. 208; for an argument that Bentley was more flexible about the role of group politics than critics give him credit for, see Robert Golembiewski, "The Group Basis of Politics: Notes on Analysis and Development," *American Political Science Review*, LIV (December 1960), 38-51.

[2]David Truman, *The Governmental Process* (New York: Alfred Knopf, 1951), esp. Chapter 2.

[3]Earl Latham, "The Group Basis of Politics: Notes for a Theory," *American Political Science Review*, XLVI (June 1952), 376-397.

[4]While the critics differ among themselves on various points, there is general agreement that group politics is only part of the total picture of the political process in any political system. See, for example, Stanley Rothman, "Systematic Political Theory: Observations on the Group Approach," *American Political Science Review*, LIV (March 1960), 15-33; and Roy Macridis, "Interest Groups in Comparative Analysis," *Journal of Politics*, XXIII (February 1961), 25-45.

[5]For example, Truman pragmatically reduces group politics to the political life of associations. (Truman, pp. 56-57).

[6]Probably the strongest statement on the differences between the party system and the pressure group system is by E. E. Schattschneider, *The Semi-Sovereign People* (New York: Holt, Rinehart and Winston, 1960), esp. Chapters 2 and 3.

[7]For an excellent discussion of the negative consequence of this narrow view which excludes class and mass politics, see Michael Rogin, *The Intellectuals and McCarthy* (Cambridge: M. I. T. Press, 1967), esp. Chapters 1 and 9.

The existence of widespread specialized associations is related to the combination of industrialization and representative democracy. Industrialization is accompanied with role specialization. The elaborate division of labor in industrialized societies encourages the formation of a diversity of narrow interests while the ideology of representative democracies tends to encourage the formation of politically oriented groups.[8] Since the combination of these factors is limited primarily to the Anglo-American and Western European countries, this definition of group politics is quite restricted.

In the first selection, F. G. Castles notes the Anglo-American bias in research on group behavior and the consequent restricted theoretical range. He points out that what constitutes a pressure group in Anglo-American countries is practically absent in under-developed nations. In the Third World "the groups which do exert pressure and struggle for power tend to be parts of the traditional aristocratic *elite,* bureaucracy, Church, or perhaps, most frequently the armed forces." Castles argues that in order to eliminate existing biases in research and theoretical restrictions it is necessary to adopt a comparative approach. As an initial step he sets out a typology of pressure groups ordered by differentiation of function into the following political systems: undeveloped, developing, totalitarian, French and Italian, Scandinavian and Low Countries, and Anglo-American. The typology takes into account the variations in which different types of groups appear in different societies and also variations in the manner in which they combine.

Different systems of group politics vary in extent and importance (1) from society to society, (2) from level to level within specific societies, and (3) from time to time within specific societies. The final selection by C. Wright Mills deals with the relative importance of the pressure group system in American society over time. Mills argues that at earlier times in American history the pressure group system was the top level of power in the United States. In the course of the industrialization of the United States, the political executive and corporate structures grew in strength and became national in scope while the components of the pressure group system (i.e., Congress, party politicians, and pressure groups) remained narrow and parochial in outlook and strength. Mills explicitly raises the issue that the top level of power in America is now held by a power elite composed of the heads of the political executive, the corporate world, and the military, while the pressure group system is now at the middle ranges of power.[9]

[8]The Gamson selection (pages 60-75) should be reviewed for the many structural limitations on the effectiveness of this ideology.

[9]For an excellent anthology of critiques of Mills' thesis from a variety of perspectives, see William Domhoff and Hoyt Ballard, eds., *C. Wright Mills and the Power Elite* (Boston: Beacon Press, 1968).

Whether or not one agrees with Mills' conclusions it is quite apparent
that the student of group politics has to raise the questions posed by Mills.
What are the political implications of the growth and centralization of government in the welfare state?[10] What effect does the economic concentration
of the post-industrial era have on the society?[11] And finally, what effect
does permanent military mobilization have on the politics of a society?[12]
Each of these forces can give rise to the importance of new types of groups
or new combinations of existing groups. In order to avoid new biases the
student of group politics must remember that the comparative approach
includes the study of group politics across time as well as across nations.

[10]For a recent study pointing out the conservative bias of the pressure group system in the
welfare state, see Theodore Lowi, "The Public Philosophy: Interest-Group Liberalism,"
American Political Science Review, LXI (March 1967), 5-24. For a view of the Welfare State as a
rationalization of industrial life, see Samuel Beer, *British Politics in the Collective Age* (New
York: Alfred Knopf, 1965).

[11]Andrew Hacker, "Power to Do What?" in *The Bias of Pluralism,* ed. William Connolly
(New York: Atherton, 1969), pp. 67-80; and John K. Galbraith, *The New Industrial State* (New
York: Signet, 1967).

[12]Marc Pilisuk and Thomas Hayden, "Is There a Military-Industrial Complex Which Prevents Peace?: Consensus and Countervailing Power in Pluralistic Systems," *Journal of Social
Issues,* XXI (1965), 67-99; Harold Lasswell, "The Garrison State," *American Journal of Sociology* XLVI (January 1941), 455-468.

Towards a Theoretical Analysis of Pressure Politics

F. G. Castles

I. The Current State of Studies

The essential point about research in the field of group behavior in Politics is that almost all contemporary study has a very restricted range. To a very great degree the study has been an Anglo-American one, and this very fact tends to restrict the theoretical orientation of the observer. We may begin by noting an important distinction in the world or pressure groups, that between "interest" and "attitude" groups. The former may be described as being "semi-permanent groups set up to protect certain sectional interests" (e.g. the British Medical Association, the Automobile Association or various trade union organizations). The "attitude" group is a temporary association which desires to achieve some specifically delimited objective. (e.g. The Campaign for Nuclear Disarmament or the temperance organizations of the early part of this century). What we must emphasize here is that the contemporary study has been almost exclusively on "interest" groups, though as we shall explain later there are good reasons for this inherent in the political structure of Anglo-American society. S. E. Finer's book *Anonymous Empire* is an example of an emphasis on "interest" groups to the exclusion of other considerations. In it he catalogues the main components of the British "group universe" as follows: the business lobby; the labor lobby; the co-operative movement; the professions; civic groups; churches and educational organizations. Those bodies which might be described as "attitude" groups are included under "civic groups," a term singularly inappropriate to the description of the more militant wing of the C.N.D. What information we have on "attitude" groups is largely the result of books appearing on the more controversial groups, e.g. Christopher Driver's, *The Disarmers* and Tom Driberg's work on Moral Rearmament. Such works are in general of an historical and descriptive nature and not intended to give any more than a generalized

SOURCE: F. G. Castles, "Towards a Theoretical Analysis of Pressure Politics," *Political Studies,* XIV (October 1966), 339-348. Reprinted by permission of the author and the Clarendon Press, Oxford.

insight into the workings of similar groups . . . in a word, they are untheoretical.

This last comment is not, however, applicable to the various studies of "interest" groups; there have been a number of suggestions as to how such activities might be analyzed. One example is given by Harry Eckstein's book, *Pressure Group Politics,* in which he analyzes the activities of the British Medical Association in the following categories:

1. The *form* of the activities: determining factors here are the structure of the particular country's government, the activities it carries out, and the general attitude to group activities within that political culture.

2. Their *intensity* and *scope:* important here we find the political mobilization of groups, the extent to which the political structure is able to fulfill demands from groups, and so on;

3. Their *effectiveness:* the groups physical resources, its size and finances and again the nature of the structure of government. Eckstein further notes that groups tend to articulate themselves on the pattern of governmental institutions. That is to say, they develop a similar hierarchy, and in the case of the B.M.A. he illustrates the close ties between the associational hierarchy and the civil service. Other issues which have received some theoretical attention have been the existence of what Galbraith calls "countervailing" pressures (for instance, the fact that the Trades Union Congress is opposed by the employers organization, the Confederation of British Industries); "over-lapping" membership and also the latent phenomenon of the "potential group," that is a group activated by a threat to implicity-held values.

Thus while it is possible to point to a certain amount of research in the field we may note certain deficiencies. Most specifically the state of research on pressure-group politics presents two basic problems if we are ever to attain some general categorisation in theoretical terms of group politics as it operates in differing political systems. These may be delineated as follows.

First, the emphasis on "interest" groups has led to a largely misconceived generalization of the categories used in their study to pressure groups as a whole. As an example we may take Finer's definition of the sum of groups, that is to say the lobby:

> The sum of organizations in so far as they are occupied at any point in time in trying to influence the policy of public bodies, though unlike political parties, *never themselves prepared to undertake the direct government of the country.*[1]

What must be noted here is that while such a definition may be entirely fitting for an "interest" group, it is by no means so obviously applicable

[1]My italics.

to an "attitude" group, such as the C.N.D. The history of this movement would indicate, that even if it was not as such an organization "willing to take over the direct government of the country," certain integral groups contemplated action whose logical consequences must have included such an act. In this context we may note various proposals for putting up unilateral candidates, "Voters Veto" (a campaign devised to see that voters did not vote for any multilateralist candidate), not to mention the activities of the Committee of 100.

Very often, too, conclusions holding true of "interest" groups are more dubious in the context of the "attitude" group. Thus the conception that the group will be articulated on the basis of government institutions it deals with seems inapplicable to a number of protest movements. Their activity is very largely restricted to "grass roots" campaigning; they attempt to activate a body of opinion behind their views, but without formal representation to the powers that be. That this is so is one reason that C.N.D. was able to preserve a loosely organized campaign structure over a number of years, a structure which at no time involved formal membership, a criterion of prime importance in determining the "effectiveness" of "interest" groups. Thus we may conclude that in any future analysis of pressure groups there is a need for greater concentration on the distinctive aspects of the "attitude" group.

The second problem we are faced with is presented by pressure-group study's very nature as an Anglo-American discipline. The modern political scientist professes to be interested in the comparative study of political institutions, but is it, in fact, possible to apply the categories developed for the analysis of "interest" groups to pressure groups in other political systems? This question is at its clearest when we ask ourselves what constitutes a pressure group in the under-developed nations. Here we find few sectional groups representing large numbers of the population; the groups which do exert pressure and struggle for power tend to be parts of the traditional aristocratic *elite*, bureaucracy, Church, or perhaps, most frequently the armed forces. Unfortunately the Anglo-American analysis of pressure groups include none of these, since they are traditionally regarded as politically neutral. But we do not need to go as far afield to see the error of this view—the French Army Revolt of 1958 and de Gaulle's subsequent rise to power are illustrative of the fact that certain circumstances (in this case the aftermath of the Indo-Chinese war and the continuing struggle in Algeria) may produce sufficient strain to activate such groups even in Western political systems. Furthermore, if we look only at European systems of government, we can see aspects of pressure politics that do not occur within the Anglo-American framework. There is, for instance, the phenomenon of the colonization of a political party by a pressure group, or the converse, where a political party controls the activities of a group; an example of the latter would be the Communist control of at least one part of the French trade union movement, e.g. the C.G.T. All this indicates the need for a comparative approach to the study of pressure groups; an approach which explains not only the variations we have noted as between "interest" and "attitude" groups, but also the cross-cultural phenomena on which we have just remarked.

II. The Structural—Functional Approach

When we say there is a need for a comparative approach we do not, in fact, mean the more conventional methods of the discipline of "Comparative Politics" are the most appropriate. Basically these methods would appear to fall into two categories.

First, there is the "country-by-country" approach. The objective here is the presentation of a political system in its total configuration. An example here would be Sir Ivor Jenning's work, *The British Constitution.*

Second, a comparison of a particular political institution as it operates in the context of differing political environments, e.g. a comparison of Second Houses in various systems of government. There is no doubt that for many purposes both methods have advantages and there is certainly no doubt that both have a large and influential body of academic adherents. Nonetheless, as B. E. Brown points out, both would seem to suffer from the same fatal weakness, that such descriptions of foreign countries are in no sense cumulative. A great deal of important information, mainly of an empirical nature, may be derived from both the above approaches, but neither is really able to relate salient features of disparate political systems. We have here what Brown calls the "layer-cake" approach, since "the result is to put one layer of information on top of another and so on until the observer runs out of countries, time or interest."[2]

As an alternative to the methods described we suggest the use of structural functional analysis as a theoretical approach capable both of helping to explain the phenomena with which we deal in politics, and also as a valid basis for comparison within and between social systems. The political system is as such specially oriented to the societal problem Talcott Parsons[3] terms as "goal attainment." Any on-going social system posits certain goals, and both their formulation and their achievement is largely carried out by the political system. That these goals be translated into concrete definitive plans of action necessitates certain requirements or functions of the political system. A possible division of these tasks facing the political system is the one presented by Gabriel Almond in his introduction to *The*

---

[2]B. E. Brown, *New Directions in Comparative Politics* (London, 1962).
[3]Talcott Parsons, *The Social System,* (London, 1951).

Politics of the Developing Areas. Here he posits a balance of input and output functions in any such system, which are as follows:

Input	Output
Political socialization and recruitment	Rule making
Political communication	Rule application
Interest articulation	Rule adjudication
Interest aggregation	

We would not suggest that this list is in any way definitive; the output factors, for instance, are very little different from the age-old division between legislature, executive and judiciary. What is important is that here we have a number of functions that any political system must by definition carry out. By comparing the style in which this is done and the institutions which are set up for this purpose, we may have a legitimate basis for the comparison of political systems; one that by relating political systems together in terms of their functions is truly cumulative. As an example we can argue that if we look at the French and British party-structures we may compare them in terms of how effectively they carry out the "aggregative" functions we have mentioned, whereas using the "layer-cake" approach the impression is of totally disparate political institutions.

Comparison on a functionalist basis is not common in political science and in the field of pressure groups the only work is again by Almond . . . this is contained in an article entitled, "Interest Groups and the Political Process."[4] It is argued here that we may distinguish at least four types of political systems in which the particular political institution termed the pressure group operates in different ways. The basis of differentiation here are the above-mentioned functions of interest articulation and aggregation. These systems are as follows.

(a) The Anglo-American: here the institutions carrying out the separate functions are sharply differentiated and each is bureaucratized; in other words pressure groups articulate interests which are aggregated by party organizations and presented as workable alternatives to the electorate.

(b) The under-developed countries: where poor political communication and consequently high degree of interest latency leads to competition for power within the framework of the traditional *élite*.

(c) France, Italy, etc.: where parties and groups are bureaucratized but are not always autonomous of each other.

(d) Scandinavia and the Low Countries: here parties tend to be aggregative and party-group relations are organized on a consensual basis.

---

[4]Published in R. Macridis and B. E. Brown (eds.), *Comparative Politics* (New York, 1964), pp. 128-36.

We shall refer to this schema again in our formulation of a typology of political systems for the analysis of pressure politics.

III. The Structural—Differentiation Approach

The functional approach solves our problem of comparison, but we have yet to find a valid theoretical distinction between "attitude" and "interest" groups. If we are to remain true to our function-comparative approach we cannot define the difference in terms of substantive differences of tactics employed by the different groups. Any distinctions drawn in this way would probably only be applicable, in any case, to the Anglo-American political system. We may, perhaps, best regard the problem as one of differing approaches to the political functions carried out in particular systems. Groups arise because they either wish to preserve the *status quo*, regain it, or because they have reasons to desire change. We may use what is called the structural-differentiation model to outline the different ways in which groups react to the strain of these problems. Basically the structural-differentiation model postulates a series of components of social action on which strain may be felt. They are:

(a) Values: these are essentially the ultimate legitimations of societal activities;

(b) norms: these are more specific regulatory principles which are necessary to realize the values;

(c) mobilization for motivation: this is component determining forms of organization of human action:

(d) situational facilities: these are means of obstacles hindering or facilitating achievement of goals.

These components are ordered in the level of generality; that is to say an attack on values necessarily undermines all the other components, whereas conflict about situational facilities need involve no other component than itself. Strain in such a system occurs when an alteration in the environment gives rise to deficits in the input of goal attainment for the acting units, such strain is removed by defining in which component of action it occurs and restructuring the components until the strain is removed and a new balance achieved. We would argue that such restructuring is typically a result of group action, brought about because acting units (in this case individuals) become aware of the manifest need for collective action to remove the source of strain.[5] The necessary condition for such a

[5]It may be argued (and has been in Mancur Olsen, *The Logic of Collective Action,* New York 1965) that for large groups, group interest and the rational self-interest of its members may be at variance. The implication being that even if acting units feel strain, this strain may

resolution is the "rational" identification of the sources of strain — the respecification of each component below it in level of generality; where this does not occur the solution is not likely to be of a type conducive to the solution of the strain.[6]

The application of this schema to the realm of "interest" groups is instructive. Groups of this kind exist to protect the interests of their members; they come into operation when they feel these interests threatened. The trade union which puts in a wage claim because it feels the interests of its members in the financial field have been neglected as compared with other sections of industry is an obvious example. Here we have a strain on the mobilization for motivation component caused by changes in the environment; the union by attempting to raise wages is trying to resolve the strain. The result is usually some compromise between the union's and the employer's interests, and at least to some extent, the balance between goal attainment in the various sections of industry is restored. Much the same can be said for attempts to better working conditions; attempts by the employers to challenge government legislation restrictive of trade, or by the B.M.A. to contract out of the Health Service. The emergence of new groups is also explicable in this way. The "potential group" arises because a strain on one of the components of social action activates latent interests (Wootton's account of the rise of the service mens organization in response to the changed conditions of the "citizens war" bears this analysis out).[7]

But structural differentiation may proceed on a less rational basis . . . here we will refer to Smelser's model for the analysis of "collective behavior."[8] Such behavior may be defined as "mobilization on the basis of a "generalized" belief redefining social action" — the defining characteristic of such a belief is its *generality* in contradistinction to "rationality." Such a belief has the function of redefining the actor's situation, but in a peculiar way which short circuits the normal process of respecification of the components of action; instead of looking for a solution at the next highest level of generality it finds a solution ready-made at the highest level and instead of restructuring each component it applies the solution at the level on which the strain is manifest. Thus the wish-fulfillment belief resolves

---

not lead to concerted group activity in defence of its interests qua group. This is, in fact, an argument against the "voluntaristic" theory of group formation, and need not apply to the "interest" groups we delineate, since these are already in existence, admittedly, and in accordance with Olsen's thesis, either on some basis of compulsion or "selective incentives." Nor need the argument apply to "attitude" groups, since they are typically small, and Olsen's theory, based as it is on the theory of "public goods" specifically exempts small groups. Moreover, although Olsen feels that his conclusions apply to ideological ("attitude") groups, he is not very sanguine of their heuristic value in this field.

[6] Talcott Parsons, "Some Considerations on the Theory of Social Change," *Rural Sociology,* vol. 26, no. 3, September 1961.

[7] Graham Wooton, *The Politics of Influence* (London, 1963).

[8] Neil Smelser, *Collective Behaviour* (London, 1962).

[9] Neil Smelser, *op. cit.,* pp. 25-26 and 120.

[10] Wayland Young, *Strategy for Survival* (London, 1959).

strain by positing absolutely efficacious generalized facilities; the norm-oriented belief resolves strain by envizaging a total reconstitution of the normative order and in a similar way the value-oriented belief resolves strain by looking to a complete modification "of those conceptions concerning nature, mans place in it, mans relation to man and the desirable and non-desirable as they relate to mans environment and inter human relationships."[9]

This analysis of collective behavior is, at the very least, partly applicable to our distinction between "interest" and "attitude" groups, and is certainly illuminating in regard to some of the manifestations of pressure politics which were inexplicable within the present framework of Anglo-American "interest" group studies. The C.N.D. may in some of its aspects be regarded as a collective-behavior movement. It posited an absolutely efficacious belief that with nuclear disarmament all international problems would be solved. The belief was a solution to the strains felt by some in a world in which the "nuclear Sword of Damocles"[10] is poised, and the individual feels he has no control whatsoever of his life chances. A lack of restructuring of the components of social action is seen in the almost total lack of any practicable proposals for disarmament with any possibility in the present state of international society. The collective-behavior framework also provides possibilities for analysis of nationalist movements, which tend to be value-oriented; the French army revolt, which involved a "generalized belief" in the inability of the civilian forces to maintain the values of French society and an equal belief that this was the sacred duty of the officer corps; and of the infiltration of groups by ideologically-oriented parties.

IV. A Typology of Pressure Politics

We are now in a position in which we may set out a typology of pressure politics. Firstly we will outline a number of political systems on the basis of their performance of political functions. These include the four outlined by Almond, but for a number of reasons we would include at least two more, both because we consider the term "under-developed" countries covers too wide a range of political phenomena, and also because we desire a complete coverage of existing types of political system. Within the structure of the systems outlined we would attempt to set out the workings of pressure politics, most especially in terms of whether groups are most typically activated on the basis of "rational" structural differentiation or on the basis of "a generalized belief redefining social action" (that is to say whether they are "interest" or "attitude" groups). One last explanatory

[9]Neil Smelser, *op. cit.*, pp. 25-26 and 120.
[10]Wayland Young, *Strategy for Survival* (London 1959).

point in connection with the latter type—the motivating generalized belief may be one of two kinds: it may be directed at societal values, or at norms, respectively the value-oriented and norm-oriented movements.

The order in which we shall discuss the various political systems will be in accord with the degree to which the two functions of interest articulation and aggregation are differentiated. As has been suggested Almond's classification for "under-developed" countries is somewhat all-embracing. As such the situation in which political communication is poor and interest latency high is most typical of the truely agrarian society untouched by Western colonialism. Once colonialism is present and any degree of modern industry introduced into the economy a number of interest groupings tend to arise creating a somewhat different political configuration. For the purposes of this exposition we shall call agrarian countries "undeveloped," the others we shall term as "developing." These are of course in some sense ideal typical constructions.

The situation as found in the *"undeveloped" system* is, perhaps, best described by Kautsky in his work *Political Change in the Under-Developed Countries.* What we have called poor political communication is manifested in a large peasant class which is almost totally unaware of the political process. The peasant is tied to the soil by the exigencies of his vocation and his horizon is bounded by the radius of the village community; his only conception of government may be an intermittent demand for taxes of corvee labour. This situation precludes the existence of associational interest groups, if only for the reason that any sort of national or even regional organization proves impossible. The middle class of trades and intellectuals tends to be small and dependent for its livelihood on the aristocratic elite, which is thus left as the only source of power in the community. Political action in such a society becomes the maneuvering of a number of aristocratic cliques for positions of power and prestige. From our point of view it may be described as being typically concerned with the groups goal attainment in the sphere of mobilization for motivation. The groups composing the aristocratic elite are typically the bureaucracy, the church, the armed forces. As Kautsky rightly suggests, changes of government occurring within a system approximating to our model of the "undeveloped" system cannot in any realistic terms be understood by the Western continua left-wing and right-wing politics. In such a society the factors preventing the growth of associational interest groups have a similar effect in inhibiting large-scale collective-behavior movements. There is little awareness of a societal pattern, the only dissidence tends to be sporadic and limited in scope—the type here is the "hostile outburst"[11] against the individual tax-farmer, rather than the system itself. (The position here has

[11]Neil Smelser, *op. cit.*

a resemblance to the description Marx gave of the reasons the French peasants were too fragmented to combine together as a class for itself in the early part of the nineteenth century.) In Weberian terms the type of political system we have described is a very close approximation to the "patrimonial" society.

The "developing" country's political system can only be appreciated through an examination of the social and economic effects of the type of industrialization that has gone on. The typical pattern is as follows:

First, colonial occupation or indirect domination through the indigenous elite lead to new industries and through them the creation of new classes. A small industrial working-class develops and an intelligentsia, often educated abroad, is at first fostered to aid industrial progress. Sometimes too there is the creation of a small indigenous capitalist class, that is to say native entrepreneurs.

Second, development is as Eisenstadt[12] suggests of a most uneven character. This can be seen in the lack of balance of processes of change between local and central levels. The colonial regime at the centre makes for reforms in administration, tax-gathering, military techniques, education and perhaps, to a certain degree initiates some sort of market economy. Often in this process they are aided by the indigenous rulers, who regarded it as the only way to maintain some semblance of their former power. Thus in Vietnam:

> After 1884, the Vietnamese monarchy showed that it had more fear of the peasantry than of the French conquerors, by coming to terms with the French. Vietnam became a protected state, where colonial administration took over all policy making and modern technical functions, leaving the mandarins with the duties of maintaining order and collecting taxes in the countryside.[13]

The objective of the régime is in certain respects to get the population to accept certain broad institutional settings organized according to the principles of what Eisenstadt terms, universalism specificity and common secular solidarity. But at the same time a conscious attempt is made to contain most change within the limits of traditional groupings. The population is "denied participation in a common political system and full integration in a common system of solidarity."[14]

The unevenness of change has an influence on the new classes resulting from industrialization. Improved political communication results from the introduction of industry (again we may note what Marx said about factory

[12]S. N. Eisenstadt, *Essays on Sociological Aspects of Political and Economic Development* (The Hague, 1961).
[13]Nguyeh Kien, *Le Sud-Vietnam depuis Dien-Bien-Phu* (Paris, 1963, p. 80).
[14]S. N. Eisenstadt, *op. cit.*

production being an impetus to the political organization of the proletariat), and so also do administrative reforms, both of which factors are conducive to the growth of associational-interest groups. We may note that even extreme penal sanctions were unable to eradicate the growth of trade unionism on the oil fields of Saudi Arabia. The new groupings are not, however, in a position to imitate the Western development of a pluralist society based on a series of groups peacefully competing for power. As we have said, they have modern values, and this is especially so of the intelligentsia which usually forms the leadership cadres, but the colonial-aristocratic régime denies them virtually all entrance to the political process. The result is the inclusion of the groups within the structure of value-oriented nationalist movements, which are specifically anti-colonial in nature. We may also note that the constellation of forces in this type of society may also force the anti-modernizing forces into the fight for independence, since the basic agent of modernization is the intervention of the colonial power. Thus at a later stage there may be conflict between the traditionalist and modern wings of the nationalist movement, but both develop in answer to the strain of modern development.

Certain typical characteristics of the nationalist movement indicate its value-oriented basis: there is a strong emphasis, for the most part, on modern, non-religious symbols of group unity and a huge expenditure of effort is made by the movement to avoid dissensus. Moreover, in contra-distinction to the colonial régime the movement is constantly attempting to get a mass popular base, that is to say it is destructive of those traditional groupings which were the best guarantee of political apathy on the part of the peasantry. The nature of the "generalized belief" is seen in a lack of emphasis on the solution of immediate social and economic problems . . . the ending of colonial rule is seen as an absolutely efficacious solution to all the problems faced.

Totalitarianism is a political system unmentioned by Almond.[15] It is that usually denoted as the "totalitarian" system. In view of the importance of this type in recent years and of some of the more ominous developments in the newly-independent countries it seems worthwhile to discuss it. The totalitarian system is characterized, at least formally, by a single and undifferentiated source of political power. It differs from the type of aristocratic-colonial régime we have outlined by the existence of intense political communication. It may be distinguished from the Anglo-American system of politics in that the modality of this communication is so designed that its major task is to relay demands from the political center of authority.

---

[15]It is unmentioned in the article on pressure groups cited earlier but Almond does deal briefly with "Totalitarianism" in an article entitled "Comparative Political Systems" also contained in R. Macridis and B. E. Brown, *op. cit.*, pp. 439 et seq.

According to Kautsky the totalitarian system may be delineated as follows:

(a) "Total terror": put in its crudest form is the fear of the "purge" or the secret police leads to social atomization. This is the state of Robespierre's "terror" when human trust becomes impossible because of the fear of denunciation. Strangely enough J. S. Mill in reflecting on what Tocqueville has to say about democracy is led to consider how to obviate this very situation: liberty is, he says,

> the necessary protection against its (democracy) degenerating into the only despotism of which, in the modern world, there is real danger— the absolute role of the head of the executive over a congregation of isolated individuals, all equals but all slaves.[16]

(b) "Total regimentation": formally the organized groups may have a similar form and nomenclature as those in the Anglo-American system, but membership is compulsory and rival organizations are not permitted. For examples we might cite the Soviet trade union structure or the Nazi Labor Front which replaced the free trade unions of the Weimar period. The new organizations lose their function of aggregating interests and formulating demands and become organizations run by the régime as organs of supervision. The more the individuals life is regulated in this way the less threat he is to the régime. We might note that even in democratic states those parties of a totalitarian persuasion attempt to emulate this feat of regulation; an example would be the set of supplementary organizations set up by the French Communist party.

(c) Total control of opinion through propaganda and the suppression of opposition views through censorship: this is of course, a facet of the peculiar modality of communication we mentioned and is itself only made possible by advances in the scientific use of the mass media. The goal of this whole operation is to satisfy the individual by identifying him with the all-embracing and omnipotent state. When we say political communication is modalized this is not to say that interest articulation does not take place. A system like "democratic centralism," for instance, is designed to relay instructions from above; it is, however, sensitive to views articulated from below and this is necessarily so since "totalitarianism" rests at least on some minimum of consent—the ruler who takes no notice whatsoever of political interests is not fated to reign for long; what is possible though, is that all accession to demands be made to look like benign wisdom from above.

The nature of the totalitarian state necessarily defines all normative change as *per se* illegitimate. Since all change of the peaceful reformist

[16]J. S. Mill, *Autobiography* (London 1924).

type is tabu, however petty the original cause for strain it takes on the form of an attack on the society's basic values:

> While individual strikes are almost impossible, and hopeless as far as potential results are concerned, there are no proper political conditions for general strikes and they can occur only in exceptional situations. Whenever individual strikes have taken place, they have usually turned into general strikes and have taken on a distinctly political character.[17]

As a general rule all attempts at normative change, not initiated by the régime itself, are identified with the outside enemy which is often used to create internal unity. An example here is the identification of non-Nazis as agents of an "international Jewish conspiracy" or the identification of the Hungarian revolutionaries with pro-Western forces, when in reality many were agitating for a more "genuinely socialist" society. This last example again points to the tendency for all movements in such systems to define their aims in terms of the value system. We may also note that the ex-colonial countries may tend towards some sort of totalitarian development, both because of the need for forced economic growth, and because, as Smelser points out, the newly legitimized government is likely to define all protest in value-oriented terms. Or as Crick puts it in his Defence of Politics:

> The struggle against imperialism has to be continued, long after the imperialists have gone, because the enemy alone creates the unity by which the governing party can hope to perpetuate itself in office.

As someone has said, "If Castro had not got the United States, he would have had to invent one."

In countries such as France, Italy and The Weimar Republic, the political system is characterized by a lack of autonomy of interest aggregation and articulation functions. The reasons for this also probably lie in uneven social and economic development as was the case in the "developing" countries. The basic structure of French industry permeated as it is by small-scale producers, has often been used as an explanatory factor for French political instability and *incivisme*. Basically, however, we may designate these systems as industrialized, and on this basis we get a similar proliferation of "interest" groups to those in the Anglo-American system. Their methods may differ in attempting to protect sectional interests, but this is very largely because of the different structure of political institu-

---

[17]Milovan Djilas, *The New Class* (London 1958), p. 110.

[18]G. Lavau, "Political Pressures by Interest Groups in France," in H. W. Ehrmann (ed.), *Interest Groups on Four Continents* (Pittsburgh, 1964) p. 76.

tions and a somewhat different political culture. Where we do find differences is in the colonization of groups by parties and the reverse phenomenon of domination of parties by groups. A further difference lies in the
greater tendency to value-orientation among the "attitude" groups. In the
case of colonization we note that in the first case we have parties imparting
a political-ideological content to groups, and in the latter the parties are
impeded from carrying out their aggregative function. As Almond puts
it, what reaches the legislature are "raw unaggregated demands or diffuse
uncompromising tendencies." Because no one party is able to form a majority government the legislature is itself unable to form an alternative source
of interest aggregation. The dominance of politico-ideological parties is
one of the many factors conducive to producing value conflict in the society. As already mentioned the Communist-controlled Confederation
General du Travail is an obvious example of this tendency. Here a contrast with the British system is instructive. The British peace movement,
and especially the C.N.D. has always tried to remain aloof from ideological
movements like the Communist Party of Great Britain; on the other hand
in France the major group, with at one time something like a million adherents, was positively identified with the Communist Party.[18] (Mouve-
ment pour la Paix). In other words, in one system the peace movement may
be largely norm-oriented, whereas in the other less differentiated system
it tends toward value-orientation. Another example would be the ex-service
movement, which in Britain after a few chaotic years settled down as the
peaceful "British Legion"[19] turned in France in the middle 1930's into the
neo-fascist Croix de Feu which in 1934 nearly brought the Third Republic
to its knees. A situation like that in France existed in an even more extreme
form in Weimar Germany; this can be illustrated by the armed conflict
of private armies financed by the political parties just prior to Hitler's
assumption of power. Groups like the army or business are likely to feel
strain under such conditions and be attracted to the value-oriented movements, which promise stability when they come to power. Here we might
cite the French army command of 1958 and the business support for the
Nazis.

In Scandinavia and the Low Countries there is, as we have suggested,
a tendency towards an aggregative party system and for relations between
parties and groups to be very largely based on consensus. To illustrate our
point a very brief summary of the Swedish position will be given. Groups
are highly organized and cover very much the same ground as that described by Finer as being applicable to Britain. The close relation between
parties and groups is seen in the proportional representation which leads
to party lists being made up largely of interest representatives in order

---

[19]Graham Wootton, *op. cit.*

to attract the floating voter. The consensual nature of relations is seen in the quite frequent cross-voting that parties permit on issues closely concerned with group interests. A further indication of the lack of dispute on basic values is seen in the reception by certain left intellectuals of the recent conservative victory in Norway. Many felt that this might in fact be of benefit to the Labour Party, which had been in office so long, in that it would give an interval for rethinking doctrine and policy.

The Anglo-American system has already been considered, especially with regard to the theory of "interest" groups, but a few observations are in order. Groups tend to be mainly of the "interest" type, they articulate interests which are aggregated by one of the two parties. These functions are almost totally autonomous. What "attitude" groups there are show a very great tendency toward norm-orientation, they are attempting to change specific rules while accepting the value framework of society. As an example we might suggest the Howard League for Penal Reform, which, using every constitutional means at its disposal, attempts to better prison conditions. The same might also be said for the vast mass of the peace movement, excluding the Committee of 100 and the British Peace Committee, neither of which are very large; C.N.D. despite its demonstrations and marches never wanted to remove atomic weapons other than by constitutional means, indeed these demonstrations were merely intended to illustrate the strength of public opinion on their side. The attempt to win the Labour Party to their side in 1960 was a case of trying to persuade what might be the future government to its way of thinking by the perfectly legal means of free discussion. Nonetheless there are a number of value-oriented movements on the Anglo-American scene, in Britain particularly they tend to be miniscule, but very vociferous. Among their numbers we find the more militant members of the peace movement, and the small fringe parties of left and right, the various Trotskyites, the Socialist Party of Great Britain and the nationalist or racialist parties of Jordan, Mosley, and others.

V. Conclusion

Politics is a study which, in so far as it is theoretical, has very little theory of its own. In one sense this article is not original since it relies very heavily on material and conceptions drawn from other sciences, in this case mainly Sociology. In a different sense, however, it is, because in bringing these new theoretical perspectives to politics it is hoped that we have learned something original about pressure groups and their behavior. What then have we learned, what are our conclusions and what is their value? This may, perhaps, best be summarized as follows.

First, taking the political systems we have outlined in order of differentiation of function, we may note that as differentiation increases so also do associational interest groups working within the structure of "rational" structural differentiation. We noted that in the "undeveloped" system such groups in the normal sense did not exist at all, that they began to develop in the "developing" system, but were drawn into the aegis of value-oriented nationalist movements. Under totalitarian régime such groups are, at least formally, the only type permitted to exist, but are in many ways bereft of their true function of interest-articulation. Only in the latter three industrialized systems does the "interest" group come into its own, and this less so in countries like France, where until very recently small-scale production and a political theory stemming from Rousseau, and intolerant of sectional interests, has prevented their full development.

Secondly, as differentiation increases we also note that those groups which are activated on the basis of a "generalized belief" tend to become norm-oriented rather than value oriented, that is to say they attack not the structure of society itself, but certain regulatory principles considered pernicious. For the reasons given we do not find either type in the "undeveloped" society, but with the "developing" country we find that almost all groups are drawn into the value-oriented nationalist movements. In totalitarian systems all movements based on "generalized belief" are suppressed, but where they come to the surface we say that they tended to be of the value-oriented kind. Lastly, it was shown that in systems like the French, that although movements based on a "generalized belief" were less frequent, they tended to be of the value-oriented type more than was the case in the Anglo-American system.

As to the value of the schema we have put forward we would suggest that it is in the tradition of the generalizing statements of the natural sciences, if nothing like as precise and exactly formulated as they are. If the framework has any validity we would maintain that we have a theoretical foundation for the analysis of group behavior in differing political systems. The incidence of specific types of group may be explained by a functional approach, and at the same time their operation may be examined either by the use of the structural-differentiation model or the collective-behavior approach, depending on whether they are "interest" or "attitude" groups.

The Theory
of Balance

C. Wright Mills

Not wishing to be disturbed over moral issues of the political economy, Americans cling to the idea that the government is a sort of automatic machine, regulated by the balancing of competing interests. This image of politics is simply a carry-over from the official image of the economy: in both, an equilibrium is achieved by the pulling and hauling of many interests, each restrained only by legalistic and amoral interpretations of what the traffic will bear.

The ideal of the automatic balance reached its most compelling elaboration in eighteenth-century economic terms: the market is sovereign and in the magic economy of the small entrepreneur there is no authoritarian center. And in the political sphere as well: the division, the equilibrium, of powers prevails, and hence there is no chance of despotism. "The nation which will not adopt an equilibrium of power," John Adams wrote, "must adopt a despotism. There is no other alternative." As developed by the men of the eighteenth century, equilibrium, or checks and balances, thus becomes the chief mechanism by which both economic and political freedom were guaranteed and the absence of tyranny insured among the sovereign nations of the world.

Nowadays, the notion of an automatic political economy is best known to us as simply the practical conservatism of the anti-New Dealers of the 'thirties. It has been given new—although quite false—appeal by the frightening spectacle of the totalitarian states of Germany yesterday and Russia today. And although it is quite irrelevant to the political economy of modern America, it is the only rhetoric that prevails widely among the managerial elite of corporation and state.

I

It is very difficult to give up the old model of power as an automatic balance, with its assumptions of a plurality of independent, relatively equal, and conflicting groups of the balancing society. All these assumptions are explicit to the point of unconscious caricature in recent statements of "who rules America." According to Mr. David Riesman, for ex-

SOURCE: From C. Wright Mills, *The Power Elite* (New York: Oxford University Press, 1956), pp. 242-268. Copyright © 1956 by Oxford University Press, Inc. Reprinted by permission. Numbered footnotes have been deleted.

ample, during the past half century there has been a shift from "the power hierarchy of a ruling class to the power dispersal" of "veto groups." Now no one runs anything: all is undirected drift. "In a sense," Mr. Riesman believes, "this is only another way of saying that America is a middle-class country . . . in which, perhaps people will soon wake up to the fact that there is no longer a we who run things and a they who don't or a we who don't run things and a they who do, but rather that all we's are they's and all they's are we's.

"The chiefs have lost the power, but the followers have not gained it," and in the meantime, Mr. Riesman takes his psychological interpretation of power and of the powerful to quite an extreme, for example: "if businessmen *feel* weak and dependent, they *are* weak and dependent, no matter what material resources may be ascribed to them."

". . . The future," accordingly, "seems to be in the hands of the small business and professional men who control Congress: the local realtors, lawyers, car salesmen, undertakers, and so on; of the military men who control defense and, in part, foreign policy; of the big business managers and their lawyers, finance-committee men, and other counselors who decide on plant investment and influence the rate of technological change; of the labor leaders who control worker productivity and worker votes; of the black belt whites who have the greatest stake in southern politics; of the Poles, Italians, Jews, and Irishmen who have stakes in foreign policy, city jobs, and ethnic religious and cultural organizations; of the editorializers and storytellers who help socialize the young, tease and train the adult, and amuse and annoy the aged; of the farmers—themselves warring congeries of cattlemen, corn men, dairymen, cotton men, and so on—who control key departments and committees and who, as the living representatives of our inner-directed past, control many of our memories; of the Russians and, to a lesser degree, other foreign powers who control much of our agenda of attention; and so on. The reader can complete the list."

Here indeed is something that measures up "to the modern standards of being fully automatic and completely impersonal." Yet there is some reality in such romantic pluralism, even in such a *pasticcio* of power as Mr. Riesman invents: it is a recognizable, although a confused, statement of the middle levels of power, especially as revealed in Congressional districts and in the Congress itself. But it confuses, indeed it does not even distinguish between the top, the middle, and the bottom levels of power. In fact, the strategy of all such romantic pluralism, with its image of a semi-organized stalemate, is rather clear:

You elaborate the number of groups involved, in a kind of bewildering, Whitmanesque enthusiasm for variety. Indeed, what group fails to qualify as a "veto group"? You do not try to clarify the hodge-podge by classifying these groups, occupations, strata, organizations according to their political relevance or even according to whether they are organized politically at all. You do not try to see how they may be connected with one another into a structure of power, for by virtue of his perspective, the romantic conservative focuses upon a scatter of milieux rather than upon connections within a structure of power. And you do not consider the possibility of any community of interests among the top groups. You do not connect all these milieux and miscellaneous groups with the big decisions: you do not ask and answer with historical detail: exactly *what*, directly or indirectly, did "small retailers" or "brick masons" have to do with the sequence of decision and event that led to World War II? What did "insurance agents," or for that matter, the Congress, have to do with the decision to make or not to make, to drop or not to drop, the early model of the new weapon? Moreover, you take seriously the public-relations-minded statements of the leaders of all groups, strata, and blocs, and thus confuse psychological uneasiness with the facts of power and policy. So long as power is not nakedly displayed, it must not be power. And of course you do not consider the difficulties posed for you as an observer by the fact of secrecy, official and otherwise.

In short, you allow your own confused perspective to confuse what you see and, as an observer as well as an interpreter, you are careful to remain on the most concrete levels of description you can manage, defining the real in terms of the existing detail.

The balance of power theory, as Irving Howe has noted, is a narrow-focus view of American politics. With it one can explain temporary alliances within one party or the other. It is also narrow-focus in the choice of time-span: the shorter the period of time in which you are interested, the more usable the balance of power theory appears. For when one is up-close and dealing journalistically with short periods, a given election, for example, one is frequently overwhelmed by a multiplicity of forces and causes. One continual weakness of American "social science," since it became ever so empirical, has been its assumption that a mere enumeration of a plurality of causes is the wise and scientific way of going about understanding modern society. Of course it is nothing of the sort: it is a paste-pot eclecticism which avoids the real task of social analysis: that task is to go beyond a mere enumeration of all the facts that might conceivably be involved and weigh each of them in such a way as to understand how they fit together, how they form a model of what it is you are trying to understand.

Undue attention to the middle levels of power obscures the structure of power as a whole, especially the top and the bottom. American politics, as discussed and voted and campaigned for, have largely to do with these middle levels, and often only with them. Most "political" news is news and gossip about middle-level issues and conflicts. And in America, the political theorist too is often merely a more systematic student of elections, of who voted for whom. As a professor or as a free-lance intellectual, the political analyst is generally on the middle levels of power himself. He knows the top only by gossip; the bottom, if at all, only by "research." But he is at home with the leaders of the middle level, and, as a talker himself, with their "bargaining."

Commentators and analysts, in and out of the universities, thus focus upon the middle levels and their balances because they are closer to them, being mainly middle-class themselves; because these levels provide the noisy content of "politics" as an explicit and reported-upon fact; because such views are in accord with the folklore of the formal model of how democracy works; and because, accepting that model as good, especially in their current patrioteering, many intellectuals are thus able most readily to satisfy such political urges as they may feel.

When it is said that a "balance of power" exists, it may be meant that no one interest can impose its will or its terms upon others; or that any one interest can create a stalemate; or that in the course of time, first one and then another interest gets itself realized, in a kind of symmetrical taking of turns; or that all policies are the results of compromises, that no one wins all they want to win, but each gets something. All these possible meanings are, in fact, attempts to describe what can happen when, permanently or temporarily, there is said to be "equality of bargaining power." But, as Murray Edelman has pointed out, the goals for which interests struggle are not merely given; they reflect the current state of expectation and acceptance. Accordingly, to say that various interests are "balanced" is generally to evaluate the *status quo* as satisfactory or even good; the hopeful ideal of balance often masquerades as a description of fact.

"Balance of power" implies equality of power, and equality of power seems wholly fair and even honorable, but in fact what is one man's honorable balance is often another's unfair imbalance. Ascendant groups of course tend readily to proclaim a just balance of power and a true harmony of interest, for they prefer their domination to be uninterrupted and peaceful. So large businessmen condemn small labor leaders as "disturbers of the peace" and upsetters of the universal interests inherent in business-labor cooperation. So privileged nations condemn weaker ones in the name of internationalism, defending with moral notions what has been won by force against those have-nots whom, making their bid for ascendancy or equality later, can hope to change the *status quo* only by force.

The notion that social change proceeds by a tolerant give and take, by compromise and a network of vetoes of one interest balanced by another assumes that all this goes on within a more or less stable framework that does not itself change, that all issues are subject to compromise, and are thus naturally harmonious or can be made such. Those who profit by the general framework of the *status quo* can afford more easily than those who are dissatisfied under it to entertain such views as the mechanics of social change. Moreover, "in most fields . . . only one interest is organized, none is, or some of the major ones are not." In these cases, to speak, as Mr. David Truman does, of "unorganized interests" is merely to use another word for what used to be called "the public," a conception we shall presently examine.

The important "pressure groups," especially those of rural and urban business, have either been incorporated in the personnel and in the agencies of the government itself, both legislative and executive, or become the instruments of small and powerful cliques, which sometimes include their nominal leaders but often do not. These facts go beyond the centralization of voluntary groups and the usurpation of the power of apathetic members by professional executives. They involve, for example, the use of the NAM by dominant cliques to reveal to small-business members that their interests are identical with those of big business, and then to focus the power of business-as-a-whole into a political pressure. From the standpoint of such higher circles, the "voluntary association," the "pressure group," becomes an important feature of a public-relations program. The several corporations which are commanded by the individual members of such cliques are themselves instruments of command, public relations, and pressure, but it is often more expedient to use the corporations less openly, as bases of power, and to make of various national associations their joint operating branches. The associations are more operational organizations, whose limits of power are set by those who use them, than final arbiters of action and inaction.

Checks and balances may thus be understood as an alternative statement of "divide and rule," and as a way of hampering the more direct expression of popular aspiration. For the theory of balance often rests upon the moral idea of a natural harmony of interests, in terms of which greed and ruthlessness are reconciled with justice and progress. Once the basic structure of the American political economy was built, and for so long as it could be tacitly supposed that markets would expand indefinitely, the harmony of interest could and did serve well as the ideology of dominant groups, by making their interests appear identical with the interests of the community as a whole. So long as this doctrine prevails, any lower group that begins to struggle can be made to appear inharmonious, disturbing the common interest. "The doctrine of the harmony of interests," E. H. Carr has remarked, "thus serves as an ingenious moral device invoked, in perfect sincerity, by privileged groups in order to justify and maintain their dominant position."

II

The prime focus of the theory of balance is the Congress of the United States, and its leading actors are the Congressmen. Yet as social types, these 96 Senators and 435 Representatives are not representative of the rank and file citizens. They represent those who have been successful in entrepreneurial and professional endeavors. Older men, they are of the privileged white, native-born of native parents, Protestant Americans. They are college graduates and they are at least solid, upper-middle class in income and status. On the average, they have had no experience of wage or lower salaried work. They are, in short, in and of the new and old upper classes of local society.*

Some members of the Congress are millionaires, others must scrounge the countryside for expense money. The expenses of office are now quite heavy, often including the maintenance of two homes and traveling between them, the demands of an often busy social life, and the greatly increased costs of getting elected and staying in office. An outside income is now almost indispensable for the Congressmen; and, in fact, four out of five of the Representatives and two out of three of the Senators in 1952 received incomes other than their Congressional salaries "from businesses or professions which they still maintain in their home communities, or from investments. Independently wealthy men are becoming increasingly

*Nowadays, the typical Senator is a college-educated man of about fifty-seven years of age— although in the 83rd Congress (1954) one was eighty-six years old. The typical Representative, also drawn from the less than 10 per cent of the adult population that has been to college, is about fifty-two—although one was only twenty-six in the latest Congress. Almost all of the Senators and Representatives have held local and state offices; and about half of them are veterans of one of the wars. Almost all of them have also worked in non-political occupations, usually occupations of the upper 15 per cent of the occupational heirarchy: in the 1949-51 Congress, for example, 69 per cent of both Senate and House were professional men, and another 24 per cent of the Senate and 22 per cent of the House were businessmen or managers. There are no wage workers, no low salaried white-collar men, no farm laborers in the Senate, and only one or two in the House.

Their major profession is, of course, the law—which only 0.1 per cent of the people at work in the United States follow, but almost 65 per cent of the Senators and Representatives. That they are mainly lawyers is easy to understand. The verbal skills of the lawyer are not unlike those needed by the politicians; both involve bargaining and negotiation and the giving of advice to those who make decisions in business and politics. Lawyers also often find that—win or lose—politics is useful to their profession of law, since it publicizes one's practice. In addition, a private law practice, a business which can be carried in one's briefcase, can be set up almost anywhere. Accordingly, the lawyer as politician has something to fall back upon whenever he is not re-elected as well as something to lean upon if he wishes when he is elected. In fact, for some lawyers, a political term or two is thought of, and is in fact, merely a stepping stone to a larger law practice, in Washington or back home. The practice of law often allows a man to enter politics without much risk and some chance of advantage to a main source of money independent of the electorate's whims.

Most of the members of Congress over the last fifteen years—and probably much longer than that—have originated from the same professional and entrepreneurial occupations as they common on Capitol Hill . . . . For those who are without private means . . . life as a member of Congress can border on desperation."* "If Federal law really meant what it seems to mean concerning the uses of cash in election campaigns," Robert Bendiner has recently remarked, "more politicians would wind up in Leavenworth than in Washington."

The political career does not attract as able a set of men as it once did. From a money standpoint, the alert lawyer, who can readily make $25,000 to $50,000 a year, is not very likely to trade it for the perils of the Congressman's position; and, no doubt with exceptions, if they are not wealthy men, it is likely that the candidates for Congress will be a county attorney, a local judge, or a mayor—whose salaries are even less than those of Congressmen. Many observers, both in and out of Congress, agree that the Congress has fallen in public esteem over the last fifty years; and that, even in their home districts and states, the Congressmen are by no means the important figures they once were. How many people, in fact, know the name of their Representative, or even of their Senators?

Fifty years ago, in his district or state, the campaigning Congressman did not have to compete in a world of synthetic celebrities with the mass means of entertainment and distraction. The politician making a speech was looked to for an hour's talk about what was going on in a larger world, and in debates he had neither occasion nor opportunity to consult a ghost writer. He was, after all, one of the best-paid men in his locality and a big man there. But today, the politician must rely on the mass media, and access to these media is expensive.† The simple facts of the costs of the

---

themselves have followed over the last decade. Between 90 and 95 per cent of them have been sons of professionals or businessmen or farmers—although at the approximate time of their birth, in 1890, only 37 per cent of the labor force were of these entrepreneurial strata, and not all of these were married men with sons.

There have been no Negroes in the Senate over the last half century, and, at any given time, never more than two in the House—although Negroes make up about 10 per cent of the American population. Since 1845, the percentage of the foreign-born in the Senate has never exceeded 8 per cent, and has always been much smaller than the percentage in the population—less than one-half of the representative proportion, for example, in 1949-51. Moreover, both first and second generation Congressmen tend to be of the older, northern and western extraction, rather than of the newer immigration from southern and eastern Europe. Protestant denominations of higher status (Episcopal, Presbyterian, Unitarian, and Congregational) provide twice the number of Congressmen as their representative proportions in the population. Middle-level Protestants (Methodists and Baptists) in the Congress are in rough proportion to the population, but Catholics and Jews are fewer: Catholics in the 81st Congress, for example, having only 16 per cent of the House and 12 per cent of the Senate, but 34 per cent of the 1950 population at large.

*From the end of World War II until 1955, the members of Congress received $15,000 annually, including a tax-free expense allowance of $2,500; but the average income—including investments, business, and professions as well as writing and speaking—of a member of the House was, in 1952, about $22,000; and of the Senate, $47,000. As of 1 March 1955, the annual salary for members of Congress was raised to $22,500.

†One veteran Congressman has recently reported that in 1930, he could make the race for

modern campaign clearly tie the Congressman, if he is not personally well-to-do, to the sources of needed contributions, which are, sensibly enough, usually looked upon as investments from which a return is expected.

As free-lance law practitioners and as party politicians who must face elections, the professional politicians have cultivated many different groups and types of people in their localities. They are great "joiners" of social and business and fraternal organizations, belonging to Masons and Elks and the American Legion. In their constituencies, the Congressmen deal with organized groups, and they are supported or approved according to their attitude toward the interests and programs of these groups. It is in the local bailiwick that the plunder groups, who would exchange votes for favors, operate most openly. The politicians are surrounded by the demands and requests of such groups, large and small, local and national. As brokers of power, the politicians must compromise one interest by another, and, in the process, they are themselves often compromised into men without any firm line of policy.

Most professional politicians represent an astutely balanced variety of local interests, and such rather small freedom to act in political decisions as they have derives from precisely that fact: if they are fortunate they can juggle and play off these varied local interests against one another, but perhaps more frequently they come to straddle the issues in order to avoid decision. Protecting the interests of his electoral domain, the Congressman remains attentively loyal to his sovereign locality. In fact, his parochialism is in some cases so intense that as a local candidate he may even invite and collect for local display an assortment of out-of-state attacks upon him, thus turning his campaign into a crusade of the sovereign locality against national outsiders.

Inside the Congress, as his constituency, the politician finds a tangle of interests; and he also finds that power is organized according to party and according to seniority. The power of the Congress is centered in the committee; the power of the committee is usually centered in its chairman, who becomes chairman by seniority. Accordingly, the politician's chance to reach a position of power within the Congress often rests upon his ability to stay in office for a long and uninterrupted period, and to do that, he cannot antagonize the important elements in his constituency. Flexible adjustment to these several interests and their programs, the agility to carry several, sometimes conflicting, lines of policy, but to look good doing it, is at a premium. Therefore, by a mechanical process of selection, mediocre party "regulars," who for twenty years or more have been firmly

---

$7,500; today, for $25,000 to $50,000; and in the Senate, it might run to much more, John F. Kennedy (son of multimillionaire Joseph P. Kennedy), Democrat of Massachusetts, was reported to have spent $15,866 in his 1952 campaign, but "committees on his behalf for the improvement of the shoe, fishing and other industries of the state, spent $217,995."

anchored in their sovereign localities, are very likely to reach and to remain at the centers of Congressional power.

Even when the politician becomes a chairman—if possible, of a committee affecting the local interests of his district—he will not usually attempt to play the role of the national statesman. For however enjoyable such attendant prestige may be, it is secondary to the achievement of local popularity; his responsibility is not to the nation; it is to the dominant interests of his locality. Moreover, "better congressional machinery," as Stanley High has remarked, "does not cure the evil of localism; indeed it may provide members with more time and better facilities for its practice."

Nonetheless, the chairman of the major committees are the elite members of the Congress. In their hands rest the key powers of Congress, both legislative and investigative. They can originate, push, halt, or confuse legislation; they are adept at evasion and stall. They can block a White House proposal so that it never reaches the floor for debate, let alone a vote. And they can tell the President what will and what will not gain the approval of the people in their district or of colleagues under their influence in Congress.

In the first and second decades of this century, only a few bills were presented during the six months of the first session or the three months of the second. These bills were considered during the ample time between committee study and their debate on the floor. Debate was of importance and was carried on before a sizable audience in the chamber. Legislation took up most of the member's time and attention. Today hundreds of bills are considered at each session; and since it would be impossible for members even to read them all—or a tenth of them—they have come to rely upon the committees who report the bills. There is little debate and what there is often occurs before an emptied chamber. The speeches that are made are mainly for the member's locality, and many are not delivered, but merely inserted in the record. While legislation goes through the assembly line, the Congressmen are busy in their offices, administering a

---

*In one state, the desegregation issue seemed to matter most; in another, an Italian, married to an Irish woman, used the names of both with due effect. In one state, a tape-recording of a candidate's two-year-old talk about whom policemen tended to marry seemed important; in another, whether or not a candidate had been kind enough, or too kind, to his sister. Here bingo laws were important, and there the big question was whether or not an older man running for the Senate was virile enough. In one key state, twenty-year-old charges that a candidate had been tied up with a steamship company which had paid off a judge for pier leases was the insistent issue expensively presented on TV. One of the most distinguished Senators asserted of his opponent—also a quite distinguished man of old wealth—that he "was either dishonest or dumb or stupid and a dupe." Another candidate broke down under pressure and confessed that he had been telling detailed lies about his war record. And everywhere, in the context of distrust, it was hinted, insinuated, asserted, guessed that, after all, the opponents were associated with Red spies, if they were not actually in the pay of the Soviet octopus. All over again the Democrats fought the depression; all over again, the Republicans were determined to put Alger Hiss in jail.

small staff which runs errands for constituents and mails printed and typed matter to them.

In the campaigns of the professional politician, insistent national issues are not usually faced up to, but local issues are raised in a wonderfully contrived manner. In the 472 Congressional elections of 1954, for example, no national issues were clearly presented, nor even local issues related clearly to them.* Slogans and personal attacks on character, personality defects, and countercharges and suspicions were all that the electorate could see or hear, and, as usual, many paid no attention at all. Each candidate tried to dishonor his opponent, who in turn tried to dishonor him. The outraged candidates seemed to make themselves the issue, and on that issue virtually all of them lost. The electorate saw no issues at all, and they too lost, although they did not know it.

As part of the grim trivialization of public life, the American political campaign readily distracts attention from the possible debate of national policy. But one must not suppose that such noise is all that is involved. There are issues, in each district and state, issues set up and watched by organized interests of local importance. And that is the major implication to be drawn from the character of the campaigns:

There are no national parties to which the professional politicians belong and which by their debate focus national issues clearly and responsibly and continuously.

By definition, the professional politician is a party politician. And yet the two political parties in the United States are not nationally centralized organizations. As semi-feudal structures, they have operated by trading patronage and other favors for votes and protection. The lesser politician trades the votes that are in his domain for a larger share of the patronage and favors. But there is no national "boss," much less a nationally responsible leader of either of the parties. Each of them is a constellation of local organizations curiously and intricately joined with various interest blocs. The Congressman is generally independent of the Congressional leaders of his party as far as campaign funds go. The national committees of each major party consist mainly of political nonentities; for, since the parties are coalitions of state and local organizations, each of them develops such national unity as it has only once every four years, for the Presidential election. At the bottom and on the middle levels, the major parties are strong, even dictatorial; but, at the top, they are very weak. It is only the President and the Vice-President whose constituencies are national and who, by their actions and appointments, provide such national party unity as prevails.

The differences between the two parties, so far as national issues are concerned, are very narrow and very mixed up. Each seems to be forty-eight parties, one to each state; and accordingly, the professional politician, as Congressman and as campaigner, is not concerned with national party lines, if any are discernible. He is not subject to any effective national party discipline. He speaks solely for his own locality, and he is concerned with national issues only in so far as they affect his locality, the interests effectively organized there, and the chances of his re-election. That is the major reason why, when he speaks of national matters, the political vocabulary of the politician is such an empty rhetoric. Seated in his sovereign locality, the professional politician is not at the summit of national, political power: he is on and of the middle levels.

III

More and more of the fundamental issues never come to any point of decision before the Congress, or before its most powerful committees, much less before the electorate in campaigns. The entrance of the United States into World War II, for example, in so far as it involved American decision, by-passed the Congress quite completely. It was never a clearly debated issue clearly focused for a public decision. Under the executive's emergency power, the President, in a virtually dictatorial way, can make the decision for war, which is then presented to the Congress as a fact accomplished. "Executive agreements" have the force of treaties but need not be ratified by the Senate: the destroyer deal with Great Britain and the commitment of troops to Europe under NATO, which Senator Taft fought so bitterly, are clear examples of that fact. And in the case of the Formosa decisions of the spring of 1955, the Congress simply abdicated all debate concerning events and decisions bordering on war to the executive.

When fundamental issues do come up for Congressional debate, they are likely to be so structured as to limit consideration, and even to be stalemated rather than resolved. For with no responsible, centralized parties, it is difficult to form a majority in Congress; and—with the seniority system, the rules committee, the possibility of filibuster, and the lack of information and expertise—the Congress is all too likely to become a legislative labyrinth. It is no wonder that firm Presidential initiative is often desired by Congress on non-local issues, and that, in what are defined as emergencies, powers are rather readily handed over to the executive, in order to break the semi-organized deadlock. Indeed, some observers believe that "congressional abdication and obstruction, not presidential usurpation, has been the main cause of the shift of power to the Executive."

Among the professional politicians there are, of course, common denominators of mood and interests, anchored in their quite homogeneous origins, careers, and associations; and there is, of course, a common rhetoric in which their minds are often trapped. In pursuing their several parochial interests, accordingly, the Congressmen often coincide in ways that are of national relevance. Such interests seldom become explicit issues. But the many little issues decided by local interest, and by bargain, by check and balance, have national results that are often unanticipated by any one of the locally rooted agents involved. Laws are thus sometimes made, as the stalemate is broken, behind the backs of the lawmakers involved. For Congress is the prime seat of the middle levels of power, and it is on these middle levels that checks and balances do often prevail.

The truly vested interests are those openly pushed and protected by each Representative and Senator. They are the parochial interests of the local societies of each Congressional district and state. In becoming vested in a Senator or a Representative they are compromised and balanced by other parochial interests. The prime search of the Congressman is for the favor he can do for one interest that will not hurt any of the other interests he must balance.

It is not necessary for "pressure groups" to "corrupt" politicians in Congress. In fact, lobbyists, in their discrete way, may at times appear as honest men, while Congressmen may appear as lobbyists in disguise. It is not necessary for members of local society to pay off the professional politician in order to have their interests secured. For by social selection and by political training, he is of and by and for the key groups in his district and state. The Congressmen are more the visible makers of pressure inside the government than the subjects of invisible pressures from the periphery. Fifty years ago, the old muckraker image of the Senator corrupted by money was often true, and money is of course still a factor in politics. But the money that counts now is used mainly to finance elections rather than to pay off politicians directly for their votes and favors.

When we know that before entering politics one of the half dozen most powerful legislators, and chairman of the Ways and Means Committee, gained prominence by promoting and organizing Chambers of Commerce in half a dozen middle-ranking cities of the nation, "without," as he says, "a cent of Federal aid," we can readily understand why he fought extension of the excess-profits tax without any reference to invisible, behind-the-scenes pressures brought to bear upon him. Seventy-eight-year-old Daniel Reed *is* a man of Puritan-like character and inflexible principle, but principles are derived from and further strengthen character, and character is selected and formed by one's entire career. Moreover, as one member of Congress recently remarked, "there comes a time in the life of every Congressman when he must rise above principle." As a political actor, the Congressman is part of the compromised balances of local societies, as well as one or the other of the nationally irresponsible parties. As a result, he is caught in the semi-organized stalemate of the middle levels of national power.

Political power has become enlarged and made decisive, but not the power of the professional politician in the Congress. The considerable powers that do remain in the hands of key Congressmen are now shared with other types of political actors: There is the control of legislation, centered in the committee heads, but increasingly subject to decisive modification by the administrator. There is the power to investigate, as a positive and a negative weapon, but it increasingly involves intelligence agencies, both public and private, and it increasingly becomes involved with what can only be called various degrees of blackmail and counterblackmail.

In the absence of policy differences of consequences between the major parties, the professional party politician must *invent* themes about which to talk. Historically, this has involved the ordinary emptiness of "campaign rhetoric." But since World War II, among frustrated politicians there has come into wider use the accusation and the impugnment of character—of opponents as well as of innocent neutrals. This has, of course, rested upon the exploitation of the new historical fact that Americans now live in a military neighborhood; but it has also rested upon the place of the politician who practices a politics without real issue, a middle-level politics for which the real decisions, even those of patronage, are made by higher ups. Hunting headlines in this context, with less patronage and without big engaging issues, some Congressmen find the way to temporary success, or at least to public attention, in the universalization of distrust.

There is another way of gaining and of exercising power, one which involves the professional politician in the actions of cliques within and between the bureaucratic-like agencies of the administration. Increasingly, the professional politician teams up with the administrator who heads an agency, a commission, or a department in order to exert power with him against other administrators and politicians, often in a cut-and-thrust manner. The traditional distinction between "legislation" as the making of policy and "administration" as its realization has broken down from both sides.

In so far as the politician enters into the continuous policymaking of the modern political state, he does so less by voting for or against a bill than by entering into a clique that is in a position to exert influence upon and through the command posts of the executive administration, or by not investigating areas sensitive to certain clique interests. It is as a member of quite complicated cliques that the professional politician, representing a variety of interests, sometimes becomes quite relevant in decisions of national consequence.

If governmental policy is the result of an interplay of group interests, we must ask: what interests outside the government are important and what agencies inside it serve them? If there are *many* such interests and if they conflict with one another, then clearly each loses power and the agency involved either gains a certain autonomy or is stalemated. In the legislative branch, many and competing interests, especially local ones, come to focus, often in a stalemate. Other interests, on the level of national corporate power, never come to a focus but the Congressman, by virtue of what he is as a political and social creature, realizes them. But in the executive agency a number of small and coherent interests are often the only ones at play, and often they are able to install themselves within the agency or effectively nullify its action against themselves. Thus regulatory agencies, as John Kenneth Galbraith has remarked, "become, with some exceptions, either an arm of the industry they are regulating or servile. The executive ascendancy, moreover, has either relegated legislative action—and inaction—to a subordinate role in the making of policy or bends it to the executive will. For enforcement now clearly involves the making of policy, and even legislation itself is often written by members of the executive branch.

In the course of American history, there have been several oscillations between Presidential and Congressional leadership. Congressional supremacy, for example, was quite plain during the last third of the nineteenth century. But in the middle third of the twentieth century, with which we are concerned, the power of the Executive, and the increased means of power at its disposal, is far greater than at any previous period, and there are no signs of its power diminishing. The executive supremacy means the relegation of the legislature to the middle levels of political power; it means the decline of the professional politician, for the major locale of the party politician is the legislature. It is also a prime indicator of the decline of the old balancing society. For—in so far as the old balance was not entirely automatic—it was the politician, as a specialist in balance and a broker of contending pressures, who adjusted the balances, reached compromises, and maintained the grand equilibrium. That politician who best satisfied or held off a variety of interests could best gain power and hold it. But now the professional politician of the old balancing society has been relegated to a position "among those also present," often noisy, or troublesome, or helpful to the ascendant outsiders, but not holding the keys to decision. For the old balancing society in which he flourished no longer prevails.

IV

Back of the theory of checks and balances as *the* mode of political decision there is the class theory, well-known since Aristotle and held in firm view by the eighteenth-century Founding Fathers, that the state is, or ought to be, a system of checks and balances because the society is a balance of classes, and that society is a balance of classes because its pivot and its stabilizer is the strong and independent middle class.

Nineteenth-century America was a middle-class society, in which numerous small and relatively equally empowered organizations flourished.

Within this balancing society there was a economy in which the small entre-preneur was central, a policy in which a formal division of authority was an operative fact, and a political economy in which political and economic orders were quite autonomous. If at times it was not a world of small entre-preneurs, at least it was always a world in which small entrepreneurs had a real part to play in the equilibrium of power. But the society in which we now live consists of an economy in which the small entrepreneurs have been replaced in key areas by a handful of centralized corporations, of a polity in which the division of authority has become imbalanced in such a way that the executive branch is supreme, the legislative relegated to the middle levels of power, and the judiciary, with due time-lag, to the drift of policy which it does not initiate; and finally, the new society is clearly a politi-cal economy in which political and economic affairs are intricately and deeply joined together.

The romantic pluralism of the Jeffersonian ideal prevailed in a society in which perhaps four-fifths of the free, white population were, in one sense or another, independent proprietors. But in the epoch following the Civil War, that old middle class of independent proprietors began to decline, as, in one industry after another, larger and more concentrated economic units came into ascendancy; and in the later part of the progressive era, the independent middle class of farmers and small businessmen fought po-litically—and lost their last real chance for a decisive role in the political balance. Already appeals to them, as by David Graham Phillips, were nos-talgic deifications of their imagined past, which they seemed to hope would dispel the world of twentieth-century reality. Such sentiments flared up briefly again in the La Follette campaign of 1924, and they were one of the sources of the New Deal's rhetorical strength. But two facts about the mid-dle classes and one fact about labor—which became politically important during the 'thirties—have become decisive during our own time:

I. The independent middle class became politically, as well as economi-cally, dependent upon the machinery of the state. It is widely felt, for exam-ple, that the most successful "lobby" in the United States is The Farm Bloc; in fact, it has been so successful that it is difficult to see it as an independent force acting upon the several organs of government. It has become meshed firmly with these organs, especially with the Senate, in which, due to the peculiar geographic principle of representation, it is definitively over-represented. Ideologically, due to the exploitation of Jeffersonian myths about farming as a way of life, large commercial farmers as members of an industry are accepted as of that national interest which ought to be served by very special policies, rather than as one special interest among others. This special policy is the policy of parity, which holds that the govern-ment ought to guarantee to this one sector of the free enterprise system a price level for its products that will enable commercial farmers to enjoy a purchasing power equivalent to the power it possessed in its most prosperous period just prior to World War I. In every sense of the word, this is of course "class legislation," but it is "middleclass legislation," and it is so wonderfully entrenched as political fact that in the realm of crackpot realism in which such ideas thrive, it is thought of as merely sound public policy.

Well-to-do farmers, who are the chief rural beneficiaries of the subsidized enterprise system, are businessmen and so think of themselves. The hayseed and the rebel of the 'nineties have been replaced by the rural businessmen of the 'fifties. The political hold of the farmer is still strong but, as a demand upon the political top, it is more worrisome than decisive. The farmers, it is true, are taken into account so far as their own special interests are concerned, but these do not include the major issues of peace and war that confront the big political outsiders today, and the issues of slump and boom, to which the farmer is quite relevant, are not now foremost in the political outsiders' attention.

II. Alongside the old independent middle class, there had arisen inside the corporate society a *new* dependent *middle class* of white-collar employees. Roughly, in the last two generations, as proportions of the middle classes as a whole, the old middle class has declined from 85 to 44 per cent; the new middle class has risen from 15 to 56 per cent. For many reasons, which I have elsewhere tried to make clear—this class is less the political pivot of a balancing society than a rear-guard of the dominant drift towards a mass society. Unlike the farmer and the small businessman—and unlike the wage worker—the white-collar employee was born too late to have had even a brief day of autonomy. The occupational positions and status trends which form the white-collar outlook make of the salaried employees a rear-guard rather than a vanguard of historic change. They are in no political way united or coherent. Their unionization, such as it is, is a unionization into the main drift and decline of labor organization, and serves to incorporate them as hangers-on of the newest interest trying, unsuccessfully, to invest itself in the state.

The old middle class for a time acted as an independent base of power; the new middle class cannot. Political freedom and economic security were anchored in the fact of small-scale and independent properties; they are not anchored in the job world of the new middle class. Scattered properties, and their holders, were integrated economically by free and autonomous markets; the jobs of the new middle class are integrated by corporate authority. The white-collar middle classes do not form an independent base of power: economically, they are in the same situation as propertyless wage workers; politically they are in a worse condition, for they are not as organized.

III. Alongside the old middle class—increasingly invested within the state machinery—and the new middle class—born without independent political shape and developed in such a way as never to achieve it—a new political force came into the political arena of the 'thirties: the force of organized labor. For a brief time, it seemed that labor would become a power-bloc independent of corporation and state but operating upon and against them. After becoming dependent upon the governmental system, however, the labor unions suffered rapid decline in power and now have little part in major national decisions. The United States now has no labor leaders who carry any weight of consequence in decisions of importance to the political outsiders now in charge of the visible government.

Viewed from one special angle, the labor unions have become organizations that select and form leaders who, upon becoming successful, take their places alongside corporate executives in and out of government, and alongside politicians in both major parties, among the national power elite. For one function of labor unions—like social movements and political parties—is to attempt to contribute to the formation of this directorate. As new men of power, the labor leaders have come only lately to the national arena. Samuel Gompers was perhaps the first labor man to become, even though temporarily and quite uneasily, a member of the national power elite. His self-conscious attempt to establish his place within this elite, and thus to secure the labor interest as integral with national interests, has made him a prototype and model for the national labor career. Sidney Hillman was not, of course, the only labor man to take up this course during the 'forties, but his lead during the early war years, his awareness of himself as a member of the national elite, and the real and imagined recognition he achieved as a member ("Clear it with Sidney"), signaled the larger entrance—after the great expansion of the unions during the New Deal—of labor leaders into the political elite. With the advent of Truman's Fair Deal and Eisenhower's Great Crusade, no labor leader can readily entertain serious notions of becoming, formally or informally, a member. The early exit of a minor labor man—Durkin—from his weak cabinet post revealed rather clearly the situation faced by labor leaders as would-be members as well as the position of labor unions as a power bloc. Well below the top councils, they are of the middle levels of power.

Much of the often curious behavior and maneuvers of the labor chieftains over the last two decades is explainable by their search for status within the national power elite. In this context they have displayed extreme sensibility to prestige slights. They feel that they have arrived; they want the status accoutrements of power. In middle and small-sized cities, labor leaders now sit with Chamber of Commerce officials on civic enterprises; and on the national level, they expect and they get places in production boards and price-control agencies.

Their claim for status and power rests on their already increased power—not on property, income, or birth; and power in such situations as theirs is a source of uneasiness as well as a base of operations. It is not yet a solidly bottomed, continuous base having the force of use and wont and law. Their touchiness about prestige matters, especially on the national scene, has been due to (1) their self-made character, and to the fact (2) that their self-making was helped no end by government and the atmosphere it created in the decade after 1935. They are government-made men, and they have feared—correctly, it turns out—that they can be unmade by government. Their status tension is also due to the fact (3) that they are simply new to the power elite and its ways, and (4) that they feel a tension between their publics: their union members—before whom it is politically dangerous to be too big a "big shot" or too closely associated with inherited enemies—and their newly found companions and routines of life.

Many observers mistake the status accoutrements of labor leaders for *evidence* of labor's power. In away they are, but in a way they are not. They *are* when they are based on and lead to power. They *are not* when they become status traps for leaders without resulting in power. In such matters, it is well to remember that this is no chicken-and-egg issue. The chicken is power, and comes first, the egg is status.*

---

*Like the corporate rich, the labor leaders as a group are not wholly unified. Yet the often noted tendency of "the other side" to regard any move by some unit of one side as having significance in terms of the whole, indicates clearly that in the views, expectations, and demands of these men, they do form, even if unwillingly, blocs. They see one another as members of blocs, and in fact are inter-knit in various and quite intricate ways. Individual unions may lobby for particularistic interests, which is one key to such lack of unity as labor as a bracket displays. But increasingly the issues they face, and the contexts in which they must face them, are national in scope and effect, and so they must co-ordinate labor's line with reference to a national context, on pain of loss of power.

The corporate executive, like the labor leader, is a practical man and an opportunist, but for him enduring means, developed for other purposes, are available for the conduct of his political as well as of his business-labor affairs. The corporation is now a very stable basis of operation; in fact, it is more stable and more important for the continuance of the American arrangement than the lifetime family. The business member of the power elite can rely upon the corporation in the pursuit of his short-term goals and opportunistic maneuvering. But the union is often in a state of protest; it is on the defensive in a sometimes actually and always potentially hostile society. It does not provide such enduring means as are ready-made and at the business elite's disposal. If he wants such means, even for his little goals, the labor leader must himself build and maintain them. Moreover, the great organizing upsurge of the 'thirties showed that officers who were not sufficiently responsive to the demands of industrial workers could lose power. The corporation manager on the other hand, in the context of his corporation, is not an elected official in the same sense. His power does not depend upon the loyalty of the men who work for him and he does not usually lose his job if a union successfully invades his plants. The upsurges of the 'thirties did not oust the managers; their responsibilities are not to the workers whom they employ, but to themselves and their scattered stockholders.

This difference in power situation means that the power of the business leader is likely to

During the 'thirties organized labor was emerging for the first time on an American scale; it had little need of any political sense of direction other than the slogan, "organize the unorganized." This is no longer the case, but labor—without the mandate of the slump—still remains without political, or for that matter economic, direction. Like small business, its leaders have tried to follow the way of the farmer. Once this farmer was a source of insurgency; in the recent past, labor has seemed to be such. Now the large farmer is a unit in an organized bloc, entrenched within and pressuring the welfare state. Despite its greater objective antagonism to capitalism as a wage system, labor now struggles, unsuccessfully, to go the same way.

V

In the old liberal society, a set of balances and compromises prevailed among Congressional leaders, the executive branch of the government, and various pressure groups. The image of power and of decision is the image of a balancing society in which no unit of power is powerful enough to do more than edge forward a bit at a time, in compromised countervailance with other such forces, and in which, accordingly, there is no unity, much less coordination, among the higher circles. Some such image, combined with the doctrine of public opinion, is still the official view of the formal democratic system of power, the standard theory of most academic social scientists, and the underlying assumption of most literate citizens who are neither political spokesmen nor political analysts.

But as historical conditions change, so do the meanings and political consequences of the mechanics of power. There is nothing magical or eternal about checks and balances. In time of revolution, checks and balances may be significant as a restraint upon unorganized and organized masses. In time of rigid dictatorship, they may be significant as a technique of divide and rule. Only under a state which is already quite well balanced, and which has under it a balanced social structure, do checks and balances mean a restraint upon the rulers.

---

be more continuous and more assured than that of the labor leader: the labor leader is more likely to be insecure in his job if he fails to "deliver the goods."

However it may be with the corporate and the political elite, there is nothing, it seems to me, in the makeup of the *current* labor leaders as individuals and as a group to lead us to believe that they can or will transcend the strategy of maximum adaptation. By this I mean that they react more than they lead, and that they do so to retain and to expand their position in the constellation of power and advantage. Certain things could happen that would cause the downfall of the present labor leadership or sections of it, and other types of leaders might then rise to union power; but the current crop of labor leaders is pretty well set up as a dependent variable in the main drift with no role in the power elite. Neither labor leaders nor labor unions are at the present juncture likely to be "independent variables," in the national context.

The eighteenth century political theorists had in mind as the unit of power the individual citizen, and the classic economists had in mind the small firm operated by an individual. Since their time, the units of power, the relations between the units, and hence the meaning of the checks and balances, have changed. In so far as there is now a great scatter of relatively equal balancing units, it is on the middle levels of power, seated in the sovereign localities and intermittent pressure groups, and coming to its high point within the Congress. We must thus revise and relocate the received conception of an enormous scatter of varied interests, for, when we look closer and for longer periods of time, we find that most of these middle-level interests are concerned merely with their particular cut, with their particular area of vested interest, and often these are of no decisive political importance, although many are of enormous detrimental value to welfare. Above this plurality of interests, the units of power—economic, political, and military—that count in any balance are few in number and weighty beyond comparison with the dispersed groups on the middle and lower levels of the power structure.

Those who still hold that the power system reflects the balancing society often confuse the present era with earlier times of American history, and confuse the top and the bottom levels of the present system with its middle levels. When it is generalized into a master model of the power system, the theory of balance becomes historically unspecific; whereas in fact, as a model, it should be specified as applicable only to certain phases of United States development—notably the Jacksonian period and, under quite differing circumstances, the early and middle New Deal.

The idea that the power system is a balancing society also assumes that the units in balance are independent of one another, for if business and labor or business and government, for example, are not independent of one another, they cannot be seen as elements of a free and open balance. But as we have seen, the major vested interests often compete less with one another in their effort to promote their several interests than they coincide on many points of interest and, indeed, come together under the umbrella of government. The units of economic and political power not only become larger and more centralized; they come to coincide in interest and to make explicit as well as tacit alliances.

The American government today is not merely a framework within which contending pressures jockey for position and make politics. Although there is of course some of that, this government now has such interests vested within its own hierarchical structure, and some of these are higher and more ascendant than others. There is no effective countervailing power against the coalition of the big businessmen—who, as political outsiders, now occupy the command posts—and the ascendant military men—who with such grave voices now speak so frequently in the higher councils.

Those having real power in the American state today are not merely brokers of power, resolvers of conflict, or compromisers of varied and clashing interest—they represent and indeed embody quite specific national interests and policies.

While the professional party politicians may still, at times, be brokers of power, compromisers of interests, negotiators of issues, they are no longer at the top of the state, or at the top of the power system as a whole.

The idea that the power system is a balancing society leads us to assume that the state is a visible mask for autonomous powers, but in fact, the powers of decision are now firmly vested within the state. The old lobby, visible or invisible, is now the visible government. This "governmentalization of the lobby" has proceeded in both the legislative and the executive domains, as well as between them. The executive bureaucracy becomes not only the center of power but also the arena within which and in terms of which all conflicts of power are resolved or denied resolution. Administration replaces electoral politics; the maneuvering of cliques replaces the clash of parties.

The agrarian revolt of the 'nineties, the small-business revolt that has been more or less intermittent since the 'eighties, the labor revolt of the 'thirties—all of these have failed and all of these have succeeded. They have failed as autonomous movements of small property or of organized workmen which could countervail against the power of the corporate rich, and they have failed as politically autonomous third parties. But they have succeeded, in varying degrees, as vested interests inside the expanded state, and they have succeeded as parochial interests variously seated in particular districts and states where they do not conflict with larger interests. They are well-established features of the *middle* levels of balancing power.

Among the plurality of these middle powers, in fact, are all those strata and interests which in the course of American history have been defeated in their bids for top power or which have never made such bids. They include: rural small property, urban small property, the wage-worker unions, all consumers, and all major white-collar groups. These are indeed still in an unromantic scatter; being structurally unable to unite among themselves, they do indeed balance one another—in a system of semi-organized stalemate. They "get in the way" of the unified top, but no one of them has a chance to come into the top circles, where the political outsiders from corporate institution and military order are firmly in command.

When the multifarious middle classes are a political balance wheel, the professional politician is the ascendant decision-maker. When the middle classes decline as a set of autonomous political forces, the balancing society as a system of power declines, and the party politicians of the sovereign localities are relegated to the middle levels of national power.

These structural trends came to political shape during the period of the

New Deal, which was of course a time of slump. That our own immediate period has been a time of material prosperity has obscured these facts, but it has not altered them; and, as facts, they are important to the understanding of the power elite today.